WHAT'S OUR PROBLEM?

WHAT'S OUR PROBLEM?

A SELF-HELP BOOK FOR SOCIETIES

TIM URBAN

WHAT'S OUR PROBLEM?
A Self-Help Book for Societies

Copyright © 2023 Tim Urban
First Print Edition Copyright © 2024 Tim Urban
All rights reserved. No part of this publication may be reproduced,
stored in a retrieval system, or transmitted in any form or by any
means, without prior permission in writing from the publisher.

Cover and Interior illustrations by Tim Urban
Cover design by Anna Dorfman
Edited by Alicia McElhone, Trish Hall, and Drew Cullingham
Print production by Scribe Media

ISBN: 979-8-9877226-3-3 (hardcover)
ISBN: 979-8-9877226-2-6 (paperback)
ISBN: 979-8-9877226-0-2 (ebook)
ISBN: 979-8-9877226-1-9 (audiobook)

To Tandice, who never planned on being married to someone who would spend six years talking about his book on politics, but here we are.

CONTENTS

INTRODUCTION: THE BIG PICTURE — 1
Hey — 9

CHAPTER 1: THE LADDER — 13
The Tug-of-War in Our Heads — 14
Vertical Thinking — 21
Intellectual Cultures — 38
Giants — 46

INTERLUDE: THE LIBERAL GAMES — 59
Designing the American Giant — 65

CHAPTER 2: POLITICS ON THE LADDER — 77
High-Rung Politics — 79
Low-Rung Politics — 86
The Golem Immune System — 92
The National Tug-of-War — 105

CHAPTER 3: THE DOWNWARD SPIRAL — 109
Shift #1: Distributed Tribalism → Concentrated Tribalism — 110
Shift #2: Concentrated Tribalism → Hypercharged Tribalism — 117
Hypercharged Tribalism — 139

Hey — 145

CHAPTER 4: RISE OF THE RED GOLEM — 149
Republicans in the Sixties — 151
Republicans in the Eighties — 163
Republicans After Reagan — 165
The Party of Trump — 178
Triumph of the Red Golem — 182

CHAPTER 5: SOCIAL JUSTICE, HIGH AND LOW — 187
Two Kinds of Social Justice — 189
Social Justice, on the Ladder — 209

INTERLUDE: THE TALE OF KING MUSTACHE — 241
Free Speech and the Marketplace of Ideas — 253

CHAPTER 6: HOW TO CONQUER A COLLEGE — 265
Idea Supremacy on Campus: Expression — 292
Idea Supremacy on Campus: Research — 301
Idea Supremacy on Campus: Education — 313

INTERLUDE: THE DIGITAL CUDGEL — 333

CHAPTER 7: HOW TO CONQUER A SOCIETY — 347
Step 1: Speech Control — 349
Step 2: Forced Listening — 380
Step 3: Forced Speaking — 403
SJF Is Bad for Almost Everyone — 437
Golems, Inc. — 448

CHANGING COURSE — 459

Cast of Characters — 474
Acknowledgments — 479
Notes — 483
Bibliography — 485
About the Author — 487

*The problem with people is
that they're only human.*
—BILL WATTERSON

INTRODUCTION
THE BIG PICTURE

Imagine if all of human history were written down in a fat book called *The Story of Us*.

Humans have been around for a long, long time—according to the most recent estimates, between 200,000 and 300,000 years.* If every page of *The Story of Us* covered 250 years of history, the book would be about one thousand pages long. To take a closer look, let's tear all the pages out and lay them on the table:

---

* AD is over two thousand years long, which sounds like a long time, until you realize that humans have been around for over two thousand *centuries*.

2 • WHAT'S OUR PROBLEM?

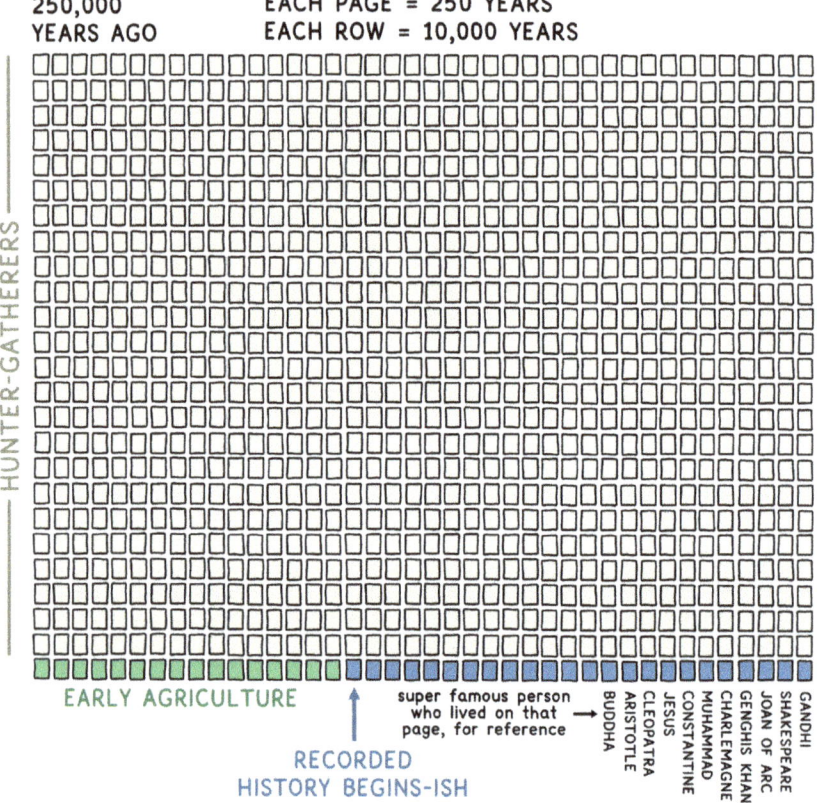

When we really zoom out, we see that most of what we consider ancient history is really just the very last pages of the story. The Agricultural Revolution starts around page 950 or 960, recorded history gets going at about page 976, and Christianity isn't born until page 993. Page 1,000, which goes from the early 1770s to the early 2020s, contains all of US history.

We're now collectively venturing into the mysterious new world of page 1,001. This excites me—and also scares me—because of three concurrent facts.

Fact 1: Technology Is Exponential
Say we went back to page 760 of *The Story of Us*, kidnapped someone, and transported them a few centuries forward to page 761. Other than

having to find new friends and make some cultural adjustments, they'd probably get along fine, because the worlds of pages 760 and 761 were pretty much the same.

For most of our history, that's what it would be like to jump forward 250 years to the next page. But the closer you get to page 1,000, the less the rule holds. Like, what if we did the same thing with someone on page 992, 998, or 999?

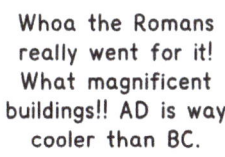

The later you lived in *The Story of Us*, the more mind-blowing it would be to jump forward to the next page. As you can see, our little person on page 999 was so shocked by the world he saw on page 1,000, he keeled over and died. We can see why when we compare page 1,000 to all the pages before it.

	PAGES 1—999	PAGE 1,000
POPULATION	under a billion people	8 billion people
TRANSPORTATION	walking, horses, camels, sailboats, rafts, canoes	steamships, trains, cars, planes, submarines, spaceships
COMMUNICATION	talking, writing letters, smoke signals	telegraph, telephone, email, text, video call
MASS BROADCAST	yelling loudly to a group of people, books (p. 998)	newspapers, radio, TV, websites, YouTube, podcasts, social media
PRODUCTION	manual tools, archaic factories	mass production, automated machines
PLUMBING	shitting in a pot, carrying water from a well, rubbing cold water on yourself	flushable toilets, running water, hot showers
MEDICINE	herbal remedies, chisel-based surgery, magic spells	vaccines, antibiotics, chemotherapy, advanced surgery, stents, pacemakers
ENERGY	pushing things with your arms, animal labor, windmills, water wheels	fossil fuels, nuclear fission, solar power
ELECTRICITY	permanent power outage	power on
WEAPONS	fists, fingernails, clubs, spears, bow & arrow, knives, cannons, guns (p. 998)	machine guns, tanks, missiles, torpedos, nuclear bombs, drones, chemical & biological weapons
COMPUTING	thinking, counting, abacus	computers
DATA STORAGE	brains, stone tablets, paper	hard drives
INTELLIGENCE	human	human and artificial
GLOBAL BRAIN	no	the internet

It's natural to assume that the world we grew up in is normal. But nothing about our current world is normal. Because technology is exponential. More advanced societies make progress at a faster rate than less advanced societies—because they're more advanced. People in the nineteenth century knew more and had better technology than people in the sixteenth century, so it's no surprise that there were more advances on page 1,000 than on page 999. Over the centuries, this builds upon itself, leading to increasingly rapid progress.* And ever since the Middle Ages ended, human technology has been advancing on an exponential fast track, leading to a world on page 1,000 that would seem like a totally different planet to humans on any previous page.

Fact 2: More Technology Means Higher Stakes

Technology is a multiplier of both good and bad. More technology means better good times, but it also means badder bad times.

On page 999 of human history, the Enlightenment and Scientific Revolution that generated vast improvements in human prosperity also generated an explosion of slavery and brutal imperialism.

Page 1,000, a time of unprecedented life expectancy, wealth, and political freedom, also saw the two most catastrophic wars in history followed by existential threats with the invention of nuclear and biological weapons and the onset of climate change.

As the times get better, they also get more dangerous. More technology makes our species more powerful, which increases risk. And the scary thing is, if the good and bad keep exponentially growing, it doesn't matter how great the good times become. If the bad gets to a certain level of bad, it's all over for us.

So far in the twenty-first century, Fact 1 and Fact 2 seem to be holding strong. The pace of change has been dizzying, with the advent of widespread internet, social media, smartphones, self-driving cars, and crypto, not to mention the dramatic leaps in AI powering many of these advances. The jump in technology from page 1,000 to 1,001 should prove to be even more extreme than the jump from 999 to 1,000—maybe many times more so. This could be unfathomably awesome. We could conquer every problem that ails us today—disease, poverty, climate change, maybe even mortality itself.

But if the catastrophes of page 1,000 were the most devastating yet, what does that mean about catastrophes on page 1,001? The same technology that has made our world magical has also opened a large number

---

* There are exceptions: seventh-century Europe (page 995) was, for instance, less technologically advanced than second-century Europe (page 993) at the height of the Roman Empire. But most of the time, technology moves in one overarching direction: forward.

of Pandora's boxes: rapidly advancing AI, cyber warfare, autonomous weapons, and bioweapons, to name a few.

With the stakes this high, we'd want to be our wisest selves. Which is unfortunate, because:

Fact 3: My Society Is Currently Acting Like a Poopy-Pantsed Four-Year-Old Who Dropped Its Ice Cream

I picture society as a giant human—a living organism like each of us, only much bigger. And when I look at the American society around me, I'm not really seeing this:

It looks more like this:

Humans are supposed to mature as they age—but the giant human I live in has been getting more childish each year. Tribalism and political division are on the rise. False narratives and outlandish conspiracy theories are flourishing. Major institutions are floundering. Medieval-style public shaming is suddenly back in fashion. Trust, the critical currency of a healthy society, is disintegrating. And these trends seem to be happening in lots of societies, not just my own.

So what's our problem? Why, in a time so prosperous, with the stakes so high, would we be going *backward* in wisdom?

This wouldn't be the first time. In 1905, philosopher George Santayana issued a warning to humanity:

> Those who cannot remember the past are condemned to repeat it.

The worrying thing about that quote is that philosopher Edmund Burke issued the same warning over a century earlier, in 1790:

> People will not look forward to posterity, who never look backward to their ancestors.

We seem to be having trouble learning an important lesson here.

When we learn a technology lesson, we tend not to forget it. The invention of the integrated circuit in 1959 was a breakthrough that launched a new paradigm in modern computing. This isn't the kind of thing we later forget, finding ourselves accidentally going back to making computers with vacuum tubes. But wisdom lessons don't always seem to stick. Unlike technological growth, wisdom seems to oscillate up and down, leading societies to repeat age-old mistakes.

As I look at the world around me today, I worry that we're on our way toward making some terrible—and preventable—mistakes. When I think about Facts 1 and 2, I picture our societies as giants trudging upward on a mountain ridge toward a glorious future—but as they move upward, the ridge gets thinner and the cliffs on either side grow steeper. The higher we go, the more deadly a fall we risk. When I think about Fact 3, I see those giants losing their composure and becoming more erratic in their steps, at the worst possible time.

If you were reading *The Story of Us* and turned the page to 1,001, everything would seem to be coming to a head, with many storylines

---

* Everything you read in this book is heavily sourced in the Notes section in the back of the book. Many of the notes also include further details or explanation if you'd like to go a level deeper on any part of the book.

suddenly converging. You'd be glued to the book, needing to find out *what happens to this species*.

Except we're not reading *The Story of Us*—we're living inside of it, as its characters. We're also its authors, writing the story as we go along.

Our responsibility is immense. If we can figure out how to get page 1,001 right, Future Us and trillions of our descendants could live high up on that mountain in what would seem like a magical utopia to Today Us. If we get page 1,001 wrong and stumble off those steep cliffs, this might be the last page of the story.

As the authors of *The Story of Us*, we have no mentors, no editors, no one to make sure it all turns out okay. It's all in our hands. This scares me, but it's also what gives me hope. If we can all get just a little wiser, together, it may be enough to nudge the story onto a trajectory that points toward an unimaginably good future.

HEY

Hey.

I know we're all intense-feeling right now after that intro, but I just want to pause for a minute and introduce myself.

I'm Tim. I spend my time writing a blog called *Wait But Why*, where I explore all kinds of things—artificial intelligence, procrastination, relationships, aliens, and lots of other random topics that interest me. Then I illustrate the writing with drawings that seem like they were done by a fourth grader but actually were done by a grown-up man. This was all going fine until a few years ago, when something began to nag at me. The society around me seemed to be devolving, and if that kept happening, none of those other topics I write about would matter. If we really were losing our grip on things, every other topic was secondary to *that* topic. So I dove in.

When I pick a topic to write about, I like to go deep down the rabbit hole. But this topic—*what's our problem?*—turned out to be a rabbit hole like no other. As I began to crawl in, I slipped and fell and ended up here. →

Normally, I spend somewhere between three days and three months learning and pondering and discussing a topic before

I know what I want to say. This one took me six years. When I finally emerged from the extended rabbit hole, I had a new perspective on the world, on politics, on group dynamics, on how we think and why we believe the things we believe. In this book, I'll share that perspective with you.

In Chapter 1, we'll get to know the book's primary tool—a framework that I've spent the past six years developing, testing, and refining. I call it the Ladder. The Ladder is a thinking lens—a pair of glasses for the brain to help us better understand the world and ourselves. It's made me a much better thinker and communicator, and I hope it will do the same for you.

In Chapter 2, we'll look at the familiar subject of politics through our unfamiliar new glasses. Instead of seeing politics as a mere horizontal axis of left, right, and center, we'll use the Ladder to supplement the one-dimensional political discussion with a badly needed vertical dimension.

In Chapter 3, we'll examine the story of our regression: how and why I believe we've been slipping down the Ladder as a society.

From there, we'll look at our current trajectory up close by examining two American stories. First, in Chapter 4, we'll turn our attention to America's Republican Party, and then, in Chapters 5 through 7, we'll take a deep dive into the controversial world of American social justice.* The tired discussions around these phenomena are, I believe, missing the forest for the trees. In both cases, the Ladder will reveal a more interesting and more useful story than is portrayed in popular discourse.

All together, our journey looks like this:

---

* While many parts of this book aren't specific to any country, others will seem America-centric. I chose US parties and movements as my case studies because I grew up within them and I understand them best. But the lessons within the case studies are both universal and evergreen. At their heart are common patterns of human nature—the same patterns that likely explain other countries right now. Both the book's lens and its lessons apply to everyone, everywhere.

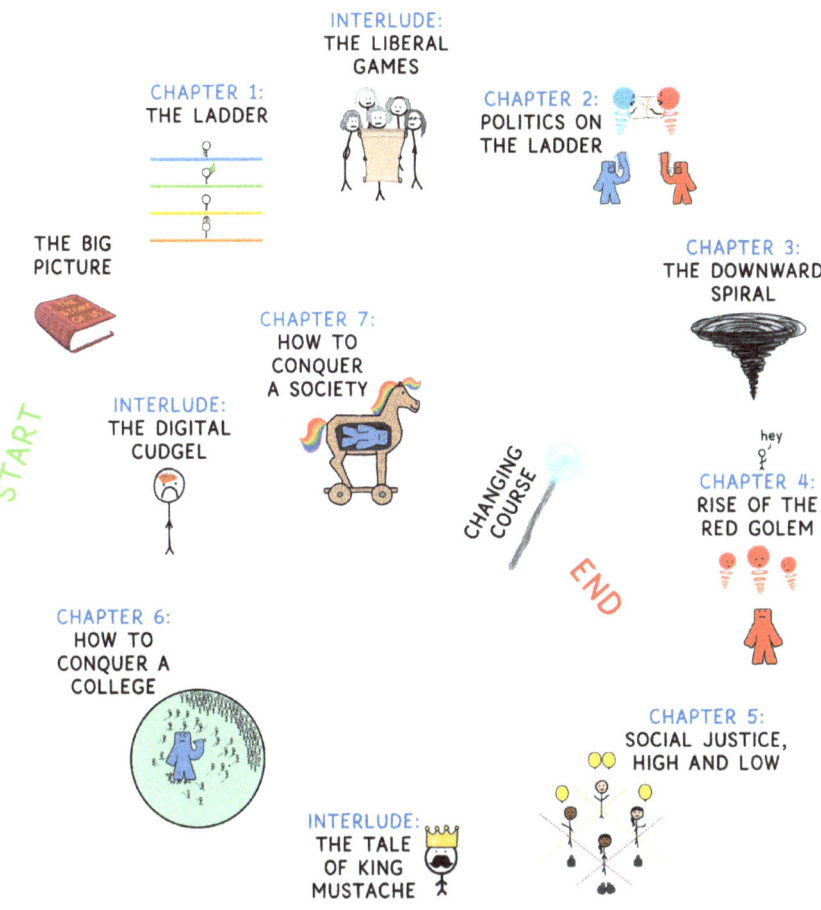

Ready?

CHAPTER 1
THE LADDER

*There is a great deal of
human nature in people.*
—MARK TWAIN

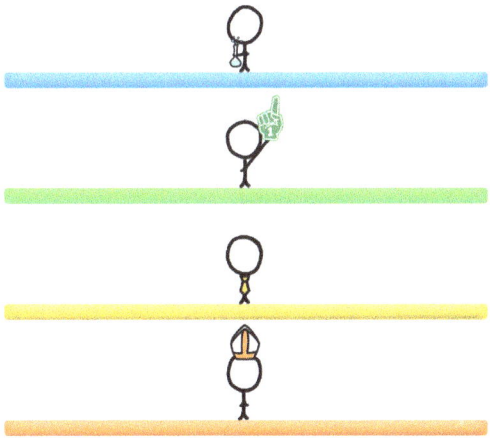

THE TUG-OF-WAR IN OUR HEADS

The animal world is a stressful place to be.

The issue is that the animal world isn't really an animal world—it's a world of trillions of strands of genetic information, each one hell-bent on immortality. Most gene strands don't last very long, and those still on Earth today are the miracle outliers, such incredible survival specialists that they're hundreds of millions of years old and counting.

Animals are just a hack these outlier genes came up with—temporary containers designed to carry the genes and help them stay immortal. Genes can't talk to their animals, so they control them by having them run on specialized survival software I call the **Primitive Mind**.

The Primitive Mind is a set of coded instructions for how to be a successful animal in the animal's natural habitat. The coder is natural selection, which develops the software using a pretty simple process: Software that's good at making its animal

pass on its genes stays around, and the less successful software is discontinued. Genetic mutation is like a bug appearing in the software from time to time, and every once in a while, a certain bug makes the software *better*—an accidental software update. It's a slow way to code, but over millions of generations, it gets the job done.

The infrequency of these updates means an animal's software is actually optimized for the environment of its *ancestors*.* For most animals, this system works fine. Their environment changes so slowly that whatever worked a hundred thousand or even a million years in the past probably works just about as well in the present.

But humans are strange animals. A handful of cognitive superpowers, like symbolic language, abstract thinking, complex social relationships, and long-term planning, have allowed humans to take their environment into their own hands in a way no other animal can. In the blink of an eye—around twelve thousand years, or five hundred generations—humans have crafted a totally novel environment for themselves, called civilization.

As great as civilization may be, five hundred generations isn't enough time for evolution to take a shit. So now we're all here living in this fancy new habitat, using brain software optimized to our old habitat.

You know how moths love to fly toward light and you're not really sure why they do this or what their angle is? It turns out that for millions of years, moths have used moonlight as a beacon for nocturnal navigation—which works great until a bunch of people start turning lights on at night that aren't the moon. The moth's brain software hasn't had time to update itself to the new situation, and now millions of moths are wasting their lives flapping around streetlights.

In a lot of ways, modern humans are like modern moths, running on a well-intentioned Primitive Mind that's constantly misinterpreting the weird world we've built for ourselves.

---

* According to biologist Richard Dawkins, future geneticists may be able to look at an individual's genome and "read off a description of the worlds in which the ancestors of that animal lived."

The good news is, our Primitive Mind has a roommate: the **Higher Mind**.

The Higher Mind is the part of you that can think outside itself and self-reflect and get wiser with experience.

Unlike the Primitive Mind, the Higher Mind can look around and see the world for what it really is. It can *see* that you live in an advanced civilization, and it wants to think and behave accordingly.

The Primitive Mind and Higher Mind are a funny pair. When things are going well, the inside of your head looks like this:

The Higher Mind is large and in charge, while its little software pet chases dopamine around, taking care of the eating and sleeping and masturbating. The Primitive Mind, at its core, just wants to survive and reproduce and help its offspring reproduce—all things the Higher Mind is totally on board with *when it makes sense*. When the Primitive Mind wants you to think and behave in a way that doesn't map onto reality, the Higher Mind tries to override the software, keeping you within the "makes sense" circle on the right:

The trouble starts when the balance of power changes.

As smart as the Higher Mind may be, it's not very good at managing the Primitive Mind. And when the Primitive Mind gains too much control, you might find yourself drifting over to the No Sense Zone.

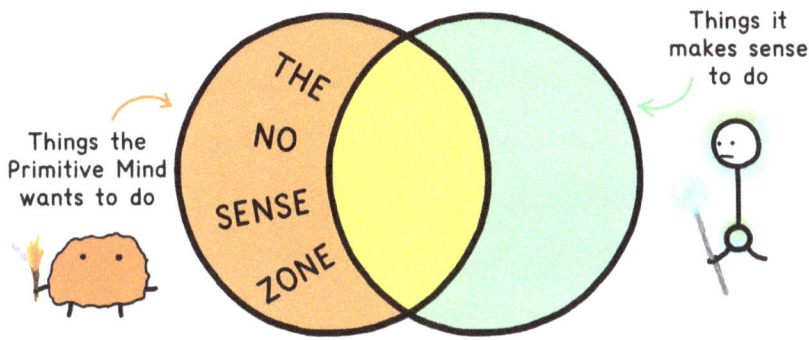

Like, we've all been here, trying to buy something at a drugstore and becoming enticed by a succulent bag of junk food.

The Primitive Mind and Higher Mind help us see what's really going on:

Like the moth flying toward a streetlight, the human Primitive Mind thinks it's a great decision to eat Skittles. In the ancient human world, there was no such thing as processed food, calories were hard to come by, and anything with a texture and taste as delectable as a Skittle was surely a good thing to eat. Mars, Inc., which makes Skittles, knows what makes your Primitive Mind tick and is in the business of tricking it. Your Higher Mind knows better. If it holds the reins of your mind, it'll either skip the Skittles or have just a few, as a little treat for its primitive roommate.

But sometimes, there you are, eighty Skittles into your binge, hating yourself—because your Primitive Mind has hijacked the cockpit.

This kind of internal disagreement pops up in many parts of life, like a constant tug-of-war in our heads—a tug-of-war over our thoughts, our emotions, our values, our morals, our judgments, and our overall consciousness.

The tug-of-war is a spectrum that we can simplify into four basic states—or four rungs of a **Ladder**.

Humans are so complicated because we're all a mixture of both "high-rung" and "low-rung" psychology.

When the Higher Mind is winning the tug-of-war, its staff illuminates our minds with clarity, including awareness of the Primitive Mind and what it's up to. The Higher Mind understands that primitive pleasures like sex, food, and all-in-good-fun tribalism like sports fandom are enjoyable, and often necessary, parts of a human life. And like a good pet owner, the Higher Mind is more than happy to let the Primitive Mind have its fun. Primitive bliss is great, as long as it's managed by the Higher Mind, who makes sure it's done in moderation, it's done for the right reasons, and no one gets hurt. In short, when we're up on the high rungs, we act like grown-ups.

But when something riles up the Primitive Mind, it gets bigger and stronger. Its torch—which bears the primal fires of our genes' will for survival—grows as well, filling our minds with smoky fog. This fog dulls our consciousness, so when we're most under the spell of our Primitive Mind, we don't even realize it's happening. The Higher Mind, unable to think clearly, begins directing its efforts toward supporting whatever the Primitive Mind wants to do, whether it makes sense or not. When we slip down to the Ladder's low rungs, we're shortsighted and small-minded, thinking and acting with our pettiest emotions. We're low on self-awareness and high on hypocrisy. We're our worst selves.

> **ON MULTIPLE MINDS**
>
> Philosophers and scientists have been grappling with the "multiple minds" idea for millennia. Plato wrote about a "charioteer" (intellect) that managed the "horses" of rational modesty and passionate insolence. Sigmund Freud's structure consisted of the "id" (primitive instinct), the "superego" (the conscience), and the "ego" that balances the two with external reality. More recently, social psychologist Daniel Kahneman wrote about "System 1" (fast, involuntary thinking) and "System 2" (slow, complex thinking that requires effort). Social psychologist Jonathan Haidt wrote about the emotional "elephant" and its rational "rider" which appears to be in control but often is not. Harvard's Todd Rogers and Max H. Bazerman wrote about the conflict between the "want self" and the "should self." Others analyze specific brain structures, distinguishing between the more rational thinking of the prefrontal cortex and the more primitive workings of the limbic system.
>
> While the Higher Mind/Primitive Mind framework in the book overlaps with elements of some of these other models, it is not meant to map perfectly onto any of them. Our characters and the tug-of-war between them will become intuitive as you read this book.

We all have our own Ladder struggles. Some of us struggle with procrastination,* an uncontrollable temper, or an addiction to sugar or gambling; others suffer from an irrational fear of failure or crippling social anxiety. We all self-defeat in our own way—in each case because our Higher Minds lose control of our heads and send us flapping our moth wings toward the streetlights.

In this book, we're going to explore a particular group of Ladder struggles—those I believe are most relevant to our big question about today's societies: What's our problem? The first stop on our journey will be our own heads, where we'll use the Ladder to help us make sense of a key process: how we form our beliefs.

---

* This book took me six years, which is at least two years longer than it should have taken.

VERTICAL THINKING

Why do we believe what we believe?

Our beliefs make up our perception of reality, drive our behavior, and shape our life stories. History happened the way it did because of what people believed in the past, and what we believe today will write the story of our future. So it seems like an important question to ask: How do we actually come to believe the things we end up believing?

To explore this question, let's create a way to visualize it.

When it comes to our beliefs, let's imagine the range of views on any given topic as an axis we can call the **Idea Spectrum**.

IDEA SPECTRUM

The Idea Spectrum is a simple tool we can use to capture the range of what a person might think about any given topic—their beliefs, their opinions, their stances.*

For most beliefs, we're so concerned with where people stand that we often forget the most important thing about what someone thinks: *how* they arrived at what they think. This is where the Ladder can help. If the Idea Spectrum is a "what you think" axis, we can use the Ladder as a "how you think" axis.

---

* The Idea Spectrum is a pretty rigid tool—it's linear and one-dimensional, and most worlds of thought are more complex and involve multiple dimensions simultaneously. But most of these worlds can also be *roughly* explored on a simple Idea Spectrum, and for our purposes, oversimplifying areas of thought to single spectrums can help us see what's going on.

To understand how our thinking changes depending on where we are on the Ladder, we have to ask ourselves: How do the two minds like to form beliefs?

Your Higher Mind is aware that humans are often delusional, and it wants you to be not delusional. It sees beliefs as the most recent draft of a work in progress, and as it lives more and learns more, the Higher Mind is always happy to make a revision. Because when beliefs are revised, it's a signal of progress—of becoming less ignorant, less foolish, less wrong.

Your Primitive Mind disagrees. For your genes, what's important is holding beliefs that generate the best kinds of survival behavior—whether or not those beliefs are actually true. The Primitive Mind's beliefs are usually installed early on in life, often based on the prevailing beliefs of your family, peer group, or broader community. The Primitive Mind sees those beliefs as a fundamental part of your identity and a key to remaining in good standing with the community around you. Given all of this, the last thing the Primitive Mind wants is for you to feel *humble* about your beliefs or interested in *revising* them. It wants you to treat your beliefs as sacred objects and believe them with conviction.

So the Higher Mind's goal is to get to the *truth*, while the Primitive Mind's goal is *confirmation* of its existing beliefs. These two very different types of *intellectual motivation* exist simultaneously in our heads. This means that our driving intellectual motivation—and, in turn, our thinking process—varies depending on where we are on the Ladder at any given moment.

In the realm of thinking, then, the Ladder's four rungs correspond to four ways of forming beliefs. When your Higher Mind is running the show, you're up on the top rung, thinking like a Scientist.

RUNG 1: THINKING LIKE A SCIENTIST

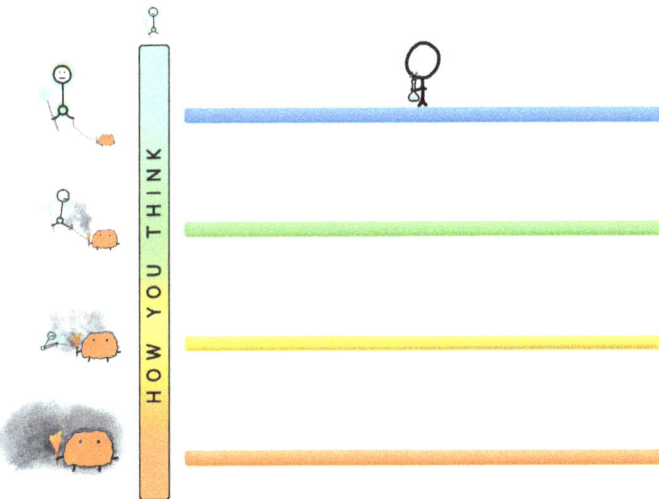

When you're thinking like a Scientist,* you start at Point A and follow evidence wherever it takes you.

---

* Of course, real-world scientists often do not think like Scientists—something we'll talk about later in the book. In this book, when we talk about capital-s Scientists, we're talking about a certain thinking process: what Carl Sagan meant when he said, "Science is a way of thinking much more than it is a body of knowledge."

24 • WHAT'S OUR PROBLEM?

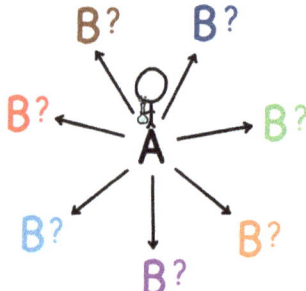

More specifically, the Scientist's journey from A to B looks something like this:

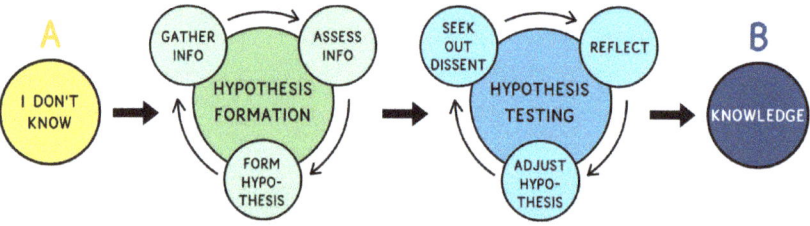

The Scientist's default position on any topic is "I don't know." To advance beyond Point A, they have to put in effort, starting with the first stage: hypothesis formation.

Hypothesis Formation

Top-rung thinking forms hypotheses from the bottom up. Rather than adopt the beliefs and assumptions of conventional wisdom, you puzzle together your own ideas, from scratch. This is a three-part process:

1. Gather information

In order to puzzle, you need pieces. Each of us is constantly flooded with information, and we have severely limited attention to allot. In other words, your mind is an exclusive VIP-only club with a tough bouncer.

But when Scientists want to learn something new, they try to soak up a wide variety of information on the topic. The Scientist seeks out ideas across the Idea Spectrum, even those that seem likely to be wrong—because knowing the range of viewpoints that exist about the topic *is* a key facet of understanding the topic.

2. Evaluate information

If gathering info is about quantity, evaluating info is all about quality.

There are instances when a thinker has the time and the means to collect information and evidence *directly*—with their own primary observations, or by conducting their own studies. But most of the info we use to inform ourselves is *indirect* knowledge: knowledge accumulated by others that we import into our minds and adopt as our own. Every statistic you come across, everything you read in a textbook, everything you learn from parents or teachers, everything you see or read in the news or on social media, every tenet of conventional wisdom—it's all indirect knowledge.

That's why perhaps the most important skill of a skilled thinker is knowing when to *trust*.

Trust, when assigned wisely, is an efficient knowledge-acquisition trick. If you can trust a person who actually speaks the truth, you can take the knowledge that person worked hard for—either through primary research or indirectly, using their own diligent trust criteria—and "photocopy" it into your own brain. This magical intellectual corner-cutting tool has allowed humanity to accumulate so much collective knowledge over the past ten thousand years that a species of primates can now understand the origins of the universe.

But trust assigned wrongly has the opposite effect. When people trust information to be true that isn't, they end up with the *illusion* of knowledge—which is worse than having no knowledge at all.

So skilled thinkers work hard to master the art of *skepticism*. A thinker who believes everything they hear is too gullible, and their beliefs become packed with a jumble of falsehoods, misconceptions, and contradictions. Someone who trusts no one is overly cynical, even paranoid, and limited to gaining new information only by direct experience. Neither of these fosters much learning.

The Scientist's default skepticism position would be somewhere in between, with a filter just tight enough to consistently identify and weed out bullshit, just open enough to let in the truth. As they become familiar with certain information sources—friends, media brands, articles, books—the Scientist evaluates the sources based on how accurate they've proven to be in the past. For sources known to be obsessed with accuracy, the Scientist loosens up the trust filter. When the Scientist catches a source putting out inaccurate or biased ideas, they tighten up the filter and take future information with a grain of salt.

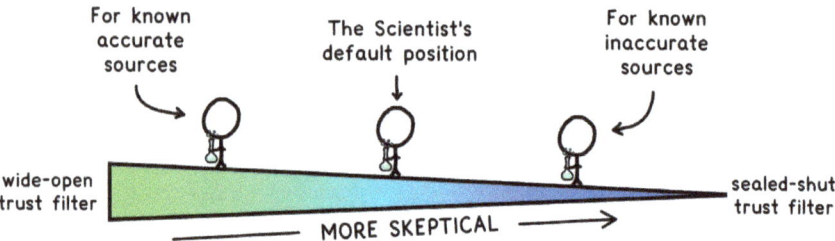

When enough information puzzle pieces have been collected, the third stage of the process begins.

3. Puzzle together a hypothesis

The gathering and evaluating phases rely heavily on the learnings of others, but for the Scientist, the final puzzle is mostly a work of independent reasoning. When it's time to form an opinion, their head becomes a wide-open creative laboratory.

Scientists, so rigid about their high-up position on the vertical How You Think axis, start out totally agnostic about their *horizontal* position on the What You Think axis. Early on in the puzzling process, they treat the Idea Spectrum like a skating rink, happily gliding back and forth as they explore different possible viewpoints.

As the gathering and evaluating processes continue, the Scientist grows more confident in their puzzling. Eventually, they begin to settle on a portion of the Idea Spectrum where they suspect the truth may lie. Their puzzle is finally taking shape—they have begun to form a *hypothesis*.

Hypothesis Testing

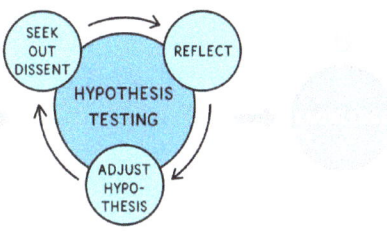

Imagine I present to you this boxer, and we have this exchange:

You'd think I was insane.

But people do this with ideas all the time. They feel sure they're right about an opinion they've never had to defend—an opinion that has never stepped into the ring. Scientists know that an untested belief is only a hypothesis—a boxer with *potential*, but not a champion of anything.

So the Scientist starts expressing the idea publicly, in person and online. It's time to see if the little guy can box.

In the world of ideas, boxing opponents come in the form of *dissent*. When the Scientist starts throwing ideas out into the world, the punches pour in.

Biased reasoning, oversimplification, logical fallacies, and questionable statistics are the weak spots that feisty dissenters look for, and every effective blow landed on the hypothesis helps the Scientist improve their ideas. This is why Scientists actively seek out dissent. As organizational psychologist Adam Grant puts it in his book *Think Again*:

> I've noticed a paradox in great scientists and superforecasters: the reason they're so comfortable being wrong is that they're terrified of being wrong. What sets them apart is the time horizon. They're determined to reach the correct answer in the long run, and they know that means they have to be open to stumbling, backtracking, and rerouting in the short run. They shun rose-colored glasses in favor of a sturdy mirror.

The more boxing matches the Scientist puts their hypothesis through, the more they're able to explore the edges of their conclusions and tweak their ideas into crisper and more confident beliefs.

With some serious testing and a bunch of refinements under their belt, the Scientist may begin to feel that they have arrived at Point B: knowledge.

It's a long road to knowledge for the Scientist because truth is hard. It's why Scientists say "I don't know" so often. It's why, even after getting to Point B in the learning process, the Scientist applies a little asterisk, knowing that all beliefs are subject to being proven wrong by changing times or new evidence. Thinking like a Scientist isn't about knowing a lot, it's about being aware of what you do and don't know—about staying close to this dotted line as you learn: →

When you're thinking like a Scientist—self-aware, free of bias, unattached to any particular ideas, motivated entirely by truth and continually willing to revise your beliefs—your brain is a hyper-efficient learning machine.

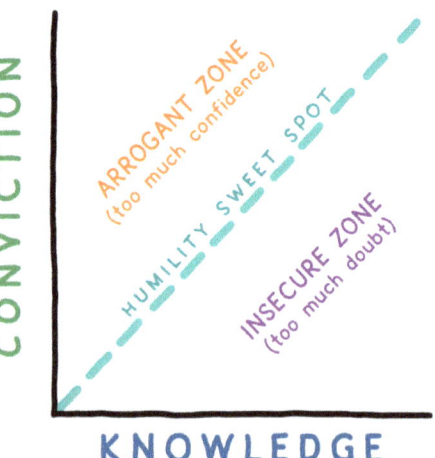

But the thing is—it's *hard* to think like a Scientist, and most of us are bad at it most of the time. When your Primitive Mind wakes up and enters the scene, it's very easy to drift down to the second rung of our Ladder—a place where your thinking is caught up in the tug-of-war.

RUNG 2: THINKING LIKE A SPORTS FAN

Most real-life sports fans want the games they watch to be played fairly. They don't want corrupt referees, even if it helps their team win. They place immense value on the integrity of the process itself. It's just…that they really, really want that process to yield a certain outcome. They're not just watching the game—they're *rooting*.

When your Primitive Mind infiltrates your reasoning process, you start thinking the same way. You still believe you're starting at Point A, and you still want Point B to be the truth. But you're not exactly objective about it.

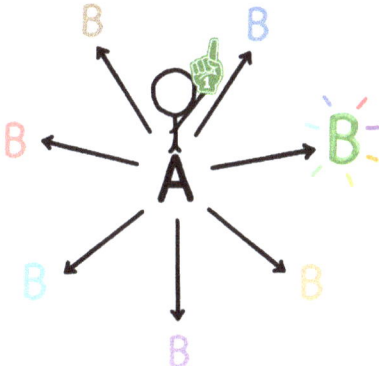

Weird things happen to your thinking when the drive for truth is infected by some ulterior motive. Psychologists call it "motivated reasoning." I like to think of it as Reasoning While Motivated—the thinking equivalent of drunk driving. As the sixth-century Chinese Zen master Seng-ts'an explains:

> If you want the truth to stand clear before you, never be for or against.
> The struggle between "for" and "against" is the mind's worst disease.

When you're thinking like a Sports Fan, Seng-ts'an and his apostrophe *and* his hyphen are all mad at you, because they know what they're about to see—the Scientist's rigorous thinking process corrupted by the truth-seeker's most treacherous obstacle: Confirmation bias.

Confirmation bias is the invisible hand of the Primitive Mind that tries to push you toward confirming your existing beliefs and pull you away from changing your mind.

You still gather information, but you may cherry-pick sources that seem to support your ideas. With the Primitive Mind affecting your emotions, it just *feels good* to have your views confirmed, while hearing dissent feels irritating.

You still evaluate information, but instead of defaulting to the trust filter's middle setting, you find yourself flip-flopping on either side of it, depending less on the proven track record of the source than on how much the source seems to *agree with you*:

So the puzzle pieces collected in the Sports Fan's head are skewed toward confirming a certain belief, and this is then compounded by a corrupted puzzling process. Compelling dissent that does make it into a Sports Fan's head is often forgotten about and left out of the final puzzle.

When it's time to test the hypothesis, the Sports Fan's bias again rears its head. If you were thinking like a Scientist, you'd feel very little attachment to your hypothesis. But now you watch your little machine box as a *fan*, wearing its jersey. It's Your Guy in the ring. And if it wins an argument, you might even catch yourself thinking, *We won!*

When a good punch is landed on your hypothesis, you're likely to see it as a cheap shot or a lucky swing or something else that's not really legit. And when your hypothesis lands a punch, you may have a tendency to overrate the magnitude of the blow or the high level of skill it involved.

Being biased skews your assessment of other people's thinking too. You believe you're unbiased, so someone actually being neutral appears to you to be biased in the other direction, while someone who shares your bias appears to be neutral.

As this process wears on, it's no surprise that the Sports Fan often ends up just where they were hoping to—at their preferred Point B.

On this second rung of the Ladder, the hyper-optimized learning machine that is the Scientist's brain has become hampered by a corrupting motivation. But despite learning less than the Scientist, the Sports Fan usually feels a little *more* confident about their beliefs.

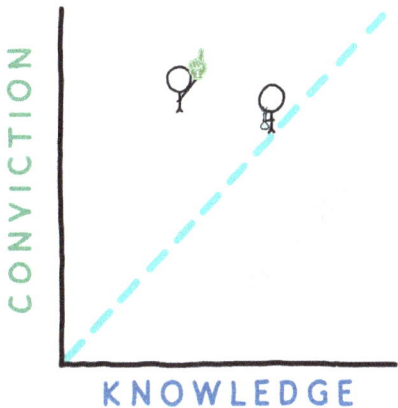

Sports Fans are stubborn, but they're not hopeless. The Higher Mind is still a strong presence in their head, and if dissenting evidence is strong enough, the Sports Fan will grudgingly change their mind. Underneath all the haze of cognitive bias, Sports Fans still care most about finding the truth.

Drift down any further, though, and you cross the Ladder midpoint and become a different kind of thinker entirely. Down on the low rungs, the Primitive Mind has the edge in the tug-of-war. Whether you'll admit it or not (you won't), the desire to feel right, and appear right, has overcome your desire to *be* right. And when some other motivation surpasses your drive for truth, you leave the world of intellectual integrity and enter a new place.

Unconvinceable* Land is a world of green grass, blue sky, and a bunch of people whose beliefs can't be swayed by any amount of evidence. When you end up here, it means you've become a disciple of some line of thinking—a religion, a political ideology, the dogma of a subculture. Either way, your intellectual integrity has taken a back seat to intellectual *loyalty*.

As we descend into Unconvinceable Land, we hit the Ladder's third rung.

---

* My copyeditor tried to change this to "inconvincible" because "unconvinceable" isn't a word. But I like "Unconvinceable Land" more, so you'll just have to deal with it.

RUNG 3: THINKING LIKE AN ATTORNEY

An Attorney and a Sports Fan have things in common. They're both conflicted between the intellectual values of truth and confirmation. The critical difference is which value, deep down, they hold more sacred. A Sports Fan wants to win, but when pushed, cares most about truth. But it's as if an Attorney's *job* is to win, and nothing can alter their allegiance.

Because would this be a good attorney?

No, it wouldn't. An Attorney is *on a team, period*.

When you're thinking like an Attorney, you don't start at Point A at all. You start at Point B. *The client is not guilty. Now let's figure out why.*

From there you'll go through your due diligence, cherry-picking evidence and piecing together an argument that leads right where you want it to.

This isn't a criticism of real-world attorneys. In an actual courtroom, the attorney's way of thinking makes sense—because each attorney's case is only *half* of what will be presented to the jury. Real-world attorneys know that the best way for the *system* to yield truth is for them to make the best possible case for one side of the story. But on our Ladder, the *cognitive* Attorney's head is like a courtroom with only one side represented—in other words, a corrupt courtroom where the ruling is predetermined.

The Attorney treats their preferred beliefs not like an experiment that can be revised, or even a favorite sports team, but like a *client*. Motivated reasoning becomes obligated reasoning, and the gathering, evaluating, and puzzling processes function like law associates whose only job is to help build the case for Point B.

If someone really wants to believe something—that the Earth is flat, that 9/11 was orchestrated by Americans, that the CIA is after them—the human brain will find a way to make that belief seem perfectly clear and irrefutable. For the Attorney, the hypothesis formation stage is really a belief-strengthening process. They inevitably end up with the same viewpoints they started with, now beefed up with a refreshed set of facts and arguments that remind them just how right they are.

In the hypothesis testing phase, the Attorney's refusal to genuinely listen to a dissenter, combined with a bag of logical fallacy tricks and their strong sense of conviction, ensures that they're an absolutely infuriating person to argue with. The Attorney's opponents will feel like they're arguing with a brick wall, and by the end, it'll be clear that nothing they could have said—nothing whatsoever—would have made the Attorney say, "Hmm that's a good point. I need to think about that. Maybe I'm wrong."

The result of thinking like an Attorney is that your brain's incredible ability to learn new things is mostly shut down. Even worse, your determination to confirm your existing beliefs leaves you confident about a bunch of things that aren't true. Your efforts only make you more delusional. If there's anything you can say about Attorney thinking, it's that it at least acknowledges the *concept* of the knowledge-building process. When you're thinking like an Attorney, you're unconvinceable, but you're not *that* big an internal shift away from high-rung thinking. From somewhere in the periphery of your mind, the voice of the Higher Mind still carries some weight. And if you can learn to listen to it and value it, maybe things can change.

But sometimes, there are beliefs that your Primitive Mind holds so dear that your Higher Mind has no influence at all over how you think about them. When dealing with these topics, ideas and people feel inseparable and changing your mind feels like an existential threat. You're on the bottom rung.

RUNG 4: THINKING LIKE A ZEALOT

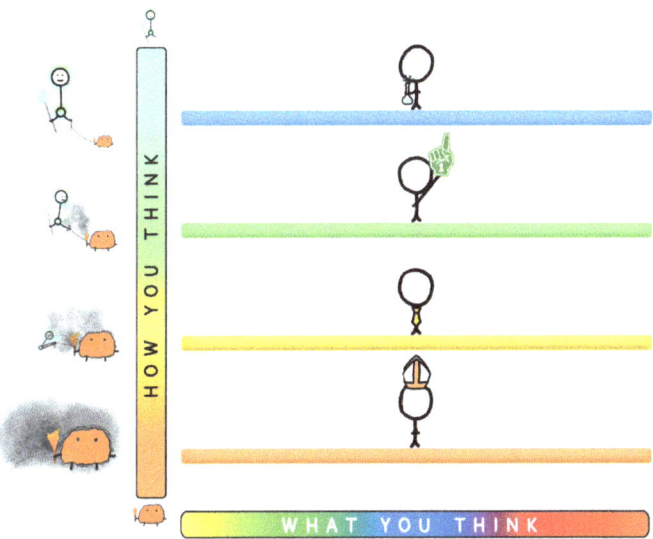

Imagine you've just had your first baby. Super exciting, right?

And every day when you look at your baby, you can't believe how cute it is.

This is the relationship Zealots have with their sacred ideas: the ideas aren't rugged experiments to be kicked around, they're fragile, precious babies to be adored and protected.

Just like no parent has to research whether their baby is lovable, the Zealot doesn't have to go from A to B to know their viewpoints are correct—they just know they are. With 100 percent conviction.*

---

* Thinking like a Zealot leaves someone low on the knowledge axis because it...

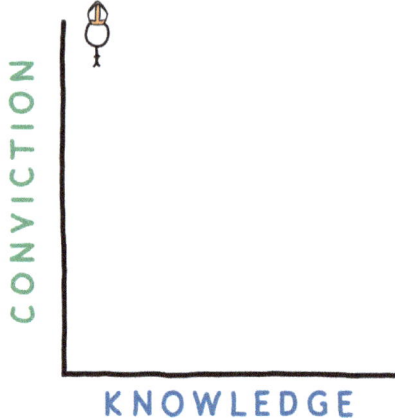

Likewise with skepticism. If someone told you your actual baby was super cute, you wouldn't assess their credibility, you'd be in automatic full agreement. And if someone told you your baby was an asshole, you wouldn't consider their opinion, you'd just think they were a terrible person.

That's why the Zealot's flip-flop goes from one extreme to the other, with no in-between.

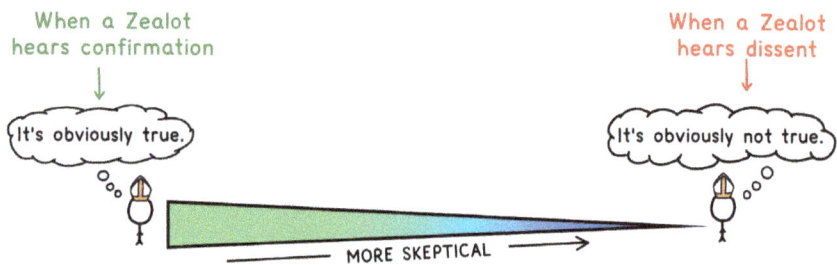

When Zealots argue, things can quickly get heated, because for someone who identifies with their ideas, a challenge to those ideas feels like an insult. It feels personally invalidating. A punch landed on a Zealot's idea is a punch landed on their baby.

...means their knowledge-acquisition mechanism isn't working correctly. It doesn't mean they're wrong about every opinion—just that when they're right, it's a credit to luck more than to their own reasoning abilities.

When the Primitive Mind is overactive in our heads, it turns us into crazy people. On top of making us think our ideas are babies, it shows us a distorted view of ourselves.

And it shows us a distorted view of the world. While the Scientist's clear mind sees a foggy world, full of complexity and nuance and messiness, the Zealot's foggy mind shows them a clear, simple world, full of crisp lines and black-and-white distinctions. When you're thinking like a Zealot, you end up in a totally alternative reality, feeling like you're an omniscient being in total possession of the truth.

High-Rung Thinking, Low-Rung Thinking

The four thinking rungs are all distinct, but they fall into two broad categories: high-rung thinking (Scientist and Sports Fan) and low-rung thinking (Attorney and Zealot).

High-rung thinking is independent thinking, leaving you free to revise your ideas or even discard them altogether. But when there's no amount of evidence that will change your mind about something, it means that idea is your boss. On the low rungs, you're working to dutifully serve your ideas, not the other way around.

High-rung thinking is productive thinking. The humility of the high-rung mindset makes your mind a permeable filter that absorbs life experience and converts it into knowledge and wisdom. On the other hand, the arrogance of low-rung thinking makes your mind a rubber shell that life experience bounces off of. One begets learning, the other ignorance.

We all spend time on the low rungs,* and when we're thinking this way, we don't realize we're doing it. We believe our conviction has been hard-earned. We believe our viewpoints are original and based on knowledge. Because as the Primitive Mind's influence grows in our heads, so does the fog that clouds our consciousness. This is how low-rung thinking persists.

---

* In case you're thinking, *I'm a really smart person, so I'm safe from the low rungs*, Adam Grant has bad news for you: "Research reveals that the higher you score on an IQ test, the more likely you are to fall for stereotypes, because you're faster at recognizing patterns. And recent experiments suggest that the smarter you are, the more you might struggle to update your beliefs."

Each of us is a work in progress. We'll never rid our lives of low-rung thinking, but the more we evolve psychologically, the more time we spend thinking from the high rungs and the less time we spend down below. Improving this ratio is a good intellectual goal for all of us.

But this is just the beginning of our journey. Because individual thinking is the center of a much larger picture. We're social creatures, and as with most things, the way we think is often intertwined with the people we surround ourselves with.

INTELLECTUAL CULTURES

We can define "culture" as the unwritten rules regarding "how we do things here."

Every human environment—from two-person couples to twenty-person classrooms to twenty-thousand-person companies—is embedded with its own culture. We can visualize a group's culture as a kind of gas cloud that fills the room when the group is together.

A group's culture influences its members with a social incentive system. Those who play by the culture's rules are rewarded with acceptance, respect, and praise, while violating the culture will result in penalties like ridicule, shame, and ostracism.

Human society is a rich tapestry of overlapping and sometimes sharply contradictory cultures, and each of us lives at our own unique cultural intersection.

Someone working at a tech startup in the Bay Area is simultaneously living within the global Western community, the American community, the West Coast community, the San Francisco community, the tech industry community, the startup community, the community of their workplace, the community of their college alumni, the community of their extended family, the community of their group of friends, and a few other bizarre
SF-y situations. Going against the current of all these larger communities combined tends to be easier than violating the unwritten rules of our most intimate microcultures, made up of our immediate family, closest friends, and romantic relationships.

Living simultaneously in multiple cultures is part of what makes being a human tricky. Do we keep our individual inner values to ourselves and just do our best to match our external behavior to whatever culture we're currently in a room with? Or do we stay loyal to one particular culture and live by those rules everywhere, even at our social or professional peril? Do we navigate our lives to seek out external cultures that match our own values and minimize friction? Or do we surround ourselves with a range of conflicting cultures to put some pressure on our inner minds to learn and grow? Whether you consciously realize it or not, you're making these decisions all the time.

Culture can encompass many aspects of interaction. A group of friends, for example, has a way they do birthdays, a way they do emojis, a way they do talking behind each other's backs, a way they do conflict, and so on. For our purposes, we'll again limit our discussion to how all this pertains to thinking, or to a group's *intellectual* culture—"how we do things here" as it relates to the expression of ideas.

In the same way the two aspects of your mind compete for control over how you think, a similar struggle happens on a larger scale over how the *group* thinks. Higher Minds can band together with other Higher Minds and form a kind of coalition, and a group's collective Primitive Minds can do the same thing. One coalition gaining control over the culture is like home-field advantage in sports—a hard one for the away team to overcome.

Let's first explore what it looks like when the Higher Minds have the reins of a group's intellectual culture.

IDEA LABS

Most of us know the term "Echo Chamber," and we'll get to that in a minute—but we sorely lack a term for the *opposite* of an Echo Chamber. When the rules of a group's intellectual culture mirror the values of high-rung thinking, the group is what I call an **Idea Lab**.

An Idea Lab is an environment of *collaborative high-rung thinking*. People in an Idea Lab see one another as experimenters and their ideas as experiments. Idea Labs value independent thinking and viewpoint diversity. This combination leads to the richest and most interesting conversations and maximizes the scope of group discussions.

Idea Labs place a high regard on humility, and saying "I don't know" usually wins trust and respect. When someone who often says "I don't know" *does* express conviction about a viewpoint, it really means something, and others will take it to heart without too much skepticism needed—which saves the listener time and effort. Likewise, unearned conviction is a major no-no in an Idea Lab. So someone with a reputation for bias or arrogance or dishonesty will be met with a high degree of skepticism, no matter how much conviction they express.

Idea Labs also love arguments. Ideas in an Idea Lab are treated like hypotheses, which means people are always looking for opportunities to test what they've been thinking about. Idea Labs are the perfect boxing ring for that testing.

Sometimes high-rung thinkers engage in *debate*, defending an idea, strenuously arguing for its validity.

Other times, they'll engage in *dialectic*, joining the dissenter in examining their idea.

They may even try flipping sides and playing *devil's advocate*, debating against someone who agrees with them in order to see their idea through another lens.

People in an Idea Lab don't usually take arguments personally because Idea Lab culture is built around the core notion that people and ideas are separate things. People are meant to be respected, ideas are meant to be batted around and picked apart.

Perhaps most importantly, an Idea Lab helps its members stay high up on the Ladder. No one thinks like pure top-rung Scientists all the time. More often, after a brief stint on the top rung during an especially lucid and humble period, we start to *like* the new epiphanies we gleaned up there a little too much, and we quickly drop down to the Sports Fan rung. And that's okay. It might even be optimal to be a *little* overconfident in our intellectual lives. Rooting for our ideas—a new philosophy, a new lifestyle choice, a new business strategy—allows us to really give them a try, somewhat liberated from the constant "but are we really sure about this?" nag from the Higher Mind.

The Sports Fan rung alone isn't a problem. The problem is that inviting some bias into the equation is a bit like closing your eyes *for just another minute* after you've shut your alarm off for good—it's riskier than it feels. Getting a little attached to an idea is a small step away from drifting unconsciously into Unconvinceable Land and the oblivion of the rungs down below. We're preprogrammed to be low-rung thinkers, so our intellects are always fighting against gravity.

This is why Idea Lab culture is so important. It's a support network for flawed thinkers to help each other stay up on the high rungs.

The social pressure helps. If high-rung thinking is what all the cool kids are doing, you're more likely to think that way.

And the intellectual pressure helps. In an Idea Lab—where people don't hesitate to tell you when you're wrong or biased or hypocritical or gullible—humility and self-awareness are *inflicted* upon you. Whenever you get a little too overconfident, Idea Lab culture pulls you back to an honest level of conviction.

All these forces combine to make an Idea Lab a big magnet on top of the Ladder that pulls upward on the psyches of people immersed in it.

But what happens when a group's Primitive Minds can run things their way?

ECHO CHAMBERS

An **Echo Chamber** is what happens when a group's intellectual culture slips down to the low rungs: collaborative low-rung thinking.

While Idea Labs are cultures of critical thinking and debate, Echo Chambers are cultures of groupthink and conformity. Because while Idea Labs are devoted to a *kind of thinking*, Echo Chambers are devoted to a *set of beliefs* the culture deems to be sacred.

A culture that treats ideas like sacred objects incentivizes entirely different behavior than the Idea Lab. In an Echo Chamber, falling in line with the rest of the group is socially rewarded. It's a common activity to talk about how obviously correct the sacred ideas are—it's how you express your allegiance to the community and prove your own intellectual and moral worth.

Humility is looked down upon in an Echo Chamber, where saying "I don't know" just makes you sound ignorant and changing your mind makes you seem wishy-washy. And conviction, used sparingly in an Idea Lab, is social currency in an Echo Chamber. The more conviction you speak with, the more knowledgeable, intelligent, and righteous you seem.

Idea Labs can simultaneously respect a person and disrespect the person's ideas. But Echo Chambers equate a person's ideas with their identity, so respecting a person and respecting their ideas are one and the same. Disagreeing with someone in an Echo Chamber is seen not as intellectual exploration but as *rudeness*, making an argument about ideas indistinguishable from a *fight*.

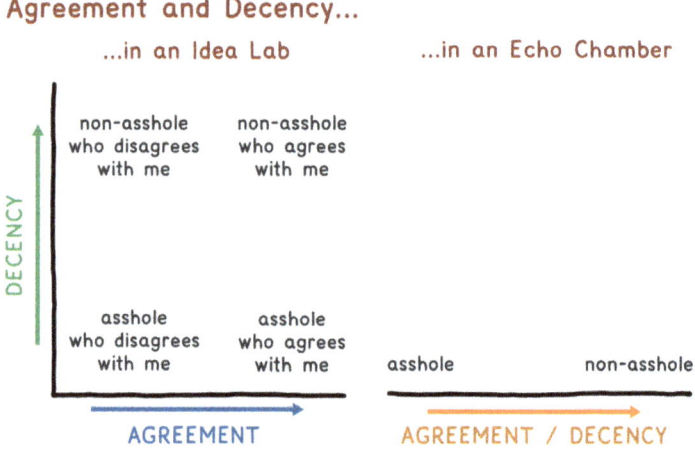

This moral component provides Echo Chambers with a powerful tool for cultural law enforcement: taboo. Those who challenge the sacred ideas are seen not just as wrong but as *bad people*. As such, violators are slapped with the social fines of status reduction or reputation damage, the social jail time of ostracism, and even the social death penalty of permanent excommunication. Express the wrong opinion on God, abortion, patriotism, immigration, race, or capitalism in the wrong group and you may be met with an explosive negative reaction. Echo Chambers are places where you must watch what you say.

An Echo Chamber can be the product of a bunch of people who all hold certain ideas to be sacred. Other times, it can be the product of one or a few "intellectual bullies" who everyone else is scared to defy. Even in the smallest group—a married couple, say—if one person knows that it's never worth the fight to challenge their spouse's strongly held viewpoints, the spouse is effectively imposing Echo Chamber culture on the marriage.

Intellectual cultures have a major impact on the individuals within them. While Idea Lab culture encourages intellectual and moral growth, Echo Chamber culture discourages new ideas, curbs intellectual innovation, and removes knowledge-acquisition tools like debate—all of which repress growth.

Spending too much time in an Echo Chamber makes people feel less humble and more sure of themselves, all while limiting actual learning and causing thinking skills to atrophy.

In a broader sense, both primitive-mindedness and high-mindedness tend to be contagious. While Idea Lab culture is a support group that helps keep people's minds up on the high rungs, Echo Chamber culture pumps out Primitive Mind pheromones and exerts a general downward pull on the psyches of its members.

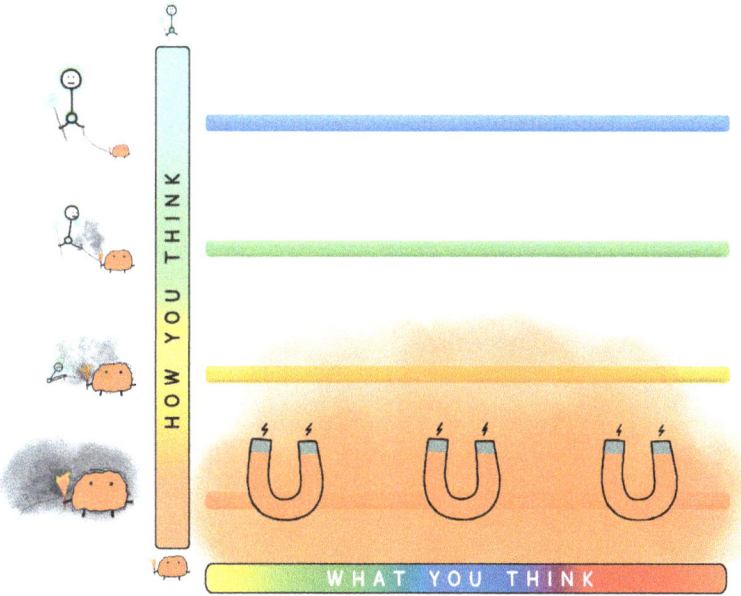

Given the obvious benefits of Idea Lab culture, it's odd that we ever go for the alternative. We eat Skittles because our Primitive Minds are programmed to want sugary, calorie-dense food. But why do our Primitive Minds want us to build Echo Chambers?

Let's zoom out further.

GIANTS

Billions of years ago, some single-celled creatures realized that being just one cell left your options pretty limited.

So they figured out a cool trick. By joining together with other single cells, they could form a giant creature that had all kinds of new advantages.

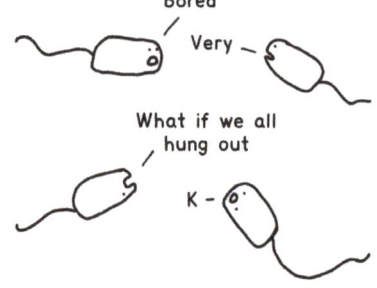

This concept—a bunch of smaller things joining together to form a giant that can function as more than the sum of its parts—is called emergence. We can visualize it using an **Emergence Tower**.

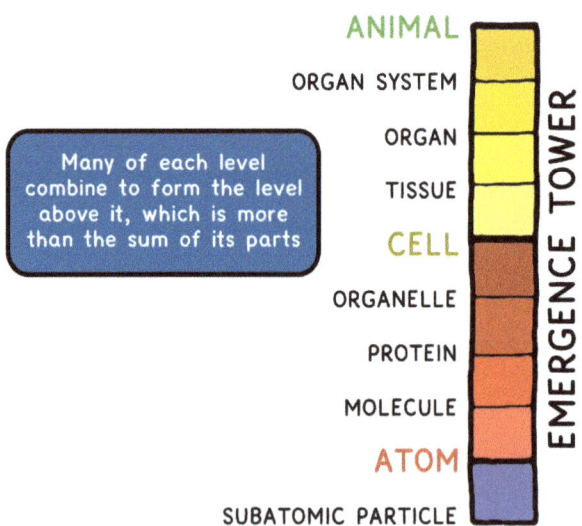

Not long after cells started joining together to form animals, some of the animals discovered that they could go up *another* level of emergence and form even bigger giants made up of multiple animals.

Sometimes, when we see animals cooperating, it seems like they're being considerate—but that's missing the bigger picture. The emergence picture.

Take ants and spiders. Ants are furiously loyal. They always put the team first. The ants I've gotten to know in my life have a long list of bad personal qualities, but "individual selfishness" isn't one of them.

Meanwhile, two rival spiders will compete with each other ruthlessly, both entirely self-interested.

So what's the deal? Are ants nicer than spiders?

No. It's just that spiders stop doing the emergence thing at the individual organism level, while ants go up a level higher—to the ant *colony*.

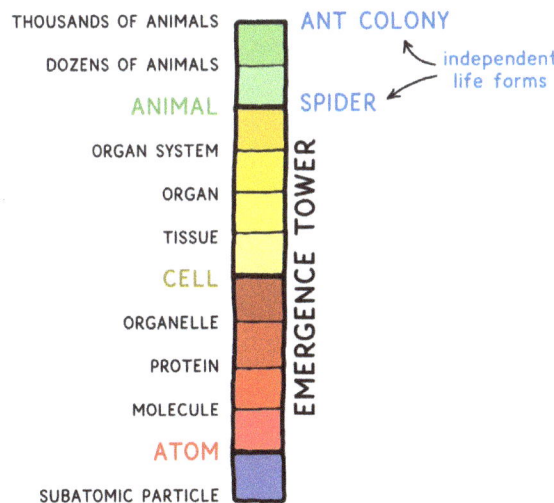

The ant colony is really the "independent life form" of the ant world. If we look at how ant colonies treat other ant colonies, it's a lot like the way one spider treats another.

Individual ants in a colony are kind of like the cells that make up your body, which cooperate with each other not because they're nice, but because they're part of a bigger life form.

Humans do emergence too—and like all things human, it's complicated.

First, in the same way we bounce up and down the Ladder, we're all over the place on the Emergence Tower.

You might wake up in the morning with your psyche firmly on the bottom of the tower, feeling like a lone individual. You head to work, where you brainstorm a project with five other people, becoming part of a six-person thinking machine. After work you join a political protest outside, losing your sense of self in the exhilaration of being a tiny piece of a thousand-person megaphone. Depending on the situation, we can act like spiders *or* ants, and everything in between. It's as if there's an elevator in the Emergence Tower, and our minds take regular trips up and down.

Second, humans form weird giants. There are all kinds of ways animal species "glue" together into higher-emergence giants. Simple creatures like ants and bees achieve cooperation on a mass scale, which comes at the expense of individual autonomy. Complex animals like wolves, lions, and dolphins are more individually independent, but they also have smaller families, which typically limits the size of the "giant" they can make.

Early humans were similar to other complex animals—limited to small, tightly knit tribes. But at some point along the way, we figured out how to hack the system. By uniting through shared beliefs, shared culture, shared values, or shared interests, we shattered the previous ceiling on giant size and achieved something other complex animals couldn't: mass cooperation.

When you take the already impressive power of human cognition and combine it with the capability of mass cooperation, you have a species with superpowers.

But here we come back to our Ladder, because the human Higher Mind and Primitive Mind each have their own way of doing emergence. Idea Labs and Echo Chambers are more than just group cultures—they're two very different ways to build a human giant.

HIGH-RUNG GIANTS: GENIES

Your brain is a giant of its own, made up of a network of eighty-six billion neurons. An isolated neuron is pretty useless.

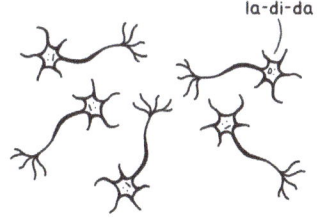

But by *communicating* with one another, a group of neurons can move upward on the Emergence Tower and combine into a single thinking system that's far more powerful than the sum of its parts: the brain.

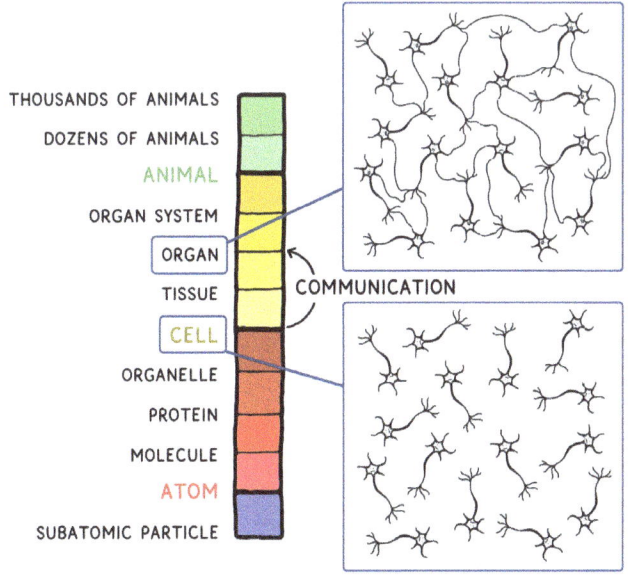

A parallel phenomenon happens a few floors up the tower, on the human level. A bunch of people together, but not communicating, is just a bunch of individual brains in the same place. Language is so important because it allows individual brains to *connect*, like neurons, to form a larger thinking system: a communal brain.

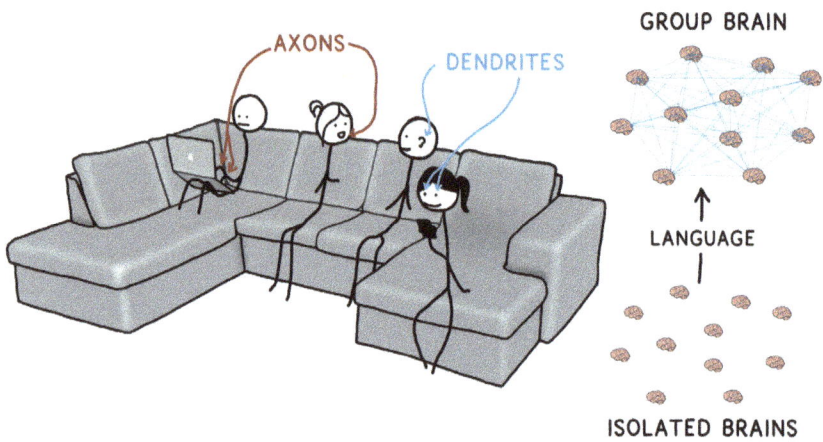

In his book *The Righteous Mind*, social psychologist Jonathan Haidt talks about how group communal brains work:

> If you put individuals together in the right way, such that some individuals can use their reasoning powers to disconfirm the claims of others...you can create a group that ends up producing good reasoning as an emergent property of the social system. This is why it's so important to have intellectual and ideological diversity within any group or institution whose goal is to find truth.

This is the magic of Idea Lab culture. While individual thinking suffers from bias, a *diversity* of biases helps the communal brain reduce blind spots. In a culture where changing your mind is encouraged, new findings spread quickly through the system, and all it takes is one member discovering a falsehood for the whole group to reject it. When disagreement is encouraged, new ideas can be tested as they're being formed, in real time, combining the knowledge-building efforts of each person into a single, dynamic process.

The result is a multi-mind thinking system that's superior to any of its individual members at learning new things and separating truth from fiction. Let's call this thinking system a **genie**.

Because genies convert disagreement into higher-level collaboration, there's nothing stopping them from endlessly scaling up. For example, a research institution is an official Idea Lab, where practices like peer review generate a hyperefficient genie. But then, research centers from different universities or even different countries can criticize or build upon each other's findings, allowing many genies to combine forces into a global supergenie.

None of this collaboration comes at the expense of the individual. Quite the opposite, as genies flourish when its members are independent thinkers. So people in a genie get the best of all emergence worlds: they can simultaneously thrive as free individuals and as smaller pieces of a larger system.

This is the Higher Mind's way of building giants. When Primitive Minds take the reins, we end up with an entirely different kind of beast.

LOW-RUNG GIANTS: GOLEMS

In 1245, the Pope approached a minister named Giovanni da Pian del Carpini with a request.

So Giovanni got on his horse and spent four months traveling three thousand miles to Mongolia—a place almost no Europeans had ever set foot (Marco Polo wouldn't begin his famous voyage for another twenty-six years). Somehow Giovanni survived the whole ordeal and, after spending four months with Mongols, made his way back to Europe.*

---

* Btw Giovanni was *sixty-five* when he started his voyage. Such an annoying thing for a senior citizen to have to deal with.

It turns out the Mongols were not overhyped. Giovanni wrote a book about how they lived and how they conducted their conquests.

According to Giovanni, the Mongol army was organized using a decimal system that worked like this:

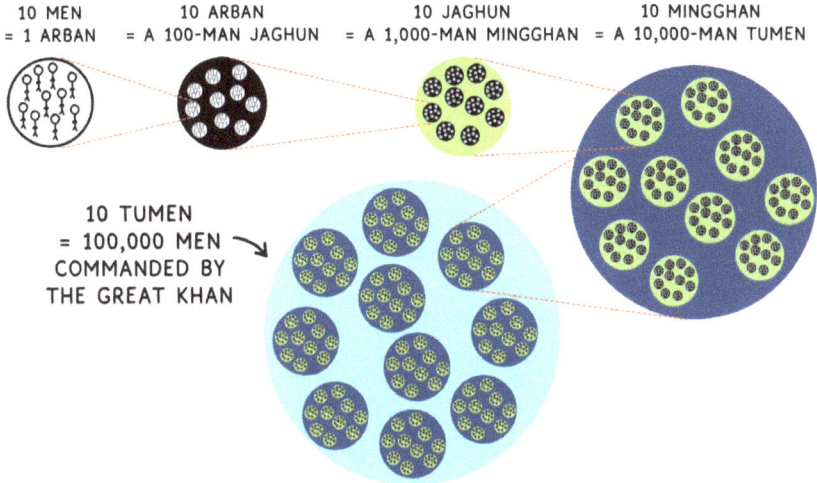

Giovanni wrote about the incredibly strict discipline Mongol rulers imposed on their army:

> When they join battle against any other nation, unless they do all consent to retreat, every man who deserts is put to death. And if one or two, or more, of ten proceed manfully to the battle, but the residue of those ten draw back and follow not the company, they are in like matter slain. Also, if one among ten or more be taken, their fellows, if they fail to rescue them, are punished with death.

Pretty happy I'm not in the Mongol army. But I'm even happier to not be in the *path* of the Mongol army. Historian J. J. Saunders writes:

> [Genghis] was adept at psychological warfare of the most horrific kind. He deliberately set out to create a reputation for ferocious terror in the expectation (often realized) of frightening whole

nations into surrendering without resistance. There is something indescribably revolting in the cold savagery with which the Mongols carried out their massacres. The inhabitants of a doomed town were obliged to assemble in a plain outside the walls, and each Mongol trooper, armed with a battle-axe, was told to kill so many people, ten, twenty, or fifty....A few days after the massacre, troops were sent back into the ruined city to search for any poor wretches who might be hiding in holes or cellars; these were dragged out and slain.

How many people can you name who lived in the 1200s? Like two, right? But you know about Genghis Khan. Everybody knows about Genghis Khan. Because Genghis Khan built one of the biggest, baddest golems in human history.

In mythology, a **golem** is a big dumb-looking monster, which makes it a perfect representation of the low-rung giant.

If the genie is the product of human collaboration, the golem is the emergent property of human obedience. Golems are what happen when humans act like ants.

Ant behavior has two components: strict conformity within the colony and total ruthlessness when dealing with other colonies.

On the internal conformity side, Mongol leaders viewed their army like a machine. If a member of a ten-man unit deserted, they saw that unit as a defective part in the machine that couldn't police itself, so they tossed it out by killing the whole unit. This may sound insane to us, but if your only goal is to create the perfect golem, this is simply like cutting out a cancerous tumor before it spreads.

On the external ruthlessness side, the Mongol army had clear rules for settled societies that lay in its path: you're with us or against us. If you immediately surrender, you'll be allowed to join our forces and live. If you resist, we will destroy you, down to every man, woman, and child.

I use the Mongols as an example because they're the extreme version of a human golem. But golems are everywhere. When a group of people exhibits a combination of strict conformity internally and an Us vs. Them mindset externally—militaries marching in unison, activists chanting a slogan, citizens raising a fist or saluting en masse, or just a group of people being super Echo-Chamber-y—that's a group of people in golem mode.

The human cognitive weaknesses a genie tries to mitigate are the golem's strengths. Confirmation-bias tricks like cherry-picking, motivated skepticism, and motivated reasoning benefit hugely from economies of scale, as the snappiest and most convincing articulations of the sacred ideas spread quickly through the system. Individual biases, all pointing in the same direction in an Echo Chamber, scale up to make the golem's ultra-biased macro-mind. And while individual minds inside a golem may have doubts about the sacred ideas, the social pressure of Echo Chamber culture keeps the giant as a whole steadfast in its beliefs. If the genie is the ultimate Scientist, the golem is the ultimate Zealot—a giant that's totally certain of itself, totally unable to learn or change its mind, and *worse* at thinking than the average human.

But golems aren't made to be good at thinking or finding the truth. The golem's specialty is brute strength. It's a group's way of turning itself into a big scary monster.

We talked about how genies can seamlessly combine forces with other genies to create supergenies. Golems scale up too, but in a very different way—based on conflict. Golems don't just prefer the Us vs. Them mindset, they rely on it. The presence of a rival golem is a critical part of what holds them together. The way golems combine forces is by sharing a common enemy. If a group of golems vanquishes their common enemy, the alliance will often fracture into smaller rival golems to maintain the Us vs. Them structure.

Let's try to jam all of this into a chart:

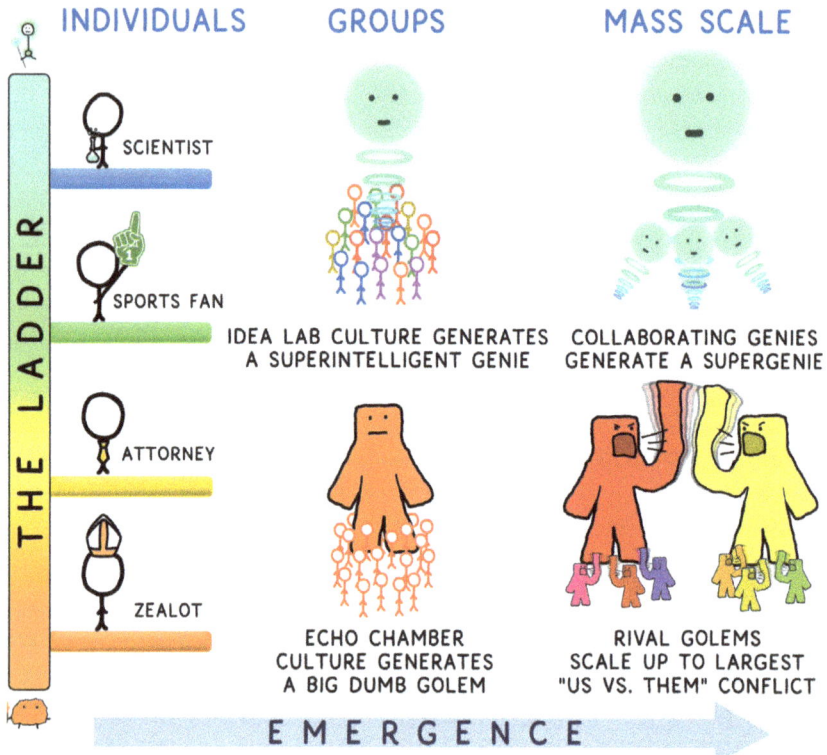

On the high rungs, individuals can thrive and grow, and human intelligence and knowledge can scale up exponentially. The low rungs squash individuality, breed delusion, and sacrifice group intelligence in favor of brute strength and large-scale conflict.

Which brings us back to the same question: Given that the high rungs are so awesome, *why are we so inclined to be down on the shitty low rungs?*

It's what our Primitive Minds are programmed to do because it was the best way to survive in our distant past. Low-rung thinking, low-rung culture, and low-rung giant-building are all ancient survival behavior—behavior that was necessary a long time ago but today seems a lot like moths flying toward streetlights.

When I look out at the world today, I see a rising epidemic of low-rung thinking and behavior. Too many of the Ladder struggles that exist in our heads, in our communities, in our political parties, and in our societies are slipping in the wrong direction.

This is the framework we'll be using throughout the book, and it can also serve as our compass. In the introduction, I compared the path of our species to a big organism trudging its way up a great mountain ridge, with steep cliffs on either side. I see the high rungs as our source of stability and positive progress, and low-rungness as the force pushing us toward those cliffs.

To give ourselves the best chance to stay up on that ridge, we need to see low-rung psychology where it resides and figure out how to outsmart it.

INTERLUDE

THE LIBERAL GAMES

Earlier, we met a bear and a bunny, in a situation that didn't go very well for the bunny.

The animal world is a stressful place to be because there are no morals, no principles, no one to make sure things are fair. The rules are simple:

**Everyone can do whatever they want,
if they have the power to do so.**

If the bear wants to eat the bunny, it can—as long as it can catch it. If the bunny prefers to keep being alive, it can—as long as it's fast enough. And that's about all there is to it.

Let's call this the **Power Games**.

For a long time, humans were like the bunny and the bear—living in some forest or grassy plain, trying to be skilled enough to feed themselves and avoid being eaten, struggling through the Power Games like all the other animals.

But the mass cooperation hack changed everything. It gave humans a tool better than any spear or bow and arrow: the genie.

If you zoom out on human history, you see over a hundred thousand years of people living in small tribes—a time during which knowledge and technological advancements happened very slowly. Then came the agricultural revolution, which brought humans together into much larger cooperative groups—and the same species started performing magic. Knowledge and technology raced forward and built vast civilizations. The people hadn't gotten smarter—but their genies had.

Larger societies yielded genies with ever bigger brains—more people comparing notes, sharing learnings, and debunking misconceptions.

The advent of writing allowed brains to communicate across time and space, enhancing the memories of genies and making them more clearheaded.

The civilization you're living in today, with all of its incredible technology, wasn't created by humans. Humans aren't nearly smart enough to do that. The amazing world around you was created by genies.

Mass cooperation got humans out of the food chain—an accomplishment that would make any bunny or bear envious. But mass cooperation has a dark side. The same emergence hack that gave us genies also generated a scarier superpredator than any bear, lion, or shark: the golem.

As everyone who fell into the expansionary path of the Assyrians, Persians, Macedonians, Romans, Huns, Muslims, Christians, or Mongols could tell you, if a golem comes your way, and you can't put up a strong enough defense, you're finished. You can live in a flourishing high-rung utopia with clear, civilized rules, but when a golem arrives at your gates, none of those rules matter if you can't beat the golem at the Power Games.

For most of our history, the only way to defend yourself against the world's golems was to be able to form an even bigger, fiercer golem yourself. Which is why much of the past ten thousand years was golems fighting other golems, with the biggest, meanest golems ruling the day.

The Primitive Mind was programmed for survival in the Power Games, and this is why we all come programmed to snap into golem mode at the drop of a hat. It's the great catch-22 of our species: the biggest threat to humanity is low-rung humanity, and low-rung humanity persists because it has often been the best defense against this very threat.

To truly free ourselves from the stresses of the animal world, we'd have to find a way to outsmart the scariest superpredator of all. A few hundred years ago, a group of rebellious thinkers started kicking around a plan they believed might be able to do just that.

• • •

PHILADELPHIA, 1776

Rebellion wasn't anything out of the ordinary in 1776, a time when many nations were on the "tyranny → coup → chaos → tyranny" merry-go-round. What was unusual about the American forefathers was their long-term plan.

Normally, the people rebel because they're annoyed about being powerless and they want to turn the tables. So a rebellion topples the tyrant, some chaos ensues, some friends murder friends, and when the dust settles, there's a new tyrant. But this was the late 1700s, and the forefathers were Enlightenment Kids.

During the Enlightenment, philosophers in parts of Europe had started talking about a new story.

The story, building on ideas that had been kicking around Western countries ever since ancient Greece, explored concepts like human rights, legal equality, tolerance, and freedom. The Power Games, the story went, were unpleasant, unfair, unproductive, and unnecessary—and they were fundamentally immoral, violating the most sacred elements of being a human.

The story was like a mind virus, and it started to spread. Before long, it had crossed the Atlantic and taken hold in minds throughout the American colonies, turning well-behaved English subjects into dissatisfied Enlightenment Kids. The American forefathers were coming of age right in the middle of all of this, and they decided to take action.

So they sent a letter to London, explaining the new situation: →

In CONGRESS. July 4, 1776.

The unanimous Declaration of the thirteen united States of America,

Dear George, Super awkward letter, but we've decided that this just isn't working for us anymore. We know we're all supposed to do what you say, but we've thought about it and it kind of seems like you're actually just a guy wearing a king costume. And we're not really sure why that means we all have to listen to you. We think it's self-evident that no one is born with the right to have power over anyone else. Except the people we own. Most of us own a significant number of people. They're a different situation. We'll explain that later. But the point is, you're just pretending to be in charge and everyone else is also pretending that you're in charge but that actually makes no fucking sense so we're gonna stop pretending. So we're just writing this letter to let you know the new situation. You should totally keep doing you, but we're gonna do us from now on. Also we want to change our accent to something less elegant and smart-sounding and it's hard to do that if we're still part of the same country. K hand's getting super tired so gonna go now bye.

King George and his parliament were terribly unamused by the development, and the British waged war. A forty-four-year-old George Washington found himself in charge of fending them off—which, hilariously, his mom apparently hated.

But George didn't let that stop him, and he and his crew, with the help of a delighted France, held off the British long enough that they finally gave up and headed back across the ocean.

The Americans had won their independence, leaving them with a rare opportunity: a chance to create a new kind of country, from scratch—a chance to take the "here's what *I'd* do if I could start my own country" fantasy and actually play it out. It was time to put the Enlightenment to the test.

DESIGNING THE AMERICAN GIANT

We can boil human activity down to a simple operation.

Human nature is a constant, and when you put that constant into different environments, it produces different behavior. That makes environment the independent variable. And human environments are complicated—they include the physical environment, the surrounding people and cultures, the prevailing beliefs and belief systems, and the laws and rules.

Many kings, emperors, and warlords of the past have done environments the Power Games way, governing with totalitarian power, strict laws, and harsh penalties in order to generate controlled and obedient behavior.

Thinkers of the Enlightenment believed they could improve upon this. They believed the same good behavior could be generated with a gentler, fairer, more hands-off form of government. I call this system the **Liberal Games**.*

Instead of being ruled by the cudgel, Liberal Games citizens would be governed by a set of *guiding liberal principles* inspired by Enlightenment philosophy.†

America's founders formalized this with the US Constitution: a set of rules that, rather than serving any particular goal or outcome, would be sacred *in themselves*. The Constitution describes a sacred *process*—a set of inviolable boundaries within which any and all national or individual goals would need to be accomplished. It outlines

> The US has long been embroiled in conflict about how well the country has actually lived up to its promises. In some obvious ways—like the fact that the country's full set of human rights initially applied only to white men—it certainly has not. We'll get into all that later in the book. The first step, though, is to brush up on what the country's promises even are. That's what we're doing in this chapter.

---

* You'll see the word "liberal" a lot in this book. I won't be using the word the way it's often used in American political discourse, as a synonym for politically left (I'll use "progressive" for that). Rather, in this book, "liberal" will always be used in the classic sense, the way it's defined by *The Oxford Encyclopedia of American Cultural and Intellectual History*: "a commitment to individual freedom and to several elements thought to be crucial for sustaining that freedom: a market economy, religious toleration, and a government constrained by law and legitimated by popular consent."

† The US was not the only country of its time to have a constitution, a representative government, or other Enlightenment-style structures. What made it unique was its ability to build these things from a blank slate, without the baggage of a monarchical past muddying the waters.

the means by which leaders would be elected, the means by which conflicts would be settled and people who broke the rules would be punished, the means by which the country could pass bills and make laws and declare war—all processes that emerged from Enlightenment values. Most importantly, the Constitution would protect the people from their own government by strictly limiting its power. The government would be the grand enforcer holding the operation together, but its use of force would be restricted beyond its core tasks.

Another critical component of the Liberal Games pertains to freedom.

One of the worst parts about living in the Power Games is the lack of freedom. Imagine that you're living with 100 percent freedom, and that all of your fellow citizens are also living with 100 percent freedom.

If everyone got along perfectly all the time, this might be able to last. But people have never gotten along perfectly all the time. In the Power Games, when there's a conflict, the rule of power kicks in and whoever has the biggest cudgel gets their way. If someone with the power to bully you decides to restrict an element of your freedom, there's nowhere to turn and no one you can appeal to.

Then comes along an even bigger bully, who gets *their* way. After a few rounds of this, the biggest bully of all is declaring the

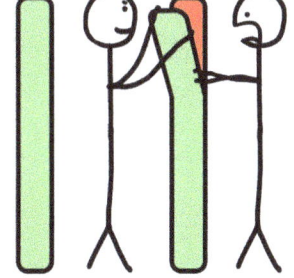

rules everyone will live by. Depending on who that person is and how they feel about you, you may find yourself with almost no freedom at all.

That's why the typical Power Games environment has a few freedom winners and lots and lots of freedom losers. Your country ends up looking like this:

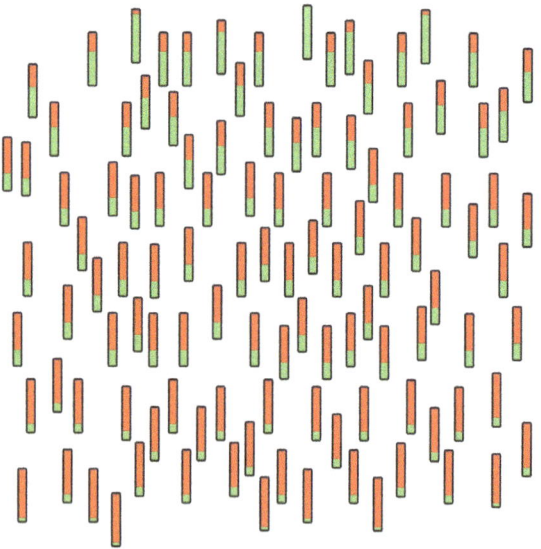

Enlightenment thinkers focused heavily on the freedom problem; a problem that the Liberal Games addresses by changing the Power Games rule—**Everyone can do whatever they want, if they have the power to do so**—into a compromise that goes something like this:

**Everyone can do whatever they want,
as long as it doesn't harm anyone else.**

Or, as it has been said:

> Your right to swing your arms ends just where another person's nose begins.

In exchange for handing over the cudgel and giving up the freedom to oppress others, you could live a life entirely free from anyone oppressing you. Pretty good trade, right? In the Liberal Games, no one would be *completely* free, but *all* citizens would be mostly free:

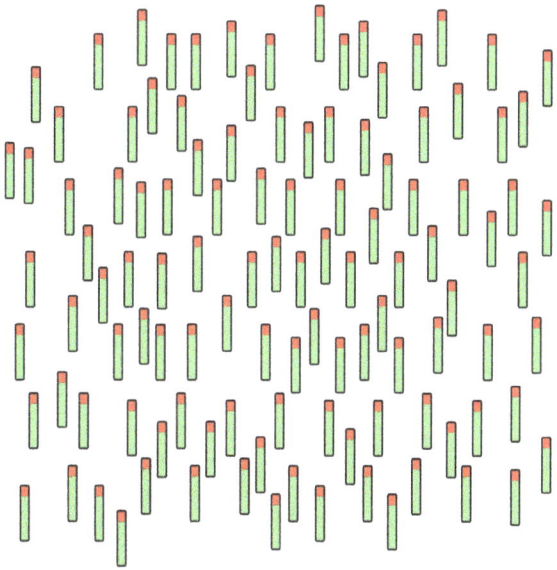

This compromise has two points baked into it. The first point—*everyone can do whatever they want*—describes what citizens *can* do. Their rights. The second point—*as long as it doesn't harm anyone else*—describes what citizens *cannot* do. Their restrictions. The US government would be responsible for both protecting citizen rights and enforcing restrictions.

Rights and restrictions are mutually exclusive: protecting citizens from a certain kind of behavior is also a decision to prohibit that behavior.

Likewise, every freedom granted to citizens is something citizens will have to live with others doing. That's why Liberal Games freedom isn't really *freedom* as much as it's a *freedom–safety compromise*. What matters is *harm*: if an action is harmful, citizens must be protected from it; if it's not harmful, it's a right that must itself be protected.

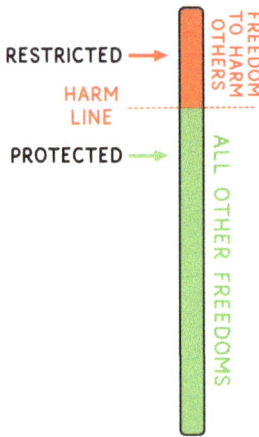

The specific definition of the harm line has been articulated by decades of judicial rulings, but at its core is the Enlightenment philosophy that individuals have a fundamental right to life, liberty, and property.

We can imagine it as two circles surrounding every citizen: a red circle of safety and a green circle of rights.

A person's green circle would give them a tremendous amount of freedom rarely enjoyed in the Power Games. But the second someone's green circle invaded anyone else's *red* circle, they'd be breaking the law and the government would be obligated to step in.*

Alongside Liberal Games rules about freedom were rules of equality. Enforcing equality of outcome, or an equal distribution of resources, would require a controlling government and a large sacrifice of individual freedom—which fundamentally conflicted with the Founders'

---

* Green circles are typically only protected in public spaces or on our own property. When you're at my party, or working at my company, or hanging out at my restaurant, or commenting on my website, I have the right to kick you out if you say something I don't like, wear something I don't like, or if I just decide I don't like you. But the second I physically assault you, kidnap you, steal your property, or do anything else that falls under the Liberal Games definition of harm, it no longer matters where we are—I've broken the law.

vision and the spirit behind the Liberal Games. Instead, they aimed for another compromise, this one between freedom and equality: US citizens would be *equal under the law* and enjoy *equality of opportunity*. (The extent to which this is actually what happens in the US is, of course, another story.)

Thinkers of the Enlightenment believed that the Liberal Games combination of freedom, safety, and equal opportunity would go beyond satisfying core philosophical tenets and generate a brilliant side effect: *fantastic productivity*.

The Liberal Games are driven by human nature, just like the Power Games are. But in the Liberal Games, a key limitation is added into the environment: *you can't use physical force to get what you want*. Where the Power Games did business by way of the cudgel, the Liberal Games would be all about persuasion.

If I want something you have, but I'm not allowed to get it by physically bullying you, then the only option I'm left with is to get you to give it to me *voluntarily*. And since you're self-interested too, the only way you'll do that is if I can come up with a "carrot"—a piece of value I can offer—that you want more than the resource I want from you.

Removing the cudgel from the game-playing options (or, rather, adding in harsh-enough penalties for it that coercion becomes an undesirable game-playing strategy) changes the game from a contest of who can be the scariest, the most dangerous, and the most intimidating, to a contest of who can provide the most *value* to their fellow citizens.

Two basic examples:

In the *economic* Liberal Games, any citizen can theoretically vie for wealth. You're free to apply for a job or start a business—but for your *pursuit* of wealth to turn into *actual* wealth, you'll need employers or customers to volunteer to trade their money for the value you can provide.

In the *political* Liberal Games, any citizen can run for office and vie for the power to allocate government muscle and funding. But to actually *acquire* that power, you have to convince other citizens to vote for you.

Without the right laws, human selfishness gets out of hand and quickly overruns everything, which is why the Primitive Mind dominates the Power Games. But the Liberal Games turn the tables on the Primitive Mind, forcing it to play by Enlightenment rules.

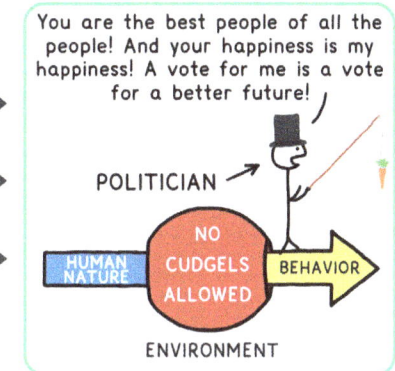
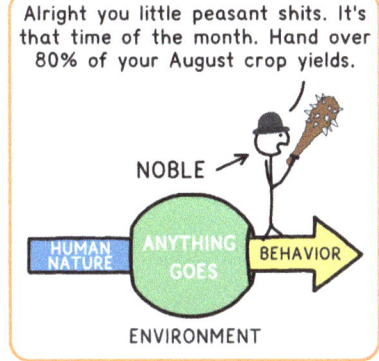

Rather than try to repress the nation's Primitive Minds, Enlightenment philosophers believed the Liberal Games would transform the fires of human selfishness into an inexhaustible, self-regulating, self-propelling *steam engine*.

On a day-to-day basis, the Liberal Games would make high quality of life a self-perpetuating phenomenon. As Adam Smith put it, "It is not from the benevolence of the butcher, the brewer, or the baker, that we expect our dinner, but from their regard to their own interest."

Over the long run, Enlightenment thinkers believed the Liberal Games would yield a giant forward arrow of progress and prosperity that would benefit all citizens. Today's hot showers and antibiotics and airplanes and mobile phones—page-1,000 luxuries the wealthiest people of the 1700s could only dream of—are testaments to the effectiveness of the Liberal Games. The genius of the Liberal Games is that it doesn't repress the Primitive Mind but redirects its energies toward productive means, while preventing those energies from conquering the society.

But perhaps the most important development to emerge from the Enlightenment was the principle of free speech. America's free speech laws would open the gates to another Liberal Games market: the marketplace of ideas, where anyone could vie for attention and influence and over time, the cream would rise to the top. Free speech would allow citizens to use golems to achieve their goals, but those golems would have to play by liberal rules—drawing their power from mechanisms like political protest and boycotts, not from physical force.

The Founders knew that they didn't have all the answers. They knew that, in the decades and centuries that would follow, the world would change. They were wise enough to know that no matter how smart they were, their country was a first draft—United States 1.0. The US was a promising child who would need to grow up into a more perfect union. With a mysterious, foggy future ahead, the Liberal Games would give the new nation a way to figure things out as it went.

But when you're dealing with humans, nothing is ever easy.

Taking the human out of the Power Games is one thing. Taking the Power Games out of the human is quite another. While the Liberal Games are the official way of doing business in the US, at the core of every US citizen and government official runs a piece of primitive software that speaks a more ancient language. Enlightenment-born constitutions put the Primitive Mind in a cage, but just how strong are those bars?

In his book *The Constitution of Knowledge*, Jonathan Rauch reminds us that "the written US Constitution is only words on paper; the real Constitution is a dense system of explicit and implicit social rules, many of which are not written down." If the Liberal Games is a brick wall, and the written Constitution provides the bricks, this dense system of social rules—of liberal *norms*—is the mortar that glues the bricks together and gives the wall its strength. No matter how many written rules there are, it is the citizens' ability to uphold liberal norms that determines the fate of the country.

This is why American history is, above all, the story of a nation's struggle against itself. The eternal tug-of-war that goes on in our heads and in our communities also rages in the mind of the big American giant. Let's see what it's made of.

CHAPTER 2
POLITICS ON THE LADDER

Knowledge of human nature is the beginning and end of political education.
—HENRY ADAMS

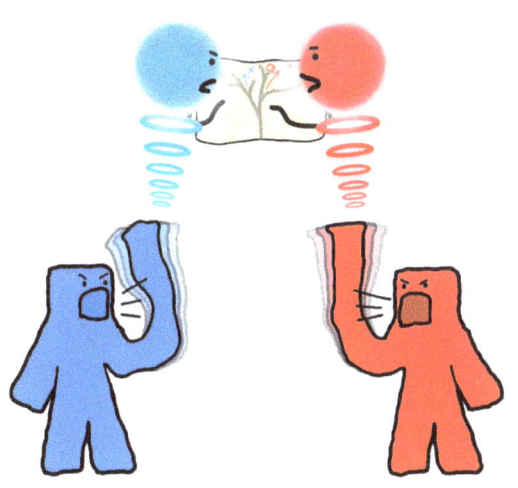

In the US, we talk about the political landscape like this:

FAR LEFT   MODERATE LEFT   CENTRIST   MODERATE RIGHT   FAR RIGHT
POLITICAL SPECTRUM

It's a two-party system, with the red conservatives on the right represented by the Republican Party, and the blue progressives on the left represented by the Democratic Party. This is a simplification: there are nuanced differences between, say, libertarians and social conservatives, or socialists and more traditional progressives. But these still all fall under the "What You Think" umbrella, which in our framework makes them all equally one-dimensional.

> **"LIBERAL" VS. "PROGRESSIVE"**
> In the US, we often use the words "liberal" and "progressive" interchangeably to mean "politically left." I'm not sure why we started doing this, but I wish we hadn't. As I mentioned, in this book, I'll use "progressive" to refer to "politically left." I'll use "liberal" in a much broader sense, referring to the Enlightenment philosophy that values individual rights, civil liberties, democracy, and free enterprise. The majority of Americans on both the political left and right would call themselves "liberals" under this definition.

We'll be using US politics as our framework's "demo system," but the same concept applies to all countries: we can give politics a vertical dimension by adding the Ladder onto the standard horizontal political axis.

Like, consider the four political thinkers on the next page. The two thinkers on the left side, at least on the topic at hand, hold common political *stances*. Same for the two thinkers on the right.

But the two high-rung thinkers have something in common—they share a certain *way of thinking* about politics. Their views may be different, but their approach is similar.

Our societies talk ad nauseam about the horizontal distinction along the political spectrum. We're experts at identifying what people think politically and grouping people that way, so we look at these four thinkers and see two left-wingers and two right-wingers.

But we're awful at talking about the vertical distinction. When I listen to arguments or read op-eds, I notice people *trying* to make high-rung/low-rung distinctions in their arguments about politicians or ideas. But without a common language, those attempts are usually misunderstood or missed altogether.

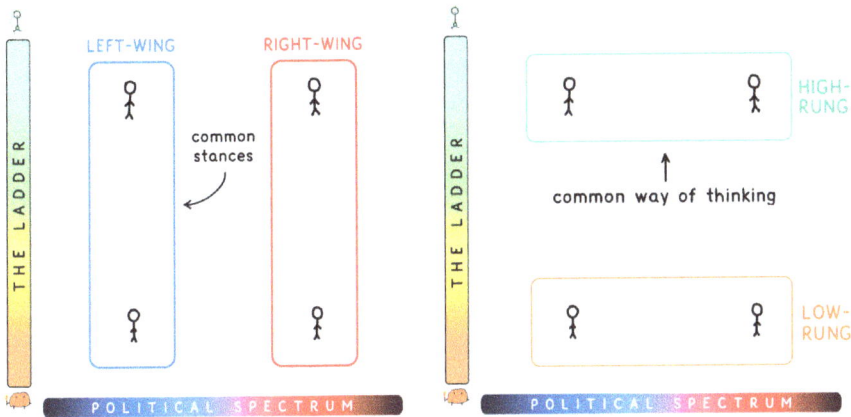

People who try to refer to our concept of high-rung political thinking often use the term "center." But center is a *What* You Think word. It refers to the middle parts of the x-axis—as if holding viewpoints in those areas is the mark of a good thinker. Likewise, people often use "far" as a proxy for "low-rung," calling, say, an uncompromising, progressive Zealot part of the "far left." This is a misnomer because A) there are plenty of uncompromising, progressive people whose views are mainstream, and B) there are plenty of people who hold radical left views who are well-informed and open-minded. Vertical terms like "high-rung" and "low-rung" make our discussions less constrained and allow us to better express what we're actually trying to say.

So let's put the horizontal discussion aside for a bit and focus in on the vertical aspect of politics.

HIGH-RUNG POLITICS

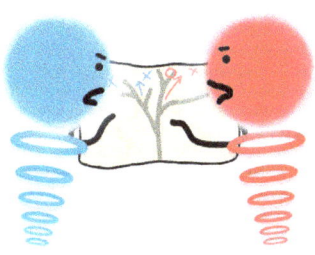

High-rung politics is the Higher Mind's way of doing politics. It places the highest value on truth. It treats political viewpoints like science experiments to be tinkered with, via criticism and vigorous debate. It is suspicious of fervent conviction and smiles upon humility, incentivizing people to say "I don't know" when they don't know and reminding them to stay humble as they learn. High-rung political culture encourages intellectual diversity and independent thought among individuals and a collaborative attitude among opposing genies.

Not everyone who participates in high-rung politics approaches politics in a perfectly non-tribal, open-minded way. In high-rung political environments, you'll find plenty of somewhat partisan, pretty confirmation-bias-y political Sports Fans. You'll also find some hopelessly partisan people mired in the low rungs, in Unconvinceable Land. But the prevailing *culture* is high rung, and the culture stands up for itself in the face of inevitable challenges from the low-rung mentality, both from within and outside the group. Low-rungers in high-rung political discussions are forced to play by the rules of high-rung discourse or they'll be socially penalized.

None of this means everyone in the high-rung political world gets along with each other. Arguments are the rule, not the exception. Most broadly, high-rung political disagreement takes place in three basic realms:

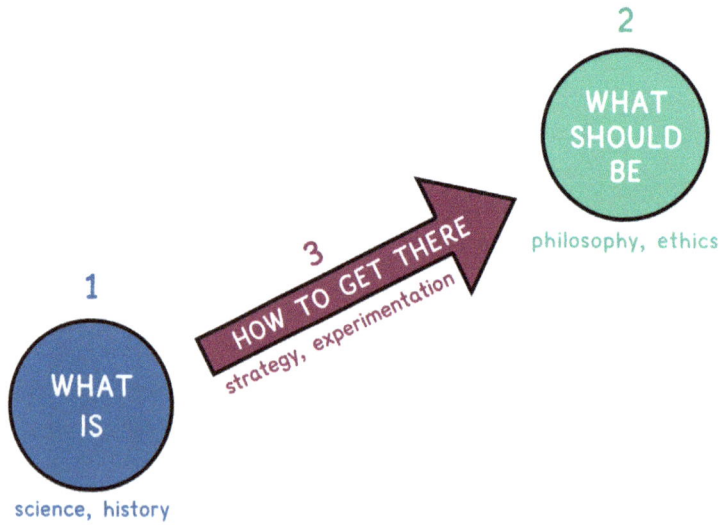

Question 1: What Is?
You can't figure out how to make a more perfect union if you don't have a good sense of the status quo. What does the population look like, and how has it evolved over time? What are the current policies, and how

do they work? Which experimental programs are being attempted, and what does the data say about their efficacy? How are resources currently distributed? Where are there problems with corruption, exploitation, or discrimination? What are the biggest threats facing the country? This is the domain of political science. Embedded in What Is, and critical to its understanding, is the study of What Has Been—i.e., how did What Is become What Is? This is the domain of history.

Question 2: What Should Be?
What Should Be is the domain of philosophy and often the subject of fierce conflict on the high rungs. The overarching goal in high-rung politics is to move toward a more perfect union, but thinkers disagree about which policies and systems are the fairest, the most morally acceptable, and the most philosophically consistent. They'll dig deep on lots of hard questions with no objectively correct answer: What should the role of government be? Which freedoms should be restricted in the name of citizen protection, and which shouldn't? When does a fetus become a human being? What are the criteria for "equal opportunity"? How big and how powerful should government be, and where should the boundaries be drawn between state and federal government power? What should the country's role be in the world, and under what circumstances should it involve itself in foreign affairs? Which resources are rights, and which are privileges? The list is long, and the debates are heated.

Question 3: How do we get from What Is to What Should Be?
What Is and What Should Be, when compared, yield the gaps between reality and the ideal—the high-rung political to-do list. Even when high-rung thinkers agree about What Is and What Should Be, they often disagree about the best way to get there. Two people who agree that the middle class should be larger than it is can completely disagree about which tax structure will best achieve the goal. Two people who feel the same way about racial injustice in the US can hold opposite viewpoints about the ethics or efficacy of affirmative action.

Parsing political arguments using these three questions can help us isolate what the arguments are really about. Many disagreements are about What Is, because figuring out what's true is anything but obvious. Sometimes thinkers who agree philosophically will disagree strategically. Some will disagree on all fronts.

Of course, politics isn't just a mishmash of arguing—in a liberal democracy, politics necessarily organizes itself into parties. Even in high-rung politics, sometimes the best way to compromise is to form two sides and go at it.

On the high rungs of US politics are two supergenies.

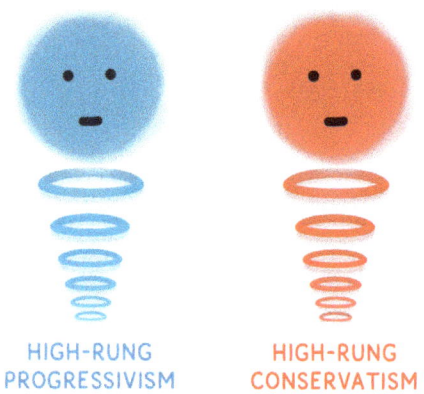

HIGH-RUNG PROGRESSIVISM   HIGH-RUNG CONSERVATISM

High-rung thinkers don't usually lock themselves into political prisons by identifying as "a progressive" or "a conservative," and individuals on the high rungs often hold progressive stances on some issues and conservative stances on others. The same high-rung thinker may choose to apply progressive pressure in the realm of drug laws and a conservative force on the country's healthcare evolution. While individuals bounce back and forth between the two camps, enough people fall into each camp on any given issue that the two genies have a constant presence.

To simplify a bit, high-rung battles in the US serve two positive purposes:

Regulating the Pace of Change

Throughout history, the terms "progressivism" and "conservatism" have each been the banner for a huge range of political, economic, social, and philosophical ideas—some that overlap, some that are unrelated to each other, and some that are totally contradictory with others. In many countries, political Echo Chambers have appropriated these words as banners for themselves and for their enemies. But it's good to remind ourselves that the words themselves have *literal* definitions, and I think those meanings provide an important and useful distinction in political thinking:

Progressivism: concerned with helping society make forward *progress* through positive changes to the status quo. That progress can come from identifying a flaw in the nation's systems or its culture and working to root it out, or by trying to make the nation's strong points even stronger. If the country is a car, progressives are in charge of the gas pedal.

Conservatism: concerned with *conserving* what is already good about society, either by fighting against the erosion of the nation's strong qualities, or by pushing back against well-intentioned attempts at positive progress that may actually be changes for the worse. In the country car, conservatives manage the brakes (and occasionally the reverse pedal).

It's easy to see why progressivism is important. No country is perfect, and you can't become a better country without making changes. Progressivism drives that change.

But conservatism is just as important. There are usually some aspects of a country that are already working well—and in these cases, the conservative impulse to resist change will be wise. Progressivism is also the generation of lots of new ideas—most of them untested—and inevitably, many of them will be bad ideas. The conservative resistance to progressive ideas provides an important filter.

These aren't binary positions but rather a spectrum that generates a rich ecosystem of disagreement on any given political issue.

OVERHAUL THE WHOLE SYSTEM	MAKE MAJOR CHANGE	ENACT CHANGE, SLOWLY AND CAUTIOUSLY	KEEP THINGS THE WAY THEY ARE TODAY	GO BACK TO HOW THINGS USED TO BE

ATTITUDE TOWARD CHANGE ON ANY GIVEN POLITICAL ISSUE

Much of high-rung politics takes place within the range of mainstream ideas, but the extreme ends of the spectrum are also important pieces of the high-rung political puzzle. People with a radical progressive mindset are the disruptors and the outside-the-box innovators—those for whom no tradition is too sacred to be questioned. People with a far-right conservative mindset are the staunchest guardians of the country's core ideals and will keep pressing to revive a long-lost way of life. These more extreme groups are also prone to believe conspiracy theories, and they're wrong more than they're right—but that's their job, because sometimes the mainstream really is wrong about something big.

In the big picture, each side of high-rung politics acts as a counterforce against the other and helps keep it in check. When the conservative genie gets riled up, it can drift too far into "Our country is perfect just as it is" or "Our country used to be perfect" territory. When the progressive genie gets out of hand, it can fall too far down the "Our country is and always has been awful" hole. The presence of its rival genie restrains each giant from becoming a caricature of itself.

Finding Happy Mediums

Some political debates aren't about whether to change but about a spectrum of possibility and where exactly on the spectrum our policies should lie.

Spectrum battles don't always map very well onto "progressive" or "conservative," and the Left and Right can flip-flop on the same issue in different eras. And that's fine—the important thing is that both sides of each issue have a genie advocating for them. This allows the marketplace of ideas to home in on a point that represents a reasonable compromise (represented below by the green arrow). As the debates rage on and public opinion evolves, the arrow's position can evolve along with it. Some very oversimplified examples of American spectrum battles:

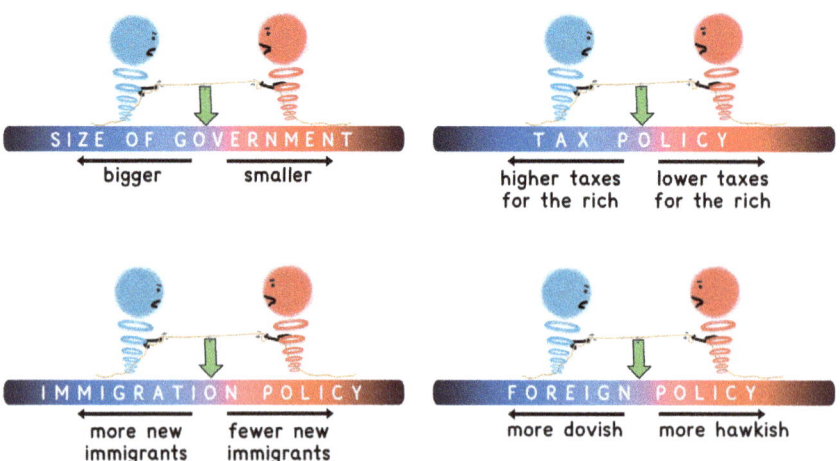

In modern-day America, the Left usually makes the case for globalization while the Right makes the argument for national interests. The Left stays wary of unchecked capitalism while the Right is wary of overreaching government. The Left focuses on protecting and lifting up marginalized groups while the Right worries about how such efforts could potentially backfire. In each case, the blind spots of one side are seen clearly by the other side, allowing the complete system to function more wisely than either side could on its own.

As fierce as the debates can be, high-rung political culture reminds its members that ultimately, they're all on the same team, working together to navigate their way up the same mountain.

People engaged in high-rung politics, without the burden of rigid attachment to any one ideology, can combine ideas from across the spectrum to form a nimble political superbrain that can respond in nuanced ways to changing times.

• • •

It would be great if this was how politics always worked. But as any Skittles eater can tell you, overriding ancient software is not easy. Each of us has a Primitive Mind in our head, and even the skilled high-rung thinkers among us are prone to morph into childish low-rungers when it comes to politics. That's no surprise: Politics deals with fairness, resource distribution, and groups of people competing for power—concepts that the Primitive Mind is programmed to freak out about because they were fundamental to ancient survival. And there's neurological evidence that politics really does ignite parts of our brain we'd associate with low-rung thinking. There's no shortage of studies showing that

---

* One 2016 study presented people with "arguments that contradicted their strongly held political and nonpolitical views." Not only were participants unlikely to change their political beliefs, fMRI data revealed that people actually processed challenges to their political beliefs with different parts of their brains than they used to process nonpolitical contradictions. Challenges to nonpolitical beliefs lit up regions of the brain involved in decision-making, while political challenges generated more activity in the emotional, fight-or-flight parts of the brain, as well as the default mode network, a group of brain regions associated with creating a sense of self and with disengagement from the external world. In the face of political dissent, participants were more likely to withdraw from the external world and go into the internally focused parts of their brains that deal with their identity, as well as the parts of their brains that deal with danger,...

politics tends to turn people into low-rung thinkers—and this is *most* pronounced in people with high levels of education.

There is a vibrant world of high-rung politics. There's just an even larger world down below, where politics is less about working together to build a more perfect union and more about the good guys triumphing over the bad guys in a political war.

LOW-RUNG POLITICS, AKA POLITICAL DISNEY WORLD

I'm pretty into most Disney movies, but especially *The Little Mermaid*, *Beauty and the Beast*, *Aladdin*, and *The Lion King*. I've never been sure if those are objectively the best four Disney movies or if everyone just loves whichever Disney movies came out when they were between the ages of seven and twelve. Either way, those are clearly the four best Disney movies.*

The thing about those movies, though, is that they're definitely not real life, right? Like, kids might think Disney movies are the way the real world is, but everyone else knows that the real world is not like Disney movies.

Right?

I thought so too. Then I started writing this book. After spending the last few years thinking about political partisanship and Echo Chambers, it hit me: a ton of Americans think they live inside a Disney movie. Let me explain.

The real world is gray, amorphous, and endlessly nuanced. But Disney movies simplify the world into a binary digital code of 1s and 0s. There's pure good (1), pure bad (0), and rarely anything in between.

...fear, and other primal emotions. And while thinking this way, their minds were far less likely to change.

* Side shout-out to *Pinocchio*, which I watched like 550 times as a child.

Real people are complex and flawed, full of faults but almost always worthy of compassion. Disney characters, on the other hand, are either entirely good or entirely bad.

1 PERFECT GOODNESS	ARIEL	BELLE	ALADDIN	SIMBA
0 UTTER EVIL	URSULA	GASTON	JAFAR	SCAR

In the real world, each turn of events is mired in potential positives and potential negatives, which is a mess to sort out. Disney movies get rid of that messiness. Aladdin gets ahold of the genie = 1. Jafar steals the genie away = 0. Disney even digitizes the weather, which is always either perfect or, when the bad guys are getting their way, stormy.

Going full binary makes sense in Disney movies. Their core audience is little kids, who aren't ready to sort through too much gray. Before a person learns to think in nuance, they first need to learn the basic concepts of good vs. bad, right vs. wrong, safe vs. dangerous, happy vs. sad.

But oversimplifying the *real* world is a bad idea—and unfortunately, that's exactly what the Primitive Mind likes to do. So low-rung politics ends up feeling, to its participants, a lot like a Disney movie.

Up on the high rungs, people know the world is a mess of complexity. They know that people are little microcosms of the messy world—each person an evolving gray smattering of virtues and flaws.

Political Disney World is much more fun. Everything is crisp and perfectly digital. Good guys and bad guys, with good ideas and bad ideas. Good politicians and bad politicians with good policies and bad policies, winning their seats in good or bad election outcomes. Right and wrong. Smart and ignorant. Virtuous and evil. 1s and 0s.

When a bunch of adults are pretty sure that they live in a Disney movie, it's usually a sign that primitive psychology has taken over and we're dealing with golems.

Both the individualism and collaboration of high-rung politics melt away on the low rungs, leaving only the rigid ant colony structure. People inside the tribe are pressured to conform, drawing unity and strength from an obsession with the common enemy and how stupid, ignorant, evil, bigoted, opportunistic, sneaky, toxic, selfish, and dangerous the bad guys are.

At the heart of every faction in Political Disney World is a guiding story: their political narrative. These narratives are all-encompassing versions of reality. They come with their own worldview, their own telling of history, and their own depiction of the present. A unique, customized Disney movie for the tribe, by the tribe.

In the US, people in the Democratic Disney kingdom see themselves as righteous citizens in a continual struggle to deliver the country to a progressive utopia even as the mean, bigoted Republicans try to pull the country backward into the land of all-powerful corporations and a government run by gunslinging misogynists and white supremacists.

The Republican Disney kingdom tells the story of honest, hard-working families doing their best to keep the country afloat as the lazy, morally defunct Democrats try their hardest to pull it down into a dystopian hell of a tyrannical government run by ivory-tower elitists that give endless handouts to hordes of dangerous immigrants.

These narratives allow believers to swap the gray mess of debates over What Is, What Should Be, and How to Get There for a clean, digitized list of issues—each with a Good, Correct Stance and an Evil, Wrong Stance. In the US narratives, the current checklist includes items like these:

✓ LEFT CHECKLIST	✓ RIGHT CHECKLIST
Roe v Wade good	Roe v Wade bad
universal healthcare good	universal healthcare bad
mainstream media fine	mainstream media bad
guns kill people	people kill people
US is a racist country	US was a racist country
protect immigrants	protect borders
tax cuts bad	tax cuts good
climate change awful	climate change overblown
raise minimum wage	don't raise minimum wage

Teammates abide faithfully by the entire list of protagonist viewpoints, and for each issue, the villain stance is seen as having zero merit.

Political Disney World narratives are also rife with outlandish conspiracy theories.

The intellectual filters of high-rung politics are great at evaluating conspiracy theories, squashing them when they're wrong but allowing true ones to work their way into mainstream consciousness. In Political Disney World, this critical sorting mechanism is nonexistent, allowing all conspiracy theories that confirm the narrative to swirl continually around each golem's thoughts. This is why so many clearly disproven wild theories never seem to die. They actually died long ago up on the high rungs, but they live on down below.

So far, we've kept our Ladder discussions mostly focused on the way we form our beliefs. But there are two other ways we'll use the Ladder as well. The second way has to do with our values and principles.

A telltale sign of Political Disney World is what we might call low-rung morality.

High-rung political thinkers will disagree about what's *morally* right and wrong as vigorously as they disagree about what's factually right and wrong. But whatever their conclusions, they apply their moral standards *consistently*—to themselves, to friends, to strangers, to foes. They work hard to avoid falling into the tribal mindset and try to maintain a balance of empathy and criticism when dealing with people on other parts of the political spectrum.

But the Us vs. Them mindset distorts our morality, generating one set of standards for Us and another for Them. When judging members of their own group, people will condone and even applaud the same behavior they see as morally reprehensible when done by their opponents.

Low-rung morality distorts our capacity for empathy. In Political Disney World, people are great at being empathetic toward members of their group, seeing the best in their intentions, and forgiving their mistakes. But we treat members of the out-group the opposite way, labeling them with dehumanizing stereotypes, assuming the worst about their intentions, and viewing any moral failing as an exposure of permanent moral bankruptcy.

When it comes to political principles, low-rung morality yields rampant hypocrisy. We can think of it like a simple Venn diagram.

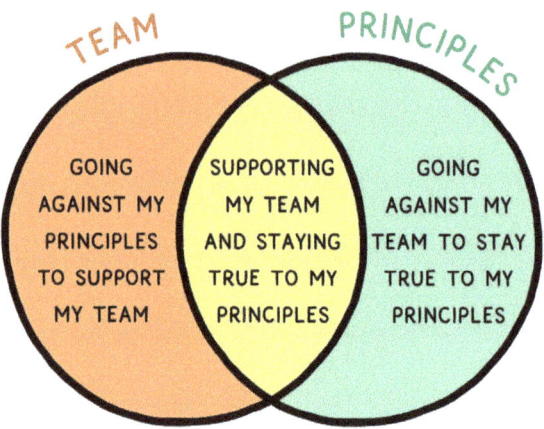

Everyone in politics spends time in the middle section of the diagram, where your team's behavior aligns with your principles—say, defending the free speech of someone you agree with—so you don't learn anything about someone when they're here. The litmus test comes when the middle section isn't an option—when your team and your principles are in conflict. High-rung political thinkers stay inside the circle on the right, criticizing their own teammates or even standing up for the other team when doing so aligns with their principles. But low-rung political culture encourages people to stay inside the left circle, keeping true to their team, even when doing so flies in the face of their principles.

We've seen a lot of this kind of hypocrisy in recent decades in the US, on issues like foreign intervention, government surveillance, aggressive executive orders, national debt, state autonomy, free speech, campaign finance reform, border policy, and political protesting. On issues like these, the stances of hyperpartisans have flip-flopped based not on consistent principle but on which party is in power.

In Political Disney World, people who claim to hold liberal values won't hesitate to go illiberal if it helps their team win. When they're unhappy with the result of an election, they insist that they're disenfranchised, that the system must be broken, that the election was manipulated by foreign powers or rigged by the opposition. When their candidate wins, they say things like "faith in democracy restored!" which translates to "democracy is only working when my candidate wins."

Alongside low-rung thinking and low-rung morality are low-rung tactics. Golems play by Power Games rules—*everyone can do what they want, if they have the power to do so.* When they do play by Liberal Games rules, it's only out of necessity, because they have to for survival's sake. When they can get away with it, golems will use whatever dirty tactics they can to defeat their enemies. Voter suppression, delegitimizing election results, censorship, obstruction, bribes, blackmail, even physical violence—it's all fair game for golems. We'll talk a lot more about high- and low-rung tactics later in the book.

Low-rung thinking, **low-rung morality**, and **low-rung tactics** all stem from the same concept: when the Primitive Mind is running the show, our minds are in ancient survival mode, and politics becomes a vehicle for tribalism. When our heads are here, truth, moral consistency, and fair play all go out the window.

	THINKING	MORALS	TACTICS
HIGH-RUNG	seek truth	moral consistency	fair play, persuasion
LOW-RUNG	seek confirmation	moral hypocrisy	cheating, coercion

The tricky thing is, when our psyches are mired in Political Disney World, we're usually too foggy to realize it. Most people reading this book will picture themselves on the high rungs. Political Disney World, we believe, is where those other shitty people are.

The distinctions we've talked about can help us evaluate where we and others *actually* are on the political ladder. Do our political views conform a little too perfectly with the exact checklist of stances on one side? Do we see ourselves and our political allies as having a monopoly on truth and moral good? Do we demonize our political opponents, feeling more disgust than empathy for them and assuming the most uncharitable interpretation of their motives? Did we feel outraged about a certain policy or tactic of the opposition and then stop feeling that way later when our own side took it up? These are all signs that you've drifted down into Political Disney World—the land of lumbering political golems.

In the Liberal Games, where physical force is off the table and information flows freely, large golems face an uphill battle. To survive, they do what any organism in a hostile environment must: protect themselves with an immune system.

THE GOLEM IMMUNE SYSTEM

A golem's lifeblood is conformity, anchored by its members' steadfast belief in its guiding narrative. The stronger and more unified the belief, the stronger and more powerful the golem.

For the same reason, doubt in the narrative is like cancer for a golem. Doubt, if allowed to fester and spread, weakens the golem and threatens its very existence.

So the golem's immune system has a simple job: keep belief strong and keep doubt out. To do this job, it uses three primary mechanisms.

Mechanism 1: Information Filtering

The simplest way for a golem to stay healthy is to control which information puzzle pieces are circulating around the system. But in a society with free speech, free press, and the internet, this can be a challenge. This is where its filters come in.

The first line of defense for a golem is the media. In today's world, every political golem has its own media channels, which serve as the giant's eyes and ears. To keep the golem strong and well-fed, these channels broadcast and sensationalize the stories that confirm the narrative. To keep the giant free of intellectual contamination, they downplay stories that challenge the narrative or neglect to report them at all. This is cherry-picking on an industrial scale, driven by market forces: to maintain the trust of the golem's members, these media sources must filter stories in a way that aligns with the golem's interests.

When dangerous dissent does manage to enter the golem's airwaves, it's handled by the second line of defense: the social pressure of Echo Chamber culture. A low-rung political tribe tends to be a motley crew.

There are the zealots, who believe every word of the narrative. The tribal people, who get off on being part of a powerful in-group and talking shit about the out-group. The opportunists, who use politics to gain social status or career advancement, to get clicks, take down their enemies, or generate profit. Some have stitched their identities so closely to their political colors that their sense of meaning, purpose, and righteousness have become one and the same with those colors. Others are the opposite: undercover high-rung thinkers who, for various reasons like geography, are mired in a Political Disney World social scene and go with the flow to avoid social conflict.

While many of these categories overlap with one another, we can simplify them into two key categories: people who believe the narrative, and people who pretend to believe the narrative.

For the golem's immune system, what matters isn't what its members are actually thinking but that they're all outwardly *saying* the right thing. Doubt in an individual's head is mostly harmless—only when they *express* that doubt does it become a danger to the system.

The powerful social incentives of Echo Chamber culture keep everyone in line. The culture rewards the continual expression of narrative-confirming sentiment, and brands ideas that threaten the guiding narrative as taboo. If the golem's media channels determine what enters the political golem's brain, social pressure provides a second filter, setting the cultural rules about how information circulates through the brain.

These filtering systems do much of the heavy lifting in keeping the golem's mind pure. But to really supercharge a golem and keep it in top health, golem immune systems supplement filtering with a second tactic.

Mechanism 2: Information Twisting

Like the human hand or the human eye, the human brain is a tool developed by evolution for a specific set of purposes. Truth wasn't one of those purposes.

We can do truth, but a human doing truth is like a dog standing on its hind legs—it's a real effort and we're not in our element. This is why we're so susceptible to reasoning errors, aka logical fallacies. The high-rung world exposes logical fallacies and roots them out, but bad reasoning thrives down below. And for the golems of Political Disney World, logical fallacies—both accidental and intentional—are an immune system superpower.

Let's look at some common ways information is twisted inside political golems.

Fallacies that misrepresent reality

Low-rung politics has a long tradition of misrepresenting reality by concocting questionable studies or misleading statistics or by spinning news stories in a way that best fits the narrative.

A common practice is what we might call **trend-anecdote swapping**.

It's simple: If you come across an anecdote that supports the narrative, you frame it as evidence of a larger *trend* to make it seem representative of broader reality. Meanwhile, if there's an actual trend happening that really is representative of broader reality—but it's a trend that makes your narrative look bad—you frame it as nothing more than a handful of freak anecdotes.

Another common fallacy has to do with **correlation and causation**. A common Statistics 101 concept is that *correlation does not imply causation*. A 2013 study found that people who have sex more often make more money. A statistics amateur might read a headline about the study and jump to the conclusion that having more sex *caused* people to make more money. Or maybe that making more money led people to have more sex. But what the study actually found was that a third variable—*extraversion*—lies behind both the sex and money trends.

There are four possible explanations for any correlation:

Possibilities if A is correlated with B:

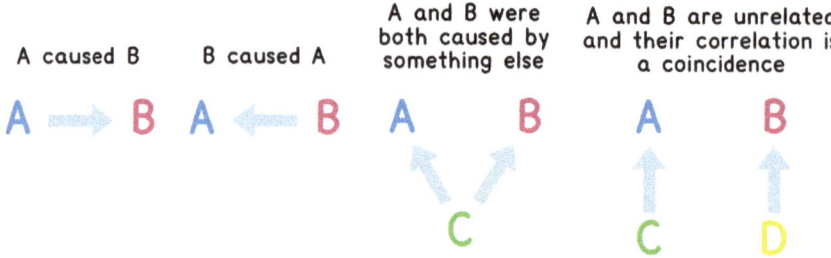

In high-rung politics, when people come across a correlation, they dig deeper to explore which of the above is actually going on. But in Political Disney World, people believe whichever explanation best supports the narrative.

Let's imagine there's a political tribe whose narrative says that dogs are almost always good boys (and anyone who says otherwise is a bigot), while most raccoons are dangerous, vile creatures (and anyone who says otherwise is a bigot). Now imagine that one week, these six news stories happen:

DOG BITES RACCOON IN PARKING LOT
RACCOON FOUND IN TRASH CAN
SIDEWALK DOG SHIT ON THE RISE
RACCOON RABIES EPIDEMIC SPREADS
LOCAL DOG FETCHES STICK LIKE A GOOD BOY
STUDY CONCLUDES RACCOONS ARE UNDERRATEDLY CUTE

The actual information at hand here suggests that both animals can be good sometimes and bad sometimes. But the required narrative leaves no room for mixed messages. Dogs are good. Raccoons are bad. Period. So the pro-dog media starts twisting things.

The anecdotes that align with the narrative (say, "raccoon found in trash can") can be reframed as trends ("yet another raccoon found in trash can"). Pro-dog media could use the correlation/causation fallacy to further nudge the day's news in their favor by fiddling with blame in two of the stories: "Dog bites raccoon in parking lot" places the blame on the dog, which conflicts with the pro-dog narrative, so it could be adjusted to the more neutral "dog and raccoon get in parking lot skirmish." The headline about dogs shitting on the sidewalk could be rewritten in a way that implies it's not caused by dogs at all: "With the city continuing to neglect dog park conditions, more dogs resort to shitting on the sidewalk."

To top things off, pro-dog media might add their own sensationalistic touch to the headlines that fit the pro-dog narrative, while downplaying those that don't. Meanwhile, pro-raccoon media has been doing all of the same things in the opposite direction. After all this twisting, the pro-dog and pro-raccoon audiences are looking at an entirely different set of stories.

Pro-Dog Headlines	Pro-Raccoon Headlines
DOG AND RACCOON GET IN PARKING LOT SKIRMISH	SAVAGE DOG THAT COMMITTED PARKING LOT MASSACRE REPORTEDLY HAD TIES TO DOG EXTREMIST GROUP
RACCOON RABIES EPIDEMIC EXPLODES, THREATENING THOUSANDS OF DOGS	PLEAS FOR AID CONTINUE TO FALL ON DEAF EARS AS RABIES RAVAGES RACCOON COMMUNITY
YOU WON'T BELIEVE THESE PHOTOS OF YET ANOTHER RACCOON FOUND IN TRASH CAN	IMPOVERISHED RACCOON LATEST VICTIM OF HARASSMENT AND DEATH THREATS AFTER TRASH CAN PHOTOS WENT VIRAL
HEROIC RESCUE DOG CONTINUES THE AMAZING TRADITION OF DOGS FETCHING STICKS LIKE GOOD BOYS	DOG FETCHES STICK LIKE AN IDIOT
DOG SHIT TROUBLES EVIDENCE OF JUST HOW BADLY THE CITY'S DOGS HAVE BEEN TREATED	SIDEWALK DOG SHIT EPIDEMIC LEAVES CITY IN SHAMBLES AS MANY RESIDENTS NO LONGER ABLE TO GO ON WALKS
RACCOON APOLOGISTS DESPERATE TO DISTRACT FROM RAMPANT RACCOON CRIME AND DANGEROUS RABIES OUTBREAK WITH A STUDY ABOUT HOW CUTE THEY ARE SMH	SCIENTISTS AGREE THAT RACCOON CUTENESS IS THROUGH THE ROOF

High-rung politics relies on a shared sense of reality—a shared understanding of *What Is*. In Political Disney World, the beliefs and viewpoints of people in different tribes are premised on entirely different versions of reality.

Fallacies that misrepresent an argument

The real test of any argument is how well it stands up to rigorous criticism. When you're confident in your viewpoint, you love a chance to throw it into the ring with other arguments and show off its strength. It works like boxing: the stronger the opponents you've beaten, the better your ranking. That's why a strong college paper always includes a strong "grizzly bear" counterargument—it lets the thesis "show off" in front of the professor.

But what if you're not so confident in your viewpoint? And you still want to make it *seem* like it can do well in the ring? As a procrastinator who wrote a lot of hasty, shitty papers in college, I can tell you firsthand that one of the trademarks of a paper with a weak thesis is an even weaker counterargument.

When exposed to high-rung opponents, oversimplified narratives are usually knocked out in the first round. So political Echo Chambers make it taboo to criticize the narrative—it's their way of banning anyone from landing a good punch.

But to generate intense conviction in its members—the belief that *of COURSE the narrative is correct*—political Echo Chambers need to make it *seem* like the narrative is a champion heavyweight boxer. So they rely on what are essentially fake fights that seem real to the Echo Chamber's members—fights where the narrative always comes out on top. They pull this off using one of the most tried-and-true tools of the low-rung intellectual world: the **straw man fallacy**.

To straw man your opponent, you invent a weak counterargument to your position and pretend that it's your opponent's position, even though it's not. It's the real-world version of what shitty college students do in their papers: conjure up a weakling opponent, pound it to the floor, and then declare victory.

The straw man makes regular appearances in political debates.

Political speeches tend to be full of straw men too.

Obama speech during the 2009 recession

Using a straw man can make you appear victorious to unwitting viewers, like a boxer who takes a swing at the balls mid-match and hopes the ref won't see it.

In Political Disney World, when a cleverly worded tweet or op-ed straw mans the opposing side, it goes viral, and soon, the farce boxing match is played on loop throughout the Echo Chamber, ad nauseam.

The straw man fallacy also has its inverse—the **"motte-and-bailey" fallacy**—which can be used as a defensive tactic. The name comes from a type of two-part medieval fortification common in Northern Europe between the tenth and thirteenth centuries. It looked something like this:

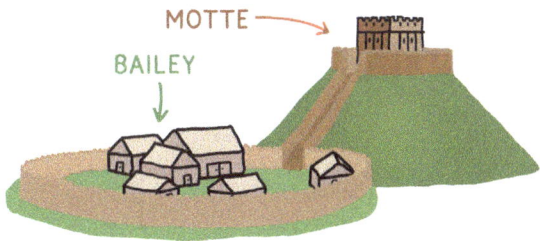

The bailey was an area of land that was desirable and economically productive to live on but vulnerable to attack and hard to defend. When the bailey was threatened, inhabitants would run up the motte and into the tower. The motte, unlike the bailey, was easy to defend and nearly impossible to conquer—so invaders who captured the bailey would be unable to conquer the whole fortification. Eventually, with arrows raining down on them from the motte's tower, the attackers would give up and leave, at which point the inhabitants could resume life in the pleasant, profitable bailey.

Philosopher Nicholas Shackel popularized the motte-and-bailey as a metaphor for a cheap argument tactic, whereby someone holding a convenient but not-very-defensible "bailey" viewpoint could, when facing dissent to that viewpoint, quickly run up the motte and swap out the viewpoint with a far stronger "motte" position. Kind of like in 2003, during the arguments about whether to invade Iraq.

Political Disney World is a land of sprawling baileys, dotted with motte hills. And if you listen carefully, you'll notice people darting up to their trusty mottes whenever their views come under fire.

The motte-and-bailey is often used alongside the straw man fallacy. Political Echo Chambers use the straw man to make their opponent's position seem weaker than it is, and they use the motte-and-bailey to make their own position appear to be more ironclad than it is.

In 2004, George W. Bush countered opponents of the Iraq War with this: "There's a lot of people in the world who don't believe that people whose skin color may not be the same as ours can be free and self-govern....I reject that. I reject that strongly. I believe that people who practice the Muslim faith can self-govern. I believe that people whose skins... are a different color than white can self-govern."

So: we just want to keep Americans safe from weapons of mass destruction (motte-and-bailey), but they don't think brown people can self-govern (straw man).

Fallacies that discredit ideas based on their speaker

Perhaps the easiest way to squash a dissenting argument is to just disqualify it right off the bat *based on who said it*, without ever addressing the argument itself. The infamous **ad hominem fallacy**.

In Political Disney World, ad hominem fallacies happen constantly, because when our minds are on the low rungs, we tend to trust people who agree with us much more than those who don't. In 2019, professors Steven Sloman and Elke Weber compiled a wide range of articles exploring the science behind political polarization. Many of the findings confirmed that people are highly uncharitable in their assumptions about those in their political out-group. For example, if an opposing candidate has mostly mainstream views but holds a few extreme positions, people tend to assume the candidate's supporters voted for them *because of*, not *in spite of*, the candidate's extreme positions—despite no evidence this is true. Another study found "constituents are likely to attribute the actions of in-group leaders as intended to benefit the country (national interests), and the actions of out-group leaders as intended to benefit the political leaders themselves (egoistic interests)"—even when the actions in question are identical.

People in Political Disney World slap a "bullshit" sticker onto an argument the second it leaves the wrong person's mouth, regardless of the argument's substance.

These two mechanisms of information control—filtering and twisting—maintain an intellectually pure environment inside the golem.

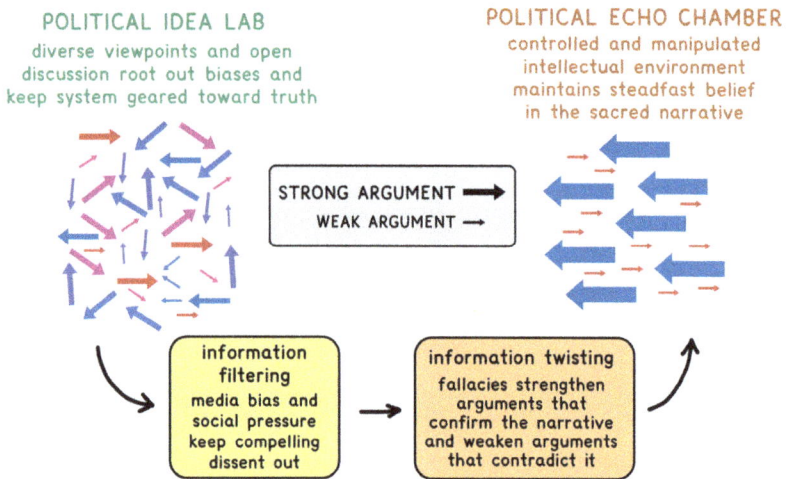

As a final safeguard to keep the tribe intact:

Mechanism 3: Confirmation Bias

When someone believes strongly in their tribe's narrative, they're usually highly motivated to continue believing it. This motivation can emerge from multiple places:

Social dependence

It's hard living in an Echo Chamber community if you don't believe the community's narrative. You either keep your mouth shut and feel distant from the other people, or you become a contrarian and, at best, find yourself in a lot of unpleasant interactions (at worst, you end up cut off from the community).

More often than not, the surrounding community is made up of beloved friends, family members, and colleagues. Even if you don't like the way they think, you still love them and very much want them in your lives. Believing the narrative makes all of this so much easier and simpler.

Intellectual dependence

An Echo Chamber makes its members feel perfectly informed while crippling them as intellectuals. It teaches them that knowledge is easy and gets them hooked on the feeling of knowing the truth about everything without having to work for it.

When you spend too much time in an environment like that, you don't just lack knowledge—your learning skills dull. People who surround themselves with Idea Lab culture get constant practice at defending their ideas and challenging others. In the Echo Chamber's safe-from-dissent space, people remain amateurs.

And the longer this goes on, the more it eats away at intellectual confidence. It's a scary feeling, but as long as the narrative really is true, it's all okay.

Self-esteem dependence

Low-rung political narratives always paint the in-group as perfectly righteous protagonists, which makes the believers feel great about themselves.

But what if the narrative isn't true?

If the narrative isn't all it's cracked up to be, its members look like brainwashed ideologues. When our heads are in Political Disney World, deep-down belief in the narrative and self-esteem go together.

Sometimes it feels like even more is at stake. We've talked about how our beliefs can become intertwined with our identity because the Primitive Mind has a hard time distinguishing between the two. When we associate ourselves with our most fervent beliefs, doubting those beliefs feels like an existential crisis. So dissent can send our Primitive Minds into fight-or-flight mode, where we lock our beliefs in a protective bunker.

If Echo Chamber culture is an external incentive to *say* the right things, these phenomena combine into an internal incentive to *believe* the right things. That motive will drive a person's psychology down the Ladder to Unconvinceable Land where any dissent that does make it into their head will run into the brick wall of confirmation bias.

The Echo Chamber environment makes confirmation bias easy. The "bandwagon effect" describes our tendency to feel that "if everyone else believes it, it must be true." Echo Chambers give their members the distinct impression that everyone believes the narrative, which alone is enough evidence for most people to stop questioning it.

There's also the "inoculation effect," a term coined by social psychologist William McGuire in 1961. The trick of many of our vaccines is to expose a person's immune system to a weak version of a dangerous virus. After the body defeats the weak version of the virus, it develops an immunity against all versions of the virus, including the strong ones. McGuire found that people's beliefs worked in a similar way: being repeatedly exposed to weak arguments for a particular position makes people dismissive of *all* arguments for that position.

In other words, if straw-man arguments are repeated enough inside a political Echo Chamber, people come to believe they are representative of what the opposition thinks. After enough of this, *any* version of dissenting arguments—even the strong ones—will be disregarded as nothing more than better-worded versions of the well-known absurd arguments. People will have become "immune" to changing their minds. The same goes for motte-and-baileys—when people continually hear their own views reframed as ironclad mottes, it can make them feel so overconfident in their beliefs they become immune to self-doubt.

The way giants treat information forms a big arrow pointing to the group's overarching motivation. For a political golem, narrative-confirming information is welcomed, spread by social incentives, boosted by fallacy distortions, and accepted uncritically. Dissenting information is hindered by the media and sharing filters, weakened by fallacy distortions, and blocked by a wall of skepticism. It's a terrible system for discovering truth, but it works great for protecting belief in a guiding narrative.

The High-Rung Immune System

Genies handle information in a completely different way. Without the burden of having to protect any particular narrative, the political high rungs don't need to control or manipulate information. Political genies are configured to root out bias and misconception and figure out the truth—so they welcome all kinds of people with all kinds of ideas, *especially* those that challenge existing beliefs.

But genies need immune systems too. All humans come programmed for low-rung thinking, and our Primitive Minds communicate with one another like wolves communicate with pheromones. While golems protect themselves against doubt, genies need to protect themselves from slipping down to the low rungs and becoming golems.

The high-rung immune system is the product of a culture of open discourse, debate, and moral consistency—and the willingness of its members to stand up for that culture in the face of inevitable attempts, from inside and out, to shut it down.

THE NATIONAL TUG-OF-WAR

So even though we talk about US politics like it's like this—

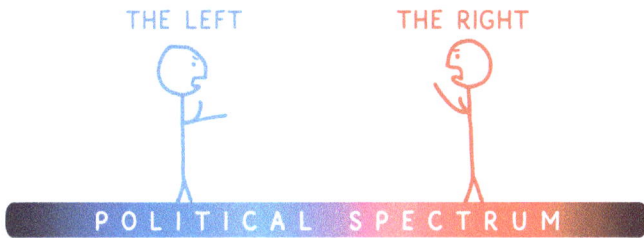

—the Ladder helps us see it's closer to something like this:

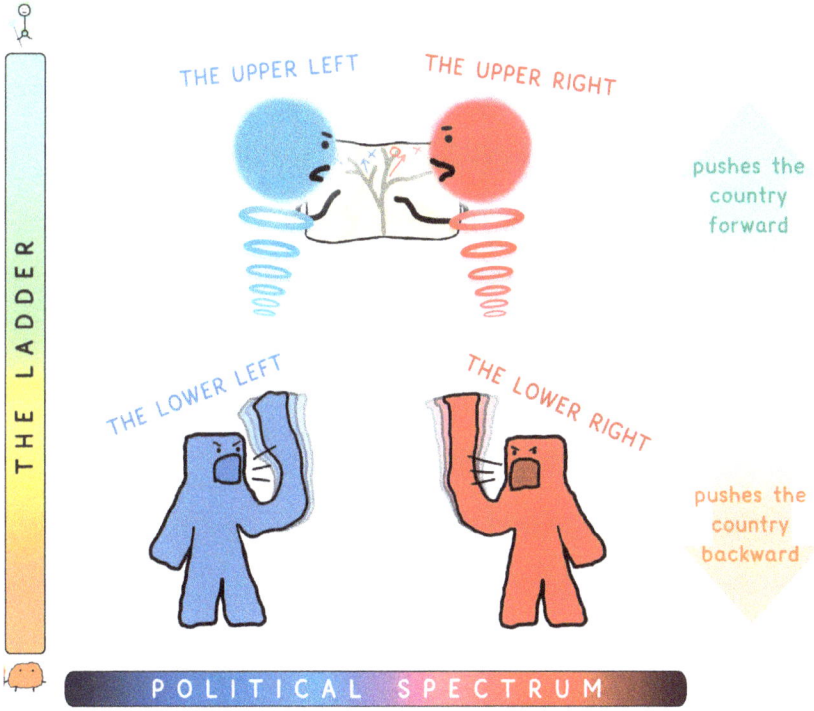

High-rung politics marries liberal laws with liberal culture to create an environment where people can enjoy the full benefits of the Liberal Games. Over time, it yields positive steps toward national improvement.

But America's political golems understand only a simpler, ancient rule book: the zero-sum Power Games. The battle of the golems ultimately hurts the country and undermines the progress of high-rung politics.

Earlier, we imagined the US as a giant organism trudging up a mountain on a mission to become a more perfect union. Splitting this organism into its component parts gives us a clearer view of what's really going on: like each of us, the national giant faces an internal tug-of-war between the high and low rungs. During eras when high-rung politics has the edge, the US can take steps up the mountain. When the golems get into a frenzy that overwhelms high-rung America, the US giant slips downward on the mountain.

None of this means the system isn't working. Modern democracies weren't built to eradicate low-rung psychology or low-rung culture. They were built to ensure that low-rung giants wouldn't be able to do what they've done throughout history: conquer the country.

In a way, the US is like an ecosystem.

In nature, an animal species is constrained from expanding endlessly by the limitations of its ecosystem—the tyranny of the predators above them on the food chain and the supply of prey below them. An ecosystem is a web made up of many species, the existence of each providing limitations on others, ultimately achieving a fragile equilibrium.

In a liberal country, communities run by high-rung and low-rung culture butt up against each other, and the boundary between them is an ecosystem equilibrium. Political genies, unimpeded, would inject the entire nation with the culture of open discussion and debate. Likewise, if a political golem had its way, it would expand and conquer the whole country, ruling the government and imposing its ideology from coast to coast. Neither the genie nor the golem can accomplish this, though, because each has an immune system that's capable of protecting itself from invasion by the other. So they coexist at equilibrium.

The Founders' hope was that something like high-rung America would prevail in the long run—that for every step backward, there would be two or three steps forward. And US history has mostly proven this correct. For all our current problems, few Americans would prefer to live in 1920s America.

But ecosystems can change.

In nature, when something changes in an ecosystem—say a species goes extinct—it has a ripple effect on the other species. The extinct species' predators may starve and go extinct, or be pruned down, while its prey, no longer being pruned by predators, grows and expands. Eventually, the chaos settles into a new equilibrium.

When we grow up within an artificial habitat that values human inventions like reason and fairness and humanity, it can be easy to forget just how tenuous that environment is. It's easy to forget that we're living in a rare anomaly within human history—an anomaly held up only by trust, cultural norms, and shared assumptions. It's easy to become overconfident in the stability and permanence of that environment and forget that the *natural* human habitat—the Power Games—is always lurking just beneath the surface.

As in every natural ecosystem, small changes in our social ecosystem can throw it into chaos. Remembering our big question—*what's our problem?*—I believe this concept offers us our first clue: our environment has been changing at breakneck speed.

CHAPTER 3

THE DOWNWARD SPIRAL

It's human nature to start taking things for granted again when danger isn't banging loudly on the door.
—DAVID HACKWORTH

With our Ladder framework in mind, let's return to the original point that got me (and now you) into this whole mess in the first place: something is wrong in America.

Some call it political polarization, or a rise in authoritarianism, or a culture war. I'd put it like this: *Golems are on the rise.*

We talked about how human behavior is what happens when you put human nature into a given environment.

So if golems are on the rise, it's not because people have changed biologically—it's because something has changed about the environment. To get a feel for how environmental changes are shaping our current political behavior, let's look at two major shifts that have transformed the American ecosystem over the past few decades.

SHIFT #1: DISTRIBUTED TRIBALISM → CONCENTRATED TRIBALISM

A diverse country like the US is ripe ground for group conflict, and its history is packed with it. Loyalist vs. Revolutionary. Federalist vs. Anti-Federalist. North vs. South. Homegrown vs. Immigrant.

There have been periods of intense political conflict—the years following George Washington's presidency, the years leading up to and through the Civil War, and the turn of the twentieth century, to name a few. In other periods, political division has taken a back seat to other types of division or to international conflicts like World War II.

The 1950s was one such period of political unity, to the point where many Americans had a genuinely hard time telling the two parties apart. Both parties were home to large numbers of conservatives and progressives, and when the talk began about national hero Dwight Eisenhower running for president in the early 1950s, it wasn't even clear which party he'd join.

But the lack of political polarization didn't mean that everyone in 1950s US politics was getting *along*.

There's an old proverb that goes like this:

> Me against my brothers; my brothers and me against my cousins; my cousins, my brothers, and me against strangers.

When I hear this, I see humans taking a ride up the elevator of the Emergence Tower—something like the comic on the next page.

This is how golems function. A golem always must be the Us in a zero-sum, Us vs. Them conflict. The thing that allows multiple golems to merge into a larger golem is a common enemy—a common *Them* that makes the golems feel like a united *Us*. When that common enemy goes away, the higher-tier cooperation melts away and golems split back into smaller competing parts.

Golems *rely* on a common enemy for unity and for might. The stronger and more dangerous the rival *Them* seems, the stronger and more united the Us group will typically be.

The proverb provides an important clue for understanding modern America. In the US, we can think of factions within a political party as the "brothers" in the proverb. That would make the two major political parties "cousins," and other *countries* "strangers."

---

* In a well-publicized 1950 paper that's in the "be careful what you wish for" hall of fame, the American Political Science Association (APSA) urged America's political parties to become more distinct and divided. They believed the two parties were both so diverse in their ideologies that it diminished the power of the voter, leaving the direction of the country subject mostly to negotiations among politicians. Voices like APSA argued that more distinct parties with a starker divide would offer voters a clearer choice and help ensure that government was a true expression of the will of the people, while also holding parties more accountable to their voters.

† Quick refresher: We talked about the Emergence Tower in Chapter 1—a visual way to think about the concept that component pieces often combine to form something that is more than the sum of its parts, like how a bunch of neurons form a brain, a bunch of ants form a colony, or a bunch of people form a genie or golem. Here, we're seeing how that same concept works up on the giant level too.

If you pay attention to the world around you, and to your own psychology, you'll spot this proverb in action. Ever notice how countries in one region of the world will often despise each other, focusing most of their national anger on each other—until there's a broader conflict or war in play, at which time they put aside their differences? How different sects of a religion in fierce conflict with each other will suddenly find common ground when a rival religion or other outside entity insults or threatens their religion as a whole? How about when rivalries in club soccer become less heated during the World Cup? Or when political factions with differing or even totally contradictory ideologies start marching in the street, arm in arm, during a national election or mass movement? I saw people travel up the emergence elevator en masse in the days following 9/11, when millions of usually unfriendly New Yorkers were suddenly holding doors for each other, showing concern for each other's well-being, and even hugging each other in the street. While an alien attack would suck overall, it would do wonders for species solidarity.

The first half of the twentieth century was dominated by world wars. International war put the US into *"my cousins, my brothers, and me against strangers"* mode, which helped the entire American "extended family" psychologically bind together as a single Us.

During the 1950s, World War II was fresh in Americans' minds, and some of that sentiment of national unity remained. At the same time, the two parties were themselves ideologically messy, with both containing a wide range of ideological positions, so "sibling" battles *within* parties were also vicious at the time.

So what is remembered as a time of relatively high political unity was actually full of division—it's just that the division was *distributed* up and down the Emergence Tower. In other words, some of the country's Primitive Minds were focused on the lower, "factions" tier of the tower, riled up about local or state politics. Others were gathered on the "parties" tier above, fixated on national politics. Others still were obsessed with international conflict up on the "countries" tier, intoxicated with patriotism and xenophobia.

Distributed tribalism can help quell the Primitive Mind's worst instincts on any given tier. Each "higher" divide helps unite the tier below (e.g., a foreign threat provides something for politicians to unite around). Each lower division helps take some of the heat off of the higher tiers (e.g., division within parties can incentivize factions to unite with like-minded politicians across the aisle). This balance prevents the rivalries on any one tier from subsuming the whole country.

But this kind of "distributed tribalism" relies on a tenuous balance. Primitive Minds gravitate toward the most intense tribal divide in their environment, and small changes to the environment can send a balanced distribution of tribalism into collapse. In the second half of the twentieth century, the pillars upholding America's political tribal balance began to crumble.

As the 1950s became the '60s, '70s, and '80s, World War II became a distant memory and the fear of Communism and nuclear war waned. International conflict that had sucked up a lot of the tribal air since the 1930s began to lose its grip over American Primitive Minds, whose thirst for common enemies increasingly turned inward to US politics. In other words, *me, my brothers, and my cousins* lost the "strangers" that helped them all unite.

Meanwhile, another environmental change was in progress.

The Ideological Purification of America's Political Parties

The 1960s was a chaotic decade in American politics, as sweeping economic programs were enacted and landmark civil rights legislation was passed, along with a Vietnam War that divided Americans more than it united them.

While all this change was happening, the country's two major political parties were trying to figure out exactly who they were and what they stood for—and the Civil Rights Movement forced the issue. The Democrats had spent decades as an awkward alliance of progressive Northerners and conservative Southerners. Civil rights had become a transcendent cause for the Democrats' young voters but supporting the movement would alienate the Southern voting bloc that Democrats needed to win elections.

Republicans, the proud party of Lincoln, came from a long tradition of fighting for the civil rights of Black Americans. They also came from a long tradition of being a largely white party with lots of voters who were icked out by multiculturalism and, in the 1960s, fearful of the rapid changes happening in the country. For these reasons, neither party was entirely for or against the Civil Rights Movement at the time.[*]

When Barry Goldwater won the Republican nomination for president in 1964, it was the first domino to fall in what would prove to be a

---

[*] Of the two parties, the Republicans were a bit more supportive of the movement. Eighty percent of the Republicans in the House and 82 percent of those in the Senate voted for the Civil Rights Act of 1964; for Democrats, it was only 60 percent in the House and 69 percent in the Senate.

seismic shift in American politics. Goldwater had campaigned against the Civil Rights Movement and had tried to appeal to Southern segregationists to woo them away from the Democrats for the first time in a century. Goldwater wasn't popular with much of his own party, and he was crushed in the general election, but he succeeded in winning an unprecedented number of the Southern states, which helped establish the Republican Party as the future home of civil rights opposition.

Political realignment tends to start off as a slow trickle, against a strong force of inertia and entrenched loyalties. But once the trickle starts, it can become a self-reinforcing process. The events of 1964 were enough to start that trickle.

Black Americans had been somewhat split in 1960, with 32 percent voting for Nixon, the Republican candidate. But after watching Goldwater spend his campaign openly flirting with Southern racists, Black Republicans were like "yeah, no" and moved en masse to the Democrats (Goldwater won only 6 percent of the Black vote), along with many other progressive Republicans.

Four years later, with the Republicans now having alienated their progressive base in return for new voters from the South, Richard Nixon doubled down on Goldwater's "Southern strategy." He was careful not to criticize the segregationists, and many have accused him of dog-whistling to Southern whites with calls for "states' rights" and "law and order."

Meanwhile, the Democrats were dealing with the rise of their own extreme faction—the young, radical, politically militant New Left, with their drugs and their campus protests and their signs and their hair and their riots. The Democrats, no longer able to rely on their Southern bloc, were hesitant to criticize the often illiberal and sometimes violent elements of the New Left.

When moderate and extreme factions are vying for a party's identity, anything but a loud, unwavering rejection of the hard-liners is an implicit admission that those factions are indeed part of who the party is. Because if that *weren't* the case, the party would of course make it crystal clear: "those people are *not* who we are." Neither party would take this stand, allowing hyperpolarizing factions to take up long-term residence in the parties' identities. Extreme factions are like repellent magnets, and the more prominent they become, the more each party becomes defined as the place for people who hate the other party's extreme faction.

This is how a trickle of realignment can quickly accelerate. Conservative Democrats and progressive Republicans are driven to switch parties by their party's growing hard-line ideological faction, which shrinks the area of overlap. Politicians respond in kind by catering their messages more to the hard-liners, which causes more defections, and ideological plurality within the parties slowly morphs into ideological purity.

In the terms of our proverb, conflict between "brothers" melted away as the parties increasingly became ideologically unified. With the "strangers" mostly gone and the "brothers" more united, the distributed tribalism of the 1950s began to rapidly collapse into a single, concentrated tribal divide between the American Left and the American Right.

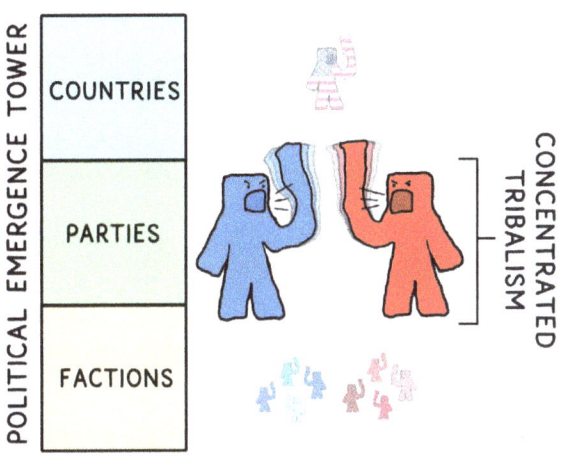

SHIFT #2: CONCENTRATED TRIBALISM → HYPERCHARGED TRIBALISM

GEOGRAPHIC SORTING

Over the past generation, Americans have become more educated, which has made them more mobile. *The Economist* notes that "45 percent of young Americans with a college degree moved states within five years of graduating, whereas only 19 percent of those with only a high-school education did."

> **DEFINING "POLARIZATION"**
>
> There are a lot of modern disagreements about political polarization—some of which seem to stem from semantic confusion.
>
> Many have pushed back against the notion that American voters have become ***ideologically* polarized**, pointing out data that suggest Americans, while more sorted in a partisan sense, have not grown more extreme in their views (i.e., there aren't fewer people in the center than there used to be). This is true—ideological sorting is far more prevalent among politicians than voters.
>
> But when many of us talk about how politically polarized America seems to be today, we're talking about something different: ***affective* polarization**, i.e., people not trusting or liking those from the other party. This *has* been on the rise—and this is the phenomenon we're mostly exploring in this chapter.

And here's the thing about mobility: if lots of people have the means to choose where they settle down, and those people tend to have even a *slight* preference to live near other people like them, everyone ends up totally segregated. This phenomenon is explained in a 1971 paper called "Dynamic Models of Segregation," and it's nicely illustrated in an interactive simulation by online creators Nicky Case and Vi Hart.

The simulation has two kinds of characters: blue squares and yellow triangles.*

These could represent people of different religions, races, socioeconomic backgrounds, or anything else.

In the simulation, there's one key metric, called "bias percentage"—a number that represents how important it is to the shapes to have neighbors that are like them. If the bias percentage were 33 percent, it would mean that the residents need at least a third of their direct neighbors to be like them, or they'll move. If one-third or more of their neighbors are like them, they'll stay.

The simulation starts with a random scattering of blue squares and yellow triangles, and it lets you set the bias percentage of the neighborhood's residents. I started by setting it to 20 percent. When I did this,

---

* All simulation images are from "Parable of the Polygons."

a few of the residents became "unhappy" and the simulation rejiggered things until every resident's 20 percent minimum similar-neighbor threshold was met. It resulted in a neighborhood that was still pretty mixed up.

But then I bumped the bias percentage up to 33 percent, which made a few more residents unhappy. To satisfy everyone, the simulation had to make things much more homogeneous.

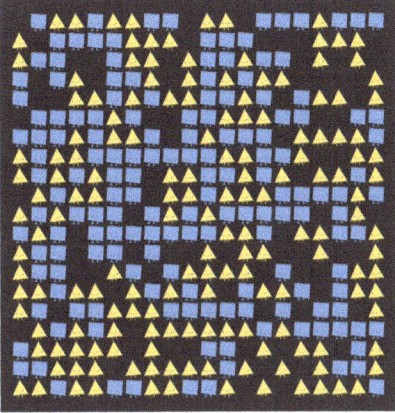

20% BIAS PERCENTAGE

When I bumped the percentage up again, this time to 50 percent—meaning the shapes are still totally fine with variety, they just don't want to be in the *minority* in their neighborhood—we end up with complete segregation:

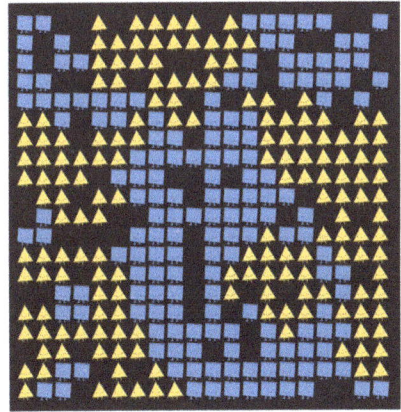
33% BIAS PERCENTAGE

50% BIAS PERCENTAGE

All it takes is a little bit of bias for almost everyone to end up surrounded entirely by people like them. As Case and Hart put it, "Small individual bias can lead to large collective bias." In a simplified simulation like this, the only way areas stay diverse—racially, ethnically, politically—is if people prefer diversity significantly *more* than they dislike being in the minority.

Now consider that alongside another fact: as the political parties purified ideologically, political identity took on more meaning. Over time, the parties also began to purify *culturally*.

Modern progressives in the US don't agree only on political stuff—they're likely to not be religious, to have gone to college, to shop at Whole Foods, to read the *New York Times*, to like backpacking and avocado toast. US conservatives, beyond their ideological similarities, often go to church, eat at Cracker Barrel, watch *Fox News*, and like NASCAR. These are, of course, massive generalizations with a million exceptions—but as the simulation shows us, even if this is a *little* true, it can have major implications.

A friend of mine just moved with his family from New York City to Vermont. When he was telling me about their new location, he emphasized that they loved their little town because it was largely progressive. Is it important to my friend to live near people who share his views on tax policy? No. What he really meant is that he and his family just want to be near "people like them." He wanted to be near the shops, activities, restaurants, and schools that people like them tend to like, near people who use their kind of slang, watch their kinds of TV shows, and vacation in their kinds of places.

In 1950, people wanted to live near people like them too—but with the political parties so mixed up, a culturally homogeneous neighborhood might still be politically diverse. Today, the parties have become proxies for two vast macro-cultures, so seeking out people like you also often means ending up surrounded by people who share your politics.

In his book *The Big Sort*, Bill Bishop examines how Americans have shifted geographically in relation to political leaning—and he found that Americans are far less likely to live in politically diverse areas than they used to be. The idea is that Americans have formed *geographical* Echo Chambers, where they find themselves surrounded by political likeness at dinner parties, at local churches and parks and businesses, and at the schools where children make their lifelong friends.

In a congressional election, pollsters define a "landslide county" as one in which the winning candidate beat the losing candidate by 20 percentage points or more—in other words, a very red or very blue county. In the 1976 presidential election, 27 percent of Americans lived in landslide counties, with the remaining 73 percent living in more politically balanced "purple" counties where the election margin was closer. By the

1992 election, the percentage of Americans living in a landslide county had moved from 27 percent to 38 percent. That number has continued to rise, with 58 percent of Americans living in a landslide county during the 2020 presidential election.

Some argue that it's not so simple. A number of experts argue that the "landslide district" numbers are more of a peculiarity of presidential elections than a general trend. Some dispute the causal relationship, arguing that political sorting is more of a reflection of people's views coming to match their surroundings than people moving to places that match their politics.

Whatever the case, most experts agree that political tribalism is on the rise. This certainly matches my observations: Americans seem to be spending a lot more time talking with those who agree with their politics than thoughtfully engaging with those who don't.

When people are surrounded by ideologically homogeneous groups, their views become more extreme. In an interesting study, researchers examined the effects of a kind of "deliberation day," when two groups of citizens from politically homogeneous areas got together to discuss hot political issues:

> Groups from Boulder, a predominantly liberal city, met and discussed global warming, affirmative action, and civil unions for same-sex couples; groups from Colorado Springs, a predominately conservative city, met to discuss the same issues. The major effect of deliberation was to make group members more extreme than they were when they started to talk. Liberals became more liberal on all three issues; conservatives became more conservative. As a result, the division between the citizens of Boulder and the citizens of Colorado Springs were significantly increased as a result of intragroup deliberation. Deliberation also increased consensus, and dampened diversity, within the groups.

So cultural sorting yields political sorting as a byproduct, and the resulting homogeneity then makes everyone's political views more extreme. You end up with increasingly partisan people, holding increasingly negative perceptions of people from the other party, which makes everyone even more determined to surround themselves with people from their own tribe. It's a classic vicious cycle.

And this is only the beginning of our environmental troubles. In the book's intro, we talked about exponential technology, and how it can be both a blessing and a curse. The tech revolution of the past thirty years has ramped up political tribalism to another level entirely.

NARROWCAST MEDIA

Here's a lens I call the Media Matrix:

Every media brand, media personality, or journalist can be plotted somewhere in the matrix.

At the top-middle of the Media Matrix is media's North Star. Here you have media sources that are rigorous about both accuracy and neutrality, trying their best to present the truth, the whole truth, and nothing but the truth—along with acknowledging when they don't know what the truth is. This is the realm of high-rung journalism.

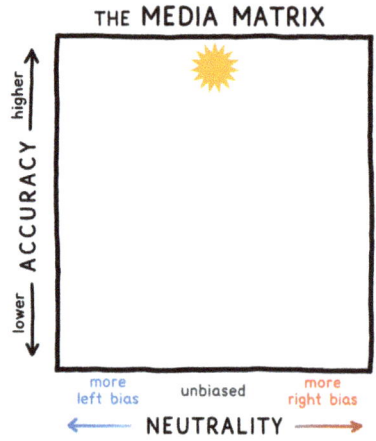

> **A NOTE ON NEUTRALITY**
> Neutrality doesn't mean portraying both political sides as equally good or equally right. It means portraying them as they are. Sometimes both sides deserve an equal share of praise or blame, in which case neutral media would report on that parallel. But when one side is behaving worse than the other side, neutral coverage portrays exactly that. Depicting both sides as equal when they're not (aka "bothsidesism") is not neutral, but is biased toward "presenting the sides as equal."

As you move to the left and right of the North Star, political bias begins to creep in.* Media voices will tell most of the story, but they may

---

* Sometimes, media slant is the result of a conscious agenda to promote one side over the other. In other cases, the intent is to be neutral, and the slant is a result of unconscious bias. Either way, the effect is the same.

omit certain unhelpful-to-their-cause facts. When you get all the way to the upper corners, you have brands with a serious bias—careful about accuracy but not about neutrality. Everything they report is carefully cherry-picked.

As you move *down* in the Media Matrix, accuracy diminishes as a core value in favor of profit, entertainment, a political agenda, or something else. A news source down here is a steadfast ally to its partisan audience, and it stays current with the latest talking points in Political Disney World, even if that means twisting stories, using misleading statistics, pulling quotes out of context, treating rumors as facts, or any other form of bullshit.

From Broadcasting to Narrowcasting

In the 1980s, most Americans got their TV news from the Rather/Jennings/Brokaw trio on CBS, ABC, and NBC; in earlier years, from nationwide titans like Walter Cronkite. In those days, networks competed to capture the largest share of American viewers. They were careful to avoid seeming politically biased, and they knew that reporting a story incorrectly could lead to damaged credibility and a loss of viewers. They were incentivized by market forces and government regulation not to stray too far from the North Star.

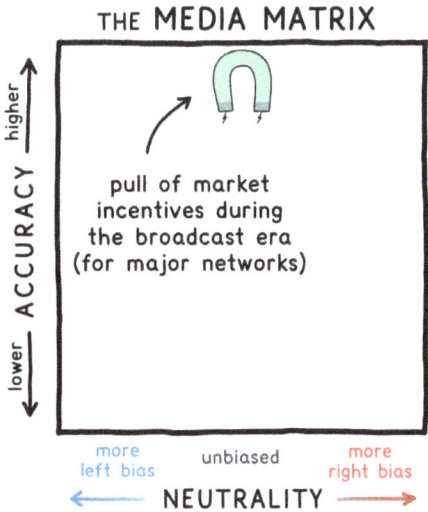

In recent decades, new technology has dramatically changed this landscape.

First, there was the explosion of cable television around 1980, and with it, the advent of twenty-four-hour cable news (CNN launched in 1980). Cable channels, with hazier expectations than mainstream networks and twenty-four hours a day to work with, could be more experimental with the way they covered the news.

Then there was the end of the Fairness Doctrine. In 1949, the FCC (the US Federal Communications Commission) established the Fairness Doctrine, which required anyone who held a broadcast license to present "controversial issues of public importance" in a "fair and balanced" manner, giving airtime to "contrasting viewpoints." In 1987, in the face of arguments that the Fairness Doctrine was in direct conflict with the First Amendment's freedom of the press clause, it was repealed.

The removal of the Fairness Doctrine was soon followed by a sharp rise in overtly partisan media. Conservative talk radio exploded onto the scene in the late 1980s, most notably with *The Rush Limbaugh Show*, which debuted to a national audience in 1988 and made Limbaugh the country's most syndicated radio host by 1991. In 1996, Fox News and MSNBC were born. Rather than broadcasting to all of America, these new media channels could *narrowcast* to a specific subset of the country.

In college in 2004, I attended a live interview with Ted Koppel, the anchor of ABC's late-night news show *Nightline*. I remember the host commenting that Koppel was famously secretive about his own political leanings. This was the standard for prominent anchors in the past, but by the end of the 1990s, a huge portion of Americans were getting their news from people whose political leaning was supremely out on the table.

While these changes were happening, the internet sprung into our lives, and with it, sites like the Drudge Report (1995), Slate (1996), the Huffington Post (2005), and Breitbart (2007), along with a trillion political blogs and YouTube channels. The internet took narrowcasting up into a new gear: full-fledged tribal media.

Meanwhile, Fox News and conservative radio continued to grow in size and influence, generating an insular right-wing information bubble that persists today. This was countered with a new genre of TV news on the left—political comedy shows. *The Daily Show* began in 1996 and became a multi-decade sensation by serving as—depending on who you ask—either the voice of reason and sanity in the face of growing right-wing madness, or a show where elitist progressives would cackle as Jon Stewart relentlessly mocked their political out-group. *The Daily Show* was followed by a slew of similar "look at how awful the Right is" comedy/news shows, hosted by *Daily Show* alums like Stephen Colbert, John Oliver, and Samantha Bee.

Narrowcast media caters to homogeneous audiences, which decreases the incentive to worry about neutrality and heightens the incentive to provide viewpoint confirmation. Rather than tell people which candidate is *likely* to win the next election like the old days, narrowcast media reaps huge rewards for telling people why their favorite candidate *ought* to win. With little risk of reputation damage for biased coverage, narrowcast media can continually bash one side while giving the other side a free pass and end up with a more loyal audience for it. If broadcast media functions like a top-rung Scientist, narrowcast media functions like a third-rung Attorney. Because when the environment changes, so does behavior.

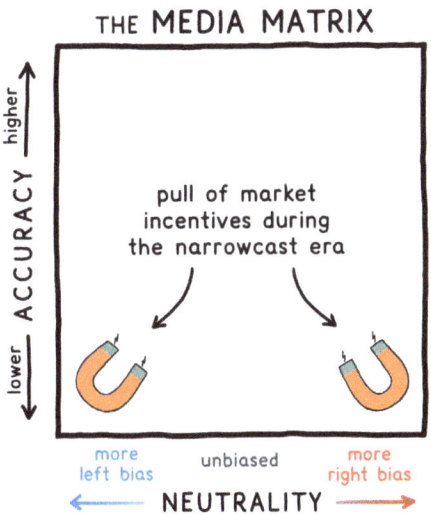

Junk Food

Many businesses have learned that a great way to make money is to sell directly to the simple, predictable Primitive Mind. To sell food to the Higher Mind, you have to worry about quality and nutrition, which is expensive and hard. Instead, you can sell Skittles to the Primitive Mind, who mistakes them for nutritious food.

If professional news coverage is nutritious food, political junk food looks like this (all actual headlines):

https://www.cnn.com › videos › politics
TRUMP DOCUMENTARY FILMMAKER SAYS THIS FOOTAGE IS THE 'SMOKING GUN'
Documentary filmmaker Alex Holder discusses an excerpt from his docuseries "Unprecedented," wherein he asks then-President Donald Trump to ...

https://www.youtube.com › watch
LAURA INGRAHAM: THE REAL TARGET OF THIS INVESTIGATION IS YOU
Laura Ingraham discusses the FBI raid on Trump's Florida home and what this overreach means for Americans on 'The Ingraham Angle.'

https://www.youtube.com › watch
'BULLST': DON LEMON FIRES BACK AT RON DESANTIS' MASKS COMMENT**
CNN's Don Lemon takes Florida Gov. Ron DeSantis to task for falsely saying, again, that masks are ineffective to combat the Covid-19 virus.

https://www.youtube.com › watch
TUCKER CALLS THIS THE MOST 'TOTALLY EVIL' THING PRESIDENT JOE BIDEN HAS DONE
Tucker Carlson joined the Guy Benson Show to talk about what he thinks is the most 'totally evil' thing Joe Biden has done as president.

https://www.thedailybeast.com › jordan-klepper-crashes-...
KLEPPER CRASHES MAGA RALLY TO CONFRONT BRAIN-WORMED TRUMPERS
The 'Daily Show' correspondent traveled to a Wisconsin MAGA rally and found some seriously deranged conspiracists.

https://www.youtube.com › watch
KAMALA HARRIS 'LAUGHS OFF' AMERICANS STRUGGLING TO AFFORD GAS
'The Big Sunday Show' panelists react to Amazon's Jeff Bezos slamming President Biden for pinning surging gas prices on gas stations and China's praise for Biden.

https://www.msnbc.com › the-reidout › reidout-blog
IN BIZARRE VIDEO, MTG ASSAULTS 'REALITY, SCIENCE, AND THE ENGLISH LANGUAGE...
Chris Hayes breaks down in laughter discussing a recent Facebook broadcast from Marjorie Taylor Greene, in which she says that Bill Gates wants people to eat artificial meat...

https://www.youtube.com › watch
FORMER CLINTON CAMPAIGN MANAGER REVEALS BOMBSHELL
Fox News legal analyst George Jarrett and Trump attorney Alina Habba weigh in on new Durham probe developments on 'Hannity.'

The confirmation promised by these kinds of headlines looks as delectable to the Primitive Mind as the sweet sustenance promised by a Skittles wrapper. Political junk food isn't geared toward learning. The headlines tell you from the get-go which side will win and which side will lose. It combines three of the Primitive Mind's favorite things: viewpoint/identity confirmation, out-group bashing, and gossip.

The explosion of the political junk food market has dragged many American minds downward into Political Disney World, the land of good guys, bad guys, and simple storylines—which in turn has continually raised the demand for junk food.

The further this cycle goes, the harder it is to reverse. Media brands that offer up one-sided tribal junk food end up alienating high-rung minds, which makes the brands that much more dependent on the junk-food-loving low-rung audience. And tens of millions of Americans end up with political diabetes.

As the media junk food industry has grown and matured, it has increasingly immersed its audience in a new, hideous genre of entertainment:

Political Reality TV

Broadcast TV news aimed to be a show about reality. Narrowcast news tries to be a reality show. Big difference.

Reality is interesting sometimes. Reality shows are interesting all the time. And what's the reality TV producer's best trick? Drama and negativity. Would anyone watch *The Real Housewives of Beverly Hills* if the characters got along most of the time? Of course not. That's why every five minutes of the show includes a conflict of some kind.

As soon as you realize that news media is also entertainment media, the constant coverage of conflict and drama makes perfect sense.

In the US, many of us are addicted to a trashy reality show I call *The Real Politicians of Washington, DC*.

The cast changes from year to year, but the formula is the same: there are whole teams of heroes and villains, lots of ongoing storylines, and endless conflict. It's a perfect vehicle for a dramatic, super-addictive soap opera.

It's not that these heavily featured politicians or the played-up storylines are unimportant. It's that we receive a totally *skewed* depiction of the *full set* of relevant political issues. The issues that make headlines day in and day out are usually overrepresented, while lots of other important political stories—like the bills being approved each week by the fifty House and Senate committees—are woefully underreported.

I recently had a chance to talk with a US representative named Derek Kilmer. Kilmer is the former head of a major congressional coalition of moderate Democrats with ninety-nine members. He's full of nuanced, measured, well-thought-out ideas for how to make the country better. Which is exactly why you've never heard of him. The editors of *The Real Politicians* waste no airtime on politicians like Kilmer because he's measured and nuanced and I'm falling asleep just writing this sentence.

Actual politics, like actual reality, is boring to most people. So tribal media brands do what reality TV producers do—they manufacture a carefully edited, fictional version of politics that's wildly entertaining.

That's why most Americans who will tell you they're passionate about politics can barely name ten current members of Congress. They probably can't name all the US representatives from their state, let alone members of their *state* legislatures. But they *can* tell you about the ten or fifteen politicians chosen by the media to be the main characters on *The Real Politicians*, along with the five or ten hot-button issues the show features in any given month.

Concentrated tribalism has led to increased division—but *The Real Politicians* adds fuel to the fire by making the distinction between the parties seem even *more* stark than it actually is.

Take the issue of climate change, where we're regularly presented with this storyline:

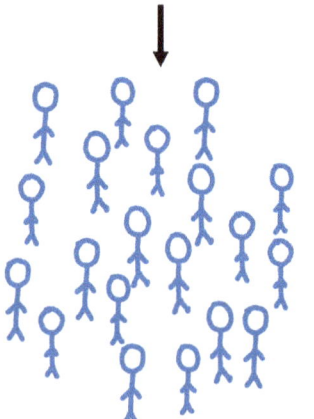
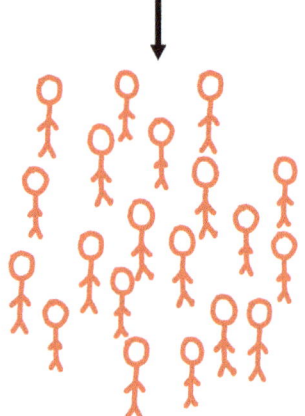

So I was surprised to see this data:

Most see environmental action as important, some lack resources to act
% who say doing things to protect the environment is...

	Important, even if it costs time or money	Important, but I don't have the time or money	Not that important right now
Total	53%	37%	9%
Rep/Lean Rep	43%	41%	14%
Dem/Lean Dem	63%	33%	4%

Which suggests that things are more like this:

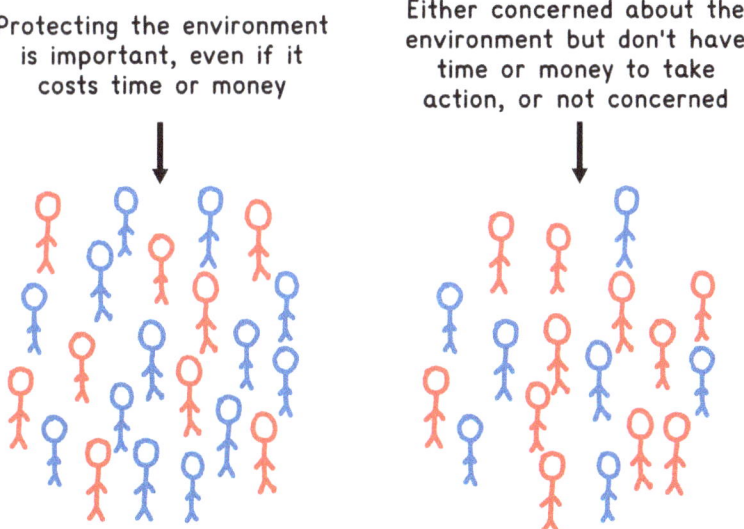

Very different story. Of course, it's also true that many Republican politicians have been dismissive of climate change. And "doing things to protect the environment" is not necessarily the same as taking action to curb emissions. But the survey makes me feel very differently about the strategies climate activists should be using to build the necessary coalition to change our trajectory.

Presenting an inaccurate version of reality breeds misplaced anger and division and hurts our ability to move toward important goals—all in the name of editing the reality show to be more entertaining with crisper, juicier storylines.

The most dramatic events on *The Real Politicians* are elections. Elections are the show's climactic season finales. And the show's editors make sure to overdramatize the shit out of them.

This is the past century of US presidential elections.

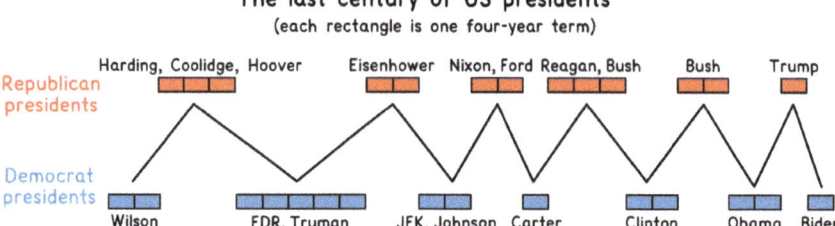

It's a clear zigzag pattern. And yet, I remember when Bush won reelection in 2004, media commentators were talking about how Democrats couldn't win races anymore for a number of seemingly rock-solid sociological reasons. Then the Democrats swept the midterms in 2006 and won the presidency in 2008.

I remember in 2012, when Obama won reelection, hearing people say that the country had fundamentally shifted, that there were more first-generation Americans than there used to be, that the Tea Party had rendered the Republican Party irrelevant, and all of this other proof that times had changed and the Democrats wouldn't ever lose a presidential election again.

Then Republicans swept all three branches of government in 2016, at which point I read all these articles about how the Left is more *culturally* powerful, but the Right is simply more *politically* powerful. I also heard a bunch of stuff about how gerrymandering ensured that the Democrats would never win back the House again. In 2018, the Democrats won the House and then swept the Congress, Senate, and presidency in 2020.

I don't know what truly motivates today's media. Maybe they make politically motivated propaganda. Maybe they make profit-motivated entertainment, which happens to double as political propaganda. Whatever the motivation, the consequence is the same: enhanced political tribalism.

Around a decade after the transformation to narrowcasting began, another technological development added even more fuel to the fire.

INTERNET ALGORITHMS

I appreciate the Google search algorithm. It filters results that are most relevant to where I live and what I'm typically interested in, and it can guess remarkably well what I want to search for after I type just a few letters, saving me the trouble of typing the whole search.

I appreciate the YouTube algorithm, which knows my favorite channels and makes sure I never miss their latest videos.

I appreciate the Facebook algorithm, which spares me the knowledge of what Jake from high school twenty years ago made for dinner last night while making sure to let me know when Jake gets engaged, so I can go look through his eighty-seven most recent photos to see the deal with his fiancée.

Internet algorithms can be great things. But new technology often comes along with unanticipated consequences.

When I'm watching a YouTube video and I glance at the thumbnails on the sidebar, I'm more likely to click on a video featuring someone explaining history or science than I am to click on a video featuring someone reviewing movies. YouTube has picked up on that, which is why I never see movie review videos on my YouTube sidebar, but I'm constantly being introduced to new history or science explainer videos.

But then one night last year, someone sent me a funny video a driver took with their phone. The driver taking the video had pissed off another driver, who opened his window and started screaming curses. The angry driver got so worked up that he swung his arm at the video-taking driver angrily, and in the process, punched *his own side mirror* off. A delight of all delights.

Then the video ended, and YouTube offered me my choice of nine more videos in the road rage genre. I clicked on one of them and watched it. Then YouTube offered me nine more. I had a lot of work to do, so I held down the Command key and clicked on all nine, opening them in nine new tabs, and watched them all. Two* hours later, utterly disgusted with myself, I pulled the dramatic "punishing Chrome by holding down Command-Q and closing all eight Chrome windows and all 127 of their open tabs" move. A nightmare waste of time. But at least it was over.

Except it wasn't over. Somewhere out there, the YouTube algorithm was baiting its Tim Urban fishhook with the best of the best road rage videos, which have reliably appeared in my YouTube sidebar ever since that regrettable night, damning me to an entire life wasted watching hilarious road rage videos.

Internet algorithms are profit-maximizing mechanisms that want to spoon-feed me whatever I'm most likely to click on. This is a win-win, symbiotic relationship—until it's not. When an algorithm is jibing with your Higher Mind, it's your friend. When it's luring in your Primitive Mind against your Higher Mind's will, the relationship is parasitic.

So how does this apply to politics? Primitive Minds like to click on political junk food. They're drawn to articles and videos that don't just report the news but sensationalize it and make it *entertaining*. The YouTube sidebar can quickly turn into a wall of *The Real Politicians of Washington, DC* content the same way YouTube inundated me with road rage videos. This feeds political tribalism and distorts our picture of reality.

Then there's social media, a phenomenon so peculiar and so specific to modern times that it would seem incomprehensible to everyone who came before us. Social media doesn't just amplify political junk food—it plays a role in shaping it. When a new political news story makes waves, thousands of hot takes quickly bubble up. It's not necessarily the most accurate takes that rise to the top† but those that are most likely to make people click the retweet or share button—those that have the catchiest wording and hit the right emotional buttons. Through an almost evolutionary process, complex topics are dumbed down and packaged into irresistible nuggets for our Primitive Minds.

---

* Four
† "The spread of true and false news online," a 2018 study that analyzed 126,000 stories tweeted by three million people, found that "falsehood diffused significantly farther, faster, deeper, and more broadly than the truth in all categories of information, and the effects were more pronounced for false political news than for false news about terrorism, natural disasters, science, urban legends, or financial information."

Only a minority of people are hyperpartisan. But internet algorithms make people who are already extreme even more extreme. On social media, these voices disproportionately drive the conversation, making people *feel* like things are even more nasty and polarized than they actually are.

In the 2020 documentary *The Social Dilemma*, computer scientist Jaron Lanier uses Wikipedia as an example to highlight the craziness of this situation:

> When you go to a [Wikipedia] page, you're seeing the same thing as other people. So it's one of the few things online that we at least hold in common. Now, just imagine for a second that Wikipedia said, "We're gonna give each person a different customized definition, and we're gonna be paid by people for that." So, Wikipedia would be spying on you. Wikipedia would calculate, "What's the thing I can do to get this person to change a little bit on behalf of some commercial interest?" Right? And then it would change the entry. Can you imagine that? Well, you should be able to, 'cause that's exactly what's happening on Facebook. It's exactly what's happening in your YouTube feed.

What happens on social media often determines what happens in the actual media. In his book *Why We're Polarized*, Ezra Klein talks about the way journalists choose what to cover—the way they decide *what is newsworthy*. "A shortcut to newsworthiness," he says, "has always been whether other news organizations are covering a story—if they are, then it's newsworthy by definition."

In the past, audience members had limited ability to influence what news was covered. But social media changes the equation. "In the modern era," Klein writes, "a shortcut to newsworthiness is social media virality; if people are already talking about a story or a tweet, that makes it newsworthy almost by definition."

It's a vicious cycle. As political junk food pulls audiences further into Political Disney World, the low-rung narratives go more viral, more often, on social media. These viral narratives are then converted into a wave of new junk food media content, which reinforces and legitimizes the ideas circulating on social media. The connectivity of the internet melds media and its audiences into a single self-perpetuating system.

It's no surprise where all this leaves us.

SEPARATE REALITIES

Pew data collected since 1994 shows us that the gap between the viewpoints of Democrats and Republicans has grown on a selection of issues across the board:

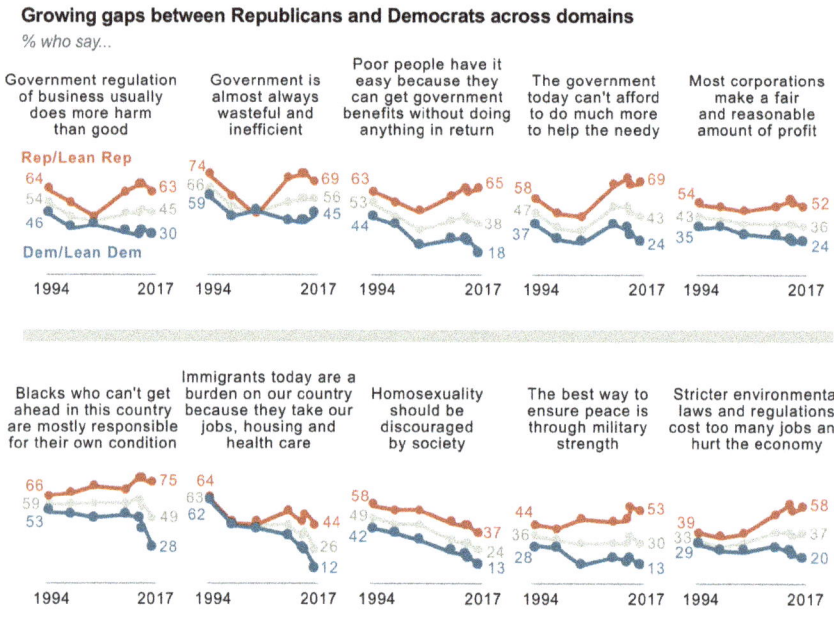

Source: Pew Research Center

Averaging out the growth of the gap in those ten graphs yields a smooth upward trend—even as gaps in viewpoints between other kinds of demographics have remained unchanged: →

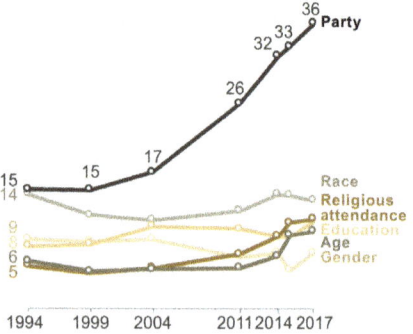

Source: Pew Research Center

When we hear about growing political division, most of us assume it means citizens are divided in their *values*—that people are unable to agree about What Should Be. But take another look at the ten questions from Pew. There's an element of What Should Be embedded in some of the questions—but mostly, they are questions about *What Is*. Many are statements about the status quo that the two political sides do not agree on.

We see the same story again and again. A 2020 poll called *Dueling Realities* found that 81 percent of Republicans believe "the Democratic Party has been taken over by socialists," while 78 percent of Democrats believe "the Republican Party has been taken over by racists." In 2022, Pew found that 72 percent of Americans believe that "on the issues that matter to them, their side in politics has been losing more often than winning" while only 24 percent felt that their side was winning more than losing—a natural result of political media that increasingly focuses on grievance and negativity.

A 2017 survey titled "The Parties in Our Heads" had an even more revealing finding: *the more political news respondents consumed, the more skewed their perception of members of the other party*.

Separate realities are a natural consequence of market incentives moving from the North Star region closer to the lower corners of the Media Matrix, where there's almost no overlap in coverage between the two sides. It makes sense that those most hooked on political media would be the most delusional, the same way political news in dog-raccoon-ville left the pro-dog and pro-raccoon crowds with totally different perceptions of reality.

A RISE IN BIGOTRY

News media is infamous for what we could call "destructive cherry-picking"—a selection bias that sees negative stories as the most newsworthy, because they draw the most interest. It's why, for example, Americans surveyed by Gallup since 1990 consistently think crime is increasing, even though in almost every one of those years, it decreased from the year before.

Destructive cherry-picking spreads fear and pessimism, and over the past twenty years, it's been steadily on the rise. In political media, this can have especially dangerous consequences.

Geographic sorting means many people barely spend time with anyone on the other political side, so the only information they have on what those people are like comes through distorted media and social media filters. The right-wing narrative floods right-wing people with anecdotes that make it seem like everyone on the left positively despises them and everything they stand for, and vice versa. Outrage about these messages then spreads like wildfire on social media.

Vocal Primitive Minds activate other Primitive Minds. Presenting people with a steady stream of "they hate you" jolts awake their Primitive Minds, in many cases filling them with reciprocal disdain, clouding their humanity, and flipping on that ancient tribal switch that makes people want to band together into golems. Portraying a society where everyone hates each other becomes a self-fulfilling prophecy. So it's no surprise that between 1994 and 2022, the percentage of people who rate the opposing party as "very unfavorable" has tripled.

It doesn't take long before this awakens the scariest human emotion of all: disgust.

Like happiness, sadness, anger, and fear, disgust is a basic emotion, meaning that it's hardwired into all humans. Basic emotions were helpful for survival in the ancient human world. A Google Images search for "disgust" shows a bunch of people, all making the same hideous face—squinting their eyes, curling up their noses, and exhaling (and if it gets really bad, exhaling turns to gagging and eventually vomiting). Scientists believe this is evolution's way of getting us to close up our incoming passages and expel outward whatever we can, in order to protect ourselves when we're in the presence of toxins or disease. We react this way to anything our primitive software believes is potentially dangerous and disease-carrying—like rotten food, blood, feces, or maggots.

The strange thing is that disgust can carry over to how we view *people*. There's a sizable amount of research that suggests that when people are exposed to something that brings out their disgust emotion, they become harsher moral judges. In one experiment, a group of Canadians were shown disturbing-but-not-disgusting images of car accidents while another was shown photos of coughing people and other disease-related visuals. Then both groups were questioned about which countries they felt Canada should try to attract immigrants from. Both groups showed a preference for immigrants from familiar countries over immigrants from less familiar countries, but the group that had seen images of disease felt this preference much more strongly. In another study, participants sitting at a dirty desk were harsher in their judgments of a series of criminal acts than participants sitting at a clean desk. In another, a wafting noxious odor made participants feel less warmly toward gay men.

Scientists use the term "behavioral immune system" to describe the theory that disgust in humans is linked to xenophobia and discomfort with practices and rituals (especially sexual) that seem foreign or different to us—an ancient impulse we developed long ago, when contact with foreign people and practices often did put you at risk of disease.

The reason I call disgust the scariest of all human emotions is that it's a trigger for dehumanization, and dehumanization is the doorway to the worst things humans do. It's not a coincidence that two of the most horrifying events in recent human history—the Holocaust and the Rwandan genocide—were made possible by disgust. Nazi propaganda constantly compared Jews to disgust-inducing animals like rats, swine, and insects. The Rwandan radio broadcasts that incited the 1994 genocide referred to Tutsis as "cockroaches" repeatedly. These are just two examples of a well-worn tradition.

Disgust fills our mind with a special kind of primitive fog—one that turns ordinary humans into psychopaths who can commit or condone unthinkable harm without remorse. Scary shit.

Geographic sorting and political junk food make a lethal combo, ripe for disgust. It's hard to feel dehumanizing disgust for people you know personally. Less hard when you rarely see your enemies in person. Less hard still when destructive cherry-picking teaches you only the worst about them. As affective polarization has risen, political opponents have gone from seeming like wrong or stupid people to seeming like disgusting people.

We like to think of bigotry as something that other people do. But we're all capable of rank bigotry when our environment pushes the right buttons in our psyche.

Political bigotry is as real as any other bigotry. In a 2014 paper on political polarization in the US, political scientist Shanto Iyengar and researcher Sean J. Westwood describe evidence that "hostile feelings for the opposing party are ingrained or automatic in voters' minds" and that "partisans discriminate against opposing partisans, doing so to a degree that exceeds discrimination based on race."*

Bigotry is at its most dangerous when it goes unrecognized. The best tools to combat bigotry are social norms that penalize its expression—but today in the US, political bigotry is rarely treated as taboo.

DOWNWARD WE SPIRAL

Human environments are made up of a complex fabric of culture, norms, values, laws, and prevailing beliefs. Changes to any element of our environment can trigger changes in other parts of the environment, which in turn can cause more changes.

We discussed the way that the advent of tribal media made people more partisan and more hooked on political junk food, and how the resulting rise in demand pushed media to be even more tribal and one-sided.

> Side by side with these macro trends are other changes political scientists have studied—like increased competitiveness for legislative majorities, changes in electoral rules, changes to campaign finance rules, and rising immigration. The extent to which these changes are causes or effects of today's political atmosphere is up for debate. I won't analyze all these here, because for our purposes, what matters is the big trend toward hypercharged tribalism, not the full array of potential causes for it.

A similar feedback loop has taken place between voters and politicians. Increasingly partisan politicians draw constituents deeper into Political Disney World, and a lower-rung electorate is more likely to reward politicians who cater to the low-rung mindset and snub the politicians who act like grown-ups.

As political tribalism has ramped up, the number of undecided votes has dwindled.† It makes less sense than it used to for candidates to try to persuade moderate voters and more sense to run hyperpartisan, negative campaigns that fire up their base and increase turnout.

---

* In 1960, only 4 percent of Democrats and 5 percent of Republicans were opposed to the prospect of their child marrying a supporter of the other party. By 2018, those numbers had skyrocketed to 45 percent of Democrats and 35 percent of Republicans. A striking trend during the same period that many other forms of bigotry waned in the US.

† One political scientist's numbers suggest that between 1980 and 2000, the number of undecided voters dropped from 22 percent of the electorate to...

And as the media's political coverage has morphed into a reality TV show, it has created an incentive system that rewards politicians who use inflammatory rhetoric. As the famously bombastic Representative Newt Gingrich has put it: "You have to give them confrontations. When you give them confrontations, you get attention." Politicians who act like children are great TV, which incentivizes the media to give them more airtime, which helps those politicians win elections, which encourages more of the same behavior.

In the first part of this chapter, we talked about how the distributed political tribalism of the 1960s coalesced into a single, concentrated tribal divide—an environment that makes a populace more vulnerable to the pull of the low rungs. When this was coupled with other changes in geography, media, and social media, it sent the country spinning down a vortex of feedback loops.

This vortex has led us to a scary place I call hypercharged tribalism.

HYPERCHARGED TRIBALISM

Hypercharged tribalism happens when a concentrated tribal divide reaches such intensity that it resembles a religious war, subsuming the entire society and the people within it. Hypercharged tribalism turns thinking, feeling human beings into loyal colony ants, overriding their intellect, their humanity, even their love of family and friends. It's

---

...7 percent. People sometimes conflate "undecided voters" with "independent voters," but these aren't the same. While the percentage of voters who label themselves as "independent" has increased since the 1980s, most Independent voters are actually quite loyal to one party. So even as the percentage of Independent voters has increased, the percentage of truly undecided voters—true "swing" voters—has decreased.

a form of group madness—a contagion that spreads like an epidemic, awakening the ancient survival instincts in millions of minds all at once, as huge groups of people slip into golem mode in lockstep.

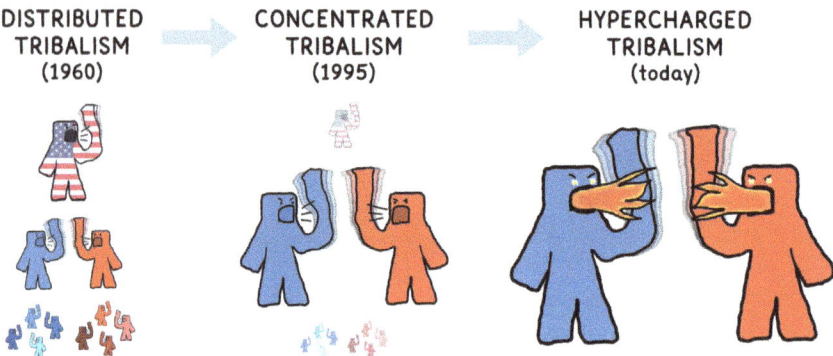

Political scientists Alan Abramowitz and Steven Webster studied an interesting metric: what we could call political *loyalty*. Over the past five decades, they looked at how districts voted in presidential elections and compared it to how those same districts voted in congressional elections. In the 1970s, the correlation was 0.54, which means that it was common at that time for Americans to vote for one party for Congress and a different one for president. That metric for political loyalty has steadily increased:

>1972–1980: **0.54**
>1982–1990: **0.65**
>1992–2000: **0.78**
>2002–2010: **0.83**
>2012–2014: **0.94**
>2018: **0.97**

A correlation of 0.7 or 0.8 would imply some seriously concentrated tribalism. A 0.97 correlation implies something more extreme. By 2018, almost *no* Americans voted for two different parties in the same election. In a span of a few decades, it has become unthinkable for Americans to vote for their out-group party, no matter *who* the candidates are.

We see the same kind of rigid allegiance when we look at how

Americans feel about different political issues. In the past, a voter could tell you their stance on guns and it wouldn't tell you much about their stances on abortion or immigration or climate change. Today, the views of Democrats and Republicans are far more predictable. Pew looks at this by analyzing "ideological consistency" among voters by plotting Americans on a spectrum from "consistently liberal"* on one end to "consistently conservative" on the other. People who adhere perfectly to one party's "opinion checklist" are plotted toward the ends, while people who hold a mix of views are closer to the center. Here are three recent snapshots:

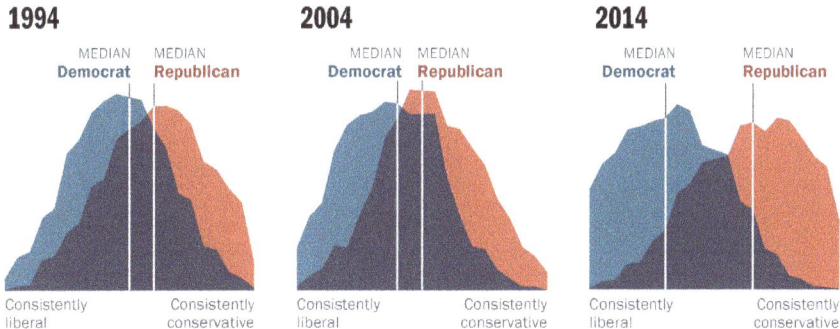

Source: Pew Research Center

This isn't going all the way back to the days of political plurality in the '60s—it *starts* in 1994. Mere concentrated tribalism wasn't enough to skew things too much—but hypercharged tribalism was.

The story with politicians is even starker. Advisory services company *National Journal* has ranked representatives along an ideological axis based on how they vote on economic, social, and foreign issues. Here's what these scores look like over four decades:

---

* Pew, like many Americans today, uses the word "liberal" the way we've been using the word "progressive." For clarity, I'll continue using the word "progressive" here.

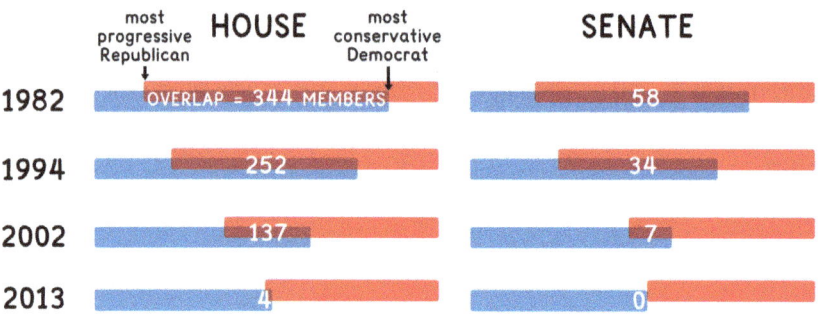

By the '80s, the Republicans had mostly become the conservative party and Democrats the party for progressives. But there was still a sizable overlap—as you'd expect from hundreds of politicians making independent decisions. Today, the overlap is *gone*. Voting against your party's ideology isn't just unpopular—it's become *blasphemy*. That's hypercharged tribalism.

One commonly cited metric to measure ideology of US representatives is something called the DW-NOMINATE, which places politicians on a liberal-to-conservative scale based on their roll call vote behavior. Here's a chart showing the gap between the mean in each party—a nice proxy for polarization:

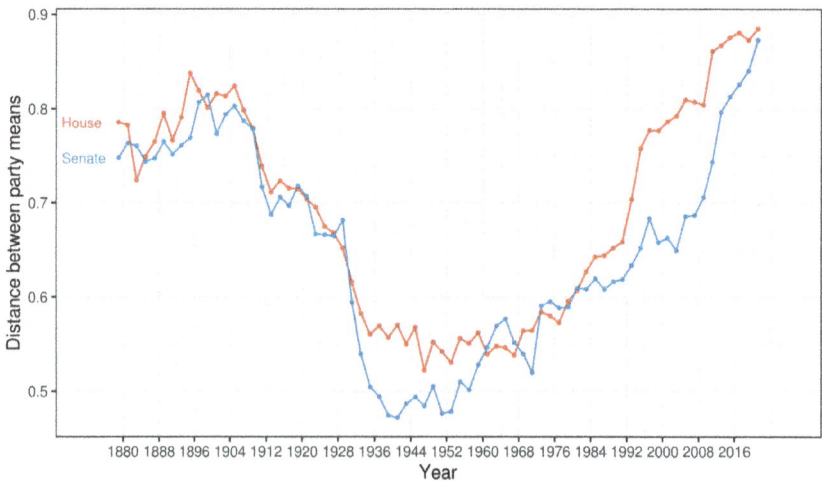

Source: Lewis et al., "Voteview: Congressional Roll-Call Votes Database."

Even the Supreme Court, supposedly a nonpartisan institution, has reflected these trends. Writing in the *New York Times*, political scientist Lee Epstein and law professor Eric Posner looked at the history of Supreme Court votes, examining the correlation between the way justices voted and the party that appointed them. The correlation did not used to be strong. In fact, Epstein and Posner write, "as late as the early 1990s, it was possible for justices to vote in ideologically unpredictable ways." In an era of hypercharged tribalism, this is no longer the case. In close votes (5–3 or 5–4), today's justices almost always vote along party lines.

According to Epstein and Posner, "For the first time in living memory, the court will be seen by the public as a party-dominated institution, one whose votes on controversial issues are essentially determined by the party affiliation of recent presidents."

Many of what we think of as hot-topic political divides today only became that way over the past thirty years. As recently as the mid-'90s, for example, people from the two parties polled about equal in their support for legalized abortion.* It's a similar story with the push for stricter gun laws, which was supported by parties in the early '90s (83 percent of Democrats, 76 percent of Republicans in 1990) but has wildly diverged since (90 percent of Democrats, 33 percent of Republicans in 2017). Republicans are far more likely to be religious today than Democrats—but in 1990, the numbers were just about the same across parties. These issues have all fallen into the grip of hypercharged tribalism.

America's two sides hate each other so much that whenever one of them emphasizes the danger of a foreign rival, the other instinctively downplays the threat and frames the concern as dishonest political maneuvering or bigotry. Even the American flag is, today, increasingly viewed by many on the left as a right-wing symbol. When a nation's Primitive Minds become maniacally fixated on a particular Us/Them divide, phenomena that would normally take some of the heat off the divide just become more fuel for it.

Hypercharged political tribalism is a magnet that pulls in everything around it. Race. Religion. Education. Media. Tech. Business. Music. Entertainment. Science. History. Sports. Thanksgiving. Christmas. In

---

* Ronald Reagan himself was conflicted about the issue, passing liberal abortion laws as governor of California in 1967, before adopting a firm pro-life stance later in his career.

the US, they've all become political. When something new happens—like Covid—it's only a matter of days before issues are parsed out, sides are taken, and the whole thing turns into yet another political proxy war. The lab leak theory becomes a right-wing thing that the Left hates. Masks become a left-wing thing the Right hates. When a society is in the clutches of hypercharged tribalism, it invades workplaces, dinner tables, churches, schools. It becomes inescapable.

As these forces have pulled more and more Americans down into Political Disney World, the macro effect is the American giant slipping downward on the Ladder, losing its giant tug-of-war more with each passing decade. A liberal society's ecosystem is supposed to yield a balance between genies and golems that keeps the golems in check—but as the US has descended down the Ladder into hypercharged tribalism, the society's high-rung immune system has begun to break down. And political golems have seized the opportunity, tramping across the land, flattening liberal rules and norms beneath their lumbering feet.

HEY

Let's pause for a little check-in. So we're here:

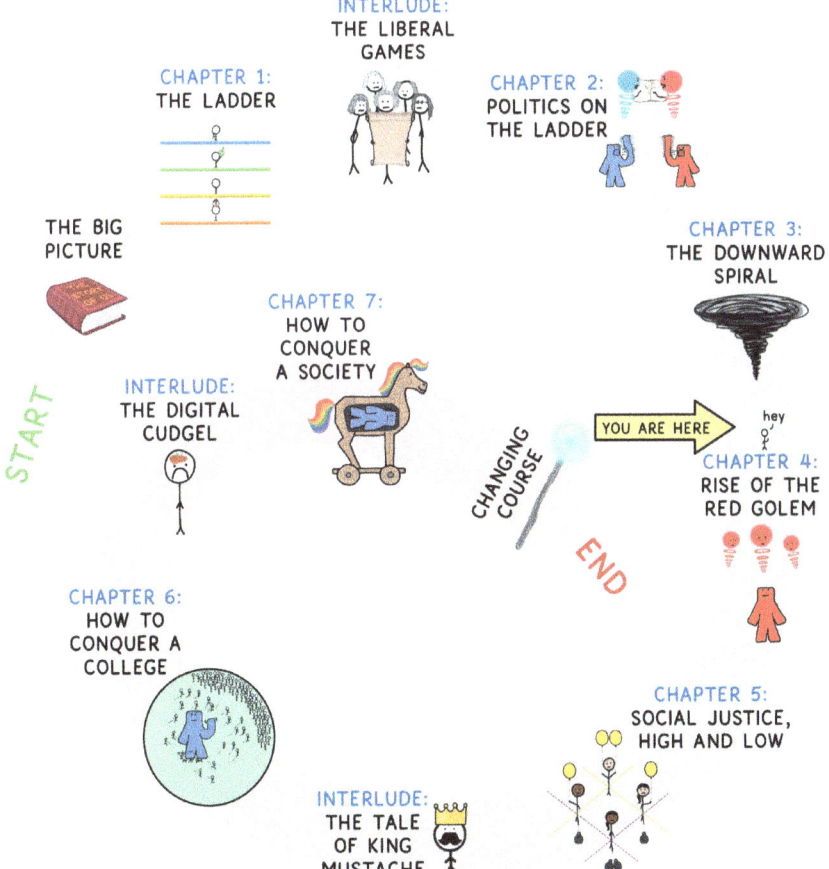

Up to this point, we've kept things pretty broad. Now it's time to get to the parts of the book that will make people do this:

We'll start our pitchfork tour in the next chapter by taking a brief trip through the history of the Republican Party. Then, in the following chapters, we'll take a Tim's-career-tanking deep dive into America's social justice movement. These phenomena have been discussed and written about a lot over the past few years, but it never feels like we're getting the stories quite right. I developed the framework in this book to give us a way to look at familiar stories through a fresh lens—a new language we can use to diagnose and discuss everything that's been going on around us.

These aren't stories about good people or bad people. They're about low-rung thinking, morality, and tactics breaking out like a virus, spreading through America's politics, its institutions, its discourse. To get out of this mess, we need to understand how we got here—so let's zoom in on it together.

Of course, the buttons of hot-button stories are typically hot for one reason: our Primitive Minds are obsessed with them. This is also why they were a challenge to write about—*my* Primitive Mind kept trying to involve itself in the writing.

Here's my plea: Make this an exercise in open-mindedness. Read the rest of this book in Idea Lab mode, asking yourself, *What if I'm wrong about some of what I think?* Hopefully, this process can help open some closed doors in your mind and leave you a little more clearheaded than you were before. Writing this book has certainly done that for me.

How we doing?

Good enough. Let's jump in.

CHAPTER 4
RISE OF THE RED GOLEM

Polarizing people is a good way to win an election, and also a good way to wreck a country.
—MOLLY IVINS

I grew up in Newton, Massachusetts, in the '80s and '90s. To live in Massachusetts, there were only two requirements: you had to be a Red Sox fan and you had to be a Democrat. Luckily, I was both.

When I was six, my first-grade classroom voted on the 1988 presidential election by circling either "Michael Dukakis" or "George Bush" on a little sheet of paper, folding it, and placing it into a shoebox on the teacher's desk. It was the first time I had been sentient for a big political event. Later that day, the teacher revealed the results:

Dukakis 20, Bush 1

As expected. It was a contest between the nice, good-guy candidate and the mean, bad-guy candidate. Of course it was a landslide.

As I grew into an adolescent and then a teen, a lot of my simple childhood beliefs grew fuzzier and more complex—but politics stayed pretty simple. There was the Obviously Good Party, who cared about poor people and equality and smiles, and there was the Obviously Bad Party, who someone only voted for if they were stupid or greedy or evil, or all three.

At eighteen, I headed to college, where most students were lying in heaps crying after Bush's victory over Gore in 2000.

At twenty-two, I left for Los Angeles, where Bush's reelection was a universal tragedy around West Hollywood brunch tables and where Obama was a ubiquitous rock star four years later.

More recently, I moved to New York City, where people referred to "these hard times" after Trump's election and there was never any ambiguity about what that meant.

That's a lotta blue. By the 2010s, I had grown up enough to be aware of political Echo Chambers and the groupthink that circulated around them. I had made friends with some smart conservatives, and I had spent a lot of time reading articles by conservative authors. I didn't want to be a groupthink Democrat. I wanted to be a cool, nuanced Independent, who understood that both sides of the political aisle had pros and cons.

But the Republicans continually made this impossible.

I had watched Bush, Cheney, and Co. start a ridiculous war in Iraq for what seemed like dishonest political motives. I had watched John McCain select the proudly anti-intellectual Sarah Palin as his presidential running mate. I had watched the Tea Party surge to prominence, with a willingness to damage the country's credit rating to maintain an incredibly rigid tax policy. I had watched the entire 2016 Republican presidential field share a near-unanimous conviction that climate change was not something to be concerned about. Out of that group, I watched Donald Trump win the nomination on a platform built on some of the lowest forms of demagoguery.

I was no longer as rosy-eyed about the Democrats as I had been as a child, but how could I possibly call myself an Independent with a straight face? I wanted *nothing* to do with the Republican Party.

Then I started writing about politics. Writing about a topic forces me to set aside my existing assumptions and dig much deeper than I normally would. Six years of digging later, I've come to see my lifelong views on Republicans as not exactly wrong—but not exactly right either.

My previous view of the Republican Party was constrained in two major ways. First, I had been looking at politics the way I had been taught to see it: along a one-dimensional spectrum that ran from far left to far right. Second, I hadn't learned enough about history—about *how* the Republican Party came to be the way it is. Expanding my scope has helped me see a more complicated, more interesting, and I believe more accurate story of the Republicans. Let's take a look.

REPUBLICANS IN THE SIXTIES

When you're immersed in the politics of your day, your country's political parties can seem static and eternal. But political parties are more like amoebas whose shapes continually adapt to changing times.

In the early 1960s, the Republican amoeba looked something like this:

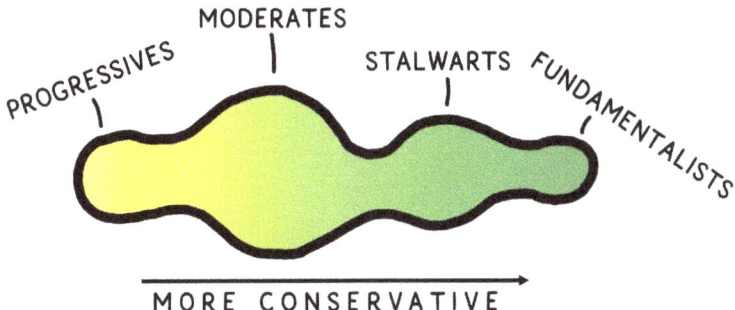

The party's wide horizontal range was reflective of the "distributed tribalism" times, when both major parties were diverse intellectual pluralities.*

During the 1950s, the moderates held the upper hand. The party, and the country, were led by President Dwight Eisenhower, the quintessential moderate—balanced, pragmatic, and nonideological. Many of the era's other prominent Republicans, like Thomas Dewey and Richard Nixon, were also broadly in the moderate camp. Arthur Larson, who was in Eisenhower's cabinet, summed up the moderate's mentality when he wrote in 1956 that "in politics—as in chess—the man who holds the center holds a position of almost unbeatable strength."

But another movement, far from the center of the chess board, was starting to gain steam. We'll call them the Republican Fundamentalists (RFs). Militant economic and social conservatives, they had come together a decade earlier as a response to Eisenhower's moderate presidency and the rise of worldwide communism. They had been the smallest of the party's factions—but by the early 1960s, they were steadily growing in influence.

As the country geared up for the 1964 presidential election, tensions were simmering within the Republican coalition. When you read about US politics of that time, you read about a horizontal tug-of-war, with the moderates trying to keep the party near the political center against the Fundamentalists' attempt to pull the party farther to the right.

---

* "Progressive Republican" might seem like an oxymoron today, but for the first fifty years of the party's existence—from Abraham Lincoln to Theodore Roosevelt—the party had a strong progressive streak. This crew shared Roosevelt's belief that progressivism was not the opposite of conservatism but rather its "highest and wisest form." Progressive conservatives of the 1960s, writes political author A. James Reichley, "remained essentially conservative in that they viewed reform as a means for preserving the underlying soundness of the existing system."

In some ways, the stances of these four groups did fall along a linear spectrum that resembles today's political axis. As you moved from left to right, the factions tended to be increasingly opposed to the New Deal reforms of the 1930s, more socially conservative, more militarily hawkish, more paranoid about the threat of Communism, and more opposed to change.

But there was something else about the Republican Fundamentalists—something beyond simply occupying the far-right section of the Republican amoeba. They did things differently than the other Republicans. These differences are almost always attributed to the group's *far rightness*—but looking through our Ladder lens, we can see that what also separated the RFs from the rest was their *low-rungness*. They were a big red golem.

RFs: LOW-RUNG THINKING

In 1964, the Ripon Society, a progressive Republican think tank, put out a widely circulated "open letter to the new generation of Republicans." In the letter, they described what they saw as the critical distinction between the "moderate" and the "extremist":

> The moderate recognizes that there are a variety of means available to him, but that there are no simple unambiguous ends....The moderate chooses the center—the middle road—not because it is halfway between left and right. He is more than a non-extremist. He takes this course since it offers him the greatest possibility for constructive achievement....Moderation is not a full-blown philosophy proclaiming the answers to all our problems. It is, rather, a point of view, a plea for political sophistication, for a certain skepticism to total solutions....In contrast, the extremist rejects the complexity of the moderate's world. His is a state of mind that insists on dividing reality into two antithetical halves. The gray is resolved into black and white. Men are either good or evil. Policies are either Communist or anti-Communist.

At first glance, this might seem like the horizontal distinction between the center of the political spectrum and its far ends. But the author is really making a vertical distinction, talking about two different *ways* of thinking and doing politics. His description of the "moderate" way—sophisticated, open to compromise, and intent on effective governance—fits perfectly with our definition of high-rung politics, and it could pertain to people anywhere along the horizontal axis. Likewise, the author's "extremist"—someone whose worldview is rigid, simplistic, and morally binary—is a great description of a low-rung political thinker.

The letter's "extremist" was a reference to the Republican Fundamentalists, who were causing a major stir at the time because their figurehead, Arizona senator Barry Goldwater, was making a run for the presidential nomination. As outlined in the Ripon letter, the RFs were sometimes more conservative than the other Republican factions, but they were *always* more rigid, speaking in vague absolutes and offering few concrete solutions. Descendants of the McCarthyites of the 1950s, the RFs also continued the tradition of promoting outlandish conspiracy theories.*

In their dealings with the other Republican factions, the Fundamentalists stood out as the most unbending and uncompromising. The other contingents, less burdened by dogmatic attachment to any one ideology, accepted intellectual plurality within the Republican Party—not because they were nice people but because they wanted to form coalitions that could win elections and solve problems. A plurality of views from across the spectrum allows a party to function as a political genie, maximizing the problem-solving tools on hand. The other factions of the party preferred sophistication over simplicity and truth over unproven conspiracy—because what people trying to solve complex problems *wouldn't*? But the Fundamentalists viewed other Republican factions more like traitors than collaborators, kind of like a golem that's unhappy to be stuck inside a larger genie.

On the principles front, the Fundamentalists were also the one Republican faction that stood firmly opposed to the Civil Rights Movement. They argued that new proposed laws that would forbid segregation and discrimination and protect voting rights would constitute

---

* The RFs cozied up with the radical John Birch Society, which liked to refer to "the Roosevelt-Truman-Eisenhower-Kennedy Administration" as part of a single continuous plot "to change the economic and political structure of the United States so that it can be comfortably merged with Soviet Russia in a one-world socialist government."

federal invasion of both states' rights and the private sector. Consistent with hard-line conservative ideology, right?

Well not really. Keeping the federal government out of the business of states and institutions is a fine conservative policy—until states and institutions are depriving citizens of life, liberty, or the pursuit of happiness. The Fundamentalists, whose rhetoric fiercely promoted individual liberty, would seemingly have been the most outraged about the violation of basic rights of millions of Americans.

Arguing that civil rights protections are beyond the domain of the federal government relied on outdated reasoning that harkened back to the country's earlier days. It's hard not to see this stance as dumping their supposed principles in exchange for a political edge—the kind of hypocrisy typical of low-rung morality.

RFs: LOW-RUNG TACTICS

In 1951, at the height of the Cold War, diplomat and historian George Kennan offered a warning to Americans. He saw communism as a serious external threat, but he was also concerned about how *paranoia* about communism could pose a danger of its own. He wrote:

> The subjective emotional stresses and temptations to which we are exposed in our attempts to deal with this domestic problem…represent a danger within ourselves—a danger that something may occur in our own minds and souls which will make us no longer like the persons by whose efforts this republic was founded and held together, but rather like the representatives of that very power we are trying to combat: intolerant, secretive, suspicious, cruel, and terrified of internal dissention because we have lost our own belief in ourselves and in the power of our ideals. The worst thing that our Communists could do to us, and the thing we have most to fear from their activities, is that we should become like them.

Kennan saw in Red Scare America a country that was failing to live up to its own standards. A country founded on free speech was suddenly cracking down on people for having the wrong ideas. And as this illiberal atmosphere normalized, the criteria for what constituted a "dangerous citizen" kept expanding. It was in this period, for example, that the chair of a Washington State investigative committee argued, "If someone insists that there is discrimination against negros in this country or that there is inequality of wealth, there is every reason to believe that this person is a Communist." New Jersey mayor Frank Hague summed up a common sentiment when he declared: "We hear about constitutional rights, free speech, and the free press. Every time I hear these words, I say to myself, 'That man is a Red. That man is a Communist.' You never hear a real American talk like that."

When it comes down to it, a country is just a bunch of people living within a culture that says "this is how we do things here." There's no law of nature that enforces those norms—only the people that make up the country can do that. That's why Kennan was so disturbed by the Red Scare. Americans had begun to violate the core norms that define the country.

By the mid-1960s, Red-Scare-style tactics had died down. But they hadn't disappeared.

The Republican Fundamentalists were major underdogs in early 1960s America. They had captured a passionate core of supporters, but those constituents were far from the mainstream. Most Americans, and even most Republicans, rejected the RFs as fringe extremists on the wrong side of history.

When you're a political underdog in a country like the US, the Liberal Games offer you two ways forward:

1. Stand firm on your positions and try to use persuasion to start a mind-changing movement that pulls public opinion toward you. If it catches on, your marginalized position can *become* mainstream.
2. Compromise on your positions to move yourself close to mainstream opinion.

But in the realm of low-rung politics, there's also a third option: change the rules of the game to a different one that you can win. If your ideas can't win a fair fight in the boxing ring, start taking cheap shots and see if you can get away with it.

When your rivals are abiding by an established set of unwritten rules, the willingness to disregard those rules can be a massive advantage— one that can equip an underdog with outsized power. This would prove to be the key to the Republican Fundamentalists' success, which happened in three stages:

Conquering the Young Republicans

National political trends often show up first on college campuses. When Americans think about college campuses in the 1960s, left-wing activism comes to mind. The New Left sprung up on campuses throughout the decade, culminating at the end of the decade in a wave of fierce protests and collisions with police. A right-wing movement also had a big presence on those same college campuses. At its core, the Republican Fundamentalists were, like the New Left, a radical, rebellious youth movement.

Under the wing of older political strategists like *National Review* publisher William Rusher and political strategist F. Clifton White, the young RFs gained a reputation for a ruthless, ends-justify-the-means approach—i.e., low-rung tactics.

One of their early targets was the highly influential nationwide organization called the Young Republicans (YR). Author Geoffrey Kabaservice tells the story of how Rusher and White's army of RFs hijacked the 1963 Young Republicans National Convention, where the organization was to elect its next national chairman:

> White and Rusher...directed the action from backstage and unleashed their full panoply of techniques. The Syndicate's forces kept [YR National Chairman Leonard] Nadasdy in the speaker's chair for a solid twenty-two hours, preventing the convention from accomplishing any business by lodging an unending series of roll calls on abstruse parliamentary points....Syndicate bullyboys reduced the proceedings to chaos with constant noise and clamor....A report on the convention by the Delaware YR delegation complained of the "people who came with the openly admitted purpose of disrupting the proceedings, so that the convention could be prolonged to the point where many delegates would be forced to return home."...The Syndicate may actually have lost the chairman's election; the chaos made a true count impossible.

In other words, while the moderates were trying to land legal punches in the ideological boxing ring, the RFs started playing by different rules, kicking out their opponents' legs and landing punches with the gloves off. They turned the contest from a match that favored the moderates to a power struggle over the boxing *rules* that favored the RFs.

Having essentially stolen the Young Republicans chairmanship, the Republican Fundamentalists shaped the YR platform to mirror their own, advocating extreme policies like abolition of the federal income tax and US withdrawal from the United Nations, and expressing support for racial segregation in the South. As the 1964 US elections approached, the RFs would take what they learned while hijacking Republican youth groups and embark on more ambitious conquests.

Conquering California

Using an emboldened army of young uber-conservatives, RFs in California orchestrated a state-wide ambush of the Republican Party's mainstream by raising large sums of money and using it to back far-right challengers for every elective office in the state.

Republican politicians across the state were taken aback by the tactics used by the RFs running against them and their supporters. One candidate for Congress complained that "they follow me around with a goon squad, call me a Socialist and say I must be a Democrat"; another called them a "hate group." An assembly candidate said his opposition accused him of being a Communist and made threatening phone calls to his wife. Another warned that the far-right militants would be the end of the Republican Party, accusing them of being "more interested in their own little game than in the party."

California GOP chairman Caspar Weinberger explained: "It is apparent an effort is being made by a small, narrowly based and heavily financed group to take over the official committees of the California Republican Party....These candidates are recognizable because they espouse only their own candidacies and they also conspicuously refuse to pledge support for the nominees of our party unless those nominees hold the same narrow views put forth by those trying to seize control of these party committees." Weinberger urged California Republicans to "recognize this hazard to our two-party system and defeat these local candidates whose real aim is the destruction of the Republican Party."

The RFs had once again changed the game from one in which they were outmatched to one that played to their strengths. By the time the other factions wrapped their heads around what was going on, it was too late. And the RFs had their sights set on the biggest prize of all.

Conquering the Presidential Primary

Since 1960, Barry Goldwater had been a linchpin of the Republican Fundamentalist movement, and these other efforts were ultimately geared toward the mission to make him the Republican nominee for president in 1964.

Goldwater's campaign epitomized each of the low-rung qualities of the RF movement. His proposals were vaguer and less sophisticated than those of the other candidates, but no candidate spoke with more zealous conviction. His messaging stood out among Republican factions in its rigidity and its negativity.

Goldwater, who campaigned on a message of liberty, and who had previously supported the Arizona chapter of the civil rights organization NAACP, was unabashed about his mission to court Southern segregationist Democrats, proclaiming in a speech: "We're not going to get the Negro vote as a bloc in 1964 and 1968, so we ought to go hunting where the ducks are." The NAACP, which had always remained politically neutral, broke with tradition to openly criticize Goldwater's "election strategy of appealing to the fear and bigotry of the few convention delegates as the means for his convention support." In June of 1964, in the heat of the primary, Goldwater was one of only six Republican senators (out of thirty-three) to vote against the Civil Rights Act.

Much of the Republican Party found Goldwater repellent, but he had built enough momentum to garner 38 percent of the popular vote in the primary, and in a crowded field, he entered the Republican National Convention as the likely nominee.*

Moderates had arrived at the convention with a glimmer of hope that they might be able to wrest the nomination from Goldwater. Their best shot was Pennsylvania governor William Scranton, who made a late entrance into the race in an attempt to thwart Goldwater's candidacy (which he allegedly called "a whole crazy-quilt collection of absurd and dangerous propositions"). Scranton supporters held signs that read "STAY IN THE MAINSTREAM," summing up the moderates' collective plea at the convention.

---

* A major boost to Goldwater came when moderate Nelson Rockefeller, an earlier front-runner, became mired in scandal after rumors of an affair and then, a 1963 marriage to a divorced woman. A month before his remarriage, he led Goldwater in the polls by 17 percentage points.

But moderates wouldn't even get the chance to make their case. Under the guidance of White and Rusher, the same Machiavellian strategists who had hijacked the Young Republicans Convention and orchestrated the hostile takeover of local California politics, the party platform committee turned the convention into a circus, much like the Young Republicans convention a year earlier. Moderates who tried to speak couldn't be heard through the blaring jeers of Goldwater supporters. Hugh Scott, a Pennsylvania senator and Scranton's floor manager, complained, "I could hardly believe the degree of inflexibility I had encountered." Eisenhower, who was in attendance, said the scene was "unpardonable—and a complete negation of the spirit of democracy. I was bitterly ashamed."

Goldwater hadn't explicitly supported white supremacist groups like the Ku Klux Klan during his campaign, but he hadn't yet denounced them either. As Martin Luther King Jr. would put it, "While not himself a racist, Mr. Goldwater articulates a philosophy which gives aid and comfort to racists. His candidacy and philosophy will serve as an umbrella under which extremists of all stripes will stand." Black attendants were the subject of racial slurs and physical harassment. Baseball legend and steadfast Republican Jackie Robinson described the Goldwater crew as "a new breed of Republican...which is seeking to sell to Americans a doctrine which is as old as mankind—the doctrine of racial division, the doctrine of racial prejudice, the doctrine of white supremacy." About his experience at the convention, Robinson put it plainly: "I would say that I now believe I know how it felt to be a Jew in Hitler's Germany."

As expected, Goldwater ended up securing the nomination. The whole ordeal was capped off by Goldwater's acceptance speech. After re-emphasizing the "with us or against us" tone of his campaign—*"Those who do not care for our cause, we don't expect to enter our ranks"*—he made, to a deafening applause, his famous two-part proclamation:

> I would remind you that extremism in the defense of liberty is no vice. And let me remind you also that moderation in the pursuit of justice is no virtue.

In a few words, Goldwater captured everything that had separated his campaign, and the Republican Fundamentalist movement that powered it, from the rest of the Republican Party. The line's focus on liberty and justice was lofty but vague, and open to a thousand interpretations.

Its proud justification of extremism during a campaign that was widely criticized for supporting extremist groups was a transparent dog whistle to racists. It offered justification for the movement's coercive, ends-justify-the-means tactics, while roundly dismissing the benefits of moderation and with it, the rest of the Republican Party.

THE BIG PICTURE WITH THE RFs

Looking at politics horizontally often misses the real story. Calling the Republican Fundamentalists the "far right" suggests that they were defined by their conservatism. But a bunch of their stances—their openness to nuclear war, their support for racial apartheid, their antidemocratic tactics at the convention—were a direct affront to conservatism. The RFs weren't the far right—they were the Lower Right.

It's not that the rest of the Republican factions were perfect high-rung genies. All political groups struggle with the vertical tug-of-war. But the other groups existed within a political culture that prevented them from drifting *too* far downward—a culture the RFs rejected.

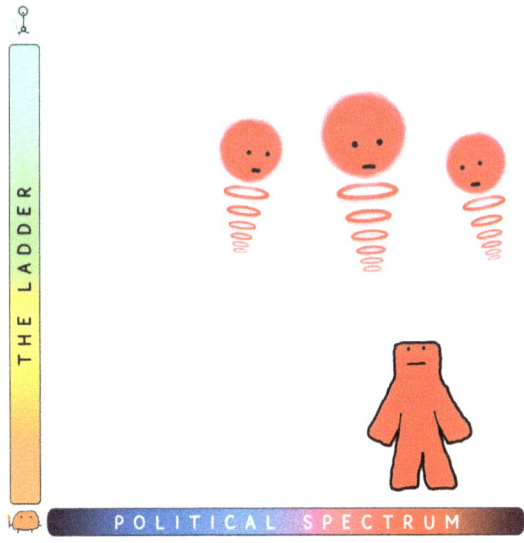

Every liberal democracy is home to political golems who would love to conquer the country—and normally, the high-rung immune system prevents those giants from doing too much harm. But that immune system is built on long-standing norms and a shared understanding of reality. Periods of upheaval shake up those structures, weakening the immune system and creating a soft spot that low-rung giants can exploit.

The chaos, division, fear, and uncertainty of the 1960s had Americans' Primitive Minds all riled up and its Higher Minds discombobulated. This combination pulled the country's center of gravity downward a bit on the Ladder. The Lower Right jumped on the opportunity and ambushed the Upper Right, knocking it on its ass.

But Goldwater's nomination was as far as the RFs would go. To win a general election, a movement needs far broader support, and Goldwater was trounced by Lyndon Johnson in the general election.

This was a story about the vulnerability of a liberal democracy, but it was also a story that illustrated America's *strength*. It's inevitable that from time to time, a golem makes a run at taking over the country and gets a bit farther than it should. The important thing is that when that happens, the country's high-rung immune system eventually kicks back in and thwarts the advance. In 1964, the red golem made a run for power, but the distributed tribalism of the time provided a robust immune system that ultimately denied the attempt.

By the end of the decade, Goldwater's candidacy was in the rearview mirror, but it had left a long-lasting imprint on the Republican Party. In 1970, Josiah Lee Auspitz, head of the Ripon Society, wrote about what he believed was "the struggle for the soul of the party." To Auspitz, the crux of this struggle was whether the Republican Party would move away from Goldwater's Southern strategy or double down on it.* But Auspitz was really getting at something bigger: the tug-of-war between those who aimed to stay true to long-standing party principles and those for whom the ends justified the means. Half a century later, it's clear that the struggle for the soul of the party was just beginning.

---

* Specifically, Auspitz described the struggle like this: "The conservative party favors an electoral strategy that courts the Wallace vote; the progressive, one that woos young, black and middle-class voters." Wallace was Alabama Democratic governor George Wallace—aka the bad guy in the movies about the Civil Rights Movement my teachers played for us in seventh grade—who famously proclaimed in his inaugural address, "segregation now, segregation tomorra', segregation forever."

REPUBLICANS IN THE EIGHTIES

Ronald Reagan began his political career in 1966 as governor of California, running on a platform very similar to Goldwater's. Reagan had even campaigned for Goldwater, making a hugely influential speech ("a time for choosing") in the run-up to the election.

But Reagan's eventual run for president in 1980 was dramatically more successful than Goldwater's in 1964, for a few reasons:

First, sixteen years of political realignment left Reagan with a far more conservative party than the one Goldwater was a part of.

Second, Goldwater was an okay politician, and Reagan was one of the most talented politicians in American history. His grace, self-deprecating humor, and grandfatherly warmth made him easy to like. Reagan was also a masterful storyteller. While Goldwater's platform had seemed like a collection of extremist positions, Reagan turned the conservative platform into a beautiful story about freedom and American idealism that tapped deeply into voters' emotions.

Finally, while Goldwater had spoken in the divisive language of Political Disney World, Reagan usually spoke to Americans' Higher Minds. His speeches were inclusive and emphasized common humanity, with lofty proclamations that all Americans were "bound together in that community of shared values of family, work, neighborhood, peace, and freedom" and convictions that "I know in my heart that man is good, that what is right will always eventually triumph, and there's purpose and worth to each and every life."

Put all that together, and the story Reagan told goes something like this: *America is a shining city on a hill, given to us by God, that represents the absolute best of humanity. It is a place where people are free, where they can live their lives with dignity, and where they can pursue their dreams. But we mustn't take these gifts for granted, as there are two forces always trying to take them away: a powerful centralized government and powerful foreign governments who do not share our values. Our federal government is meant to protect citizens, not control their lives, and no government will ever be better at making decisions and driving prosperity than are free citizens. Abroad, we will foster peace through strength and help the world become a freer place. I believe we will succeed, and America will remain a beacon of hope for all the world's people.*

This story appealed to a wide range of voters, from the staunchest conservatives to the center-right moderates, and easily won Reagan two presidential elections.

Of course, while Reagan is an icon to many, there's also no shortage of people who detest his policies. These people say his supply-side economics made the rich richer, enhanced income inequality, and expanded the deficit. They see his American idealism as chauvinistic and his belief in rugged individualism as callous toward those most in need. They call him a warmonger who used the Cold War to justify the overuse of force in Central America and elsewhere. They point to him being on the wrong side of history with his stances against gay rights and his stoking of racial resentment.

Most of these criticisms, though, are *horizontal* disagreements. Reagan was very, very conservative and highly ideological. Of *course* progressives detest his policies. A lot had changed between 1964 and the Reagan Era, as the parties became more ideological and political tribalism homed in on the national divide. Reagan was a reflection of that change. His success was a testament to how united in its conservatism the Republican Party had become.

But Reagan was also a reflection of something that had mostly held strong: America's high-rung immune system. Reagan was for the most part a high-rung president, both in his oratory and in his governance. His common-humanity rhetoric was clearly an asset in a country that, despite a heated political divide, still felt a sense of unity and shared patriotism. In office, Reagan typically governed the high-rung way: steadfast about principles but flexible about policies. He compromised with progressives on many occasions and in doing so, was able to enact a huge amount of change. His ability to govern pragmatically is evidence that high-rung politics was still possible in Washington.

The Reagan Era illustrates how concentrated political tribalism, though tense, is not necessarily destructive. If you look back at American history, there's an ebb and flow between distributed and concentrated tribalism. In the context of the country's past, the evolution that had happened between the post-WWII era and the Reagan years seems like a normal part of a healthy country's political cycle. Periods of polarization may even be necessary at times to break society out of a stubborn status quo.

What's dangerous about concentrated tribalism is what it leaves us *vulnerable to*. When a single divide becomes central in a society,

Primitive Minds take notice, awakening dormant tribal instincts. The social pressure of invigorated Echo Chambers begins to stifle discourse and dull group intelligence. Opposite sides of the divide rile each other up with dehumanizing, common-enemy rhetoric, which can generate a vicious cycle of resentment and revenge. If concentrated tribalism goes the wrong way, things can quickly spiral downward.

Reagan was a transcendent figure who essentially became the founder of the modern Republican Party. A party whose identity had been hazy since the 1930s suddenly knew exactly what it was: the Party of Reagan.

But a vertical struggle was about to heat up.

Reagan was more than a presidency—he was a *movement*. Movements can light up both our higher and lower instincts, and even movements that start out on the highest rungs tend to develop a dark shadow—a low-rung counterpart riding along in parallel, like two trains riding side by side. When the movement is in the early stages and on the way up, the distinction between the trains can be masked by the exhilaration of change. The question is what happens when that phase dies down and the two trains start to diverge on where they want the movement to go. It's only a matter of time before most movements hit that fork in the road.

Republicans up and down the Ladder held Reagan as their hero, but the Upper Right and Lower Right trains wanted to take the party in very different directions.

What no one in the '80s could have foreseen was the way technology was about to totally transform the country. It turns out that the elevation of Reagan to iconic status in Republican circles coincided with the beginning of a slide downward into the era of hypercharged tribalism.

And for the big red golem, opportunity knocked.

REPUBLICANS AFTER REAGAN

Newt Gingrich was never a hard-line conservative. In the 1960s, he had been a supporter of progressive Republican Nelson Rockefeller, and he has called himself a "Theodore Roosevelt Republican." He was a supporter of affirmative action who would go on to criticize the party for not being more proactive on civil rights issues.

But Gingrich was a wizard at the dark art of low-rung politics.

During his 1978 campaign for Congress, he spoke to a group of College Republicans and told them that "one of the great problems we have in the Republican Party is that we don't encourage you to be nasty." He told them: "Every one of you is old enough to have been a rifleman in Vietnam....This is the same business, we're just lucky, in this country, we don't use bullets, we use ballots instead. You're fighting a war. It is a war for power."

This mindset may have turned off Republicans of the Eisenhower Era, but by 1978, when Gingrich won his first election, the Democrats were starting their twenty-fifth straight year as the majority in the House of Representatives.

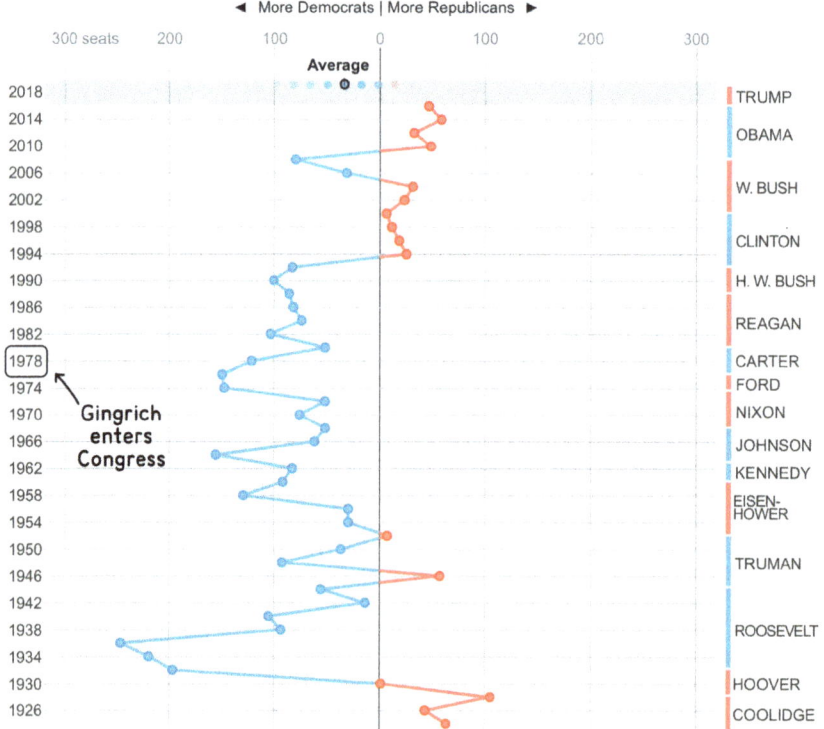

Original source: FiveThirtyEight

During this long tenure, the Democrats were known to bully the Republicans with policies that abused their power, like excluding them from committees or denying them staff. Gingrich and other Republicans were frustrated and worried that, because Democrats had more money and more power, as well as help from left-leaning media, there was no end in sight to their stranglehold on Congress. When a group feels unfairly treated and hopeless about the future, a politician like Gingrich becomes more appealing.

Gingrich entered Congress determined to reverse the fortunes of the Republicans, and he got innovative. He wanted to reframe congressional elections to be less about the actual people running for Congress and more about a national tribal war between the Left and the Right. As Gingrich gained more seniority over the following sixteen years, he emphasized a culture among Republican politicians of distrust and disgust for Democratic leadership and helped make it taboo to say anything to legitimize them. (In 1990, he sent a memo to Republican candidates recommending specific adjectives for them to use in their description of the Democrats: "betray," "decay," "anti-flag," "anti-family," "pathetic," "lie," "cheat," "radical," "sick," and "traitors," among others.) He concocted a strategy of publicly trashing Congress as corrupt and ineffective, even though he was a part of it, knowing that anger with Congress would hurt the majority party most—and then helped to make his depiction of a broken Congress a self-fulfilling prophecy by putting pressure on Republican representatives to vote against anything Bill Clinton proposed after he took office.

These strategies began to pay off, and by the early '90s, the Republicans had momentum. In the run-up to the 1994 midterm elections, Gingrich encouraged Republican congressional candidates to run not on local issues, as was the tradition, but to frame the election in national terms, as a referendum on the recently elected Bill Clinton. Gingrich was joined in this effort by the radio host Rush Limbaugh, who in the late '80s had quickly become a conservative megastar. This was enough to push the Republicans to victory in 1994, winning a majority in both houses for the first time since the '50s.

During the same era, another master strategist was at work. Conservative strategist Grover Norquist, in his role as head of the political advocacy group Americans for Tax Reform, wrote a pledge that obligated signatories to "oppose any and all efforts to increase the marginal income tax rates for individuals and/or businesses."

The idea was that any Republican politician who didn't sign the pledge, or any who did and then broke it, would have their career destroyed. In 2005, Norquist explained to journalist John Cassidy the mafia-esque way he hoped to blacklist three such dissidents:

> The next Republican Presidential candidate will be a Republican governor who did not raise taxes. People who raise taxes—their aspirations for higher office have been destroyed. Mitch Daniels will never be anybody's Vice President. Bob Riley will never be President. Bill Owens, who I considered a Presidential contender, he will never be President. He slit his own throat.

Straight out of the Genghis Khan school of using fear to enforce conformity.

These coercive low-rung tactics resembled those used by F. Clifton White and William Rusher, the strategists who orchestrated Goldwater's siege in the 1960s. By the '90s, though, these kinds of tactics were endorsed by the whole Republican Party, not just a fringe faction.

While these forces were permeating the party's culture in Washington, narrowcast media was taking the country by storm, as Fox News and conservative talk radio became political megachurches with charismatic preachers like Limbaugh, Sean Hannity, and Bill O'Reilly. These figures repeatedly told their million-voter congregations that they were in the midst of a culture war with the other half of their country. The sermons were peppered with conspiracy theories.

At the 1992 Republican National Convention, on one of the biggest political stages in US politics, Republican strategist Pat Buchanan made a speech hammering in the same messaging. After lavishing praise on Ronald Reagan, Buchanan pronounced:

> There is a religious war going on in this country. It is a cultural war, as critical to the kind of nation we shall be as was the Cold War itself, for this war is for the soul of America. And in that struggle for the soul of America, Clinton & Clinton are on the other side, and George Bush is on our side....We must take back our cities, and take back our culture, and take back our country.

The big idea was clear: people like us—the kind of people who like Ronald Reagan—are on one side of a war for the soul of America, and we need to vanquish our enemies on the other side.

But the thing is, Reagan hadn't used this tone at all. He had asked, "How can we love our country and not love our countrymen?" and far from trying to stoke a culture war, he'd say things like, "There are no words to express the extraordinary strength and character of this breed of people we call American."

Reagan believed opposing politicians should work together and come to compromises, and he encouraged a culture of individual thinking and open disagreement. He demonstrated this in his governance (e.g., he raised taxes and levies multiple times while in office) and said it plainly in speeches. He'd preface calls for Republican unity with qualifiers like this: "The Republican Party, both in this state and nationally, is a broad party. There is room in our tent for many views; indeed, the divergence of views is one of our strengths….Unity does not require unanimity of thought."

The Republican Party of the 1990s was doing the opposite, treating Reagan's platform like the party's Ten Commandments and enforcing fealty to it with loyalty oaths.

If you're looking at politics horizontally, the '90s Republicans might seem *kind of* like Reagan, just more hard-nosed. But looking at the vertical story, the '90s Republicans were becoming the *opposite* of Reagan.

This theme continued into the twenty-first century. The George W. Bush administration regularly used Us vs. Them rhetoric when building support for the War in Iraq. Their message—"either you're with us, or you're with the terrorists"—sounds more like Joe McCarthy than Reagan. And given that Reagan's number one bogeyman was government overreach, it's hard to see him approving of the many big government and sometimes even authoritarian policies of the Bush administration (the government surveillance program called the Patriot Act comes to mind—likely named as such to imply that anyone who opposed it was, again, unpatriotic).

By the time Barack Obama came to office, these trends had only intensified. The Tea Party movement burst into prominence, and with the help of right-wing media (by 2010, Fox News profits had crossed $700 million—more than the combined profits of MSNBC and CNN), Republicans in 2010 elected a wave of the most conservative representatives in almost two hundred years.

Buchanan's culture war rhetoric in 1992—which was seen as extreme enough back then to receive a strong backlash from most of America—was now par for the course. Geoffrey Kabaservice writes, "Republican leadership sponsored and spoke at Tea Party rallies at which demonstrators equated Democrats to Nazis and charged that Obama was a foreign-born dictator ravaging the Constitution." This didn't just apply to smaller races. Gingrich himself ran for president in 2011 and for a while was the front runner. Journalist Hendrik Hertzberg picked out some highlights from his campaign speeches:

> President Obama's actions cannot be understood except as an expression of "Kenyan, anti-colonial behavior." Liberals constitute a "secular-socialist machine" that is "as great a threat to America as Nazi Germany or the Soviet Union." There is "a gay and secular fascism in this country that wants to impose its will on the rest of us" and "is prepared to use violence."…In San Antonio, Gingrich declared, "I am convinced that, if we do not decisively win the struggle over the nature of America," his grandchildren will live "in a secular atheist country, potentially one dominated by radical Islamists and with no understanding of what it once meant to be an American."

In 1963, the Ripon Society had called the Goldwater faction "a coalition of all who are opposed to something…singularly devoid of positive programs for political action."

With the Republicans of the Obama Era, the "coalition of all who are opposed to something" was back. Republican leaders like Mitch McConnell declared that "the single most important thing we want to achieve is for President Obama to be a one-term president." Their chief strategy to accomplish this, beyond a blanket party ban on optimism, unifying rhetoric, or cooperation, was to be a force of pure obstruction, vilifying and rejecting anything that Obama proposed. Republicans even voted against bills they *themselves* had created, once Obama came out in support of them. The Republican Senate blocked or delayed routine cabinet nominations and judicial appointments throughout Obama's time in office, capping this off by refusing to even hold a hearing for Obama's 2016 Supreme Court nomination, Merrick Garland.*

And of course, there was the whole debacle in 2011 over the debt ceiling.

---

* The justification given by the Senate was that it's not right for presidents to fill Supreme Court seats in the last year of their term—rather, the government should "let the people decide" what they want when they elect their next president. This principle lasted exactly four years, when Ruth Bader Ginsburg passed away with only months to go in Donald Trump's term, and the Republican Senate, still in the majority, broke their own rule and filled the seat.

The 2011 Debt Ceiling Fiasco

Every year, after a bunch of squabbling, the two parties attempt to agree on a budget for the next fiscal year. If the budget involves spending more money than the US will make in revenue during that period, the result is a deficit—something that has become commonplace for the US.

Let's say in a given cycle, the deficit is X dollars. That means that the agreed-upon budget will entail the US borrowing X at some point during the cycle in order to fully fund the obligations dictated by the budget. This will raise the cumulative national debt, and the way the rules work, increases to the debt must be approved by Congress. So Congress approves the "debt ceiling increase," the Treasury borrows X, and all payment obligations are made.

This means Congress essentially has to approve the X loan *twice*—the first time when they agree upon a budget, and a second time when the actual borrowing happens. The first time, during budget negotiations, is the actual approval—the second is mostly a redundant formality.

Congressman Dick Gephardt thought it was pointless too, so in 1979 he created a new rule called the Gephardt Rule, which was simple: when a new budget is passed, if it includes new borrowing, the debt ceiling *automatically* goes up to match what will be needed. Basically, it got rid of the redundant second approval.

But in 1995, Republican-majority Congresses began waiving the Gephardt Rule during the passage of certain budgets, again forcing the Treasury to pointlessly ask Congress if it can borrow the money it needs to carry out Congress's agreed-upon budget.

So why would anyone ever waive the Gephardt Rule, if doing so makes things less efficient?

Well for one, marketing.

The Republicans wanted to pass budgets as usual and plan to pay for them, but they also wanted to put on a little show for the country during the second step to make it clear how much they hated borrowing.

This seems nonsensical, but the Republicans knew that most Americans didn't fully understand the fine print of government rules and would assume the Republicans were objecting not to meeting existing obligations but to the spending *itself*. Democrats, not to miss out on the fun, did the same thing the next decade when the Bush administration needed to raise the debt ceiling.

Typically, though, the grandstanding would end, and the debt ceiling would be raised in time to get the country's bills safely paid.

When you read about these stupid situations, there seems to be a theme: members of the government know that the party making the fuss about raising the debt ceiling is just grandstanding for political points. The legislators in charge have already gotten private confirmation from the obstructing party that they won't actually let the US miss its payments. In other words, the obstructors put on their show, but they give a little wink to the other party.

By 2011, Congress had raised the debt ceiling sixty-seven times since 1960, which is why none of this should be interesting. But that year, in 2011, when it was time for the Treasury to go off and pay the bills, this happened:

This wasn't the usual showboating about the debt ceiling increase—there was no wink. The Republicans made it clear they would *actually* let the US default on their payments, which would lead to a damaged credit rating and be catastrophic for the US economy and long-term US credibility.

The Republican demands, among other things, were that a long-term deficit-reduction bargain had to be reached, and that bargain could include not even one dollar of tax hikes. Rather than try, probably unsuccessfully, to achieve this rigid set of terms during the next budget negotiations, they tried to force preapproval from the Democrats by holding the country hostage. This standoff went on until just two days before the US would begin defaulting on payments, when a small deal was struck that Republicans could proudly tell their base included not a cent of tax increases. Four days later, Standard & Poor's lowered America's credit rating for the first time in history from the top score of AAA to AA+, where it still sits over a decade later.

The Republicans had used a routine administrative procedure as a political cudgel. The next day, Mitch McConnell, the leader of the Senate Republicans, shared his thoughts on the debacle: "It set the template for the future....I expect the next president, whoever that is, is going to be asking us to raise the debt ceiling again in 2013, so we'll be doing it all over." In 2013, they repeated the ordeal.*

THE POWER GAMES IN WASHINGTON

Former Republican staffer Mike Lofgren writes about how Thomas Jefferson believed the Senate should work:

> In his "Manual of Parliamentary Practice," Thomas Jefferson wrote that it is less important that every rule and custom of a legislature be absolutely justifiable in a theoretical sense, than that they should be generally acknowledged and honored by all parties. These include unwritten rules, customs and courtesies that lubricate the legislative machinery and keep governance a relatively civilized procedure.

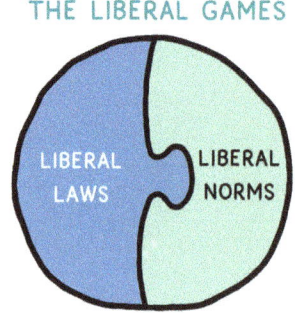

In other words, the way the American system was set up, there would be no way to craft a perfect set of laws for every situation. So a shared adherence to "how we do things here" is critical to make the government functional. For a Liberal Games government to work, it requires two puzzle pieces: certain laws *and* a certain culture.

---

* In early 2023, the debt ceiling once again became front-page news during Representative Kevin McCarthy's bid to become Speaker of the House. To win the necessary votes from the hard-liners in his own party, McCarthy made a series of concessions, including a pledge that there would be no increase to the debt ceiling without major, controversial spending cuts. This tees up what will likely be another debt ceiling fiasco later in 2023.

The opposite of the spirit Jefferson wrote about is what we might call "legal cheating." Legal cheating doesn't break the written law—it finds the soft spots held up only by unwritten rules, and it breaks *those* rules. Technically, the Senate majority has the power to block opposing presidents from appointing justices. Technically, Congress has the power to legally hold the country hostage using the debt ceiling to force a negotiation. It's legal. But in a system whose function relies on unwritten norms, it's also cheating.

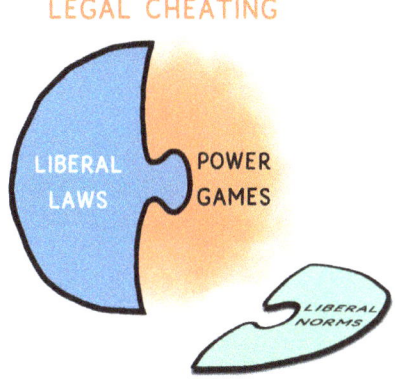

And that's the scary thing about the US system—if parties ramp up the legal cheating and things get too Power-Games-y, at some point it crosses a line where the system stops working. And no law can prevent that from happening—only the high-rung immune system can.

When the immune system is strong, legal cheaters are roundly criticized by members of both parties, and by voters, and the threat is extinguished—kind of like the widespread backlash against the Goldwater campaign in 1964. But in an atmosphere of hypercharged tribalism, people with high-rung instincts can become timid about standing up to norm-breakers in their own party. Once this happens, legal cheating runs rampant. Even if most people in the group disapprove of low-rung tactics, there will always be some willing to grab a cheap advantage, and if the culture has stopped standing up for itself, the cheaters will get away with hitting below the belt and change the entire game.

Once Power Games start, they escalate in a tit-for-tat way, which ends up being worse for everyone. It's like the prisoner's dilemma. If both parties play by Liberal Games rules, it's like both sides getting "one year in prison." Like we saw with the escalating Republican Fundamentalist heists of 1964, this presents an opportunity for one party or faction to carry out a surprise attack with low-rung tactics. Catching their opponents off guard, they can snag a short-term gain (grabbing a "zero-year sentence" and sticking their opponents with ten years). Soon, both parties are playing the Power Games to avoid getting screwed, and everyone ends up with five years in prison.

> **THE PRISONER'S DILEMMA**
>
> There are a number of variations on the prisoner's dilemma, but I'm using the numbers from this one: Two criminal partners are arrested and thrown into separate jail cells to await their fate. The police give both prisoners a chance to betray the other and testify to their partner's guilt, and both prisoners are told the following rules (without any way to communicate with each other):
>
> - If both prisoners stay loyal and refuse to betray their partner, both will be sentenced to **one year** in prison
> - If one betrays and the other stays loyal, the betrayed prisoner gets **ten years** in jail and the betrayer gets **zero years**
> - If both betray each other, both are sentenced to **five years**
>
> The dilemma is that if you're one of the prisoners, no matter what the other one does, it's selfishly better for you if you betray and worse to stay loyal (if your partner betrays you, you also betraying will knock your ten-year sentence down to five; if your partner stays loyal, betraying your partner will knock your one-year sentence down to zero). But if both prisoners make this rational selfish decision, both end up worse off (five-year sentences) than if they had both acted irrationally and stayed loyal (one-year sentences).

Modern US politics has seen a steady increase in both parties swapping out Liberal Games norms for Power Games ruthlessness, breaking long-established customs for a short-term edge and leaving both parties as prisoner's dilemma losers. I discussed one example of this—debt ceiling shenanigans—but I could have just as easily talked about the soaring use of the filibuster, strategic redistricting (aka gerrymandering), voter suppression, or rules around campaign finance. In each case, legal cheating has run rampant and made the government less functional.

Nearly all the Liberal Games norms broken by Republican politicians have also been broken by Democrats. But the Republicans seem to have tumbled farther and faster.

One telling situation is the party factions. In Congress, one of the largest Democratic factions is a caucus called the New Democrats—as of December 2022, 99 of 218 (45 percent) House Democrats were members. Their core values statement is one of moderation. They say they're "committed to pro-economic growth, pro-innovation, and fiscally responsible policies," that they're "a solutions-oriented coalition seeking to bridge the gap between left and right by challenging outmoded partisan approaches to governing," and that the challenges ahead are too great "to refuse to cooperate purely out of partisanship."

The largest faction of the Republican Congress, by far, is the Republican Study Committee (RSC), with 143 of 213 House Republicans as members (67 percent) in 2022. The faction's stated mission is "to bring like-minded House members together to promote a strong, principled legislative agenda that will limit government, strengthen our national defense, boost America's economy, preserve traditional values and balance our budget." Nothing about cooperation with Democrats or bridging the gap between left and right. The Democratic Party equivalent—the Congressional Progressive Caucus—had 97 members (44 percent) in 2022.

As another indicator, a large 2013 survey of county-level party leaders found that while Democratic leaders preferred extremist candidates to centrist candidates at a ratio of 2:1, the ratio for Republican leaders was 10:1. This is a big deal in a country where the parties themselves have a huge influence over who gets elected.

As for why the Republican decline has been more pronounced, one reason might be that the Republican base is more homogeneous—ethnically, religiously, ideologically. To win elections, Democrats have needed to appeal to a more varied demographic, so they couldn't afford to be as rigidly ideological, preaching a singular story like the Republicans.

The average Republican voter also favors a more ideologically extreme party than the average Democrat: According to a 2018 Gallup poll, 57 percent of Republicans wanted their party to become more conservative, compared with only 41 percent of Democrats who wanted their party to become more liberal. And only 37 percent of Republicans wanted their party to become more moderate, compared with 54 percent of Democrats.

Then there's the fact that in the recent political environment, Republicans have been more likely to win elections without capturing a majority of the vote. Both parties have done their fair share of gerrymandering, but the Republicans, who control more state legislatures, had until 2022 been more egregious about it. Throughout the 2010s, Republicans needed to win only about 45 percent of total votes for Congress to win the House majority, compared to the Democrats needing to win more than 55 percent of voters to be the majority party. The same phenomenon exists in the Senate, where all states have the same two seats, leaving low-population states (which typically vote Republican) overrepresented.* With their ability to win rural states, Republicans have been able to win the Senate majority while losing the aggregate popular vote for Senate. Likewise in presidential elections where, because of the electoral college system, two of the past three Republican victories have come while losing the popular vote, something that hadn't happened since 1888. All of this has stuck the Democrats with the burden of having to win the center and freed up Republicans to be more ideological.

By the end of Obama's presidency, the Republican Party had sold off so many little pieces of itself that it bore little resemblance to the party of Reagan. Republican tribalism had become the party's most sacred value. What mattered most was Republican victory in a war against the Democratic enemy, even if that victory had to come at the expense of nearly every core value Reagan had preached. As the 2016 election unfolded, this would become all too apparent.

THE PARTY OF TRUMP

The Party of Reagan and the Party of Trump wear the same Republican uniform. But under the uniform, almost nothing is the same.

---

* According to Kean University provost David Birdsell, by 2040, about 70 percent of Americans are expected to live in the fifteen largest states, represented by only thirty senators. The other 30 percent of Americans will be represented by seventy senators.

Reagan's aim to appeal "to your best hopes, not your worst fears; to your confidence rather than your doubts" had, thirty years later, become Trump's demagogic appeal to the lowest parts of human nature.

Reagan's dignified message of common humanity—to love your countrymen the way you loved your country—had become Trump's crusade against the common enemies of Blue America and the media, told with twenty-five thousand tweets.

During Reagan's 1980 campaign, he called America "a refuge for all those people in the world who yearn to breathe free." Trump began his campaign by calling America "a dumping ground for everybody else's problems," following up with his infamous "When Mexico sends its people, they're not sending their best....They're sending people that have lots of problems, and they're bringing those problems [to] us. They're bringing drugs. They're bringing crime. They're rapists. And some, I assume, are good people." When Reagan painted his vision of America as a shining city on a hill, he said, "And if there had to be city walls, the walls had doors and the doors were open to anyone with the will and the heart to get here." Trump would lead his rallies in the chant "Build the wall! Build the wall!"

Reagan's warning to foreign governments who are "the enemies of freedom" became Trump's open admiration of authoritarian leaders like Vladimir Putin, Recep Tayyip Erdoğan, and Kim Jong Un.

Reagan had kept the Birch Society and their conspiracy theories at arm's length, referring to them as a "lunatic fringe" at a 1965 Republican fundraiser. Trump not only embraced brazen conspiracy theorists like Georgia representative Marjorie Taylor Greene during his time as president—he *was* a conspiracy theorist, spearheading, for example, the "Birther" claim in 2010 that Obama was not an American citizen.

Reagan's recipe to make America great—"There are no great limits to growth because there are no limits of human intelligence, imagination, and wonder"—was the American people. Trump's recipe was himself: "Nobody knows the system better than me. Which is why I alone can fix it."*

It's not that Trump's base didn't have valid concerns.

Looking at congressional districts where Trump made gains in 2016 over Romney four years earlier tells a story of economic despair. These districts had experienced recent drops in median income and employment levels. They stand out on metrics that measure rotting

---

* Reagan didn't grab anyone by the pussy. Trump did grab people by the pussy.

infrastructure and the shuttering of business establishments. In 2019, nearly all of the country's wealthiest fifty districts, by household income, were represented by Democrats, which could understandably leave many Republican voters feeling excluded from elite America. It's the same story with education. When you rank districts by the percent of adults with a bachelor's degree, forty of the top forty-two districts vote Democratic, and all of the top seventeen. Throughout this stretch, Republicans have been the primary punching bag of a condescending coastal elite that lectures them on political correctness and white privilege. They've entirely lost trust in a mainstream media they see, not without justification, as biased against them. And the Republican Party that was supposed to be looking out for them has, many of them argue, become corrupted by special interests and left them in the lurch.

Trump's supporters have plenty of justification to feel grievance and to demand major change. But for the Party of Reagan, Trump seems like a strange choice.

There was a brief moment, in the run-up to the 2016 election, when many prominent Republicans stood firmly opposed to Trump. Ezra Klein writes:

> Ted Cruz called Trump a "pathological liar," "utterly amoral," and "a narcissist at a level I don't think this country's ever seen." Rick Perry said Trump's candidacy was "a cancer on conservatism, and it must be clearly diagnosed, excised, and discarded." Rand Paul said Trump is "a delusional narcissist and an orange-faced windbag. A speck of dirt is way more qualified to be president." Marco Rubio called him "dangerous" and warned that we should not hand "the nuclear codes of the United States to an erratic individual."

But once it was clear the tide was turning, nearly all major Republicans—including Cruz, Perry, Paul, and Rubio—pulled a 180 and backed Trump. The party of the strictest fiscal conservatism during Obama's presidency now supported a president who disregarded long-held conflict-of-interest rules and spent more on his own lifestyle in office than any president in American history. The party of self-proclaimed "constitutionalists" got behind a president who routinely ignored constitutional protocol, who threatened to jail and blackmail his opponents, and who pardoned supporters who engaged in criminal acts.

When people are so fixated on the horizontal political battle that they stop caring about the vertical axis entirely, they forget who they are. They forget what actually matters.

Reagan once spoke about the peaceful transition of power:

> The orderly transfer of authority as called for in the Constitution routinely takes place, as it has for almost two centuries, and few of us stop to think how unique we really are. In the eyes of many in the world, this every four-year ceremony we accept as normal is nothing less than a miracle.

This has been a mainstay position of every modern American president, which makes sense, because it is the defining practice of any healthy democracy.

But in a debate before the 2016 election, Trump declared: "I will totally accept the results of this great and historic presidential election, *if I win*." In a debate before the 2020 election, Trump again made it clear that he would not accept the results if he lost. True to his word, after losing, he spread the unfounded conspiracy theory that he had won the 2020 election in a landslide. Then he tried to overturn it. Trump coerced state officials, calling Georgia's secretary of state during the vote count with a request: "I just want to find 11,780 votes." He pressured governors to replace existing electors with new ones who would promise to cast their votes for Trump. Using a memorandum written by his legal advisor, John C. Eastman, he tried to persuade his vice president, Mike Pence, to delay certification of the election or even to straight up declare him the winner. Mike Pence ultimately said no—had he not, the country would have found itself in an unprecedented national crisis. When these efforts fell short, Trump told a crowd of supporters in Washington: "We're gonna walk down to the Capitol. Because you'll never take back our country with weakness. You have to show strength."

Everyone knows what followed, but I'm not sure everyone realizes just how bad it was. Testimony later given under oath described a violent, organized attack armed with guns, Tasers, and tear gas that quickly overwhelmed police officers. Here's one officer testifying:

> For the first time, I was more afraid working at the Capitol than during my entire Army deployment to Iraq...What we were

subjected to that day was like something from a medieval battlefield. We fought hand-to-hand and inch-by-inch…It was a prolonged and desperate struggle. I vividly heard officers screaming in agony and pain just an arm's length from me.

Another:

At some point during the fighting, I was dragged from the line of officers into the crowd. I heard someone scream, "I got one!" as I was swarmed by a violent mob. They ripped off my badge. They grabbed my radio. They seized the ammunition that was secured to my body. They began to beat me, with their fists and with what felt like hard metal objects….I heard chanting from some in the crowd, "get his gun" and "Kill him with his own gun."…I was electrocuted, again and again and again with a Taser….I had been beaten unconscious and remained so for more than four minutes…. At the hospital, doctors told me that I suffered a heart attack, and I was later diagnosed with a concussion, traumatic brain injury and Post Traumatic Stress Disorder.

All together, the assault on the Capitol left 150 law enforcement officers injured—head wounds, broken bones, damaged spinal cords. One died of a stroke the following day after being sprayed by an irritant during the protest. In the months that followed, four of the officers who were there that day would commit suicide.

In October 2021, Trump wrote about the incident: "The insurrection took place on November 3, Election Day. January 6 was the Protest!"

TRIUMPH OF THE RED GOLEM

Political parties are amoebas that change their shape over the decades, but it happens slowly enough that it can be hard to see in real time. It took decades for the Party of Lincoln to become the Party of Theodore Roosevelt and decades more for it to turn into the Party of Eisenhower. Thirty years of party realignment transformed the Party of Eisenhower into the Party of Reagan. Today, anyone still calling it the Party of Reagan is living in another era.

Political transformations don't happen because everyone in the party changes their mind. They happen because at some point, a movement within the party builds enough support that a tipping point is crossed, like a tug-of-war where the status quo side finally loses its footing. Supporting the new movement, rather than criticizing it, starts to become the winning political strategy. Momentum keeps building until campaigning for the party's old values and against the new movement's values becomes political suicide. Old-school politicians are forced to jump on board with the new values,* switch parties, or retire.

The Ladder helps us see a more complete story here. Many of Trump's policies are closer to the center than the far right. But he's as low-rung a president as we've had—fundamentally antidemocratic in a way none of his predecessors were. This is a vertical struggle.

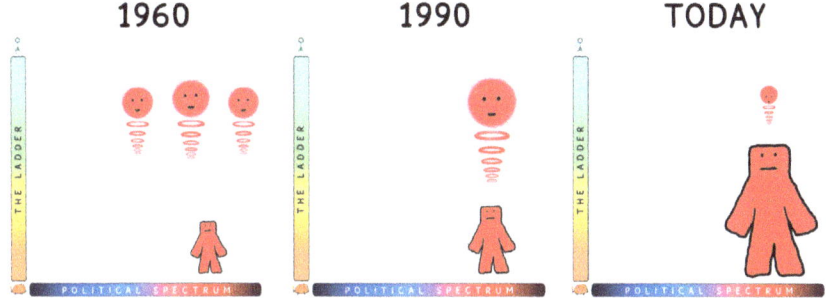

When a vertical tug-of-war goes wrong, the golem gains the upper hand. High-rung politics itself becomes political suicide. Which is exactly what happened in the aftermath of the 2020 election.

As in 2016, Republican leaders in 2020 at first dismissed Trump's claim that the election was wrongfully stolen from him. But the tug-of-war had moved too far downward, and politicians quickly read the signs. In the 2022 midterms, more than half of Republican nominees denied or questioned Biden's 2020 victory. Those who didn't openly campaign on this premise mostly refrained from outwardly refuting it, and the few who did were strongly rebuked, ostracized, or booted

---

* Quintessential example: Republican New York Representative Elise Stefanik, who transformed herself from a moderate, critical of Trump, to a self-proclaimed "ultra-MAGA" Trump supporter. This totally turned her career around and elevated her to the top ranks of the party.

altogether from their positions by the rest of the party. It had become taboo within the Republican Party to stand in support of the most basic democratic concept.

No political party will ever be a shining example of high-rungness. But the modern Republican Party has allowed itself to become *defined* by low-rung thinking, morality, and tactics.

	THINKING	MORALS	TACTICS
HIGH-RUNG	seek truth	moral consistency	fair play, persuasion
LOW-RUNG	seek confirmation	moral hypocrisy	cheating, coercion

The scary thing about the Republican story isn't that there is a red political golem that does golem things like trying to grab power by breaking the rules, by enforcing conformity, by undermining trust in the electoral process. Political golems are an inevitability within any liberal democracy. The scary thing is that it's *succeeding*.

Zooming back out, we're reminded that this is a story about the American ecosystem. The Republicans have contributed to the vortex that has brought us to this point, but their trajectory is also a *reflection* of the larger changes that have been taking place. Republican voters and politicians are caught in the vortex like everyone else.

Trump was elected in a hypercharged America—a place where tribalism beats truth and Power Games beats liberal norms. Trump beat the other candidates because he understood better than anyone how to play this new game on this new playing field. Until that environment changes, America will remain vulnerable to opportunistic demagogues.

Growing up, when I observed the Republicans and thought, "Whatever my problems with the Left, the Right is *definitely* not for me," I wasn't entirely wrong. The Republican Party I grew up with was, for the most part, what I thought it was. But I was missing the real story.

I mistakenly thought that what I objected to was "the Right." But the Right wasn't the problem. The problem was the *Lower* Right. The problem wasn't too much conservatism, it was too *little* conservatism. I hadn't understood that high-rung conservatism is a critical part of a healthy country and that the Republican Party I knew was actually *depriving* my country of it.

I also mistakenly thought that, since the problem was on the right, there could never be reason to worry about the other side of the spectrum.

But the low rungs span the whole political spectrum, and the vortex affects the whole country. I didn't understand at the time that the same ecosystem changes that had disabled the high-rung immune system on the right could do the very same thing much closer to home.

CHAPTER 5

SOCIAL JUSTICE, HIGH AND LOW

Human nature is potentially aggressive and destructive and potentially orderly and constructive.
—MARGARET MEAD

Back in 2012, life was simple for blue America.

But over the past decade, a new movement sprung onto the scene, causing all kinds of rifts.

These rifts began brewing in America in 2014 and 2015 and rapidly ramped up every year thereafter. There have been moments during these years when the topic of "wokeness" seemed to move to the back burner, but it was never long before it returned to the front burner of American political and cultural consciousness. This has proven to be more than a phase—it's one of the defining stories of the modern political era, and one I believe we're in the middle, not the end, of.

I first turned my attention to the topic in early 2016. I was both concerned and fascinated to see so many people I knew who were once politically united, now suddenly so at odds.

Arguments about "Social Justice Warriors" and "identity politics" were followed by arguments about #metoo and the "Intellectual Dark Web." Debates about free speech on campuses paved the way for debates about online censorship. Disagreements about Black Lives Matter and white supremacy and cancel culture evolved into battles over diversity trainings and critical race theory in schools, which then became schisms over transgender athletes and children at drag shows.

The specifics have changed and so have the buzzwords, but underneath it all is a single overarching story. I've studied it closely for almost seven years now, trying to lift up the layers and see what's really going on. What lies at the heart of these rifts? Are they based on fundamental differences or deep misunderstandings? Are people disagreeing about What Should Be or about What Is? Most importantly, is there a way out of this mess, and if so, what does that look like?

I'm convinced this is one of the most important stories of our time and something that can provide major clues to our big question: *What's our problem?*

The story of wokeness[*] is about so much more than wokeness: It's about individual and group psychology, about cowardice and courage, about battling narratives. Above all, it's about how societies work, and how they can stop working.

TWO KINDS OF SOCIAL JUSTICE

LIBERAL SOCIAL JUSTICE

When the Liberal[†] Social Justice (LSJ) activist looks at the United States, they see two stories.

The first is a great story of liberalism: a country founded by Enlightenment Kids, based on Enlightenment values, built to protect the sacred rights of life, liberty, and the pursuit of happiness, premised on the

---

[*] "Wokeness" is the current fashionable buzzword, and it too will probably be replaced by something else soon. It's also a term loaded with culture-war baggage, so I won't be using it very much.

[†] As before, "liberal" here will refer to liberalism regardless of party, not the way it's often used in the US, synonymous with "left-wing."

notion that all men are created equal. Not all Americans would enjoy equal success in the pursuit of happiness, but they'd all have an equal opportunity to shoot for their dreams. This is the story written in pen across American lore.

The second story is the one written in invisible ink. In certain key moments, America's founders seemed to be all about Enlightenment values...until those values conflicted with their personal or political goals.

Painting source: Howard Chandler Christy, Signing of the Constitution

In those cases, they added a little metaphorical edit to their founding documents, in invisible ink.

We hold these truths to be self-evident, that all white *men are created equal, cause I mean, come on*

In his "I Have a Dream" speech, Martin Luther King Jr. talked about this:

> When the architects of our republic wrote the magnificent words of the Constitution and the Declaration of Independence, they

were signing a promissory note to which every American was to fall heir. This note was a promise that all men—yes, black men as well as white men—would be guaranteed the "unalienable rights" of "life, liberty and the pursuit of happiness." It is obvious today that America has defaulted on this promissory note insofar as her citizens of color are concerned. Instead of honoring this sacred obligation, America has given the Negro people a bad check, a check which has come back marked insufficient funds.

If the words written in normal ink are promises, each invisible asterisk represents a broken promise—an add-on written by people with the power to violate the system, at the expense of others and to the detriment of the entire US project.

Liberal Social Justice activists simply want the country to live up its stated promises. They're on a mission to root out old invisible ink, wherever it's still hiding, and to thwart the inevitable attempts at new violations.*

The struggle is never-ending. Fill in the "____-American" blank with nearly *any* nationality, ethnicity, or belief system, and you could write books about their struggle to be included in the promises of "life, liberty, and the pursuit of happiness" and "all men are created equal." That's the bad news about the US.

The good news about the US is that many of these struggles for equality have made remarkable progress. Since its founding, people have immigrated to the US because they were being treated unfairly somewhere else. What made America different was the ability for unequally treated groups to *do* something about it, nonviolently, and actually see results.

This is where Liberal Social Justice activists come in. They know that progress in the face of injustice is possible, but they also know it doesn't happen on its own. As slave-turned-statesman Frederick Douglass put it, "Find out just what any people will quietly submit to and you have found out the exact measure of injustice and wrong which will be imposed upon them."

---

* Invisible asterisks span a wide range of areas—from political corruption to crony capitalism to voter suppression. Liberal Social Justice activism is a subset of broader invisible asterisk hunting. It deals with the ways in which historically marginalized demographic groups are getting a raw deal.

From women's suffrage to civil rights to second-wave feminism to LGBTQ rights, the American twentieth century was jam-packed with trailblazing social justice movements. These movements overturned discriminatory laws, dismantled oppressive institutions and cultural norms, and debunked long-standing pseudoscientific beliefs about the superiority or inferiority of groups.

For the most part, these movements were carried out in the spirit of liberalism. They rode on the premise that the country's wrongdoings happened not *because* of their founding liberal values but because the country fell *short* of them. And they brought about change using the system's own liberal tools: free speech, free assembly, free press, due process, and voting.*

The essence of Liberal Social Justice is the two-part belief that America has made great strides away from its oppressive past and that there is still much work to be done. This kind of self-critical patriotism has been a consistent feature of modern American progressivism, from Martin Luther King's speeches to Barack Obama's presidential campaigns.

To help clarify our terms, let's imagine a modern liberal society as a pyramid.

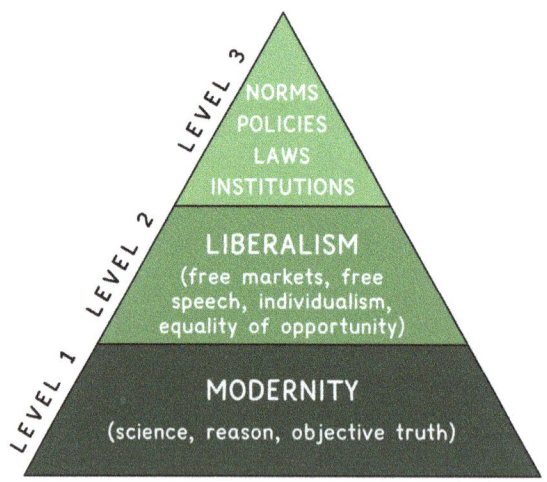

---

* Their use of civil disobedience—like MLK's many arrests—wasn't about challenging the liberal systems of the Constitution, it was about purposefully breaking laws that *conflicted* with the Constitution in order to expose elements of society that weren't working the way they were supposed to.

At the foundation of the pyramid is a basic principle of modernity: the notion that people can learn what is objectively true, using the methods of science and reason. Atop that foundation are core liberal ideals that emerged from the Enlightenment, like free speech, free markets, and equality of opportunity. Finally, on the top level of the pyramid are the laws, norms, and institutions the society builds to safeguard the ideals on the levels below.

Liberal Social Justice activists are often highly progressive when it comes to Level 3, which they believe is full of problems that need fixing, many of which lead to direct violations of Levels 1 and 2. To use a social justice example, a Level 3 problem might be hiring discrimination against non-white applicants. This is a glitch in Level 3 that has the effect of reducing equality of opportunity, a Level 2 staple. So activists would employ working parts of Levels 1 and 2 to try to repair the glitch—say, using research institutions to collect statistics on this phenomenon, and then using free speech, free press, and free assembly to get the word out, build awareness, and change behavior.

But the story of social justice has grown more complicated in recent years. Another player has emerged that has both added firepower to recent Liberal Social Justice movements and undermined their progress.

SOCIAL JUSTICE FUNDAMENTALISM

The woke movement is much more than a cultural phenomenon—it's rooted in a distinct set of ideas and philosophies. To understand what's going on today, we have to take it apart and look at how it was built.

One of the primary roots derives from Marxism. Marxism and liberal progressivism might seem to have a good amount in common. They're both on the political left, both looking at the world through a lens of the little guy's struggles against entrenched power and oppressive systems, and both in conflict with conservatism. But they're fundamentally opposed to each other. The thing the liberal progressive considers the foundation of a good society, liberalism, is the very thing the Marxist wants to dismantle.

Liberal progressives and liberal conservatives are at odds over Level 3 of our pyramid—

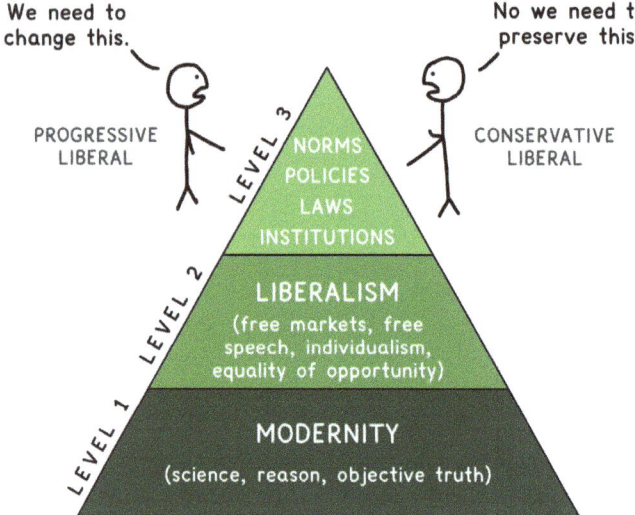

—but they share an overarching goal to preserve Levels 1 and 2. In other words, *both* groups are conservative when it comes to Levels 1 and 2.

Marxists, and their neo-Marxist descendants, don't think this is progressive enough. They believe the founding liberal ideals of countries like the US are fatally flawed and inevitably create a horribly lopsided structure whereby ruling classes use and abuse oppressed classes. They argue that the freedoms of liberal systems don't really make people free—rather, they give the upper classes the freedom and the tools to exploit everybody else. To really fix society, they say, you need to go deeper into the pyramid and overhaul *Level 2*.

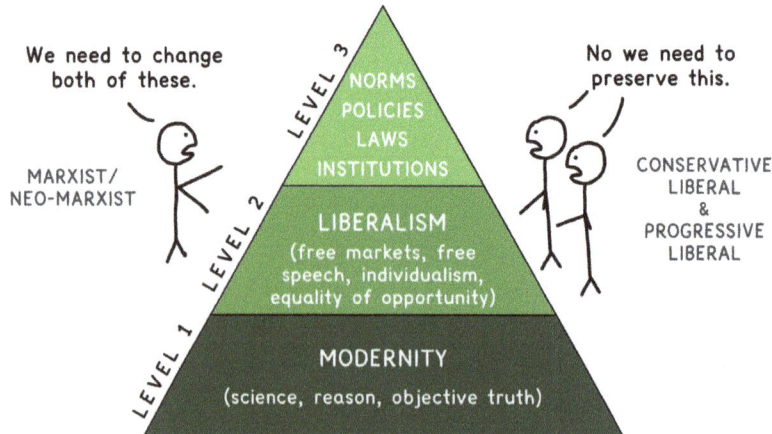

Neo-Marxism Comes to America

The Great Depression was no surprise to Marxists around the Western world. Karl Marx's famous prediction—that the breakdown of capitalism would give way to the new world order of communism—seemed to be happening before their eyes.

There was just one problem. None of the Western countries, with their flailing economies, were turning to communism. Places like the US and the UK were sticking with capitalism, while in other places, like Germany and Italy, economic collapse had given way not to communism but fascism.

In Frankfurt, Germany, a group of discouraged neo-Marxist philosophers, known today as the Frankfurt School, got thinking. In standard Marxist fashion, they saw liberal societies as exploitative and fatally flawed. They subscribed to the classic Marxist notion of *false consciousness*—the idea that revolution is prevented by the oppressed believing that the status quo is simply the natural order of things. This was, they believed, what led so many people to support capitalism or fascism even though it was against their interests to do so.

But they also believed traditional Marxism needed an update. So they came up with a kind of Marxism 2.0: Critical Theory. Critical Theory updated the Marxist model by broadening the focus beyond economic class oppression to subtler deceptive systems, like pop culture, education, and institutional structures. They wanted to understand how these systems might entrench uneven power dynamics and leave the oppressed classes so blind to their own oppression that they even embraced it.

Then came the Nazis.* The Frankfurt School thinkers, many of whom were Jewish, left Germany. A number of them ended up in New York City where, by the 1960s, their influence had helped ignite the radical young New Left. The New Left was politically militant, skeptical of capitalism, and even willing to suppress their opponents' free speech rights to achieve their objectives. As influential Frankfurt transplant Herbert Marcuse (often called the father of the New Left) wrote in 1965, "It should be evident by now that the exercise of civil rights by those who don't have them presupposes the withdrawal of civil rights from those who prevent their exercise."

---

* To put it lightly

In the early 1980s, neo-Marxist political theorists Ernesto Laclau and Chantal Mouffe wrote about the "crisis of Marxism" that had developed as experiments in communism sputtered around the world. In an influential article and subsequent book, they discussed recent efforts to center the Marxist framework around "a new privileged revolutionary subject which might come to replace the working class." They wrote that, among others, "women, national, racial and sexual minorities" were considered "popular candidates for the carrying out of this new role."

In other words, there was a burgeoning movement to replace class politics with *identity politics* as the organizing vehicle of modern Marxism.

Around the same time, new academic fields of study centering around identity—African American Studies, Gender Studies, Queer Studies—emerged and began to spread. These areas of scholarship generally centered around an Americanized version of Critical Theory, and many of the fields acknowledge this social justice/Critical Theory fusion with names like critical race theory, critical gender studies, etc. Many have called this fusion Critical Social Justice.

Adherents of the new fields of Critical Social Justice asked the radical, revolutionary questions characteristic of Marxism. They were skeptical of liberalism, suspicious of false consciousness, and focused on how oppression might manifest in unexpected places. The authors of *Critical Race Theory: An Introduction* lay it out like this: "Unlike traditional civil rights discourse, which stresses incrementalism and step-by-step progress, critical race theory questions the very foundations of the liberal order." Marx, never satisfied to merely analyze the world, famously wrote, "The philosophers have only interpreted the world, in various ways. The point, however, is to change it." The disparate fields of Critical Social Justice took on this thinking, geared not only toward education but also activism.

They also reflected a Marxist cynicism that represented a departure from the patriotic tone of previous eras of social justice rhetoric. While liberals see instances of oppression as shameful flaws in an otherwise noble project, Critical Theorists see instances of oppression as evidence of the country's *true* nature and founding purpose. Derrick Bell, a former Harvard legal scholar and a key figure in the formation of critical race theory, developed what he called the "interest conversion principle." Bell believed that progress for Black Americans happened only when the progress served white interests, and that the progress would be taken away as soon as it no longer fit with the self-interested white agenda.

Critical Social Justice was a US-specific version of the Marxist mindset that resonated with many Americans. But to truly become a Marxist framework, the disparate fields of Critical Social Justice would need *unity*. While the protagonists of the old story—the working class—were united by their economic positions, social justice movements are separate struggles, each with a unique character and unique goals. Addressing this problem, Laclau and Mouffe wrote that "unity must be constructed" by way of "a far-reaching transformation in the way that the forces of the left are organized and function."

In the late 1980s, Critical Social Justice scholars began to develop a framework that would achieve this "far-reaching transformation" and bind the various social justice struggles together.

Privilege

In 1989, Peggy McIntosh, the associate director of the Women's Studies department at Wellesley College, published an essay called *White Privilege: Unpacking the Invisible Knapsack*. She begins like this:

> I have often noticed men's unwillingness to grant that they are overprivileged, even though they may grant that women are disadvantaged. They may say they will work to women's status, in the society, the university, or the curriculum, but they can't or won't support the idea of lessening men's.

McIntosh then goes on to say that she believes that she and other white people are in a similar position to men with regard to race—that "there was most likely a phenomenon of white privilege that was similarly denied and protected." She described this white privilege as "an invisible weightless knapsack of special provisions, maps, passports, codebooks, visas, clothes, tools and blank checks."

McIntosh then offers forty-six examples of the kinds of special tools in the invisible knapsack of the white person. Here are a few:

> I can if I wish arrange to be in the company of people of my race most of the time.

> If I should need to move, I can be pretty sure of renting or purchasing housing in an area which I can afford and in which I would want to live.
>
> I can turn on the television or open to the front page of the paper and see people of my race widely represented.
>
> I can go into a music shop and count on finding the music of my race represented, into a supermarket and find the staple foods which fit with my cultural traditions, into a hairdresser's shop and find someone who can cut my hair.
>
> If a traffic cop pulls me over or if the IRS audits my tax return, I can be sure I haven't been singled out because of my race.

Reading through the list, it seems that McIntosh is sometimes talking about wealth or class privilege and other times talking about *majority* privilege, as many of the items on her list would, for example, imply similar "Asian privilege" in Asian countries. Others, though, point to specific instances of race-related unfairness—like her reference to housing restrictions or traffic stops.

The notion of privilege draws on the idea of false consciousness—that people born into a country of systemic imbalance may have their "scale calibrated" such that the status quo *feels* normal and fair, even when it's not. As such, those privileged by the only system they've ever known, as well as those disadvantaged by it, may fail to recognize anything is wrong.

In a 2012 TEDx Talk, McIntosh puts a visual to it: "an imaginary line of social justice that is parallel to the floor." When you're on the line, she says, "things feel fair." Privilege, to McIntosh, raises a person *above* the line, while oppression pushes a person beneath it. Let's make our own version of this visual, thinking of privilege like a balloon and oppression like a weight.

This is a big step toward a Marxist framework, because it gives a unifying word to the "upper" and "lower" side of each social justice struggle. "Ruling" and "working" classes become "privileged" and "oppressed" demographics.

The struggles themselves, though, are still different and separate. That same year, a new idea would tie it all together.

Intersectionality

In 1989, Kimberlé Crenshaw, a law professor and student of Derrick Bell's, published a paper in the *University of Chicago Legal Forum* called "Demarginalizing the Intersection of Race and Sex."

Crenshaw explains that combatting discrimination "along a single categorical axis," like race *or* gender, may still leave "those who are multiply-burdened," like Black women, vulnerable. As one example, she points to a 1976 court case in which five Black women sued General Motors for discrimination specifically against Black women, citing the company's near nonexistence of Black female employees. The court ruled against the women, seeing no evidence that General Motors discriminated against A) women, or B) Black people, and so rejected the claim. But the women hired by GM were almost all white, and the Black people hired by GM were almost all men. Crenshaw argues that not viewing Black women as their own identity group left them vulnerable to discrimination that would remain invisible if discrimination were only examined using separate, single axes.

Crenshaw called this idea "intersectionality." Under the premise that it was insufficient for identity-related struggles to be addressed individually, intersectionality was the notion that these fields must be brought together into a cross analysis.

According to Crenshaw, the baggage Black women carry at their identity "intersection" is sometimes even greater than the sum of the baggage Black men and white women carry—like at General Motors, where they were completely shut out of the company.

Crenshaw uses Black women as her primary example, but she points out that the idea of intersectionality could be applied to two or more social justice movements of any kind. Taken to its full extent, intersectionality can be used to arrange every demographic group in society into a hierarchy of oppression, which she explains with this metaphor:

> Imagine a basement which contains all people who are disadvantaged on the basis of race, sex, class, sexual preference, age and/or physical ability. These people are stacked—feet standing on shoulders—with those on the bottom being disadvantaged by the full array of factors, up to the very top, where the heads of all those disadvantaged by a singular factor brush up against the ceiling. Their ceiling is actually the floor above which only those who are not disadvantaged in any way reside.

Crenshaw's basement concept was a way of binding the various arenas of social justice into a single, vertical power hierarchy. We can think of it as the **Intersectional Stack.**[*]

---

[*] When I refer to "privileged" and "oppressed" people or groups in this book,...

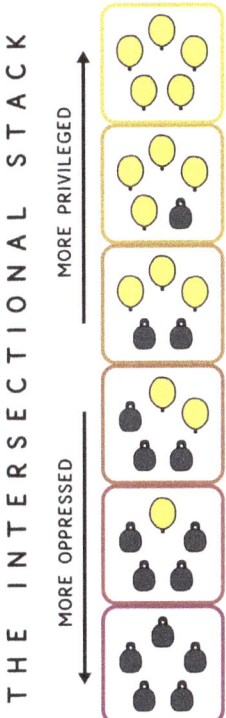

Enter Postmodernism

Liberals and Marxists fundamentally disagree about liberalism, but they both subscribe to the basic ideas of modernity. Modernity, as I mentioned, emphasized the notion of objective truth that anyone, anywhere could work toward using scientific methods. As philosopher Thomas Paine described it:

> Science, the partisan of no country, but the beneficent patroness of all, has liberally opened a temple where all may meet....The philosopher in one country sees not an enemy in the philosopher of another: he takes his seat in the temple of science, and asks not who sits beside him.

...I'm referring to the way intersectional theory sees things. So when I write "a privileged person," for example, it's shorthand for "a person intersectional theory deems to be privileged."

This idea was once revolutionary. In premodern times, it was common for different humans to believe in different denominations of truth—like, for example, the prominent religious doctrines, each of which had its own version of the truth. Modernity replaced faith-based thinking and divine authority with the idea of a single objective truth and a universal process for discovering it.

Postmodernist thinkers take issue with this. A philosophy that emerged in France during the 1960s, postmodernism takes Critical Theory to the next level. Postmodernist thinkers like the critical approach but don't think Critical Theory takes it far *enough*.*

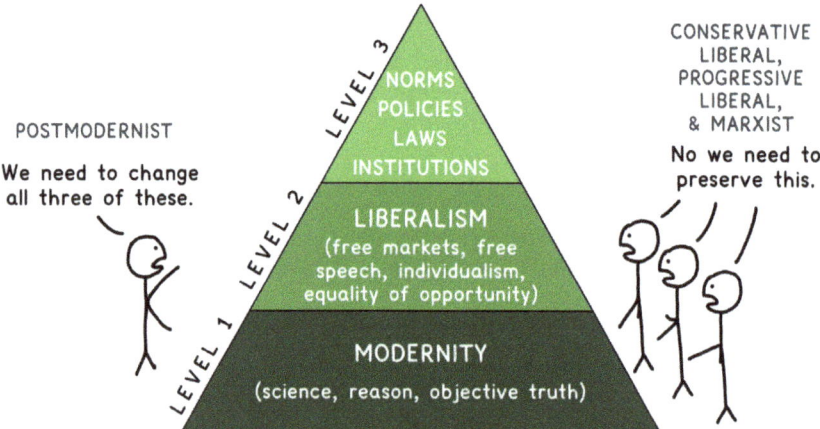

Postmodernists are radical skeptics who see nearly *all* beliefs as false consciousness. They believe that power is exerted not only through economic oppression or cultural brainwashing but through every element of a society—through all layers of the pyramid. The whole society is permeated with a "metanarrative" that's so well embedded in the minds of citizens that it feels like the natural order of things.

To postmodernists like Michel Foucault and Jean-François Lyotard, religions, political theories, and even science were bad, nonsensical metanarratives—systems of thought that serve the interests of the powerful and legitimize their dominant position. Others argued that the

---

* The pyramid offers a cool way to visualize the concept of being politically "radical." The more radical a political movement or line of thought, the deeper down in the pyramid it wants to enact change.

way language divided the world into binary categories—male/female, fact/fiction, science/art, etc.—was also a social construction that helped entrench power by assigning superiority to one half of the binary and inferiority to the other.

Remember the Scientist, Sports Fan, Attorney, and Zealot? That's a framework of modernity—one that sees the scientific method not as an arbitrary metanarrative but as a universal truth-seeking process that actually *can* lead thinkers in the direction of objective truth. Our discussion framed the Ladder as a hierarchy, with the best truth-finding thinking at the top and the worst at the bottom.

Many postmodernists would call this a delusion that has me falling hook, line, and sinker for the dominant metanarrative surrounding me. They believe *any claim to objective truth* is an illusion—and that in labeling scientific thinking as "high-rung thinking," I'm just another Zealot elevating one metanarrative above the rest. The postmodernist's goal was not to discover the truth but to "deconstruct" our notions of knowledge and discourse to look at what they're made of and how they work.

By the 1980s, just as neo-Marxism had gone out of fashion, postmodernism had also begun to wane in influence. But many of the same activists who revived neo-Marxism by marrying it with a social justice framework would soon give postmodernism new life.

A Philosophical Merger

In her landmark 1991 paper, "Mapping the Margins" (written two years after her initial paper on intersectionality), Kimberlé Crenshaw writes:

> I consider intersectionality a provisional concept linking contemporary politics with postmodern theory.

As the idea of intersectionality rose in prominence, Crenshaw and others began to infuse Critical Social Justice with a postmodern way of thinking.

While postmodernism offered broad analysis rather than ideas for real-world action, the Critical Social Justice framework was specifically geared toward making change. The *fusion* of the two created a new beast—one with both the deconstructive capability of the postmodernists and the political drive of Marxists and Critical Theorists.

The identity politics lens of Critical Social Justice made the often-vague postmodern notions of power more clearly defined and more applicable to politics. On the flip side, postmodernism broadened the scope of Critical Social Justice. The Critical Social Justice premise that white supremacist, patriarchal, heteronormative power was embedded in cultural, institutional, and legal systems could stretch into a much further-reaching premise that this power was embedded in the fundamental mechanisms of modern civilization: knowledge, language, discourse, science, reason, and the very notion of objective truth. All of these mechanisms, through the lens of postmodernism, could be analyzed as socially constructed "systems of domination" that served to legitimize, maintain, and perpetuate privilege and oppression.

This fusion was the genesis of a new ideology I call **Social Justice Fundamentalism (SJF)**.

SJF is a philosophical Frankenstein. It's the Marxist framework, applied to American social justice, merged with the postmodern rejection of modernity, while swapping out postmodern skepticism toward all metanarratives with a total embrace of the SJF metanarrative.

Over the past thirty years, the SJF narrative has grown increasingly radical and developed from a handful of academic papers into an all-encompassing worldview.

The subsects of Social Justice Fundamentalism, developed in academic fields like critical race theory, women's studies, queer theory, and postcolonial theory, center around their own theories about humans and identity—but they share a belief in one overarching concept:

The Force

In 2014, at a conference on race and pedagogy, four professors read out a passage to a room of educators, which they said described their "core tenets":

> Racism is an institutionalized, multi-layered, multi-level system that distributes unequal power and resources between white people and people of color, as socially identified, and disproportionally benefits whites. All members of society are socialized to participate in the system of racism, albeit within varied social locations. All white people benefit from racism, regardless of intentions. No one chose to be socialized into racism, so no one

1930s

MARXISM
Society is a struggle between the ruling class and the working class, with power being exerted through politics and economics.

↓

CRITICAL THEORY
(Marxism 2.0)

Society is a struggle between **the dominant class and the oppressed class**, with power being exerted through politics, economics, **culture, and institutions**.

LIBERALISM

1960s

CRITICAL THEORY 2.0
(the New Left)

Society is a struggle between **the dominant class and the oppressed class**, with power being exerted through politics, economics, **culture, and institutions**, and the suppression of rights is sometimes necessary to achieve justice.

LIBERAL SOCIAL JUSTICE
(1965)

Demographic groups like women and Black people are oppressed in society by racism and sexism in laws and cultural norms, breaking the promises of a liberal society. Movements that leverage liberal rights and appeal to common humanity are necessary to change minds and bring society closer to its liberal ideals.

POSTMODERNISM

Dominant groups in societies hold power over oppressed groups through language, morality, science, and basically anything else you can think of.

↓

CRITICAL SOCIAL JUSTICE
(identity politics)

Society is a struggle between identity divisions like white/black, men/women, and straight/gay, with power being exerted through politics, economics, culture, and institutions, and the suppression of rights is sometimes necessary to achieve justice.

1980s

↓

CRITICAL SOCIAL JUSTICE 2.0
(intersectionality)

Society is an intersectional struggle between privileged identities and oppressed identities, with power being exerted through politics, economics, culture, and institutions, and the suppression of rights is sometimes necessary to achieve justice.

1990s

SOCIAL JUSTICE FUNDAMENTALISM

Society is an intersectional struggle between privileged identities and oppressed identities, with power being exerted through politics, economics, culture, institutions, language, morality, science, and basically anything else you can think of, and the suppression of rights is sometimes necessary to achieve justice.

LIBERAL SOCIAL JUSTICE

Demographic groups like women, people of color, LGBTQ, and immigrants are disadvantaged in society by certain illiberal systems and norms, breaking the promises of liberalism. Movements that leverage liberal rights and appeal to common humanity can change minds and bring society closer to its liberal ideals.

is quote-unquote "bad," but no one is neutral. To not act against racism is to support racism. The default is racism. Racism must be continually identified, analyzed, and challenged. No one is ever done. The question is not, "Did racism take place?" but rather, "How did racism manifest in that situation?" The racial status quo is comfortable for most whites. Therefore, anything that maintains white comfort is suspect....Resistance is a predictable reaction to anti-racist education and must be explicitly and strategically addressed.

Perhaps no passage better represents the essence of Social Justice Fundamentalism.

When physicists look at the world, they see gravity, electromagnetism, the strong nuclear force, and the weak nuclear force—the four fundamental forces of nature—at work. Everything else is at the whim of those forces, playing by their rules. By infusing the identity politics of Critical Social Justice with the conception of power as an all-encompassing social driver, the scholars of Social Justice Fundamentalism have come to see society as being run by a similar set of fundamental forces: white supremacy, patriarchy, heteronormativity, and others. But intersectionality provided SJF with something physicists haven't yet discovered: a unifying theory of everything. Intersectionality weaves the fundamental forces of social justice into a single exertion that permeates all aspects of human existence—every interaction, every assumption, every social norm. I call it **the Force**.

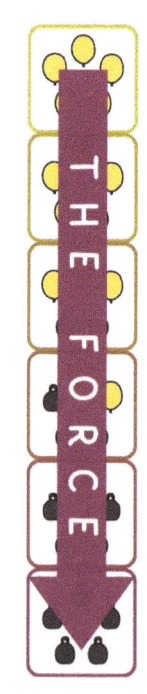

According to Social Justice Fundamentalism, whether consciously or not, the people who designed societies embedded them (and all of the institutional and cultural systems within them) with the Force, which ensures that they and others like them would forever be in a position of dominance.

SJF proponents don't use the term "the Force," but in their writings, you can hear them describe it. Robin DiAngelo, author of the mega-bestseller *White Fragility*, believes that racism flows through "cherished ideologies" like "individualism" and "meritocracy," through not some but "all institutions." Duke professor Eduardo Bonilla-Silva says most colleges and universities are "white-oriented" and "reproduce whiteness through their curriculum, culture, demography, symbols, traditions, and ecology." SJF proponents argue that concepts like the scientific method, hard work, a respect for authority, planning for the future, private property, competition, and politeness are all oppressive systems through which the Force exerts itself.

In her 2020 bestselling book *Caste*, journalist Isabel Wilkerson uses the term "caste" as her word for the Force:

> As we go about our daily lives, caste is the wordless usher in a darkened theater, flashlight cast down in the aisles, guiding us to our assigned seats for a performance....As a means of assigning value to entire swaths of humankind, caste guides each of us often beyond the reaches of our awareness. It embeds into our bones an unconscious ranking of human characteristics and sets forth the rules, expectations and stereotypes that have been used to justify brutalities against entire groups within our species....Caste is the powerful infrastructure that holds each group in its place.... Its very invisibility is what gives it power and longevity...it is an ever-present through line in the country's operation.

Liberal Social Justice generally defines a concept like "racism" to mean discrimination, bias, or negative stereotyping against individuals or groups based on immutable characteristics like skin color, sex, or sexual orientation. Social Justice Fundamentalism sees racism not merely as a certain way of thinking or of treating people, but as an expression of the Force. Since the Force goes in only one direction, so must the words (e.g., "only white people can be racist"). Since the Force is all-pervasive and systemic, so is racism. When an SJF activist says that "all white people are racist," they're not referring to the behavior of individual white people but to the way Syracuse professor Barbara Applebaum describes it in her book *Being White, Being Good*: "White people, through the practices of whiteness and by benefiting from white privilege, contribute to the maintenance of systemic racial injustice."

These particular passages were about racism, but you could also substitute "racism" for sexism, homophobia, transphobia, xenophobia, or any other word for identity-related bigotry or oppression, because the Force applies to all parts of the SJF narrative. Queer theorists like Judith

Butler, for example, believe that most of what we think of as gendered behaviors are actually social performances that serve to reinforce the dominance of men over women. In SJF, it's as if society is a play, people the actors, and the Force the playwright.

The narrow focus on the Force is a key distinction between Social Justice Fundamentalism and Liberal Social Justice. In the world of Liberal Social Justice, the Intersectional Stack is indeed a valid lens to examine one form of justice discrepancy in society. But it's only *one* of many such axes, along with others which arrange people according to wealth, intelligence, talent, attractiveness, temperament, age, geography, family structure, family connections, quality of upbringing, education, and others. Each axis burdens certain people with baggage and lifts others up with balloons. But SJF, depicting society through the lens of the Force, sees the Intersectional Stack as by far the most meaningful axis of advantage and disadvantage. We see this in the way it defines key terms: while Liberal Social Justice considers many forms of diversity—racial, ideological, socioeconomic, geographic, etc.—in SJF, "diversity" almost always means "racial diversity."

Along the same lines, believers in Liberal Social Justice see society as a product of many social elements—power, culture, competition, integrity, altruism, persuasion, compassion, forgiveness, etc.—while SJF views society mostly in terms of power. In SJF, power among groups is *the* governing force that determines why things are the way they are, how they got that way, and how things will go in the future.

The two lines of thinking also differ in their approach to solutions. While Liberal Social Justice tries to make improvements using liberal means like science, free speech, and voting, SJF sees liberalism *itself* as an element of the Force. As Black feminist scholar Audre Lorde famously put it: "The master's tools will never dismantle the master's house. They may allow us temporarily to beat him at his own game, but they will never enable us to bring about genuine change." When the premise is that oppression is etched into the very DNA of a nation, the only way to truly fix things is to get out the wrecking ball, overthrow the entire system, and start from scratch. Both Liberal Social Justice and Social Justice Fundamentalism want to make major change, but the kind of change SJF wants to make goes far deeper and is much more revolutionary.

SOCIAL JUSTICE, ON THE LADDER

So far, this has been a horizontal discussion. Defining leftness as "how deep into the pyramid your progressivism goes," Social Justice Fundamentalism is certainly a very far-left, radical ideology, while Liberal Social Justice occupies a more moderate position.

But as we've discussed, far left doesn't imply anything about the ideology's *vertical* position on the Ladder. The high rungs are expansive and inclusive, and the radical lens of the far left can be a valuable piece of the high-rung superbrain. The far left serves as society's extreme skeptic, interrogating the status quo down to its foundation. They'll often be wrong, but from time to time, they discover something important and act as the catalyst of major change.

There are plenty of far-left thinkers up on the high rungs—the kind who like to disagree, are willing to change their mind, are morally consistent, non-tribal, etc. Of course, there are plenty down on the low rungs too.

I dedicated such a large portion of this book to Social Justice Fundamentalism because I'm convinced it's not only far left but *lower* left. And I believe the ideology has become the guiding dogma of a growing low-rung political behemoth: the SJF golem.

We'll talk about the golem and what it's doing in Chapters 6 and 7. First, let me explain why I think the ideology itself is a classic product of the low rungs. I'll sort my reasoning into three buckets:

1. SJF IS UNSCIENTIFIC

In Chapter 1, we discussed the difference between high- and low-rung thinking.

High-rung thinking abides by the spirit of the scientific method. It's an exercise in humility, starting with Point A—"I don't know"—and then working toward truth by way of reason and evidence.

But SJF treats its own worldview as an axiom. We saw this in the passage I quoted above, the one written by four professors:

> The question is not, "Did racism take place?" but rather, "How did racism manifest in that situation?"

In SJF, asking "did racism take place?" is like asking "did gravity take place?" The answer is yes, of course. This is the opposite of the scientific method, starting at Point B—"I know"—and working backward from there.

High-rung thinking values nuance, seeing complex topics in shades of gray. But SJF tends to simplify a messy gray world into binary 1s and 0s: white/POC, privileged/oppressed, colonizer/colonized, racist/anti-racist. It's the kind of digital thinking characteristic of Political Disney World narratives.

High-rung thinking is data-driven, working off the idea that strong beliefs must be capable of being supported or falsified by evidence. But SJF's vague, all-encompassing claims (e.g., "All members of society are socialized to participate in the system of racism") are neither provable nor falsifiable—yet the SJF narrative is utterly certain in its worldview. This makes SJF a matter of faith more than science.

And the way SJF proponents talk about the Force, while presenting it as an academic theory, it often *does* sound more religious than scientific.

Here's Robin DiAngelo describing racism in a 2016 talk at Evergreen College:

> DIANGELO AND KENDI
>
> Robin DiAngelo and Ibram X. Kendi are two of the best-known and most influential proponents of what we're calling Social Justice Fundamentalism. Through their papers, talks, and mega-bestselling books, each has had profound impact on classroom education, academia, corporate recruiting and training, and government policy. They are only two of many prominent SJF activists, but I'll reference them frequently because their words have made a particularly large impact on today's US society.

There is no avoiding it. We all collude with it...recognize that it's ongoing, that you're never finished, that 24/7 the forces around us push and seduce and compel us to participate and the only way to not collude is to actively, intentionally, and strategically seek to resist those forces, and as soon as we're complacent, we get sucked back in.

Another prominent voice in the world of SJF is Ibram X. Kendi, whose ideas rose to prominence in 2016 with his first bestselling book, *Stamped from the Beginning*, and then shot into the stratosphere with his 2019 mega-bestseller *How to Be an Antiracist*. In *How to Be an Antiracist*, Kendi writes with the same kind of language as DiAngelo: "Denial is the heartbeat of racism, beating across ideologies, races, and nations. It is beating within us."

This kind of thinking runs throughout the SJF narrative and serves as the basis for the policies those activists promote. A good example are beliefs about "equity."

Equality and Equity

There's a meme that has been passed around a lot over the past few years. Here's one version of it:

The assumption is that **everyone benefits from the same supports**. This is equal treatment.

Everyone gets the supports they need (this is the concept of "affirmative action"), thus producing equity.

All 3 can see the game without supports or accommodations because **the cause(s) of the inequity was addressed**. The systemic barrier has been removed.

Source: MobilizeGreen

The meme depicts social inequality—the kind that makes living and succeeding harder for someone of one demographic group than someone of another, *even if* those two people are identical in every other way.

That's what the meme's left pane is getting at: three people, all supposedly enjoying equal opportunity, except there's a wooden fence there that blocks one of the people from the "success" enjoyed by the other two.

If the left pane is What Is, the right pane is What Should Be—a world with no wooden fence of systemic injustice.

Liberal Social Justice activism tries to tear down what remains of the fence using the tools of liberalism—the scientific method, vigorous discourse, and political activism—to change minds, build broad coalitions, and eradicate injustice.

But removing the wooden fence is complicated and takes time. Which is where another idea comes into play: equity.

Equity says that fairness should account for both the current and lingering effects of the wooden fence and make adjustments to bring the playing field closer to true level ground. The boxes below the feet of the people in the meme are those adjustments.

This is the logic behind affirmative action. Affirmative action policies in the US began in the 1960s. Harvard Law School lays out the basic definition:

> **Affirmative action** or **positive discrimination** is the policy of favoring members of a disadvantaged group who are perceived to suffer from discrimination within a culture...intended to promote the opportunities of defined minority groups within a society to give them equal access to that of the privileged majority population.

The quest for success is intergenerational, as wealth and connections accumulate over long periods of time. In the case of Black Americans, slavery ended around five generations ago. The racial apartheid of the Jim Crow era, which began in the American South shortly after the US Civil War and ended with the civil rights movements in the 1960s, was in full force just two generations ago. Other injustices like housing discrimination, hiring discrimination, and unequal treatment by police persisted beyond the 1960s, affecting the current and previous generation. That's a pretty big pile of double standards impeding the progress of Black Americans for many consecutive generations. Over time, that compounds into a sizable wooden fence. Affirmative action policies aim to offset the effects of the fence in the present and accelerate the process of eradicating the fence for future generations.

But in a country premised on equality, mitigating injustice using equity boxes is tricky business. Which is why Liberal Social Justice activists tend to advocate for them sparsely—and mainly in instances when the effects of the policy will be positive-sum.* The thing about moving

---

* In the case of affirmative action, proponents argue that more diverse campuses,...

those boxes around is that if activists are wrong about the specifics of the fence, moving boxes may be counterproductive and potentially a form of injustice itself. So Liberal Social Justice gets really specific about the nature of the fence, backing up its assertions where possible with empirical evidence, before making major adjustments in the name of equity.

Social Justice Fundamentalism talks a lot about equity too, but two SJF tenets lead to a very different solution:

*The wooden fence is the **only** possible explanation for disparities between groups*

When Liberal Social Justice scholars see a disparity between groups in society, it forms a question mark in their heads. Maybe the disparity is the result of injustice—of some inequality of opportunity (say, discrimination, systemic sexism, racist legal structures, or lingering effects of historic injustice)—or maybe the disparity is caused by any number of other factors that don't necessarily imply injustice has happened (say, varying cultural values, varying group interests, or varying geography). They'll investigate and try to get the answer.

When SJF activists see the same disparity, there's no question mark: it is proof of injustice. Any disparity among identity groups is a product of the Force. In his book *Stamped from the Beginning*, Kendi sums up the SJF position:

> We have a hard time recognizing that racial discrimination is the sole cause of racial disparities in this country and in the world at large…When you truly believe that racial groups are equal, then you also believe that racial disparities must be the result of racial discrimination.

This distinction lies behind a major difference between the liberal and SJF worldviews. The liberal mindset aims for equality of opportunity, and any affirmative action measures are geared toward that goal. This mindset assumes that, for lots of potential reasons, equality of opportunity may often yield inequality of outcome. But SJF, believing

---

…workplaces, and leadership make society richer and more productive for everyone. Critics of affirmative action question its fairness and its effectiveness in achieving equity and point out ways in which it may backfire.

that any disparity between groups can only be the result of injustice, sees equality of opportunity and equality of outcome as one and the same. Any instance of inequality of outcome between groups is, in SJF, *evidence* of the presence of a wooden fence—and therefore, a just society should take measures to ensure equal outcomes.

The **only** solution to the wooden fence is wooden boxes

While liberal activists usually think of "equity boxes" like affirmative action policies as one of many possible solutions (and often, a last resort), SJF activists see them as the *only* effective response to past or present injustice. Kendi expresses the SJF view like this:

> The only remedy to racist discrimination is antiracist discrimination.
> The only remedy to past discrimination is present discrimination.

SJF activists look at societal institutions through a zero-sum lens. Groups that are overrepresented got there by oppressing those who are underrepresented, and the only way to help those at the bottom is to take from those at the top. Ensuring equal outcomes trumps individual rights.

The tricky thing about this kind of reasoning is that society is *full* of disparities of every kind. Take a look at this chart, compiled by data scientist Zach Goldberg, which shows the average income of America's many different ancestry groups:

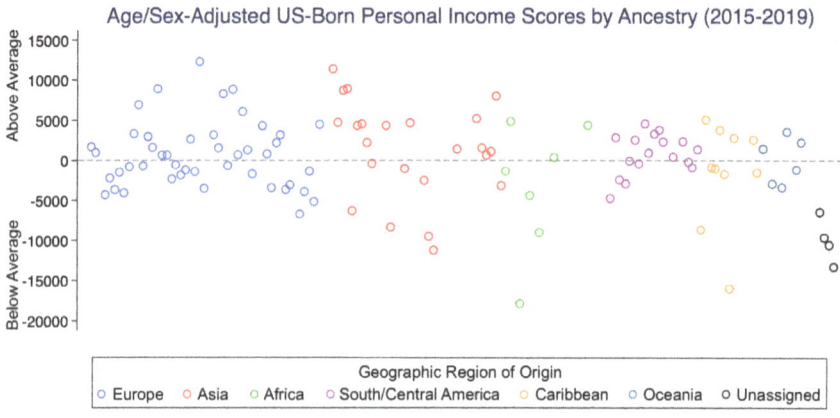

Source: Zach Goldberg

The SJF narrative doesn't have room for this kind of messiness, so it applies its key tenets selectively to disparities that fit within the narrative. For disparities that favor a group higher up on the Intersectional Stack (say, white Americans out-earning Hispanic Americans, or men being overrepresented among software engineers), it says injustice is the cause and equity boxes are a necessary remedy. For disparities that go in the other direction (say, Asian Americans outperforming white Americans on standardized tests, or women being more likely than men to attend college), correlation no longer implies causation, and no equity boxes are warranted. Certain disparities may be more likely than others to be a sign of underlying injustice, but a hard rule about which must and must not be injustice is dogma more than analysis.

This will be a theme: extreme assumptions and extreme policy prescriptions, applied only when they fit within the SJF worldview.

Such a narrative, built on clear-cut explanations and unquestioning certainty, makes things easy for its believers. The scientific method is *hard* and the SJF way of thinking removes that burden. But this ease comes with a tradeoff because certainty is a burden of its own. When a group of people relies on total belief in a single narrative, they must go to great lengths to control the flow of information and enforce intellectual conformity within their ranks. Which brings me to the next bucket:

2. SJF IS ECHO CHAMBER-Y

In 1938, blues musician Lead Belly sang a song he wrote about "the Scottsboro boys," a group of Black teenagers who were sent to jail after being falsely accused of raping two white women on a train (one of the women later admitted it was a made-up charge). After the song, Lead Belly talked about the case and advised fellow Black Americans "to stay woke—keep their eyes open."

Stay woke.

The term has been a part of the Black American lexicon for a very long time. In more recent years, the term has evolved from the way Lead Belly was using it—warning Black people to stay alert to dangerous situations that might arise—to a broader meaning about staying aware of racist systems of oppression. After the release of Erykah Badu's 2007 song "Master Teacher Medley," with a chorus that repeated the line "I stay woke," the term exploded into the mainstream.

Over recent years, the word has evolved to take on yet a new meaning: believing and promoting the Social Justice Fundamentalist worldview.

In contrast, Liberal Social Justice has no single narrative. It's a big Idea Lab—a supergenie made up of collaborating smaller genies, which are made up of independent individual minds. It's a messy space that includes libertarians, socialists, and all the ground in between, arguing about everything from affirmative action to individual accountability to the lingering effects of historical injustice to the nuanced definitions of concepts like fairness, justice, and equality.

The fundamentalists believe in a single narrative, and their movement is premised on shared certainty in that narrative. To be woke is to believe. It's to abide by the SJF position on affirmative action, individual accountability, and historical injustice. It's to define fairness, justice, equality, diversity, inclusion, and equity the precise way they're defined by SJF doctrine.

In religious or political groups bound by shared belief, belief itself is typically tied to social status. From medieval Christianity to modern North Korea to every hard-line cult you can find, the coolest way to be cool is to talk about how great the leaders and their ideas are and how awful the out-group is, and the fastest way to get yourself in big trouble is to openly question those ideas. The specifics vary but the concept is the same: the social environment incentivizes ideological conformity.

The same social environment makes any departure from the sacred beliefs taboo. In SJF circles, dissenting from the party line will often get someone slapped with socially disastrous labels like racist, misogynist, or transphobic.

I've talked about this with SJF proponents who have countered that what I see as social rules enforcing conformity are actually based in theory and reflect, if anything, deep humility. They're referencing something called standpoint theory.

Standpoint Theory

Standpoint theory, a concept that emerged from Marxist theory and has since been adopted more broadly by Social Justice Fundamentalism, argues that different identity groups have special access to different kinds of knowledge. The idea is that if society is a river and the Force is the current, oppressed groups, who spend their lives swimming against the current, develop intimate knowledge of the current that privileged people, always swimming *with* the current, can't access. Put another way: The dominant perspective is understood by everyone, because it's everywhere, all the time, while the oppressed perspective is only understood by the oppressed. So the words of people from oppressed groups should carry extra weight, because they carry more knowledge.

Standpoint theory is the philosophical backdrop behind the popular four-word SJF reprimand: *stay in your lane.*

"Stay in your lane" means: If you're white, your words carry little authority on race issues. If you're a man, you should refrain from weighing in about women's movements like #metoo and the debates around rape culture on campuses. If you're not Muslim, you should defer to those who are on the topic of Islam. If you're a cisgender heterosexual, check your privilege before offering your two cents on LGBTQ issues.

On one hand, most liberals would agree that standpoint theory gets at something undeniable: different people have different life experiences, some of which are related to their group identity, and these experiences offer them specific insights that people from other groups may not grasp. In 1965, literary and civil rights icon James Baldwin said:

> In the case of the American Negro, from the moment you are born every stick and stone, every face, is white. Since you have not yet seen a mirror, you suppose you are, too. It comes as a great shock around the age of 5, 6, or 7 to discover that the flag to which you have pledged allegiance, along with everybody else, has not pledged allegiance to you. It comes as a great shock to see Gary Cooper killing off the Indians, and although you are rooting for Gary Cooper, that the Indians are you. It comes as a great shock to discover that the country which is your birthplace and to which you owe your life and identity has not, in its whole system of reality, evolved any place for you.

What Baldwin describes is a reality for many Black Americans, but not for white Americans. No matter how hard white Americans try, they can't fully know what it's like to experience the particular kind of "great shock" Baldwin describes.

But to the liberal mindset, specific life experience is only one form of knowledge, alongside another: the universal experience of being human. When trying to understand another person's point of view, a liberal thinker aims for the *humility sweet spot* that acknowledges both each person's uniqueness and all people's shared humanness.

To use myself as an example, having a major procrastination/perfectionist problem opens an empathy window to anyone with *any* form of self-defeating tendency. When I see someone who struggles with their diet, I don't think, *Why don't they just eat healthier? It's not that hard.* I think, *This is their version of procrastination.* Without having experienced their *specific* struggle, I can appreciate just how awful and difficult it must be.

Likewise, I'm not Black, but when I hear people talk about what it's like to be Black in America, I don't think, *I can't imagine what that must be like!* I *can* imagine it. Because I remember what it was like when, as a Jewish kid, I first learned that antisemitism was a thing. It was scary and upsetting and infuriating. It changed the way I thought about the world and history and a lot of other things. Is this the same experience as being Black in America? No. My ancestors weren't enslaved here. I looked at leadership in America and saw Jews well represented. For the most part, Jews were portrayed just fine in the media and in movies. At least in my particular life, no anti-Jewish slur could have felt as bad to me as the way the n-word, used in a derogatory way, must feel to Black people. But my own life experience gives me a *glimpse* of what it must be like to be Black in the US—and a glimpse can go a long way.

But then passages like the one above from Baldwin are a reminder that a glimpse also doesn't go *all* the way. Imagining a different struggle than your own is an exercise in extrapolation—it's an educated guess. But it's not knowledge. At the humility sweet spot, a person gives themselves the right amount of credit for what they *do* know about someone else and also the proper level of respect for what they *don't* know.

Social Justice Fundamentalism rejects this kind of balanced approach in favor of the more extreme take of standpoint theory: that having a certain skin color or gender or sexual orientation grants one full access to a set of experiences that others have no access to at all—not even a glimpse. Suggesting otherwise is seen as a microaggression (in academic papers, a common item on lists of sample microaggressions is, "As a woman, I know what you go through as a racial minority").

Under this reasoning, SJF activists dismiss dissent from anyone in a privileged demographic by discrediting the speaker straight off the bat.

The most famous instance of this is Robin DiAngelo labeling disagreement from a white person as "white fragility," but there are lots of other versions too. Women's and Gender Studies professor Alison Bailey refers to dissent from the privileged as "privilege-preserving epistemic pushback." Philosophy professor Kristie Dotson frames it as "pernicious ignorance." Education professor Alice McIntyre uses the term "white talk," which Alison Bailey describes as "designed, indeed scripted, for the purposes of evading, rejecting, and remaining ignorant about the injustices that flow from whiteness and its attendant privileges."

These are all different ways to say the same thing: if you are a member of a privileged group, any disagreement from you is invalid. At best, it's ignorance. At worst, outright bigotry.

So perhaps what I'm viewing as social pressure to agree with the narrative is really just this:

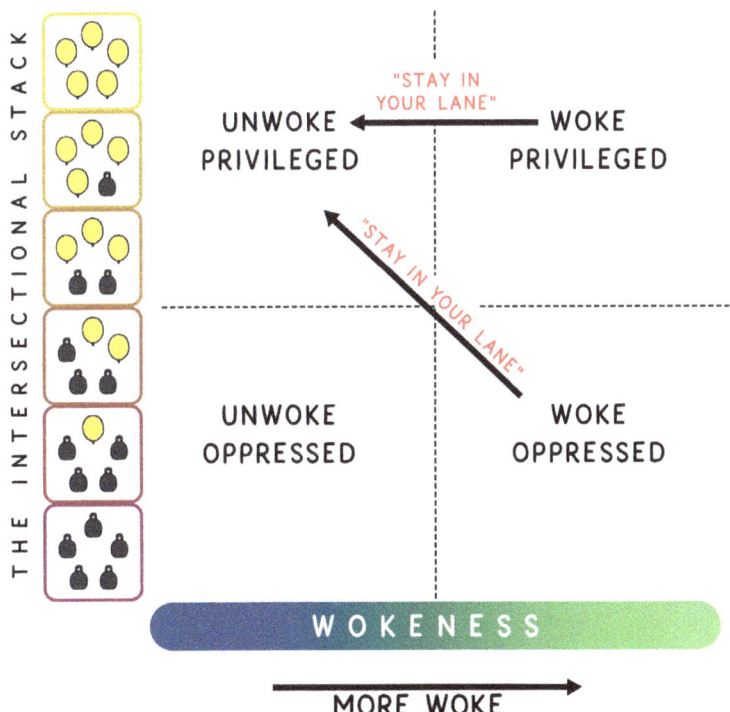

But again, things get tricky when they get messier—like when someone from that *lower left* quadrant disagrees with the SJF narrative.

There's a lot of data showing that progressive activists, as a group, are overwhelmingly white, wealthy, and college educated. So it's unsurprising that SJF activists, many of whom hail from high-ranking universities, often seem to match these demographics. This creates an odd contradiction: most of the people speaking with authority about how members of privileged groups should take a back seat on issues of oppression are members of privileged groups.

Standpoint theory is supposed to invalidate what these mostly white scholars have to say about a topic like racism. But for their own ideas, these scholars make an exception. Likewise, standpoint theory would have these scholars defer to the opinions of more oppressed people—even when those people disagree with SJF. But again, we see an exception.

Writer and activist Coleman Hughes told this story in a 2018 podcast interview with economist Glenn Loury:

> Being in class at Columbia, I've been in a class where the teacher said to the whole class, "All students—all people of color are victims of oppression." Right? This professor happened to be white, but it wouldn't have mattered if she was Black because I don't define myself that way. I think it's just untrue as a matter of fact, for me and for most Black people I know. It's profoundly disempowering and even somewhat offensive to be labeled in that way without one's permission. But the social dynamic in the classroom was such that had I raised my hand and said, "Actually, I disagree," it would have been tantamount to social suicide.

In a 2014 paper about classroom instruction, Robin DiAngelo and coauthor Özlem Sensoy include a list of problematic viewpoints that they believe should not be permitted in a social justice classroom. This is one of their sample cases: "How do you respect differences and affirm everyone's perspectives when a student of Color claims that racism doesn't affect him?" They use this as an example of a time when the traditional classroom mantras "respect differences" and "affirm everyone's perspectives" should *not* be honored.

The authors don't believe this hypothetical student of color—or real-life Coleman Hughes—is trying to be deceptive, but that they are victims of false consciousness. They've been trained to uphold the society's dominant narrative, unconsciously aiding in their own oppression.

SJF applies the same judgment to people from oppressed groups who vote the wrong way. In November of 2022, after Ron DeSantis fared especially well with Latino voters in Florida's gubernatorial election (winning 58 percent), journalist Jemele Hill commented on the story by tweeting, "That proximity to whiteness is a real thing. Also reminds me of an adage I heard a long time ago about how the oppressed begin to take on the traits of the oppressor."

One of the most common pleas from SJF activists is to "*listen* to people of color," to "*listen* to women," to "*listen* to LGBTQ people." But when what these people say doesn't jibe with the SJF narrative, SJF stops listening.

British blogger Tomiwa Owolade, who is Black, talked about this phenomenon, summing up the message like this: "If you disagree with me, you can't be thinking for yourself"—a message he calls "both racist and arrogant."

Sometimes, the reaction is worse than just patronizing.

Conservative radio talk show host and 2021 California gubernatorial candidate Larry Elder, who is Black, talks about the wide array of insults that are regularly hurled at him by the radical social justice crowd:

> Token. Boot licker. Uncle Tom. Sambo. Sambo Tom. Coconut, as in brown on the outside, white on the inside. Oreo, same concept. The anti-Christ. Because they've got to malign someone like me. I am a bigger threat to their whole ideology than anybody else.... Therefore, I can't just be dealt with with facts and rebutted with facts, I've gotta be maligned. I've gotta be cast away. I've gotta be treated as if I'm Darth Vader....It's bigotry. I don't have the same right to have an opinion as somebody else.

In some cases, the SJF mindset will make SJF alignment a prerequisite for membership in an oppressed group.

Tech mogul Peter Thiel made a speech at Donald Trump's 2016 convention, saying: "I am proud to be gay. I am proud to be a Republican. But most of all I am proud to be an American." In response to Thiel's open conservatism, *Advocate*, a gay magazine, published an article called "Peter Thiel Shows Us There's a Difference between Gay Sex and Gay" that argued, "By the logic of gay liberation, Thiel is an example of a man who has sex with other men, but not a gay man. Because he does not embrace the struggle of people to embrace their distinctive identity." Making a similar point, SJF activist Nikole Hannah-Jones once tweeted: "There is a difference between being politically black and being racially black."

When standpoint theory butts heads with the SJF narrative, in the form of a member of an oppressed group challenging the narrative, the SJF narrative tends to prevail. Like the SJF rules about disparity implying injustice, standpoint theory seems to apply *selectively*.

Ultimately, what makes a speaker of any group valid in the eyes of SJF is agreement with SJF. That's the definition of an Echo Chamber.

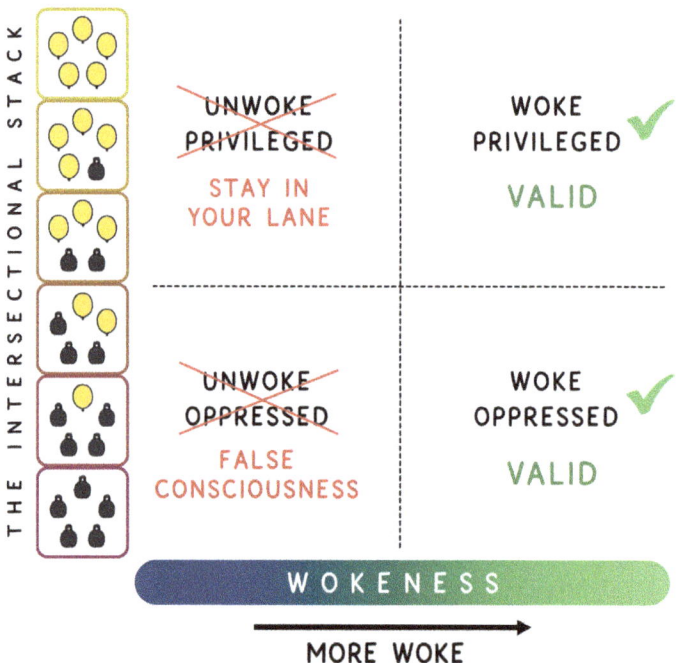

3. SJF IS MORALLY INCONSISTENT

In a society, there are generally two kinds of tolerance: legal and cultural. The legal rules apply to everyone. But any social group, whether it be a household, group of friends, private university, or political movement, can draw a *second* line on the freedom/safety graph: the cultural tolerance line.

Cultural intolerance can't put people in jail, but it *can* ruin people's lives. If 99 percent of a country's citizens agree that you're intolerable, you'll be banished to the fringes of society as a pariah. A guy with a swastika tattooed on his forehead won't be put in literal jail, but he'll be banned from 99.9 percent of social circles, essentially sent to social jail.

In this way, every subculture, movement, or other private club is like its own little country within a country, with its own tolerance rules overlaid on top of the broader national rules.

One mark of high-rung morality is tolerance *consistency*. Humans are hardwired to be hypersensitive to the concept of fair vs. unfair, so whatever a society's or community's specific rules around what's

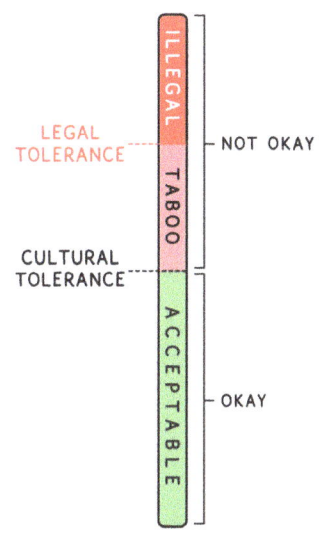

tolerable or intolerable, it's usually a good sign if the same rules apply to everyone. We can think of this like a flat seesaw. When things aren't morally consistent—when different groups are held to different standards—it's like a slanted seesaw.

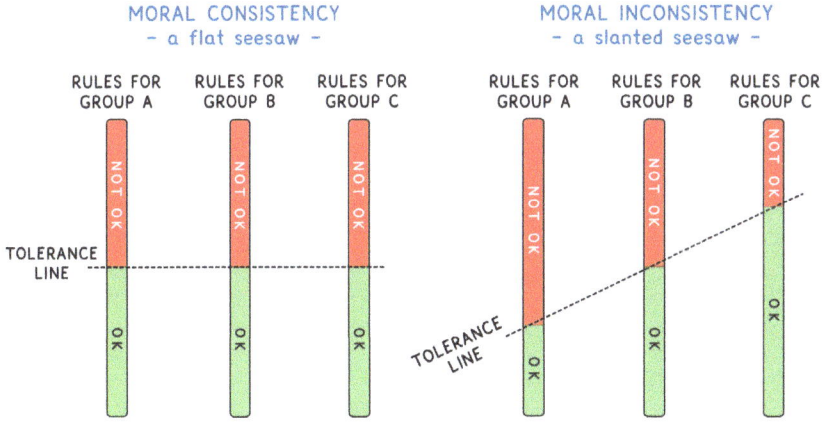

A good litmus test of moral consistency is the headline test.

If I show you three headlines—"man assaults woman," "gang murders man," "man and woman have consensual sex"—I assume you'd have plenty of information to assess your tolerance level of all three.

But if we presented the same challenge to a white person living in rural Mississippi in 1955, they might have a problem.

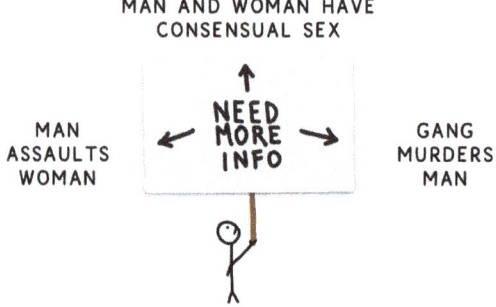

During the US South's Jim Crow era, white people were high status, Black people were low status, and tolerance was *status dependent*. If you equalized for status by making the race of all parties in each headline the same, the 1955 Mississippi person's judgments would probably be in the same ballpark as yours above. But fiddle around with the races in the headlines and, for some, everything changes:

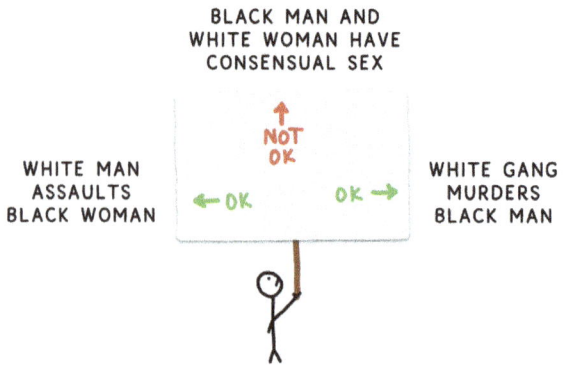

When the moral seesaw is slanted by race, the race of the parties involved is a *critical* piece of moral information. In the Jim Crow South, a Black man assaulting a white woman would be seen as a *far* worse offense than it would be if the races were reversed. A Black man having consensual sex with a white woman would be viewed as a heinous crime—so heinous that if the man were murdered by a white gang for it, it might seem like a tolerable reaction against an intolerable crime. In the infamous case of Black fourteen-year-old Emmett Till, merely whistling at a white woman was seen as so intolerable that not only was he murdered for the offense, but the *lynching* was seen as tolerable enough that the killers received full acquittal in court. That's about as slanted as seesaws come.

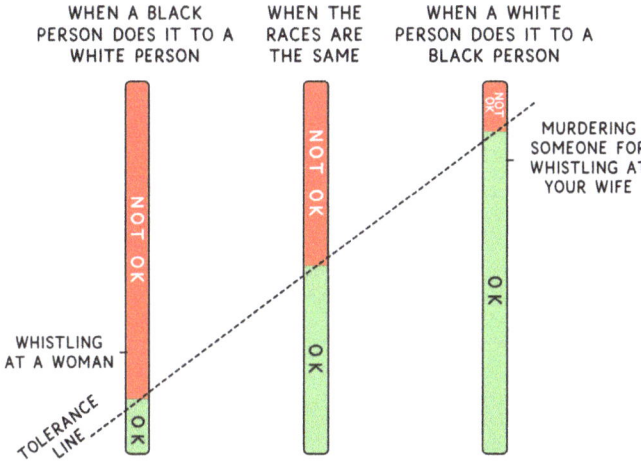

Following decades of political progress, many of history's slanted seesaws have been leveled out. But SJF argues that today's US isn't all that different from the Jim Crow South—the oppression is just better disguised. To apply a corrective counterforce, they flip the seesaw in the other direction regarding what is tolerable. A few examples:

Macroaggressions, Microaggressions

One of the tenets of SJF is that racism = prejudice + power, and power only moves down the Intersectional Stack, not up it. Therefore, there's no such thing as racism against white people, who reside at the top of the stack. Declassifying racism toward whites as racism reclassifies it as tolerable. And when a culture normalizes behavior that had previously been considered unacceptable, that behavior typically starts to happen more.

In 2019, the *Washington Post* published an opinion piece titled "Can Black Women and White Women Be True Friends?" in which the author explained why she believed the answer is no:

> Generally speaking, it's not that I dislike white women. Generally speaking, it's that I do not trust them. Generally speaking, most black women don't....This is what black women know: When push comes to shove, white women choose race over gender: Every. Single. Time....The brutal truth is that many white women, like much of white America in general, do not consider black women vulnerable. Which means they do not consider us to be fully human....Friendship is not possible between a human being and one who doubts her humanity.

These kind of negative generalizations of a giant group of people—"white women"—would certainly qualify as racist under the liberal definition of racism. Within SJF, it's just the expression of an exasperated Black woman living within the Force.

In 2018, *Vice* made a short documentary, aired on HBO, called "What It's Like to Take a Vacation Away from White People," about a tour company that arranges retreats to Costa Rica, with one guiding rule: no white guests allowed. In the documentary, the head of the tour company, Andrea X, explained the reasons behind the no-whites policy:

> We needed a safe space that was out of the United States to hold certain conversations, and just to heal. I don't think we can do that in the United States. I think that we're suffering, and suffocating, and just dying every single day trying to survive there.

This is the way a number of Black Americans had come to feel at the time. But she continued:

> I decided one day to just eliminate white people from my personal life. And ever since then, my life has been way more breezy....I feel like white people shouldn't have passports, because they've done

enough—especially white Americans. Leave them in the United States. They do not need to come here....My tip to white people is to let us have our space, let us have our room, and go hang out with other white people.

In *Vice*'s description of the documentary, they support the narrative that oppression in the US justifies Andrea X's language:

At a time when white supremacist groups march out in the open, and the president disparages African countries as "shitholes," it's not surprising many Black Americans are feeling isolated and unsafe in communities and workplaces. Some are turning those frustrations into acts of self-preservation, spending significant money to get outside of the country—away from the people who make them feel that way.

There's also the term "whiteness," which in SJF almost always carries a negative connotation. In SJF, whiteness is not a skin color, it's part of the Force: an oppressive system that pervades society and benefits white people while harming non-white people. Popular websites like Everyday Feminism hold trainings like "Healing from Internalized Whiteness," wording that sends a clear message: it's not that some white people do bad things, *whiteness is bad*.

This sentiment was echoed in a 2021 *New York Times* opinion piece, in which a woman who put up a little library in a Black neighborhood wrote about her feelings when a white couple stopped by one day to check it out:

Instantly, I was flooded with emotions—astonishment, and then resentment, and then astonishment at my resentment. It all converged into a silent scream in my head of, Get off my lawn!...What I resented was not this specific couple. It was their whiteness, and my feelings of helplessness at not knowing how to maintain the integrity of a Black space that I had created.

What would typically be considered intolerable language about race in modern America is perfectly tolerable within SJF. Meanwhile, as the tolerance line has moved "up" regarding treatment toward white people, the line has moved down for racism going in the other direction.

Take the microaggression. Coined by psychiatrist Chester Pierce in 1970, the term was popularized by counseling psychologist and diversity training specialist Derald Wing Sue in a 2007 paper. Sue defines racial microaggressions as "brief and commonplace daily verbal, behavioral, or environmental indignities, whether intentional or unintentional, that communicate hostile, derogatory, or negative racial slights and insults toward people of color." He includes a sampling of what would qualify. Here are a few:

"Where are you from?"
"You are so articulate."
"I don't see color."*
"America is a melting pot."
"There is only one race, the human race."
"I'm not racist, I have several Black friends."
"I believe the most qualified person should get the job."
Mistaking a person of color for a service person.
Asking an Asian person to help with a math or science problem.

The same narrative that defends overt racism toward whites inconsistently maintains that minor insensitivities qualify as a form of bigotry.

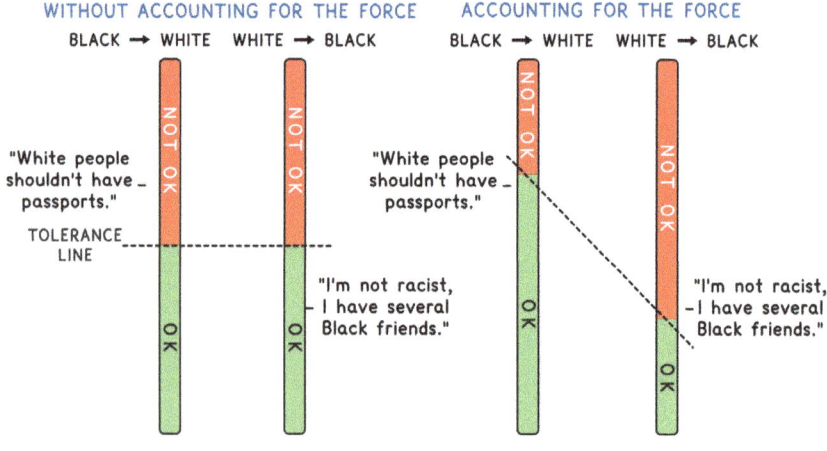

---

* To SJF activists, colorblindness is the exact wrong goal. To be colorblind, they believe, is to accept and ignore the Force instead of fighting against it—to turn a blind eye not just to color but to the struggles faced by people of color.

Social Justice Fundamentalism views the Force like a one-way physics vector that factors into the equation in both cases. Just as the Force "subtracts" harm from the behavior of oppressed people directed at privileged people, it "adds" harm to the words and actions privileged people emit toward oppressed people. So what might normally be considered overt racism, minus the Force, becomes tolerable, while what might seem like a minor faux pas, plus the Force, becomes an intolerable act.

This explains certain news stories that may otherwise seem perplexing. Like the time a Gap ad drew outrage because, amid a group of photos of little kids hanging out in different poses, one showed a white girl resting her elbow on the head of a younger Black girl. While this may not seem problematic to many people, the [elbow + Force] sum pushed the ad into intolerable territory for SJF activists. (After the ensuing criticism, the Gap apologized and withdrew the ad.)

Or a public feud in 2015, when pop singer Taylor Swift tweeted the following at rapper Nicki Minaj:

> I've done nothing but love & support you. It's unlike you to pit women against each other. Maybe one of the men took your slot.

I'll leave it to Taylor and Nicki fans to get to the bottom of all that. But what caught my eye was a paper about the incident by two professors, Judy L. Isaksen and Nahed Eltantawy. They wrote:

> By unpacking Swift's message through the lens of microaggressive theory, we find that her tweet is riddled with unconscious microinsults and sadly exemplifies the extent of her blinding white privilege as well as the oppressive nature of her postfeminist sensibilities.

In a chapter of *White Fragility* called "White Women's Tears," Robin DiAngelo recounts a staff meeting she led, where she explained to the white women in the room why crying in the meeting would be unacceptable:

> As the meeting started, I told my fellow white participants that if they felt moved to tears, they should please leave the room... there is a long historical backdrop of Black men being tortured

and murdered because of a white woman's distress, and we white women bring these histories with us. Our tears trigger the terrorism of this history, particularly for African Americans.

In a passage from her 2021 book, *Nice Racism*, DiAngelo criticizes the act of white smiling, arguing that "over-smiling allows white people to mask an anti-Blackness that is foundational to our very existence as white."

For DiAngelo, [tears + the Force] and [smiling + the Force] are both intolerable.

A cousin of the microaggression is the phenomenon of cultural appropriation. Many people would agree that it's good to be sensitive about objects and symbols that are sacred to certain cultures, and that treating those objects with mockery or disrespect (or claiming credit for them) is not a kind thing to do. Many would also argue that this is worse when a historically powerful population in a society does this to a sacred object of a historically marginalized population. In a multiethnic country like the US, this is obviously a super complicated issue with very blurry lines.

But for SJF activists, privileged groups getting anywhere *near* sacred objects of oppressed groups will spark outrage. Like in 2018, when a photo of a white girl wearing a traditional Chinese dress to her prom caused an internet uproar. Or in 2020, when the pop singer Adele posted a photo of herself with Bantu knots in her hair and a Jamaican flag bikini top while at a festival celebrating Black culture, which was met with a storm of backlash. In SJF, *sacred object* becomes *any object*. *Mockery or disrespect* becomes *any form of usage*. Because they are adding the Force into the equation.

Innocence and Guilt

Women have spent a huge part of the past—in the US and nearly everywhere else—living under a slanted seesaw. For centuries, women have been prohibited from learning how to read, attending university, voting, and entering the workplace. They've been treated like lower caste members within their own marriages, expected to "honor and obey" their husbands and to endure marital physical abuse that for a long time was largely considered tolerable (and legal) behavior. Women have suffered at the hands of cultural norms that believed "boys will be boys" and that accepted a certain level of sexual assault and demeaning harassment at work and in public as par for the course.

Thanks in part to a long history of progressive activism, these conditions have improved considerably, while modern movements continue to push Western societies closer to true gender equality.

But again, Social Justice Fundamentalism views it differently. These activists don't believe gender equality is anywhere near being achieved, or even possible at all, as they see today's Western women as victims of the Force (in this case, "the patriarchy"). As such, they apply the same kinds of tolerance double standards around gender as they do around race.

In many illiberal Power Games societies of the past (and present), justice has worked like this: for less powerful people, the rule is "guilty because accused" or "guilty because of who you are," while for more powerful people it is "automatically innocent." In other words, the rule in a dispute was "believe powerful people."

In the Liberal Games, justice systems were built to level the legal playing field. When a conflict occurred in the US, all parties, regardless of who they were, would be subject to the same due process and given a fair trial.

In a perfect liberal justice system, no one would be punished unfairly, and no guilty deed would go unpunished. But no justice system will ever be perfect, and it's critical to prevent innocent people from being unfairly punished. So in liberal societies, the accused are given the benefit of the doubt—they're presumed innocent until proven guilty.

At least that's the part written in pen. At times in US history, the justice system has been overwritten with invisible ink. The acquittal of Emmett Till's killers suggests that in an interracial conflict in the Jim Crow South, the real rule was "believe white people."

Women have spent a lot of time on the losing side of the justice equation. Accusations of rape and sexual abuse often lack hard evidence, which has left many female victims not being believed and many men being given the benefit of the doubt. Historically, these kinds of cases have been closer to "believe men" than should be the case in a just system.

Liberal Social Justice has launched movement after movement aimed at leveling the justice seesaw. But here again, SJF aims to remedy one form of double standards by applying new double standards in the reverse direction. When it comes to rape and assault, instead of trying to figure out ways to get every case right, the SJF mantra has been: "believe women." In an article in *The Atlantic*, Helen Lewis writes:

"Believe women" was intended to capture an undeniable truth: Sexual harassment and sexual assault are so endemic in society that they make the coronavirus look like a rare tropical disease. False allegations do exist, but they are extremely uncommon.... When thousands of women tell us that there is a problem with sexual aggression in our society, we should believe them. That broad truth, however, tells us nothing about the merits of any individual case. And as my colleague Megan Garber has written, "Believe women" has evolved into "Believe all women," or "Automatically believe women." This absolutism is wrong, unhelpful, and impossible to defend. The slogan should have been "Don't dismiss women," "Give women a fair hearing," or even "Due process is great."

Rather than try to level the justice seesaw, "believe women"—or, sometimes, "believe all women"—*flips* the seesaw in the other direction to apply a counterforce.

Now and Then

At college in the early 2000s, at a Halloween party, I remember seeing a white person I knew coated in brown face paint, as part of an elaborate Mr. T costume. I didn't think much of it at the time.

Today, I know that blackface was a trademark feature of nineteenth- and early twentieth-century minstrel shows, where white actors would paint their faces black and act out denigrating racial stereotypes, received by raucous laughter from all-white audiences.

But while a large portion of my own schooling focused on the racist history of the US, it wasn't until sometime in the 2010s that I learned about the troubling history of blackface. Over the past decade, as blackface has become a major topic in Western countries, I and many others have become educated about its meaning. With today's awareness about blackface, that Mr. T portrayal would be an open defiance of a widespread taboo and a dismissal of the well-known reasons for the taboo. But I don't look back to that Halloween party and think, *Wow, that person was an awful racist—who knew!* I look back and assume that they shared my ignorance and, in light of what they now know, wouldn't consider repeating the costume today.

This kind of thing happens a lot in a rapidly changing society. Much of what's considered racist or misogynist or homophobic today was broadly culturally acceptable in the past. As the old saying goes, *autres temps, autres mœurs*. Other times, other customs. While it's certainly admirable to have been ahead of your time on a moral issue, punishing or disgracing someone for saying or doing something in the past that was prevalent at that time but considered taboo today makes little sense.

As an example, it's easy to imagine a future in which eating animals is widely considered an unspeakably vile act. In that world, with that moral embedded in everyone's consciousness, eating animals would probably become very uncommon—something done by only the most morally bankrupt people. But if those future people looked back at our times and assumed that everyone who ate meat in the 2020s must have been morally bankrupt, that wouldn't really make sense. Even if the harm of meat-eating practices is the same across time, the people engaging in those practices should be judged with their times in mind.

In some cases, SJF activists agree with this logic. In 1958, a student wrote to Martin Luther King Jr. with this question:

> I am a boy, but I feel about boys the way I ought to feel about girls. I don't want my parents to know about me. What can I do? Is there any place where I can go for help?

To which King responded:

> Your problem is not at all an uncommon one. However, it does require careful attention. The type of feeling that you have toward boys is probably not an innate tendency, but something that has been culturally acquired. Your reasons for adopting this habit have now been consciously suppressed or unconsciously repressed. Therefore, it is necessary to deal with this problem by getting back to some of the experiences and circumstances that lead to the habit. In order to do this I would suggest that you see a good psychiatrist who can assist you in bringing to the forefront of conscience all of those experiences and circumstances that lead to the habit.

The LGBTQ website PinkNews defends King with the same logic I used above:

Though Dr. King's response may seem ill-informed by modern standards, his advice to the boy is remarkably calm and polite, given the fears and active scaremongering about gay people at the time. The rights activist was tragically assassinated in 1968, one year before the Stonewall riots birthed the gay rights movement—so we will never know his true considered feelings on the matter.

In other words, *autres temps, autres mœurs*.

But when the past actions are by someone in a privileged group, the SJF mindset abandons "other times, other customs" in favor of "other times, judged by *today's* customs"—a stance summarized by *New York Times* writer Jamelle Bouie in 2019:

> Blackface is so thoroughly associated with the worst of American racism that we should expect immediate condemnation of politicians and public figures who have any association with it, even if it's a decades-old offense.

According to this framing, the student I saw in blackface, regardless of the context of the time when it happened, should be haunted by the incident today and forever forward. This is the sentiment behind recent uproars about decades-old blackface offenses, as politicians, actors, talk show hosts, and musicians have all come under fire.

• • •

We talked earlier about the headline test as a way to measure moral consistency. The kinds of double standards we've just looked at—around language, judgment, forgiveness—leave SJF activists with the same headline difficulties as the white person in 1955 Mississippi. If shown a set of headlines that only referred to Person A and Person B, without the parties' identities provided, SJF activists would be stuck in the "need more info" camp, not knowing how outraged to be.[*] Looking at it that way, SJF morality might seem like the picture of low-rungness.

SJF activists would probably counter that what I'm calling double standards are in fact a step in the right direction—a necessary corrective

---

[*] Modern media seems to be highly aware of this, which is why the race of the parties involved is so often specified in today's headlines.

response to the pervasive systemic injustice we've been referring to as the Force.

The problem with this line of reasoning is that it rides entirely on the Force being everything SJF says it is—but as touched on above, SJF tenets are not exactly scientific. The SJF narrative warrants being treated, at best, as a set of hypotheses. And if the narrative is questionable, then so is the justification for SJF's wide array of moral double standards.

Certainty in the Force is the linchpin of SJF morality. Remove that, and these counterforce measures look less like justice and more like two simultaneous forms of bigotry:

1. Hard Bigotry Against Privileged Groups

Bigotry never feels like bigotry to the person committing it. The left-wing brand of bigotry—the kind directed at people deemed to be powerful and privileged—is especially easy to justify, as it takes some deliberate thinking to remember that the targets can still be victims.* It's the brand of bigotry famously employed by groups like the Maoist Revolutionaries and the Rwandan Hutu militia. But the Nazis—more of a right-wing movement—used it too. Hitler didn't talk about the Jews only as outsider scum, he also talked about them the way left-wing movements talk about their enemies: as powerful, privileged manipulators who were pulling the strings of society in secret, hard-to-see ways.

Saying you're a crusader against hate and oppression doesn't mean that you actually are. Being tolerant, fair, and humane to some people and not others is the definition of intolerance and inhumanity. *Everyone is principled when it comes to people and ideas they're tribally aligned with—a person's moral integrity is judged precisely by how well they apply their principles to the people they can't stand.*

When a person or group fights for "justice," it can mean two things: The first is "justice" as in a fair society. The second is "justice" as in "bring justice to wrongdoers"—aka revenge. Beneath all the SJF language about remedying past discrimination with present discrimination, there's a spirit of revenge in the double standards. Privileged groups have had it too good, for too long, and they deserve to be knocked down a peg today.

---

* The right-wing brand of bigotry, by contrast, is more typically directed at groups deemed to be inferior or outsider.

The effect of this is to punish entire demographic groups as payback for what some people in those demographic groups—often people no longer alive—have done. From a liberal perspective, this is just a new form of injustice, an attempt for two wrongs to make a right.

Some people may roll their eyes at the notion that bigotry against privileged groups does much harm, arguing that these groups are not especially vulnerable. Even if we accepted that, there's another kind of bigotry in play here as well:

2. Soft Bigotry Against Oppressed Groups

Quick story: I was with a bunch of friends recently and we played Pictionary. It was all adults playing except one couple's seven-year-old son who also joined the game. When it was his turn to draw, competing against one of the adults, the unwritten rule was clear: the kid should probably win. So the competing team would go slower than usual to let the other team guess the kid's drawing first. When he did a decent drawing—which was not often—the rule was again clear: praise the shit out of his drawing skills. Anyone who made fun of his drawing the way they would if he were an adult would be an obvious asshole.

Using different rules and lower standards for children makes sense. But when you apply different standards to different demographic groups in a society, you're treating groups of adults like children. Which is awfully patronizing.

This is what some call "the soft bigotry of low expectations."

Helen Pluckrose talks about how she believes this affects women:

Intersectional feminism cultivated a culture of victimhood, negatively impacting all women in society but particularly young women....If [men] call out to us or proposition us, we should be terrified. If obnoxious men attempt to grope us or succeed, we have experienced an appalling sexual assault from which we may never recover. Not only are we oppressed by seemingly all men but by anyone expressing anti-feminist ideas or feminist ones we don't like. More than this, we are rendered "unsafe" by them....It is hard to imagine how women manage to survive leaving the house at all.

We already heard about *White Fragility* author Robin DiAngelo telling her class that white women would not be permitted to cry in front of Black people, because of the trauma it might inflict (not the kind of protection often offered to adults). Here's another of DiAngelo's stories:

I am coaching a small group of white employees on how racism manifests in their workplace. One member of the group, Karen, is upset about a request from Joan, her only colleague of color, to stop talking over her. Karen doesn't understand what talking over Joan has to do with race; she is an extrovert and tends to talk over everyone. I try to explain how the impact is different when we interrupt across race because we bring our histories with us. While Karen sees herself as a unique individual, Joan sees Karen as a white individual. Being interrupted and talked over by white people is not a unique experience for Joan, nor is it separate from the larger cultural context. Karen exclaims, "Forget it! I can't say anything right, so I am going to stop talking!" The episode highlights Karen's white fragility.

Rather than Karen engaging with Joan's ideas the way she would with anyone else's, DiAngelo wants Karen to see a Black woman and think, *Okay, it's a Black woman, don't interrupt her, don't disagree with her, don't make her feel uncomfortable in any way*. In other words, don't be herself when interacting with her. It feels a bit like how you treat a kid playing Pictionary.

Soft bigotry isn't just about how people from marginalized groups are treated—it's also about the standards they're held *to*. Author and Muslim reformer Maajid Nawaz explains this side of things:

The racism of low expectations: to lower those standards when looking at a brown person if a brown person happens to express a level of misogyny, chauvinism, bigotry, or anti-Semitism and yet hold other white people to universal liberal standards. The real victim[s] of that double standard are the minority communities themselves, because by doing so, we limit their horizons; we limit their own ceiling and expectations as to what they aspire to be; we're judging them as somehow that their culture is less civilized; and of course, we are tolerating bigotry within communities and the first victims of that bigotry happen to be those who are weakest from among those communities.

This may feel like a compassionate gesture toward marginalized groups, but really, it's just patronizing. I would never want to live in a country where it was socially acceptable for my particular demographic group to engage in bad behavior. It would make me feel excluded, like I was sitting at society's children's table. And plenty of women, LGBTQ people, and people of color feel the same way.

So yeah

This is why I think Social Justice Fundamentalism is a low-rung ideology. SJF activists wear the same "social justice" uniform worn by Liberal Social Justice activists, but underneath that uniform they're as different as can be. SJF's worldview sees society not as a collection of complex individuals but as a zero-sum struggle of monolithic groups fighting for power. Its core ideas tend to be rigid and unfalsifiable, more dogma than science. Its intellectual immune system enforces conformity and filters for confirmation over truth. It encourages moral hypocrisy and even bigotry in its adherents. From every angle we examine, SJF matches up with the classic characteristics of a low-rung ideology.

Of course, this is just what my hypothesis says. I'm not an expert on politics, progressive activism, or what I'm calling Social Justice Fundamentalism. I've tried hard to stay neutral, but as someone who fervently believes in liberal values, I'm inevitably going to be a bit biased against an ideology that rejects them. From where I'm sitting, I'm bound to have some blind spots when analyzing concepts like standpoint theory and cultural appropriation. Surely, SJF activists would see me as the delusional low-rung one in this discussion. I acknowledge all of this.

But here's the thing: whether I'm off base or on point is beside the point.

As a liberal, I welcome Social Justice Fundamentalism into the marketplace of ideas. A rich marketplace of ideas is made rich by a wide variety of ideas and worldviews. SJF is, without a doubt, a radical left ideology, and the *job* of the radical left is to be intensely critical of the status quo and skeptical about traditions and institutions. In the case of SJF, I don't doubt that some elements of what I've been calling the Force are very real, and it's a good thing that SJF activists continually push more moderate progressives to keep their attention on those possibilities.

And even *if* I'm totally right and SJF is indeed a not-so-productive, low-rung ideology—even that's okay. Messy liberal democracies will always be home to low-rung movements. Not only does the Constitution not forbid tribal Echo Chambers—*it actively protects them*. In a liberal country, any group can believe any damn thing they want and that's okay…as long as they don't *force* their views on anyone else. Any group can make rigid Echo Chamber rules about what can and cannot be said *within* their social community…as long as membership in that community is entirely *voluntary*.

As long as a group is abiding by the sacred liberal rule when it comes to dealings with people and groups outside itself—*live and let live*—they're no problem for a liberal democracy. It's when a group breaks that code, trying to forcefully expand into places they shouldn't, that we have a problem.

Low-rung movements are inevitable in liberal democracies, but when they become forcefully expansionist *golems*, it's like a benign tumor that starts to metastasize. It's then that a society's high-rung immune system is obligated to wake up and stop the expansion.

	THINKING	MORALS	TACTICS	
HIGH-RUNG	seek truth	moral consistency	fair play, persuasion	
LOW-RUNG	seek confirmation	moral hypocrisy	cheating, coercion	

My big problem with Social Justice Fundamentalism isn't the ideology itself. It's what its scholars and activists started to do sometime around 2013—when they began to wield a cudgel that's not supposed to have any place in a country like the US.

INTERLUDE

THE TALE OF KING MUSTACHE

Once upon a time, in a land far, far away, there was a little kingdom called Hypothetica, ruled by the benevolent King Longbeard. Hypothetica was known for its vibrant discourse. Citizens held salons in teahouses to discuss and debate issues of philosophy, literature, history, and politics. People visited the kingdom's amphitheaters to hear prominent intellectuals speak or to see a play or a concert by one of the kingdom's many artists. At the center of the kingdom was the grand library, which held thousands of books on almost any topic you can imagine.

But one day, King Longbeard died, leaving the throne to his son, King Mustache.

During the early days of his reign, King Mustache grew frustrated that the crowds didn't cheer for him as loudly as they had cheered when his father would address them. He heard whispers that people missed the days when his father was king, and he even heard one rumor that some people were mocking his mustache. He grew more and more insecure with every week.

Finally, King Mustache decided to take matters into his own hands by enacting a new policy. He announced it on the palace steps to a great crowd: "Anyone who is heard criticizing King Mustache or mocking his mustache will be put to death."

The crowd stirred uncomfortably, and a few people cried out: "That is not how we do things in Hypothetica!" King Mustache grew red in the face and yelled: "Guards, put everyone who just protested to death!"

The king's guards were taken aback by the order. They all knew that none of them wanted to carry out the order, and they all knew that if they stood together in refusal, the king would have no choice but to rescind the order.

But no guard wanted to be the first to speak out and refuse the order—because they knew that if no one else joined them, they would be executed along with the dissenters. After a few tense seconds of silence, someone finally spoke. "Hang the traitors!" shouted a junior member of the king's guard. Terrified of being seen as unsupportive of the king, others quickly joined in, calling out, "Hang the traitors!"

One hour later, the five most vocal protesters were hanging in the public square. After that, no one criticized King Mustache.

A few months later, the king decided to send his army on a crusade to conquer the neighboring kingdom, Neverlandia. This, he believed, would make everyone realize how great and powerful a king he was. He announced the plan on the palace steps.

"But we're a peaceful kingdom! We don't attack our neighbors!" yelled a shopkeeper from the crowd.

King Mustache grew red in the face. "Hang that man!" he ordered. After a second or two of silence, the king's guard seized the man and strung him up in the square. That was the last time anyone dared defy King Mustache.

Soon, all the talks in the amphitheater were about how great King Mustache was. The plays and concerts were all about the glory of the wars he was waging. The king's guards burned all the library books the king disapproved of. The bustling teahouses grew quiet, as most people chose to keep their conversations to the privacy of their own homes.

A portrait of King Mustache was placed in every classroom in Hypothetica, and for years to come, students would read tales about how their brave king saved Hypothetica from being conquered by the evil Neverlandians.

• • •

Putting the Higher Mind and Primitive Mind aside for a minute, let's break every human into two parts another way: their Outer Self and their Inner Self. The Inner Self represents what a person thinks; the Outer Self represents what a person *says*. If we take any given topic, we can depict each of their viewpoints by where they're standing on the Idea Spectrum, and by the color of their head:

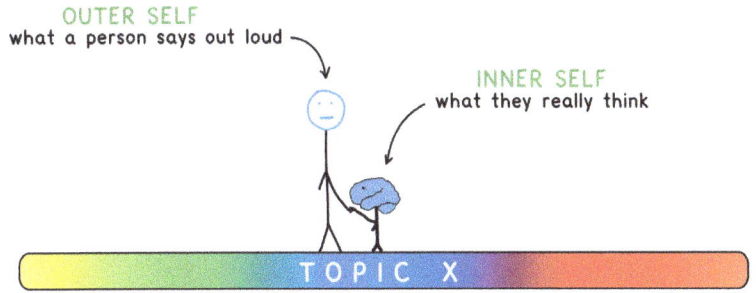

We can combine these using a shorthand notation:

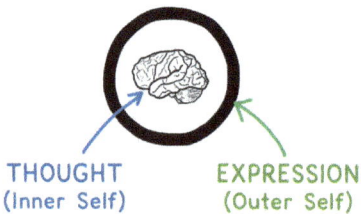

And we can color these to show what a person is thinking (brain color) and what they're saying (ring color). When a person is being honest and saying what they really think, the two colors are the same, allowing the thoughts of the Inner Self to pass unimpeded through the Outer Self and out into the world.

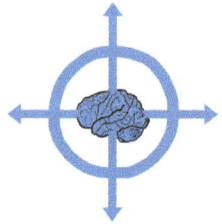

So, for example, when three people are having a conversation about a topic and everyone is saying what they really think, their brains link together into a three-brain thinking system:

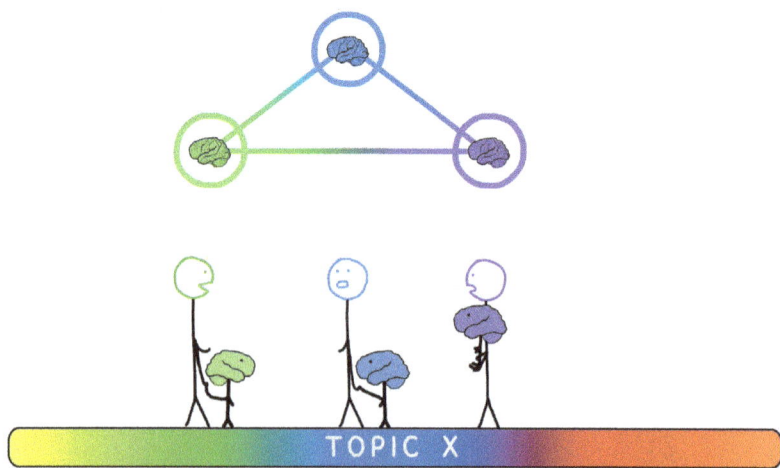

We can use this system to visualize the story of Hypothetica. On a particularly controversial topic, the Inner Selves of the Hypothetican citizens might have looked something like this:

We can organize these Inner Selves by stacking them along the Idea Spectrum. Smoothing it out gives us a visual representation of what Hypotheticans think about Topic X. Let's call it the **Thought Pile**.

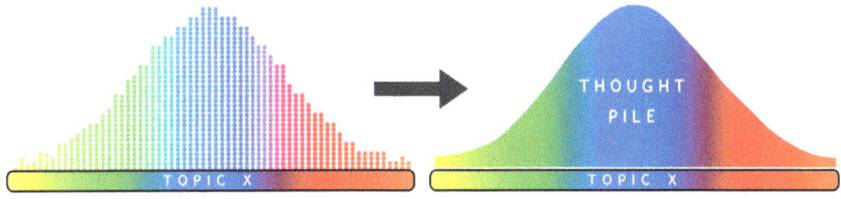

In Chapter 1, we saw how human brains can have emergent properties, combining together into larger superbrains called genies. This only happens when the brains actually *connect*, which they do by way of expression. King Longbeard encouraged open discourse, allowing Hypothetican citizens to combine their brains together into a big Hypothetican genie.

Small conversations alone can't make a very large genie. Hypothetica's public venues—its teahouses and amphitheaters—help meld the kingdom's disparate conversations together into a single larger conversation.

If the Thought Pile depicts what citizens are thinking, we can use a **Speech Curve** to illustrate what they're *saying*. The more a certain viewpoint is being expressed, in conversations and in public venues, the higher the Speech Curve over that point in the Idea Spectrum. So when people are all saying what they're thinking about a given topic, the Speech Curve matches the shape of the Thought Pile, sitting neatly on top of it:

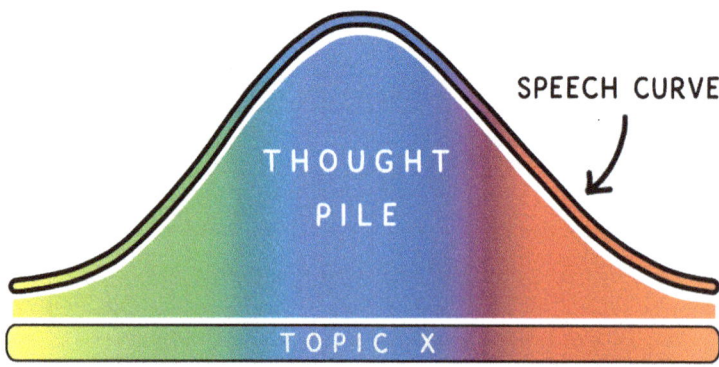

King Mustache was especially unhappy about one particular topic of conversation. His decree that criticizing him was illegal was his attempt to lay down an electrified "censorship fence" across the topic that would severely punish anyone who dared to cross it.

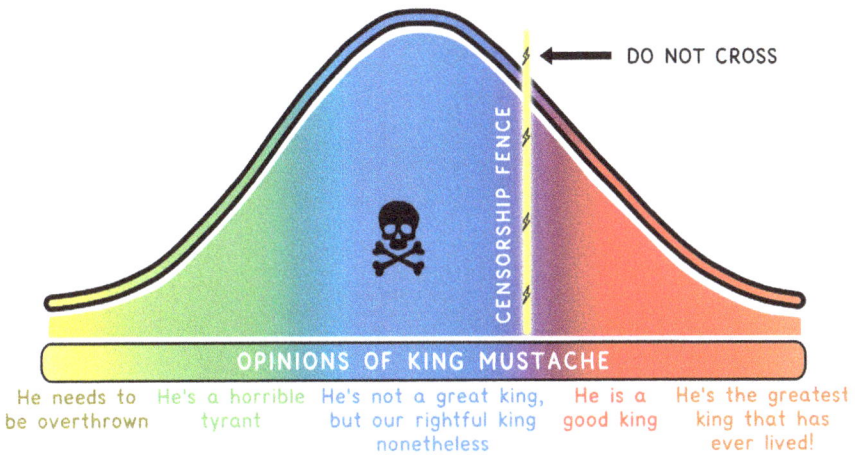

The king's open challenge to the free speech tradition was a pivotal moment of truth in Hypothetica. Would the guards and citizens stand up for that tradition or give in to the king?

Had the police and military stood together against the order, the king's fence would be proven to be but a figment of his imagination. But when the guards carried out the order and people were actually killed, the electric fence—and King Mustache's authority—became very real.

Citizens' Inner Selves could still think freely, but King Mustache's now-very-scary policy kept everyone's Outer Selves contained to the reddish-orange part of the spectrum.

When a person isn't allowed to say what they think, their ideas become quarantined inside their head, isolated from the outside world. From the communal brain perspective, where each individual human mind is a single neuron in a larger brain, it's as if the axons of the neurons have been hijacked, and any real neural communication ceases.

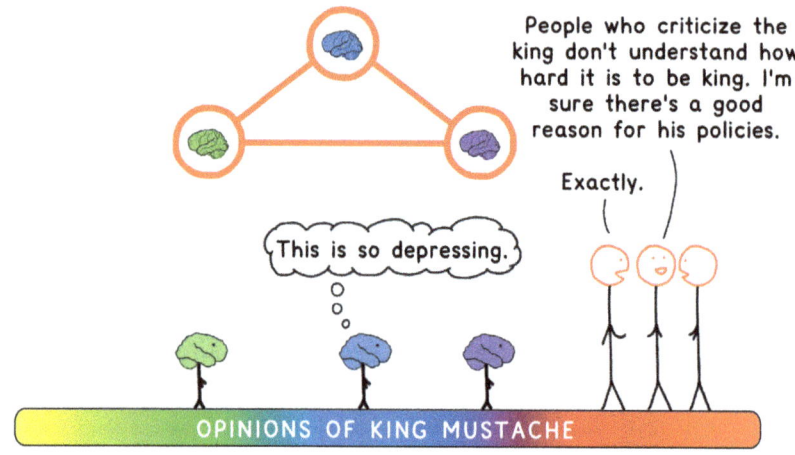

The result was that on the topic of King Mustache's awesomeness, Hypothetica now looked like this:

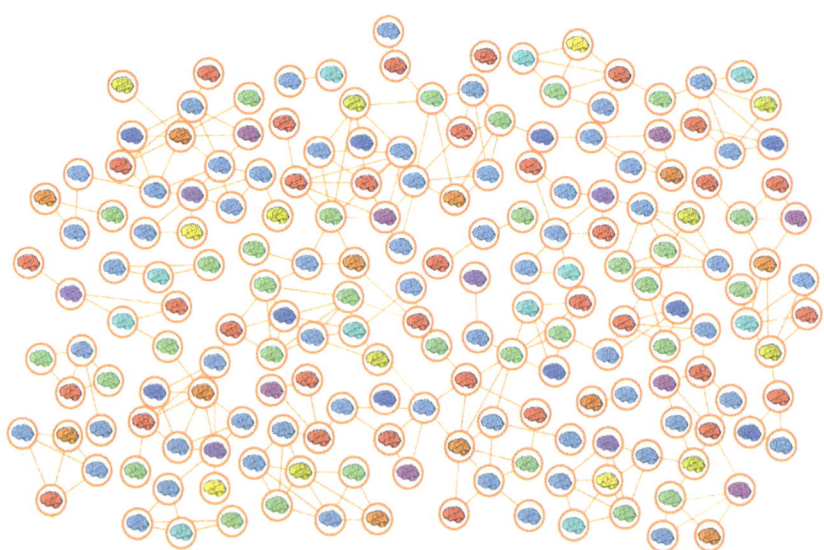

The kingdom's public venues, with the king's cudgel looming over them, also quickly fell in line. With people no longer saying what they were thinking, the Speech Curve separated from the Thought Pile. Silenced areas of the Thought Pile fell dormant, and the kingdom's minds could no longer form a genie. What was once a land of thriving discourse and higher-emergent thinking became a rigid Echo Chamber.

Meanwhile, especially on large platforms, the king's preferred viewpoints were then repeated ad nauseam—receiving a far *brighter* spotlight than public opinion and public interest would normally warrant.

Censorship takes a single region formed by an aligned Thought Pile and Speech Curve and turns it into three regions by generating these two "censorship gaps":

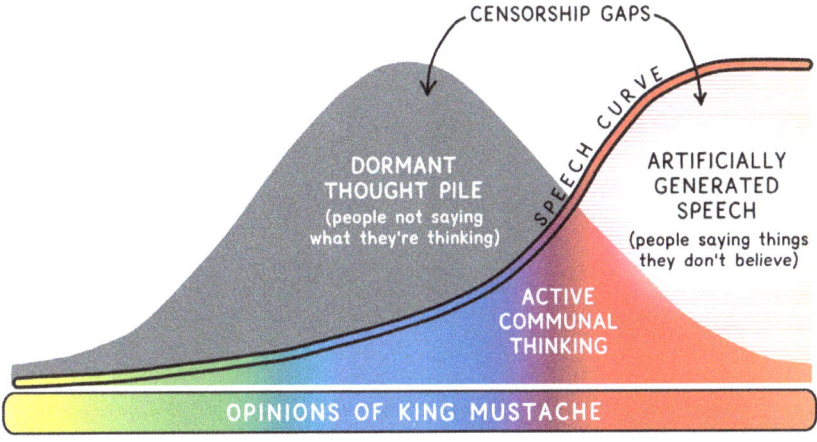

Censorship doesn't have to be airtight to accomplish its goal. For example, a small intimate group might begin to be honest with each other, forming a tiny, undercover Idea Lab within the larger Echo Chamber:

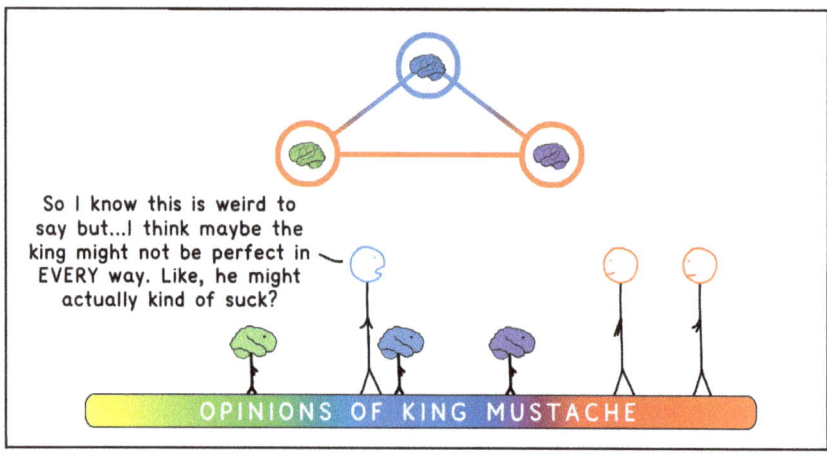

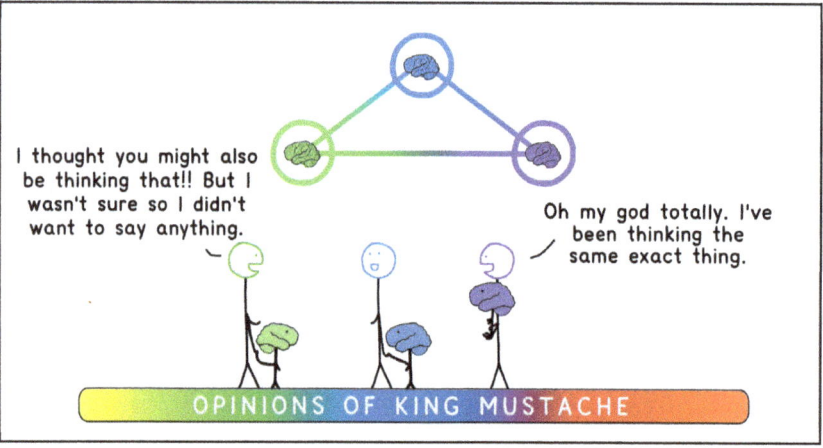

But if a ruler can block ideas from being spoken in more public spaces, forbidden ideas are still *quarantined* within small, isolated pockets. If people will speak openly in private but still abide by the censorship rules in public, they *appear* to everyone else to hold the king's preferred views.

Containing the expression of banned viewpoints to small groups prevents the viewpoints from *traveling* anywhere and gaining any momentum within the national giant's big brain.

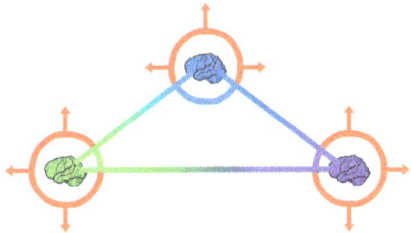

We think of censorship as control over what people can say. But the concept of emergence reminds us that human *giants* only "think" by way of conversation—which means that censorship is really control over what the *giant* can *think*. For a giant, censorship is *mind* control.

If *everyone* spoke out against the king, he wouldn't stand a chance—but that takes a coordinated effort. And if just one person speaks out against the king, they're a traitor and they'll be executed. This traps the populace in a kind of prisoner's dilemma. Without the confidence that everyone will join them in their treason, no one will want to risk speaking out. If someone does speak out, no one will want to join them out of fear that *they'll* be the only one to join in, which would spell their own doom. So even if *every single citizen* wants to overthrow the king, and even if everyone *knows* everyone else wants to overthrow the king, the censorship policies prevent the *giant* itself from being able to act.

And then something else starts to happen.

The illustrations we've been using display a cross section of everyone's head that shows *us* what people are both saying and thinking. But for each citizen, what others are thinking is hidden from sight. So if you're this person—

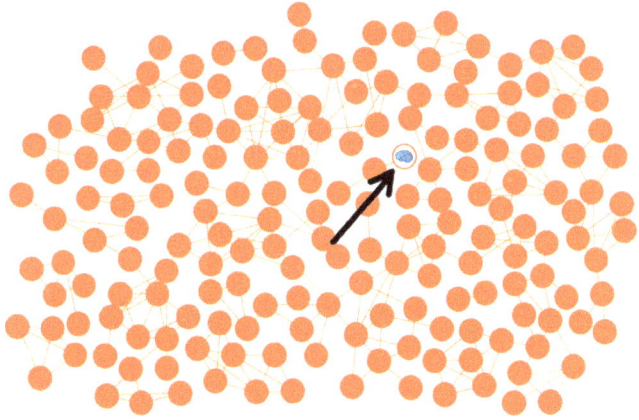

—despite actually being surrounded by tremendous viewpoint diversity, you may start to wonder if you're the only person thinking what you're thinking. Seeing only everyone's orange exterior, you might assume everyone actually believes the orange viewpoint.

A phenomenon that psychologists call "pluralistic ignorance" begins to set in: when no one believes, but everyone *thinks* that everyone believes. Over time, hearing everyone expressing the same viewpoint, people start to doubt their own beliefs and assume that if everyone is saying it, there must be something to it.

As belief in the king's narrative grows, the iron grip of censorship gets even tighter, as believers become loyal soldiers ready to turn in neighbors who speak treason, even in private. Over time, the Thought Pile itself begins to distort.

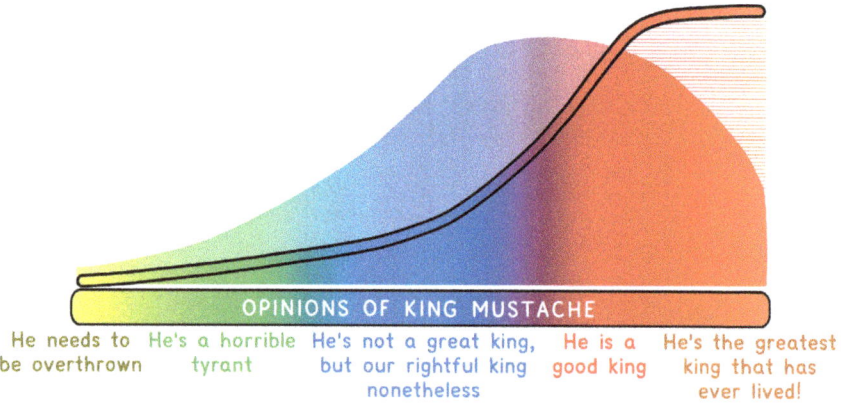

Many young Hypotheticans, raised entirely on the king's version of reality, come to believe wholeheartedly that their king is righteous and his policies noble. They then pass the story into the heads of their own children.

Controlling what people can say controls what the giant can think—which eventually leads to controlling what individuals think. Over time, a superintelligent genie turns into a mindless golem.

This is the true power of censorship. And once a society succumbs to censorship, they can get stuck in it for a long time.

• • •

Throughout human history, clever opportunists have discovered that if you could control what people say, you could write the story people believed. You could dictate the values, the morals, and the customs. You could decide who the good guys were and who the bad guys were. You could create the laws, dole out the rewards, and inflict the penalties. If you could write the narrative, the group became your marionette.

The most effective puppet masters came up with depictions of reality that tapped directly into people's Primitive Minds. Some would stoke fear with stories of imminent danger or invoke rage toward a common enemy to fuel the Primitive Mind's natural fires. Or they might write stories of their own ruthlessness and inflict fear of torture and death on subjects. Others would claim knowledge of the divine in order to bring the afterlife into the picture and drive incentives to astronomical heights.

Stories like these encourage the formation of the low-rung kind of giant: the golem. They activate behaviors like conformity and obedience that make a population easy to control. They ignite psychology like self-sacrifice and out-group dehumanization that are perfect for tyrants trying to win wars for territory and resources.

But none of this works on a giant that can think for itself. The high-rung kind of giant—the genie—is not easily controllable or brainwashable. This, perhaps above all, was the defining insight of the Enlightenment.

FREE SPEECH AND THE MARKETPLACE OF IDEAS

The tale of King Mustache—and so many real-world instances like it—is why the US has the First Amendment:

> Congress shall make no law respecting an establishment of religion, or prohibiting the free exercise thereof; or abridging the

freedom of speech, or of the press; or the right of the people peaceably to assemble, and to petition the Government for a redress of grievances.

Pulled out from the larger group of First Amendment liberties, we see that the American notion of free speech comes down to ten words:

Congress shall make no law abridging the freedom of speech

Congress shall erect no electric fences. Congress shall exercise no mind control over the giant.

These ten critical words mean that speech of any kind is always legal and protected. Well, not speech of *any* kind. Remember the freedom/safety compromise. When speech infringes upon a citizen's *red* circle rights, it's not allowed:

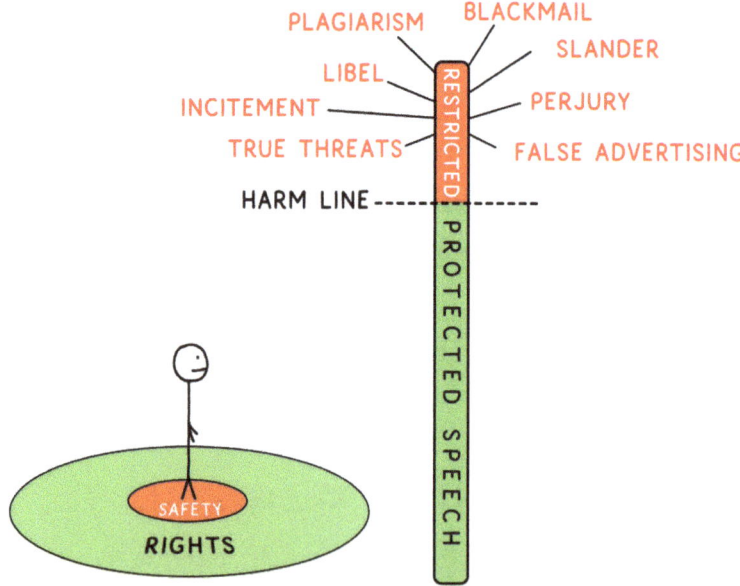

But aside from carefully delineated instances carved out in case law, speech is almost never illegal.

Free speech means that even the most vile and objectionable ideas can be aired freely. This is critical, because governments that enact censorship policies rarely call them "censorship" policies—they usually say they're banning some form of vile or objectionable speech. And so often, what rule-makers happen to find objectionable is criticism of themselves and their policies. The ability to restrict blasphemy is the ability to censor.

In Hypothetica, we saw how the power to censor became the gateway to other kinds of power. That's why free speech is often referred to as not just any right but *the* fundamental right.

Beyond protecting against tyranny, free speech laws open the gates to a dynamic free-speech market—the marketplace of ideas. In the marketplace of ideas, scientists freely do their research, philosophers freely philosophize, activists freely protest, journalists freely report, and artists and comedians freely challenge norms and test the edges of what's socially acceptable. If the market's "supply" is made up of the ideas of millions of free-speaking humans, "demand" consists of millions of free-listening ears. To win the key currency of the market—attention and influence—ideas have to outcompete other ideas in the market.

In the same way that a free economic market has a natural tendency to push bad products to the fringes while elevating the best, the marketplace of ideas serves as a vast information filter. Ideas are stripped naked and analyzed from every angle. This exposes and embarrasses false or unwise ideas and prevents them from spreading too widely. The marketplace of ideas is messy, and it doesn't always succeed at sorting right from wrong and good from bad, but it's a far better system than the alternative: allowing the most powerful people to decide what's true and what's good.

The marketplace of ideas is like a giant communal brain that allows the country to think for itself and, over time, point the country in the direction of truth and progress. The national genie.

HOW THE AMERICAN BRAIN LEARNS

On any given topic, at any given point in time, there will be a wide range of what people believe to be true or good. But typically, the ideas that carry the most power will be those held by the most people—the mainstream ideas.

The mainstream ideas are taught in schools, dictate broad cultural norms, and show up as slogans in political campaigns. Even though plenty of individual citizens will disagree with them, the ideas at the top of the Thought Pile are what the big *communal* brain "thinks" at any given point in time.

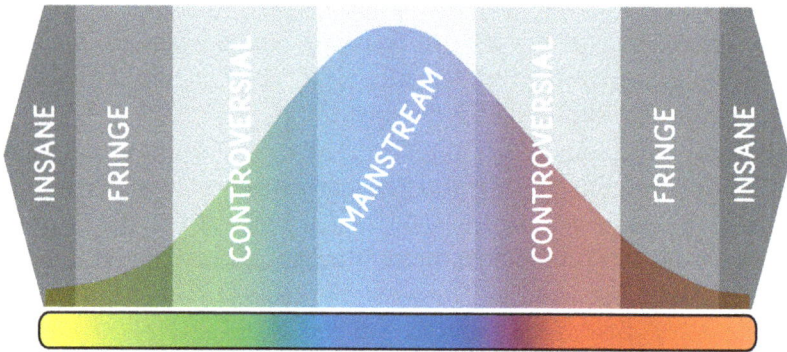

The combination of free speech and representative government means one person with a good idea can freely speak out about it and start a *mind-changing movement* that, if successful enough, can eventually change the big brain's mind and drive the country's evolution. This is how, over time, the giant national brain can make its own decisions, learn new things, and grow wiser.

Take the history of smoking. The modern cigarette was invented in the 1880s and exploded in popularity in the US in the first half of the twentieth century. Americans went from smoking an average of fifty cigarettes per adult per year in 1880 to over two thousand by the mid-1940s. Throughout these decades, it was a mainstream view among Americans that smoking was a relatively harmless habit.

The communal US brain believed that smoking was harmless—a narrative that was continually promoted through mainstream channels. Ads portraying cigarettes in a positive, beneficial light were everywhere. Cigarettes were culturally cool and commonly associated with movie stars and other icons. You could light up in airplanes, restaurants, offices, hospitals, and most other places.

But there was another viewpoint out in more controversial territory:

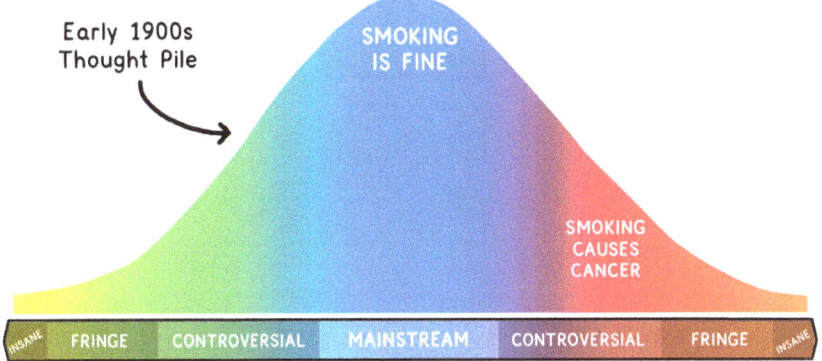

Early in the twentieth century, research began to appear linking smoking to all kinds of health problems. And people began to talk about it.

People don't like having their beliefs challenged or their favorite habits disparaged. Companies profiting from the status quo *really* don't like alternative viewpoints. So, the new anti-smoking position was attacked from all sides.

For a while, the attacks were effective. Forty years after the early evidence surfaced linking smoking to cancer, a 1954 Gallup survey found that 60 percent of Americans answered "no" or "unsure" to the question "Does smoking cause lung cancer?" But the marketplace of ideas eventually separates the truth needle from the haystack of falsehoods, and the anti-smoking voices didn't fade away—they got louder.

In 1964, the US Surgeon General issued the first public report on smoking, outlining the negative effects. As evidence piled up about the dangers of secondhand smoke, more people in the marketplace began to protest cigarette smoking being legal in indoor spaces. Parents whose minds had changed about cigarettes became more likely to prohibit their children from smoking. Politicians, noticing the shifting tide of public opinion, began to outlaw cigarette ads and ban smoking in enclosed spaces like restaurants and airplanes.

As the big US giant's answer to "Does smoking cause lung cancer?" shifted from "no" to "yes," the percentage of Americans who smoked dropped from 47 percent in 1953 to 14 percent in 2017.

The "smoking causes cancer" advocates conquered the Thought Pile by *pulling* it toward their viewpoint—and in the process, pulling the Thought Pile *away* from the "smoking is fine" viewpoint.

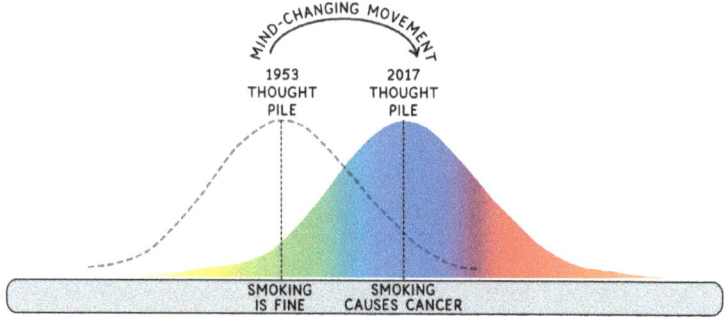

As the Thought Pile slid, so did culture, politics, laws, and behavior. All of this happened against the tremendous force of a large industry's fight for survival. The newer narrative had truth on its side, and in a free marketplace of ideas, truth usually prevails.

The same process that makes the national giant more knowledgeable can also drive its moral growth.

In 1958, 96 percent of Americans disapproved of interracial marriage. The 4 percent who approved were on the far fringe:

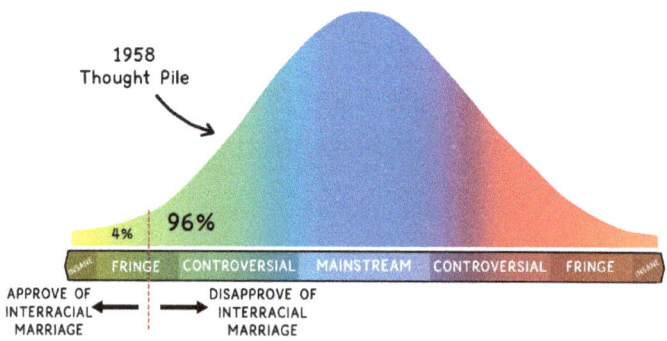

In 1958, almost everyone in the US bought into the "interracial marriage is immoral" viewpoint. Today, most of us see that fringe 4 percent as the wise ones, but this was anything but obvious at the time. Without free speech, that extremely unpopular viewpoint may have never been publicly expressed.

Instead, over the next half century, this small group of fringe activists shouted their unpopular views into the marketplace of ideas, igniting a mind-changing movement that spread until the change of mind had reached the center of the US giant's consciousness.

U.S. Approval of Marriage Between Black People and White People, 1958–2021
Do you approve or disapprove of marriage between Black people and White people?

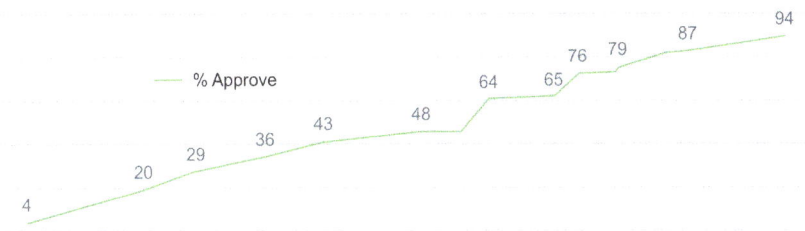

Source: Gallup

When the national brain changes its mind, politicians follow. The Overton window is a newish term—named after late political scientist Joseph Overton—but it's a concept as old as democracy itself: that for any political issue at any given time, there's a range of ideas the public will accept as politically reasonable. Positions outside of that range will be considered by most voters to be too radical or too backward to be held by a serious candidate.

It's as if the Thought Pile is filled up to a point with water, and politicians who venture beyond the Overton window will drown.

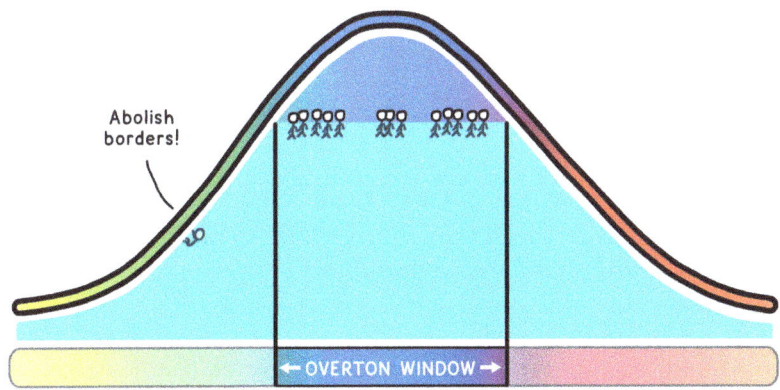

As the national brain's views evolve and the Thought Pile oozes its way along the Idea Spectrum, the Overton window is carried with it. When this happens, politicians have no choice but to adapt to the times or lose relevance. We can see this in the history of interracial marriage:

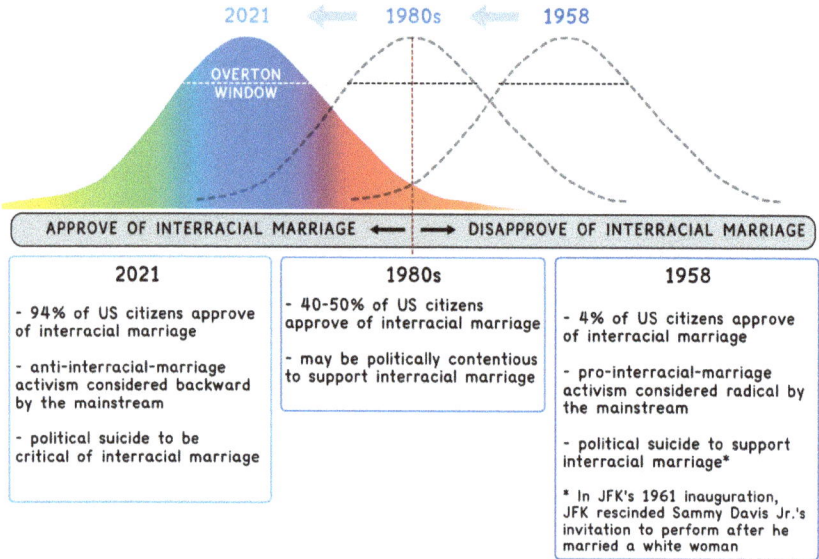

While most political squabbling happens within the Overton window, big-picture change is driven by a second set of battles, over *exactly where the edges of the window lie*. If promoting Policy A would mean political suicide, it isn't even eligible for debate. If its proponents want their chance to duke it out in the political ring, they first have to figure out how to shake that stigma.

We can see this in the history of gay rights in the US. In his book *Kindly Inquisitors*, author and activist Jonathan Rauch describes what it was like to be gay in the US in 1960:

> Gay Americans were forbidden to work for the government; forbidden to obtain security clearances; forbidden to serve in the military. They were arrested for making love, even in their own homes; beaten and killed on the streets; entrapped and arrested by the police for sport; fired from their jobs. They were joked about, demeaned, and bullied as a matter of course; forced to live by a code of secrecy and lies, on pain of opprobrium and unemployment; witch-hunted by anti-Communists, Christians, and any politician or preacher who needed a scapegoat; condemned as evil by moralists and as sick by scientists; portrayed as sinister and simpering by Hollywood; perhaps worst of all, rejected and condemned, at the most vulnerable time of life, by their own parents.

In a dictatorship, gay rights advocacy, considered deeply offensive to most people in 1960, would probably have been censored. But in a country that protected free speech, Rauch talks about how things changed:

> In ones and twos at first, then in streams and eventually cascades, gays talked. They argued. They explained. They showed. They confronted....As gay people stepped forward, liberal science engaged. The old anti-gay dogmas came under critical scrutiny as never before. "Homosexuals molest and recruit children"; "homosexuals cannot be happy"; "homosexuals are really heterosexuals"; "homosexuality is unknown in nature": The canards collapsed with astonishing speed.
>
> What took place was not just empirical learning but also moral learning. How can it be wicked to love? How can it be noble to lie? How can it be compassionate to reject your own children? How can it be kind to harass and taunt?...Gay people were asking straight people to test their values against logic, against compassion, against life. Gradually, then rapidly, the criticism had its effect. You cannot be gay in America today and doubt that moral learning is real and that the open society fosters it.

By 2008, the US brain had given homosexuality a lot of reflection, and it had changed its mind considerably on the topic. But it hadn't quite changed its mind on gay *marriage* yet. Most likely sensing that the pro-gay-marriage stance was still below political sea level, Democratic presidential candidates Barack Obama and Hillary Clinton played it safe:

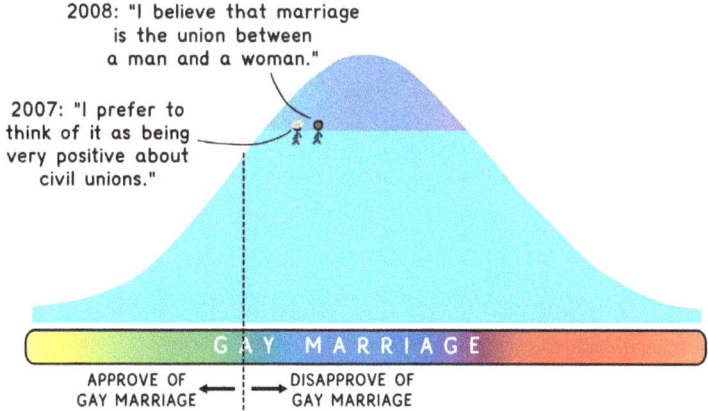

But a mind-changing movement had caught fire, and the national Thought Pile was on the move. Only four years later, things had shifted. And suddenly, Obama and Clinton's views on gay marriage had "evolved":

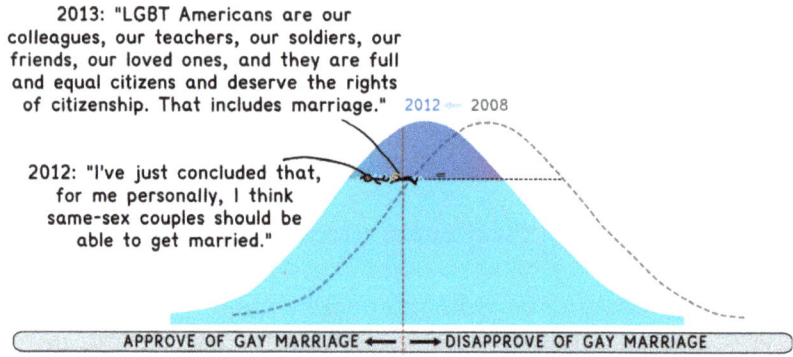

The Supreme Court had undergone the same "change of heart," and in 2015, they made it mandatory for states to recognize gay marriage.

Oppression has been a regular feature of human societies since the dawn of time, and in the Power Games, the primary tool to fight oppression has been violence. Free speech offers a better way. The rich are protected and empowered by their money, the elite by their connections, the majority by their vote, while minority views often end up left out. But free speech gives the powerless a voice—the ability to spark a mind-changing movement that gains so much momentum, it moves our beliefs and our cultural norms, which in turn moves the Overton window, which moves policy, and then law.

Throughout American history, free speech has been much more than protection against tyranny. It's been the country's brain, its compass, and its conscience.

Of course, a country like America isn't quite as simple as I've presented it here. Let's not forget about the lumbering golems of Political Disney World.

POCKETS OF HYPOTHETICA

While all Americans live in a free speech country, not all Americans enjoy the full benefits of free speech. Laws like the First Amendment make free speech possible, but only within the right *culture* does the freedom come to fruition. What's needed is an environment where open discourse is "how we do things here." Idea Lab culture is the critical second piece that completes the free speech puzzle.

In Echo Chamber cultures—where harsh social penalties are imposed for saying the wrong thing—freedom of speech all but vanishes, along with the presence of the marketplace of ideas. In countries like the US, you're so free that you're *free to be unfree*, if you so choose. Echo Chambers are like mini-dictatorships inside a larger free speech zone—a place where the culture is playing the role of King Mustache.

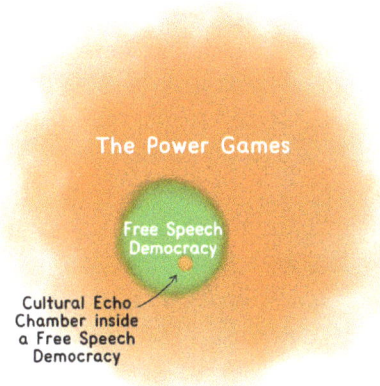

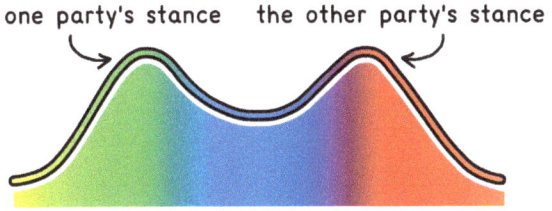

Political Echo Chambers are like frozen spots in the giant national brain—places where the flow of thinking isn't driven by open discourse but by allegiance to certain political narratives. This distorts the marketplace, on hot political topics, into a less efficient camel shape.

The science and business worlds can advance quickly because bad ideas fail quickly. Political Echo Chambers (aka political golems) allow bad ideas to live on for longer than they would in a more typical marketplace. With so many voters locked into the major low-rung narratives, politicians have to spend a lot of their energy catering to those narratives. Political golems make the national brain less intelligent, less adaptable, less rational, and less wise.

But while political golems can slow progress, free speech means they cannot stop it. Earlier, we talked about how low-rung thinkers can exist within an Idea Lab. They may not be on the high rungs themselves, but in an Idea Lab, they're forced by the culture to play by high-rung rules. Free speech laws are a national version of Idea Lab culture. They ensure that the inevitable golems in the country, though not on the high rungs themselves, are forced to "live and let live" in their dealings with other giants, preventing them from messing with the marketplace of ideas and hindering the formation of supergenies. Free speech means that no one person, or golem, can play King Mustache with the country by determining the narrative it believes. The US is still driven by a narrative, but that narrative is ultimately written, and continually edited, by the American people.

At least that's how it normally works. In our modern age of hypercharged tribalism, this system is under strain. Across the political spectrum, golems that don't represent mainstream thought have, in recent years, become unusually powerful—powerful enough to threaten the working order of the national communal brain.

Which brings us back to Social Justice Fundamentalism.

CHAPTER 6

HOW TO CONQUER A COLLEGE

No tendency is quite so strong in human nature as the desire to lay down rules of conduct for other people.
—WILLIAM HOWARD TAFT

In 2017, a small college in Washington State called Evergreen State was briefly all over the news. Every April since the 1970s, the campus had held a "Day of Absence"—a day when a number of students and faculty of color voluntarily refrained from showing up on campus in order to highlight their contributions to the college. Bret Weinstein, a professor at the school and a long-time advocate of social justice causes, says he was always supportive of the spirit behind the annual event.

But in 2017, organizers of the event announced a new twist. For that year's Day of Absence, it would be the white students and faculty invited to stay "absent" and attend off-campus programming, while people of color would come to campus to hold seminars on race, equity, inclusion, and privilege.

Weinstein was like, "Wait what? No" and sent out an email to campus faculty protesting the flipped Day of Absence. He said:

> There is a huge difference between a group or coalition deciding to voluntarily absent themselves from a shared space in order to highlight their vital and under-appreciated roles...and a group or coalition encouraging another group to go away. The first is a forceful call to consciousness which is, of course, crippling to the logic of oppression. The second is a show of force, and an act of oppression in and of itself....On a college campus, one's right to speak—or to be—must never be based on skin color.

His email quickly made the rounds, and not long after, a large group of students confronted him outside his classroom, accusing him of being a white supremacist, demanding his resignation, and interrupting his attempt to explain his position by chanting, "Hey hey! Ho ho! Bret Weinstein has got to go!"

Later that day, hundreds of students met with the school president about the controversy, discussing their grievances with explanations like "fuck you and fuck the police!" and "whiteness is the most violent fucking system to ever breathe!" The school supplied food and water for the meeting, which protesters announced was only to be consumed by people of color, and white protesters were told to stand in the back of the room.

The next day, students took the school's president, provost, and other senior administrators into an office and kept them captive there until their demands were accepted. Students blocked the doors to the building with furniture to make sure no one could enter or leave the building, chanting, "2-4-6-8, this time you cannot escape!"

While this was going on, the head of the campus police contacted Bret Weinstein and told him students were going around the parking lot, car to car, looking for him, and advised him not to come to campus. The police chief warned Weinstein: "We can't protect you, because the president has told us to stand down."

In the aftermath of the protests, Evergreen asked Weinstein and his wife, Heather Heying, professors there for fifteen years, to resign. And they did.

DINNER TABLES

Let's imagine two neighbors: High-Rung Heidi and Low-Rung Lola. Heidi's dinner parties have an Idea Lab culture, where people treat ideas like science experiments. Lola's dinners happen within an Echo Chamber culture, where people treat certain ideas like precious babies. Remember, this whole thing:

In a liberal country like the US, Heidi and Lola can happily coexist as neighbors, both free to host dinner parties their own way.

Things might get tricky, though, when Heidi invites Lola to one of her dinner parties. It would be a clash of intellectual cultures, and something would have to give. At the dinner, Lola would have two options:

1. **She could accept the prevailing culture**. She'd probably be uncomfortable with all of the disagreement, and with the inevitable offensive views that would be part of it.
2. **She could issue a *challenge* to the culture by becoming openly offended**. This would be an attempt to impose the rules of Lola's preferred Echo Chamber on Heidi's dinner party.

In the second scenario, High-Rung Heidi and her other guests would have two options:

1. **Temporarily cede the culture to Lola**. Accommodate her sensitivities and after the initial conflict, avoid controversial topics for the rest of the night.
2. **Refuse to cede the culture to Lola**. Tell Lola they think she's being overly sensitive and go on with their discussion.

We can generalize the scenarios like this:

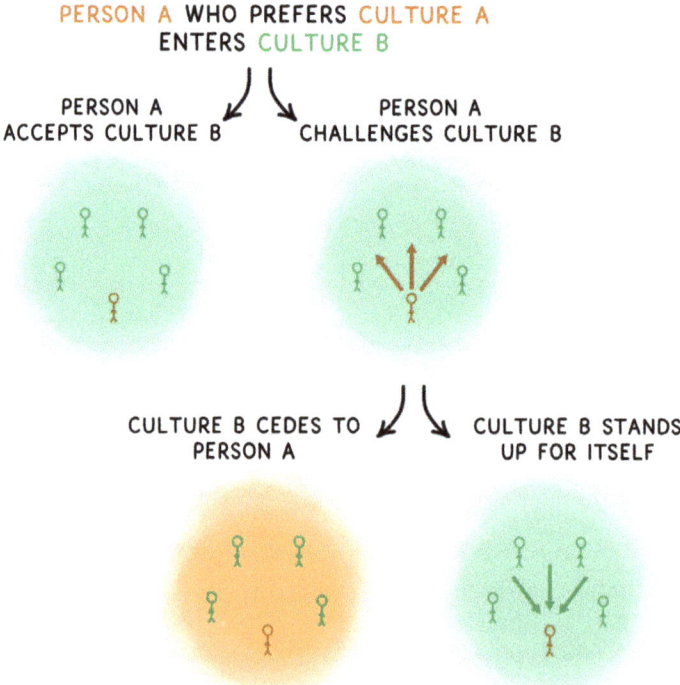

All of these outcomes are fine, because if anyone's not happy about the situation, there's an easy fix: Heidi and Lola don't have to be friends. They can stop inviting each other to dinner or politely decline each other's invitations.

This is a metaphor for how a larger liberal society like the US works. Americans are free to spend their time in Idea Labs or Echo Chambers. Americans are also free to challenge the culture around them, and cultures are then free to give in to the challenge or to defend themselves against it.

The result is a country where Idea Labs and Echo Chambers can live and let live. Echo Chambers are protected against the free flow of ideas by the golem's low-rung immune system (all those filters and fallacies we looked at in Chapter 2). Idea Labs are protected against expansionist golems by the genie's high-rung immune system: a vigorous free speech culture that stands up for itself in the face of attempts at low-rung bullying. By definition, this makes the country itself a giant Idea Lab—a giant dinner party that's home to a huge variety of ideas.

THE COLLEGE DINNER TABLE

There's a Wikipedia page that lists hundreds of university mottos from schools across the globe. If you search the page for the word "truth," you see that it appears 144 times. In the US alone, there are 38 universities with "truth" in their motto. As an undergrad at Harvard in the early 2000s, I walked past the school's seal hundreds of times.

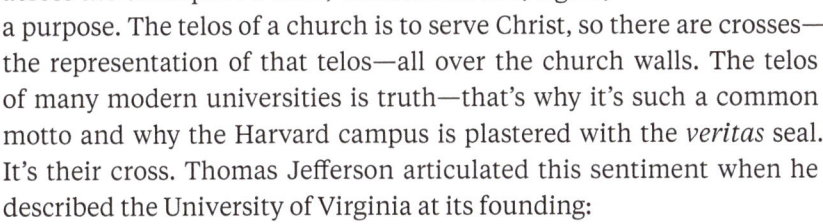

VE-RI-TAS. Truth. Set in stone on the entrance to the school.

If you've ever studied philosophy, you've come across the concept of a telos, which is an end, a goal, a purpose. The telos of a church is to serve Christ, so there are crosses—the representation of that telos—all over the church walls. The telos of many modern universities is truth—that's why it's such a common motto and why the Harvard campus is plastered with the *veritas* seal. It's their cross. Thomas Jefferson articulated this sentiment when he described the University of Virginia at its founding:

> Here we are not afraid to follow truth wherever it may lead, nor to tolerate any error so long as reason is left free to combat it.

This was Jefferson's way of saying, "This is how we do things at the UVA dinner table." The *veritas* seal on the entrance to Harvard and dozens of other schools sends the same message: this is how we do things here.*

Truth is the primary value of high-rung intellectual culture, so a *veritas* campus should function like High-Rung Heidi's dinner table: an Idea Lab full of open discourse, vigorous debate, and a wide variety of viewpoints. This applies to two core purposes: knowledge discovery, and education.

On the knowledge discovery front, research conducted at the university is subject to a gauntlet of criticism that filters out bias, falsehood, and shoddy methodology. Only research that manages to pass through this filter sees the light of day and enters wider society.

On the education front, on top of feeding students lots of "knowledge fish," schools teach students *how to fish*—helping them become skilled truth-finders themselves. A *veritas* campus trains students to think like top-rung Scientists who are conscious of their own biases, adept at the arts of balanced skepticism and intellectual humility, and suspicious of unearned conviction.

Of course, plenty of the individuals at a truth-mottoed university at any given time will inevitably be mired in low-rung thinking, attached to their existing viewpoints and hostile toward dissenting ideas. At some point along the way, each of these people allowed "getting it right" to take a back seat to "feeling right" in their mind, subconsciously abandoning the *veritas* seal at the entrance of their head. Like Low-Rung Lola, these thinkers often socialize with like-minded people and form little Echo Chamber dinner tables within the campus's larger marketplace of ideas. Inside these intellectual safety bubbles, thinkers can play King Mustache, laying down their electric taboo fences at will and imposing them on their friends through social penalties.

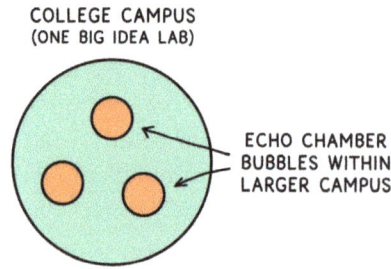

---

* The extent to which universities have lived up to the promise of a "truth" telos is more complicated. Many universities, including Harvard, have grappled with competing values like religion or political ideology.

But the *veritas* seal on the university entrance makes a crystal clear statement about how things are done at the *big* campuswide dinner table. The seal is a promise: if the low-rungers attempt to challenge that culture and impose their Echo Chamber upon the whole campus, they'll be shot down by the prevailing culture.

But over the past decade, Social Justice Fundamentalism has managed to usurp these norms on many college campuses, replacing the truth-seeking system with something directly opposed to it: **idea supremacy**.

WHAT IS IDEA SUPREMACY?

Glad you asked.

> **Idea supremacy = low-rung thinking + authoritarianism**

Let's line up three low-rung thinkers on an axis of authoritarianism:

In the scenario where Lola tried to enforce her Echo Chamber upon Heidi's party, she was being a social bully. It might not be admirable, but it doesn't violate any liberal rule. If Lola pushed it to the limit, she might cut Heidi out of her life for disagreeing with her views, or Heidi could cut ties with Lola for being a Zealot. No big deal.

Idea supremacy extends beyond friendships. An idea supremacist tries to enforce their Echo Chamber upon a much wider space. A classroom, a company, a social media platform. The most egregious form of idea supremacy happens in places that *center* around high-rung culture—places where free speech and open discourse are core values, necessary for optimal function. When a person or group pulls a Lola in that much larger kind of "dinner table," it's a threat to the very soul of the place.

When this happens, it's a pivotal moment of truth for the people who inhabit the high-rung space. If the culture stands up for itself in the face of the challenge with a loud, proud *"that's not how we do things here,"* the attempt at idea supremacy fails and the open discourse is protected. If the culture doesn't, the culture is ceded to the idea supremacists, and the space is transformed into an Echo Chamber.

While Heidi and her guests could freely choose whether to cede their culture or not, people in a classroom or company or any other officially high-rung space have an *obligation* to stand up for the culture and reject the challengers.

College campuses are clearly the kind of dinner table that *relies* on open discourse to uphold the telos of truth.

Liberal Social Justice never requires idea supremacy. It's very much at home in a *veritas* environment. In the 1960s, it was the social justice activists who were arguing hardest on behalf of *veritas* values. It was Mario Savio, an antiwar socialist who fought for civil rights for Black Americans, who led the Berkeley Free Speech Movement, aiming to "bring the hard light of free inquiry to bear upon important matters of the sciences but also the social sciences…asking that there be *no*, no restrictions on the content of speech save for those provided by the courts." This makes sense—only in an environment of free inquiry can you discover the truth about where injustice lies and spark movements to make change.

Social Justice Fundamentalism on campus is more like Lola at Heidi's dinner table. In Chapter 5, we looked at how and why SJF tends to contain itself within Echo Chambers. Ideologies with extreme narratives and unbending certainty about their worldview don't typically jibe with an environment of open inquiry and rigorous criticism. And for a long time, SJF was contained to small pockets on campuses, existing peacefully within the larger high-rung culture.

But as SJF evolved, this began to change. Let's pause our look at colleges for a minute and talk about this evolution.

THE SJF MUTATION

Social ecosystems, like animal ecosystems, exist in fragile balance. Animal ecosystems can be disrupted when one species undergoes a mutation—like when a virus does only minimal damage to a host species and then mutates and is suddenly much more dangerous.

The same idea can apply to social ecosystems. A golem's behavior is driven by the narrative that binds it together. If that narrative mutates, so does the golem's behavior.

The SJF narrative and its surrounding culture have rapidly evolved over the past thirty years, which has caused equally rapid behavioral changes in SJF believers. Two notable phenomena are at the heart of these changes: victimhood culture and concept creep.

Victimhood Culture

We've talked a lot about intellectual cultures. In their book *The Rise of Victimhood Culture*, sociologists Bradley Campbell and Jason Manning explore the idea of *moral cultures*. They outline what many sociologists believe are the prevailing moral cultures of the Western world through recent history.

The first type of moral culture they describe is **honor culture**:

> In honor cultures, it is one's reputation that makes one honorable or not, and one must respond aggressively to insults, aggressions, and challenges or else lose honor. Not to fight back is itself a kind of moral failing…People socialized into a culture of honor often shun reliance on law or any other authority even when it is available, refusing to lower their standing by depending on another to handle their affairs.

Campbell and Manning believe that honor cultures "tend to arise in places where legal authority is weak or nonexistent and where a reputation for toughness is perhaps the only effective deterrent against predation or attack"—but that as countries have become safer and more lawful, honor culture has given way to its opposite: **dignity culture**.

Dignity, say Campbell and Manning, "exists independently of what others think, so a culture of dignity is one in which public reputation is less important. Insults might provoke offense, but they no longer have the same impact as a way of establishing or destroying a reputation for bravery." They elaborate on this:

It is even commendable to have thick skin that allows one to shrug off slights and insults, and in a dignity-based society parents might teach children some version of "sticks and stones may break my bones, but words will never hurt me"—an idea that would be alien in a culture of honor. People are to avoid insulting others, too, whether intentionally or not, and in general an ethic of self-restraint prevails.

So in an honor culture, the cool kids go apeshit when their enemies insult them. In a dignity culture, it's cooler to show a thick skin and shrug off disrespect.

Unsurprisingly, there are way fewer fights and duels in dignity cultures. But inevitably, certain conflicts will escalate beyond the "turn the other cheek" threshold. Here's where dignity cultures get nuanced:

> When intolerable conflicts do arise, dignity cultures prescribe direct but non-violent actions, such as negotiated compromise geared toward solving the problem. Failing this, or if the offense is sufficiently severe, people are to go to the police or appeal to the courts—it would be wrong for them to take the law into their own hands. For offenses like theft, assault, or breach of contract, people in a dignity culture use law without shame. But in keeping with their ethic of restraint and toleration, it is not necessarily their first resort, and they might condemn many uses of the authorities as frivolous.

There's a *specific* thickness to the dignity culture skin—a Goldilocks zone between "oversensitive/overdramatic" and "unprotected from harm."

In recent years, in certain pockets of the Western world—certain SJF-y pockets—dignity culture has been replaced by what Campbell and Manning call **victimhood culture**. Victimhood culture "rejects one of dignity culture's main injunctions—to ignore insults and slights—and instead encourages at least some people to take notice of them and take action against them. The idea is that such offenses do cause harm, just like violence."

This sounds a lot like honor culture, with one major difference. In honor culture, when people "take action against" those who have insulted them, that action is direct physical confrontation. Victimhood culture doesn't encourage direct confrontation, physical or verbal.

Instead, wronged people are supposed to go straight to the authorities, or appeal to a support group, to have the wrongdoer punished.

In other words, victimhood cultures "combine the sensitivity to slight that we see in honor cultures with the willingness to appeal to authorities and other third parties that we see in dignity cultures. And victimhood culture differs from both honor and dignity cultures in highlighting rather than downplaying the complainants' victimhood."

We can sum it up using a playground interaction:

Some researchers believe the rise of victimhood culture is part of a broader trend, partially explained by the changes in how young people in the West, or at least in the US, are raised. In their book *The Coddling of the American Mind*, Greg Lukianoff and Jonathan Haidt write:

> Children today have far more restricted childhoods, on average, than those enjoyed by their parents, who grew up in far more dangerous times and yet had many more opportunities to develop their intrinsic antifragility. Compared with previous generations, younger Millennials and especially members of iGen (born in and after 1995) have been deprived of unsupervised time for play and exploration. They have missed out on many of the challenges, negative experiences, and minor risks that help children develop into strong, competent, and independent adults.

Haidt and Lukianoff believe these changes in childhood experiences have left many of today's young people reliant on an authority to resolve conflict—which maps onto the way conflict is handled in victimhood culture.

This broader phenomenon is intensified within the world of Social Justice Fundamentalism, where victimhood has come to be treated as a form of status.

The most important kind of victimhood in Social Justice Fundamentalism is *identity* victimhood: the position of your group on the Intersectional Stack. As we saw in the last chapter, SJF applies very different moral standards to those deemed to be privileged vs. oppressed. This may explain the handful of recent stories of white people who work in fields that deal with oppression being caught assuming fake marginalized identities (with the case of Rachel Dolezal, a white former college instructor who pretended to be Black for years, being the most famous). In a 2021 article in *The Atlantic*, journalist Helen Lewis tells the story of Jessica Krug, a white, Jewish professor who, for years, pretended to be Black. She writes: "The white, Jewish Jessica Krug *could* have had an academic career. What she would not have had was moral authority."

A second form of victimhood—*experience* victimhood—is based on having experienced harm. Experience victimhood grants people an elevated social position throughout society, not just within SJF, as it is human nature to treat a suffering person with extra kindness. Hearing about someone's suffering reminds us of their humanity, which in turn reminds us to treat them with humanity.

But wherever there's good will, profiteers will be there trying to exploit it.

People faking illness is so common that there's a term for it: Munchausen syndrome.* In their book *Dying to be Ill*, Marc Feldman and Gregory Yates explain that people who pretend to have cancer or other illnesses cannot "resist the pull of obtaining attention or sympathy...these patients fabricate disease and illness in order to reap the rewards of the *sick role*, which include entitlement to support from others, exemption from social obligations, and a general state of being in need of help, or deserving of special allowances."

---

* Most scholars actually call it "factitious disorder"—but Munchausen syndrome is the better-known term.

In Social Justice Fundamentalism, the victim experiences that matter most are those of oppressed people harmed by privileged people—so while faking cancer may not translate to enhanced status in the SJF world, faking being the victim of a hate crime *will*.

Many of us are well acquainted with the story of Jussie Smollett, the actor who in 2019 told police he was attacked in the street by two men wearing ski masks. According to Smollett, the men beat him up while calling him racist and homophobic slurs (Smollett is Black and gay) and saying, "This is MAGA country," before leaving him there with a noose tied around his neck. Smollett immediately received an outpouring of love and support from across the internet. Except it turned out that it was all a hoax, orchestrated by Smollett, who was then convicted on five counts of making false police reports.

This is Social Justice Munchausen syndrome.

Smollett is a high-profile case, but over the past few years, as victimhood culture has spread, there have been literally hundreds of hate crime hoaxes (for a sampling, see endnote).

None of this is to downplay the prevalence of *real* hate crimes—just like analyzing Munchausen syndrome isn't downplaying real cancer cases. It's just that it's pretty hard to picture Black Americans in South Carolina in 1925 orchestrating fake attacks. Or Jews in Germany in 1938. Or LGBTQ people in Afghanistan today. We have fake hate crimes in the US because they're socially rewarded by a culture in which victimhood enhances one's status.

Victimhood culture encourages people to define themselves by their suffering, their trauma, their vulnerability. Popular YouTuber Olivia Sun talks about the effects of victimhood culture on Tumblr: "Being chronically on Tumblr in the early 2000s did something awful to me: It made me desire intense depression…Tumblr, which is kind of like the blog version of Twitter, made being sad an essential part of what made you interesting, and so it led to romanticizing mental illness….Tumblr allowed us to masochistically indulge in self-pain because we received attention, support, and hashtag 'you're so relatable' comments because of our pain."

So, young SJF adherents are part of both a generation susceptible to victimhood culture and a political group whose social structure and worldview further encourage it. But social victimhood can't happen on its own—it requires a *victimizer*. And as the supply of victimhood has been driven upward culturally, so has the demand for victimizers. Which brings us to our second phenomenon.

Concept Creep

Psychologist Nick Haslam writes about "concept creep," which describes the way that perceptions of harm have been rapidly evolving:

> Concepts that refer to the negative aspects of human experience and behavior have expanded their meanings so that they now encompass a much broader range of phenomena than before. This expansion takes "horizontal" and "vertical" forms: concepts extend outward to capture qualitatively new phenomena and downward to capture quantitatively less extreme phenomena.

So something like this:

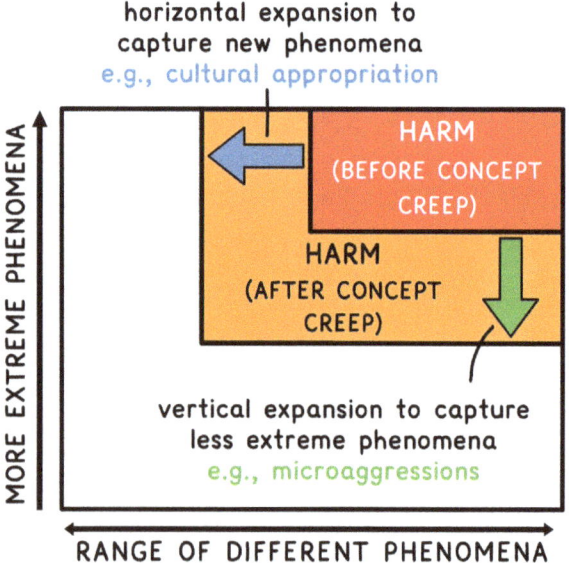

In 2018, a group of scientists led by Harvard psychologist Daniel Gilbert found that "people often respond to decreases in the prevalence of a stimulus by expanding their concept of it." As a consequence, "social problems may seem intractable in part because reductions in their prevalence lead people to see more of them."

It's as if we like to keep our perception of the world at a constant. So when the world changes, instead of allowing our perception of the world to change, we alter our standards and our definitions to keep our perception the same.

In the world of social justice, this phenomenon can be a positive thing. It's the *job* of the progressive to never be satisfied with progress. Social justice activists are proud of the giant strides they've made, but they remain hard at work on the challenges still facing historically marginalized people. Reacting to decreases in the prevalence of harms like racism, sexism, and homophobia by expanding the definition of those concepts can help activists address the nuanced ways oppression can persist long after the more blatant instances have been curtailed.

But SJF has taken this concept and turned a slight, potentially useful distortion into something more extreme. When concept creep gets out of control, it allows a far wider range of behaviors to qualify as bigotry, abuse, and trauma, which means a far wider range of people viewing themselves as victims of bigotry, abuse, and trauma. It also turns a far wider range of people into bigots, abusers, and traumatizers. Many more victims = many more villains.

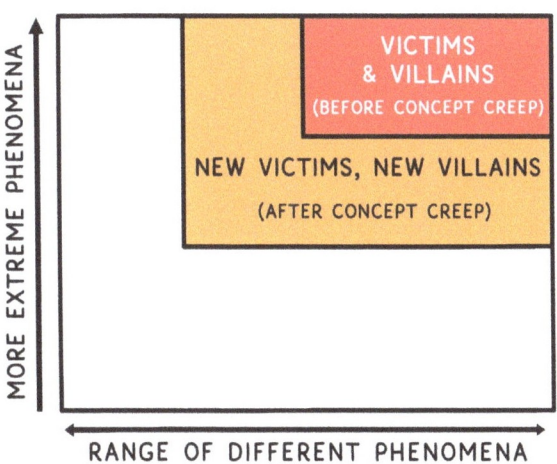

Perhaps the most impactful example of concept creep has been the evolution from "words can be hurtful" to "words can be an act of violence." This directly contradicts the liberal mindset, in which speech is seen not as violence but as the critical *alternative* to violence. But over the past decade, open disagreement with the SJF narrative has regularly been labeled as "violence."

Now think back to the other component of victimhood culture—the part that encourages appealing to authorities to punish harm-doers. What happens when you combine an increasing number of perceived villains with an increasing inclination to *punish* villains?

A Justification for Idea Supremacy

No group says, "We're an Echo Chamber, and we've decided we're going to try to use coercion to impose idea supremacy on everyone else." It's almost always framed as a noble group of people trying to do good.

The one caveat a liberal society places on their guiding mantra—"live and let live"—is the harm principle. *Everyone can do whatever they want, as long as it doesn't harm anyone else*. When harm is happening, "live and let live" no longer applies.

This, of course, makes the definition of harm critically important. When concept creep turns dissent itself into an act of unacceptable harm—an act of racism, of transphobia, of violence—punishing those who dissent becomes not only justified but *imperative* in order to protect people's safety. This is how idea supremacy, through the lens of SJF, can appear to be righteous activism.

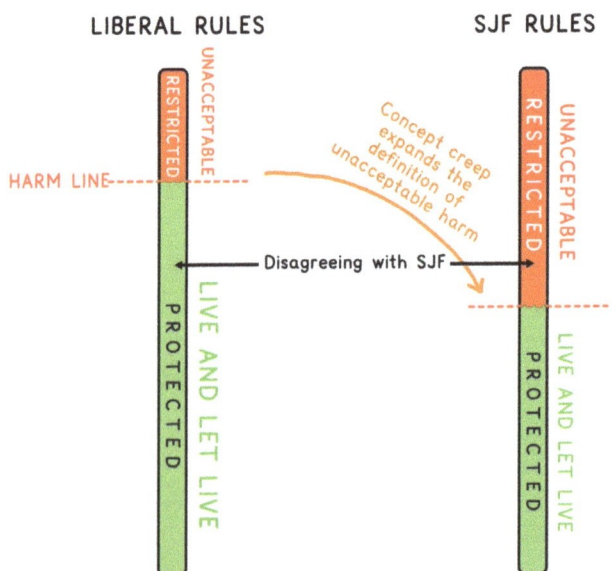

The crucial mutation that happened to SJF ideology wasn't the development of victimhood culture or concept creep or the extreme notion of an all-encompassing Force*—it was what these changes yielded when combined together: the transformation from a golem that minds its own business to one that tries to conquer the surrounding environment.

Attempting to impose idea supremacy is one thing—actually pulling it off is another. To successfully enforce idea supremacy in a liberal environment, you need to find a way to breach its high-rung immune system.

Which brings us back to Evergreen.

EVERGREEN'S COLLAPSE

A filmmaker named Mike Nayna made a documentary about the Evergreen shitshow. It's about halfway through the documentary that the widely discussed Day of Absence drama starts. But I was most interested in the first half of the documentary, about the six-month *lead-up* to the drama.

Weinstein explains how he believes the story started:

> We hired a new president at the college. He set in motion a committee to study the question of equity on our campus and to propose some solutions to problems.

But when, at a major staff meeting, one of the members of this Equity Committee read out the committee's beliefs, there didn't seem to be much left to study. They read out, word-for-word, that statement on racism by the four professors that I quoted in Chapter 5—the one about racism being permanently embedded in everything, about the question being not "Did racism take place?" but "How did racism manifest in that situation?"

---

* Quick refresher: The Force is my term for the guiding principle of Social Justice Fundamentalism—the idea that American and other Western societies are embedded at every level by identity-based oppression. The oppression always goes in the same direction, downward on the Intersectional Stack, with cisheterosexual, white, able men at the top and women, people of color, and LGBTQ people down below. According to the SJF narrative, every interaction, every assumption, every social norm is an expression of the Force, whether we're conscious of it or not.

These sentiments were right in line with the words of Robin DiAngelo, who had said this during a talk on the campus a few months earlier:

> An anti-racist frame understands racism as a system....It's embedded in the fabric of the society, in all the institutions, the norms, the practices, the policies, the way that history is told, and it functions to ensure an unequal distribution of basically everything between people of color as a whole and white people as a whole.

Social Justice Fundamentalism had clearly made its way to Evergreen. But an extreme ideology isn't what turned Evergreen into a place where Bret Weinstein and his wife were forced to resign for standing up for basic liberal principles. It was the notion that the ideology *may not be challenged*.

Weinstein identified the moment he believes it became clear that the ideology was sacred. He talks about a conflict he had at a faculty meeting with Naima Lowe, a media studies professor at the school who he believed was instigating much of the tension around race at Evergreen.

> There were all these allegations about white supremacy at Evergreen, and every so often, somebody...asked about, "Okay, where is this white supremacy? Can we see it? Can we evaluate it?" And [Lowe] said, "To ask students who are suffering from white supremacy to tell us about instances of white supremacy is itself racism. We must stop asking them because we are inflicting harm on them asking for evidence." And the phrase she used, she said: "To ask for evidence of racism is racism with a capital R." And as she said, "racism with a capital R," she leaned forward in her seat, and she looked directly at me....I sat in my chair, and I said, "Are you talking to me?" and she said, "Yes." And I looked around the room, and nobody said a word.

Weinstein responded to Lowe by saying that a quick look at his history would make it clear that he wasn't a racist. But then the chair of the faculty spoke up:

> The chair of the faculty said, "Bret, this is not the place to defend yourself against accusations of racism." And I said, "That's fine.

Where is the place?" And then the faculty member who leveled the accusation says: "You should not expect a place to defend yourself against accusations of racism." And I looked around the room. The president of the college is sitting there. The provost of the college is sitting there. And nobody said a word.

In the SJF Echo Chamber, challenging SJF is prohibited. Outside the Echo Chamber in the school's larger *veritas* culture, all ideas are supposed to be questioned and criticized. Like someone trying to enforce the rules of a church group on a science laboratory, Naima Lowe issued a challenge to Evergreen culture—an attempt to impose the rules of the SJF Echo Chamber on the entire faculty.

It was a cultural moment of truth at Evergreen.

And I looked around the room. The president of the college is sitting there. The provost of the college is sitting there. And nobody said a word.

When King Mustache announced the new censorship laws, laying down what he insisted was an electric fence in his country's marketplace of ideas—that was his attempt at idea supremacy. When the king ordered dissenters to be hanged, the country faced its moment of truth. When no one stood up for the dissenters, allowing their executions to take place, the king's idea supremacy became *real*. It was not King Mustache's orders but the failure of others to defend the country's constitution that gave the fence its *electricity*.

On her own, someone like Naima Lowe can attempt to impose idea supremacy on the Evergreen campus, but they're not likely to succeed. It was the silence of the rest of the faculty—the failure of the campus's high-rung immune system to kick in and stand up for free speech culture—that gave the SJF fence its electricity at Evergreen. The silence sent a clear message to everyone: Bret Weinstein, who tried to cross the SJF speech fence, has now been branded a racist. Anyone else who challenged the Equity Committee in the future would be too.

Once a liberal institution's high-rung immune system is seen as breachable, things can quickly spiral downward. To see how, let's make a hypothetical campus diagram, arranging the people on a campus— administration, faculty, and students—based on two criteria: their level of **belief in a certain ideology (Ideology X)**, and their level of intellectual **authenticity**:

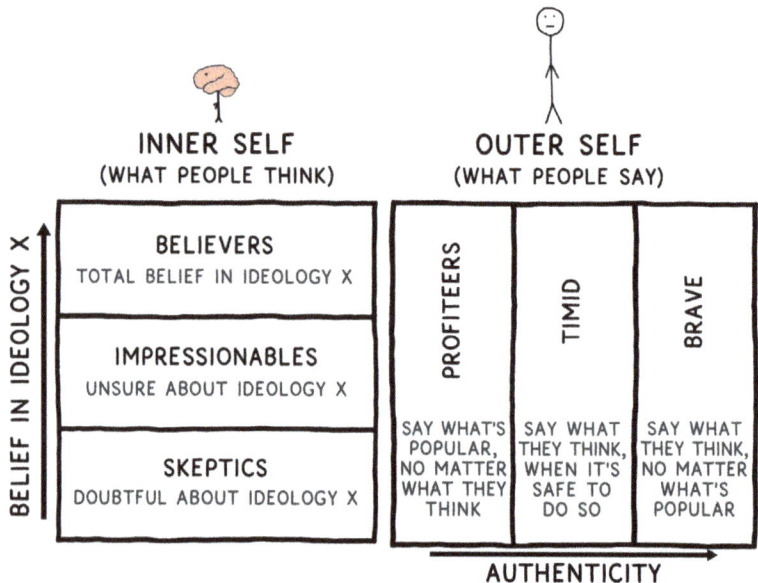

The Belief axis has to do with the Inner Self: what people actually *think* about Ideology X. The Authenticity axis is about what people *say* they believe—i.e., how well their Outer Self matches their Inner Self. People on the far left of this axis are called "profiteers" because they say what they say for reasons other than true intellectual expression—for financial or professional gain, to project a certain image or attain a certain status, or simply for social acceptance.

Putting these two axes together, we can divide a campus into six general groups of people regarding their relationship with Ideology X. →

In a liberal environment like a modern college campus, a metaphorical boxing ring would form around Ideology X and the proponents and skeptics would go at it. Whichever group proved to hold sounder viewpoints and better arguments would eventually persuade the impressionables, who tend to believe whatever the prevailing views are. If the Ideology X proponents were consistently coming out on top in arguments, it would probably also become fashionable around campus to say you were a believer—so the profiteers, who do whatever's fashionable, would be gung ho about Ideology X. If things were reversed, the profiteers would join the crowd in shaking their heads at those silly people who believed Ideology X.

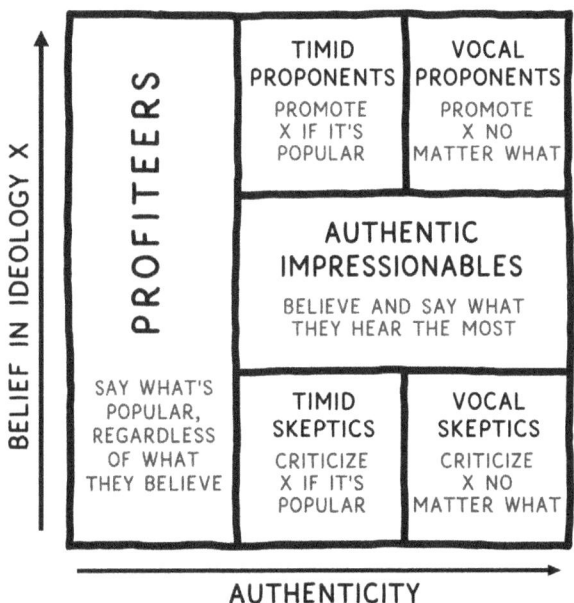

As Social Justice Fundamentalism rose into the zeitgeist over the past decade, we'd expect to see a lot of boxing matches between SJF proponents and SJF skeptics.

But what happens when staff meetings start going the way they did in the Evergreen story?

That was a story of a vocal SJF skeptic, Weinstein, arguing to uphold basic liberal ideals and asking for evidence of claims that were the basis of major proposed changes on campus—and being *burned* for it. When it becomes social and perhaps career suicide to attempt to get in the ring with a certain ideology, a bunch of things quickly change:

1. All but the bravest skeptics go from vocal to timid and silent.
2. SJF proponents, now protected against anyone challenging their ideas, become even more vocal about their beliefs.

---

* We're using this diagram to categorize people on a college campus, but the same diagram applies to how any human environment relates to any set of ideas.

3. Profiteers, seeing the new way the wind is blowing, become vocal SJF proponents.
4. Impressionables, now hearing nearly everyone around them talking about SJF as if it were obvious, established truth, come to be SJF believers.

As the cultural tide shifts, the cost of open resistance grows.* For college students who could become social pariahs, for faculty who have built careers at the university and rooted their families nearby, it's just not worth it to stand up to the tide. So the college's high-rung immune system vanishes.

SJF CHALLENGES EVERGREEN CULTURE

EVERGREEN CEDES TO SJF ✓

EVERGREEN STANDS UP FOR ITSELF ✗

According to the documentary, with Evergreen's high-rung immune system disabled, SJF activists began to unilaterally enact sweeping changes to school policy. Every faculty member was required to submit an annual report on their growth relative to their personal

---

* The scarier it gets to speak out, the more that line between the timid skeptics and vocal skeptics moves to the right. If it gets bad enough, all skeptics go timid, leaving no vocal skeptics on campus.

racism—information that would affect promotion and firing. Every new applicant, in any department, would be judged on their prior engagement with social justice issues. The speech rules of the SJF Echo Chamber became the speech rules across campus, as a *veritas* campus was converted into a sanctuary for a sacred ideology.

This is how it appears SJF conquered Evergreen. Not the Liberal Games way, via persuasion in the intellectual boxing ring, but the Power Games way, using coercion to declare itself the boxing champion without ever having to put on the gloves.

I don't blame Evergreen students for what went down at the school. It's a lot to ask of young adults to listen to authority figures, at a place that promised to educate you, and to conclude that you're being led in the wrong direction. The bandwagon effect kicks in, in which lots of people believing something seems to be evidence that the belief must be true. And so, lots of well-intentioned, impressionable young minds had come to believe that a vocal SJF skeptic like Bret Weinstein had no place on their campus.

In the final moment of truth for Evergreen in this story, the school stated the values they now stood for in the clearest way possible. Weinstein—one of the last vocal skeptics at Evergreen—was eradicated from the system.

WHY CAMPUS IMMUNE SYSTEMS HAVE FAILED

Liberal societies are home to plenty of people and groups that don't actually believe in the liberal mantra "live and let live" and would like to enforce their will over others. But the system is designed to keep ambitious golems in check, and usually, it does.

When a liberal institution *is* conquered by a golem, we should all take notice and ask why. College campuses have always had low-rung groups in their midst. Why would Evergreen's high-rung immune system suddenly collapse in 2017?

In Chapter 3, we looked at a broad political trend in the US as the country moved from distributed tribalism to concentrated tribalism to hypercharged tribalism. Evergreen's collapse, I believe, was only possible because of a major environmental shift that has taken place at many US colleges over the past few decades, one that mirrors the country's broader political trend.

From Plurality to Purity

University faculty have always skewed progressive. In the past, the ratio of progressive to conservative professors was in the 2:1–4:1 range. But over the past thirty years, that ratio has grown far more extreme. One large 2021 study looked at 12,372 professors at the most elite universities in every US state, noting their political party registration. STEM fields have maintained a semblance of ideological diversity, with a Democrat to Republican ratio of 4.5:1 in chemistry and 5.5:1 in mathematics. Psychology (11.5:1) and philosophy (11.4:1) were far more lopsided, while English (26.8:1), sociology (27.0:1), and anthropology (42.2:1) were more homogeneously progressive still. By far the most lopsided ratio emerged from "interdisciplinary studies"—the category that is home to most social justice classes. These areas were so politically homogeneous, the study's author says, that "I could not find a single Republican with an exclusive appointment to fields like gender studies, Africana studies, and peace studies."

The study also looked at professors' political donations between 2015 and 2018, which is one possible proxy for political *fervor*. The ratio of donation dollars to the Democrats vs. the Republicans was 21:1 overall. These ratios were the most lopsided at top-ranked colleges, like Harvard ($96 donated to Democrats for every $1 donated to Republicans), Brown (113:1), and Cornell (196:1). At Yale, Princeton, Dartmouth, Penn, Duke, Berkeley, Georgetown, Caltech, and Johns Hopkins, the ratio was infinite because not a single professor donated to the Republicans.

A 2018 study by the same author looked specifically at liberal arts colleges. Using a sample of 8,688 tenure-track, PhD-holding professors from 51 top-ranked liberal arts colleges, they found that 78.2 percent of the academic departments had either zero Republicans on the faculty or "so few as to make no difference." Again, the highest ranked schools were the most extreme. Here are the top six liberal arts schools, where there were eleven *total* registered Republicans:

College	US News Rank	Sample Size	Not Reg.	Reg. but No Party	Dem.	Rep.	D:R Ratio
Williams	1	254	71	50	132	1	132:1
Amherst	2	184	42	37	102	3	34:1
Wellesley	3	240	53	48	136	1	136:1
Swarthmore	4	182	51	6	120	1	120:1
Bowdoin	6	166	24	26	107	2	53.5:1
Pomona	7	195	41	29	119	3	39.7:1

Source: Academic Questions

When we look at college administrators, the people who write policy and hire faculty, we see the same extreme skew. A 2018 survey found that the progressive to conservative ratio among college administrators is a whopping 12 to 1. In the *New York Times* in 2018, the survey's author Samuel J. Abrams wrote: "It appears that a *fairly* liberal student body is being taught by a *very* liberal professoriate—and socialized by an *incredibly* liberal group of administrators."

Once a trend toward purity starts in a cultural environment, it tends to gather momentum. As campuses have slid from bluish-purple to pure blue, we should expect the emphasis on viewpoint diversity to wither away, replaced by increasing hostility toward the shrinking intellectual minority.

A 2021 report by Eric Kaufmann for the Center for the Study of Partisanship and Ideology found that 62 percent of conservative graduate students agree that "my political views wouldn't fit, which could make my life difficult," compared with 8 percent of progressive graduate students. Writing about his report in *Newsweek*, Kaufmann explains:

> In the U.S., a staggering one in three conservative graduate students or academics has been disciplined or threatened for discipline for their views. Meanwhile, 75 percent of conservative academics in the social sciences and humanities in the U.S. and Britain say their departments are a hostile environment for their beliefs. In the U.S., fully seven in 10 conservative academics in the social sciences or humanities say they self-censor.

As increasingly homogeneous campuses become increasingly difficult places for conservatives to work, fewer conservatives go into academia in the first place, further enhancing homogeneity. It's a vicious cycle.

---

* One telling trend: In 2014 the website FiveThirtyEight published statistics about commencement speeches across the top sixty national and liberal arts universities, specifically looking at instances in which the address was given by a political figure. In 2003 and 2004, thirty commencement addresses at these sixty top schools were given by political figures: sixteen progressive, fourteen conservative. Ten years later, at the same sixty schools, there were twenty-five commencement speeches by political figures in 2013 and 2014: twenty-five progressive, zero conservative.
† In Chapter 3, we saw this phenomenon play out in the feedback loop that led to the ideological purification of America's two political parties.

This trend is a direct affront to the *veritas* seal. Humans, individually, are often bad at truth. Even the most seasoned intellectuals can be biased, especially when it comes to theories they've spent their careers developing. But when a bunch of people get together and their ideas can clash freely in the ring, they form a genie and *collectively* can be pretty good at truth. There's only one way a scholarly institution, full of biased thinkers, can keep itself consistently pointing toward truth: every theory that emerges must survive a gauntlet of people trying to prove it wrong.

When university faculty was at a 2:1 or even 4:1 political ratio, there was still enough ideological diversity to maintain a marketplace of ideas. A vocal conservative minority could provide a vital dissenting perspective to progressive theories. When that dissent filter vanishes, the campus becomes, ideologically, more like a church group than a science lab. As psychologist Sally Satel writes, "political biases that distort researchers' work...counterbalance one another. In American universities today, those biases generally point in the same direction."*

A homogeneous environment makes for a weak high-rung immune system that can be exploited by the dominant ideology's low-rung counterpart.

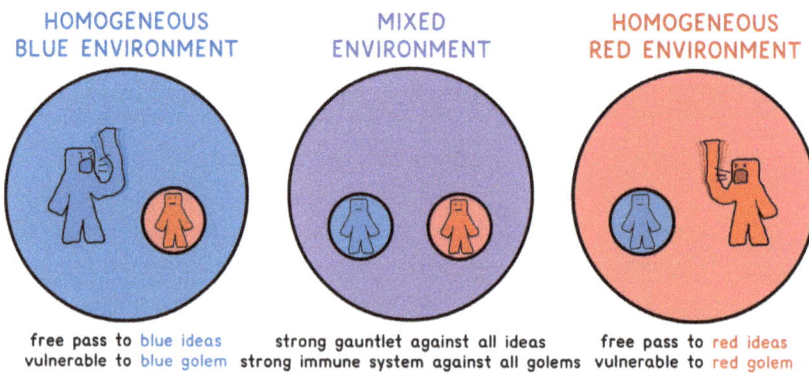

---

* We can think of this like a courtroom. When both sides of a case are properly represented, neither attorney can get away with too much BS because one attorney yells out "objection!" when the other tries something sneaky. Politically homogeneous universities are like courtrooms with only one attorney. Not only is the other side not properly represented, but the dominant side can get away with more bias, more straw-man arguments, and more motte-and-bailey defenses when there's no opposition there to yell "objection!"

It's hard to push back against your own political tribe—especially in a time of hypercharged political tribalism throughout the country. The loss of ideological diversity in academia did away with the very people who would have been on the front lines against an attempted hijacking by a blue golem.

Add to all this the fact that social justice has been *the* most emotional and passionate cause on America's Left—on both the high and low rungs. When an issue becomes sacred to a community, it raises the social stakes. Growing up in a progressive suburb, I would have rather been labeled almost *anything* other than "racist" or "sexist" or "homophobic." In a progressive environment, these terms described the worst possible kind of person.

Concept creep has then taken those powerful words, so loaded with negative meaning, and cheapened their meaning *without* cheapening the punch they pack. As journalist Coleman Hughes put it, "We're operating on like, five or ten different definitions of racism simultaneously at the moment as a society. And yet the word 'racist' carries a severe stigma. So the stigma is very precise, but the definition is very vague."

At Evergreen, no one was going to be hanged in the public square. But the fear of being branded a bigot had essentially the same effect. People who would normally stand up for a colleague and friend in the face of an unwarranted public smear stayed silent.

The 1950s saw an unusual wave of illiberalism: the Red Scare. The specifics of that moment—postwar uncertainty, widespread fear of the threat of foreign influence and nuclear war, loyalty and patriotism being elevated to sacred values—left a liberal society especially vulnerable to a particular kind of accusation: *Communist.*

On today's college campuses, the combination of ideological homogeneity and the sacredness of social justice, alongside the backdrop of the country's hypercharged political tribalism, similarly created an unusual vulnerability to a particular golem: Social Justice Fundamentalism.

• • •

In my conversations over the past few years, when I've brought up a story like Evergreen's, a common response has been something like, "Sure, there are extreme anecdotes, but this isn't actually a big concern." I understand that instinct. Telling a sensational story and presenting it as evidence of a larger problem stinks of cognitive fallacy. But while it is one of the more sensational campus stories of recent years, Evergreen is no anomaly.

Across the US, Canada, the UK, and elsewhere, as stories of campuses being overrun by SJF went viral, SJF activists on many campuses grew bolder. Every time a vocal skeptic like Bret Weinstein was burned for trying to stand up to the cultural hijacking, would-be vocal skeptics at other schools saw the warning in bright lights. Fear has gone viral. Silence has gone viral. Idea supremacy has gone viral. At universities all around the US and other liberal societies—from the Ivy League to flagship state schools to small private colleges—stone *veritas* plaques have fallen like dominos.

While this book isn't nearly long enough for a comprehensive review of what's happened to academia over the past decade, I'll go through a sampling of stories to emphasize the scope of the problem. Each of the following stories is an example of idea supremacy in action—each is evidence of a high-rung immune system that's not functioning properly. I've grouped the stories into three broad categories: expression, research, and education.

IDEA SUPREMACY ON CAMPUS: EXPRESSION

College campuses play regular host to public speakers, public debates, and speaker panels. Our Ladder can help us see how different audience members might experience a talk. The authoritarian axis can help us see the fuller picture.

Check out the image on the following page. When these six characters agree with what a speaker is saying, they're nearly indistinguishable as they all sit in the audience thinking "great talk!" It's when we look at audience members who *disagree* with the speaker that the differences show.

We've talked a lot about the differences between these characters, but as far as a liberal college campus is concerned, there are only two groups here: five people, none of whom violate a liberal environment's "live and let live" ethos, and the idea supremacist, who does.

It's only the idea supremacist on campus who says, "*No one* on campus is allowed to express ideas I find reprehensible, whether I'm in the room or not." Which is another way of saying, "No one on campus is allowed to *hear* ideas that I find reprehensible."

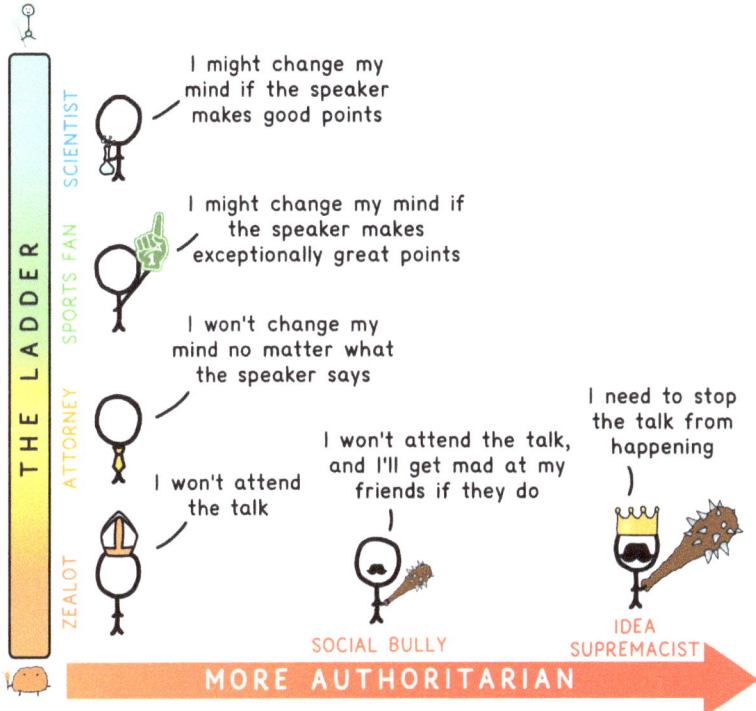

Idea supremacy is at odds with the basic ideals of a college campus. And yet, over the past decade, idea supremacists have succeeded again and again at canceling speaker events they don't approve of.

Disinvitations and Shutdowns

Plan A for idea supremacists, when a speaker they detest is invited to campus, is to get the invitation revoked and the event canceled before it even happens. Zachary Wood, a student at Williams College who self-identifies as a liberal Democrat, joined an alumni-funded speaking series at the school called "Uncomfortable Learning." But when he invited author Suzanne Venker to give a talk titled "One Step Forward, Ten Steps Back: Why Feminism Fails," a group of students decided that that topic was too uncomfortable even for Uncomfortable Learning and their protests got the talk canceled. Wood was drawn to the series because, "As a Black man, I don't need to be protected from offensive ideas. I'd rather hear them for myself—and challenge them." The student newspaper at Williams felt differently, explaining that the disinvitation was necessary, because of "the potential damage of introducing harmful thoughts into the safe space that is so vital to the College's ability to nurture and educate."

The past decade saw a cascade of stories about speakers being disinvited under the same type of reasoning. Supreme Court Chief Justice John Roberts at Butler. Former Deputy Secretary of State Robert Zoellick at Swarthmore. In 2021, a planned lecture at MIT by geophysicist Dorian Abbot was canceled by the school following outrage on social media over the fact that Abbot had published a *Newsweek* op-ed critical of diversity, equity, and inclusion initiatives.

The women at Smith College never had a chance to hear from Christine Lagarde, the first female head of the International Monetary Fund and first female finance minister of a G8 nation after protests led her to withdraw from the event. For the same reasons, students at Rutgers were never able to hear a planned commencement address by Condoleezza Rice, the only Black female secretary of state in US history.

Ayaan Hirsi Ali, a Black woman born in one of the most oppressive patriarchal societies in the world, was a child victim of female genital mutilation in Somalia. After fleeing a forced marriage to her cousin, she was granted asylum in the Netherlands, later becoming a member of the Dutch parliament and a prominent feminist. Her invitation to speak at Brandeis was canceled because the particular patriarchy she criticized was Islamism. In the UK, similar reasoning barred ex-Muslim Maryam Namazie from speaking at the University of Warwick.

FIRE (the Foundation for Individual Rights and Expression), a nonprofit group dedicated to protecting free speech rights on college campuses,* has documented more than one hundred successful disinvitations since 2015. But the disinvitation is only Plan A. When a disinvitation effort fails, campus idea supremacists turn to Plan B: the shutdown.

---

* FIRE has been incorrectly called a conservative organization by its critics. In fact, FIRE is politically neutral and regularly criticizes illiberal behavior by the Right as well as the Left. The organization more often criticizes illiberalism from the Left because its primary focus has been on higher education, where the Left variety is more prominent.

In a campus shutdown, protesters will either physically block attendees from entering the building where the talk is supposed to happen, or they'll attend the event themselves only to drown the speaker out with shouts, chants, banging on drums, or by pulling the fire alarm once the talk starts. The result is usually a canceled event.

Christina Hoff Sommers is a second-wave feminist who is very vocal in her criticism of third-wave feminism and other elements of Social Justice Fundamentalism. When she went to speak at Lewis & Clark Law School, a group of students crashed the event and interrupted the talk with chants and shout-downs. The students who had attended the event actually stood up to the protesters and said they wanted to hear her talk and that the Q&A was the place for protest. A classic moment of truth for the university: Do they side with the students who organized the event or with the protesters trying to kill the event? The school cut the speech short.

In many cases, the school doesn't even have a choice. When political commentator Heather Mac Donald showed up at Claremont McKenna to share her views on police shootings, the intense, screaming shutdown of her event by hundreds of students—an event that 100 students had signed up for—left campus officials so concerned for the speaker's safety that they changed the plan, recording the talk in an empty room. Whether they agreed with Mac Donald or not, students at Claremont McKenna concerned about police shootings might have benefitted from hearing from someone the *New York Times* has called an "influential institute thinker," who has spent decades writing about police-related issues. Instead, the only thing students heard that night were continuous chants: *"from Oakland to Greece, fuck the police!"*

Perhaps most notoriously, student protesters at Middlebury shut down an event with controversial social scientist Charles Murray, during which a professor who disagreed with his views was going to debate him on stage. Before any words could be exchanged, a large group of students in the audience stood up and, echoing the tenets of SJF, recited in unison: "Science has always been used to legitimize racism, sexism, classism, transphobia, ableism, and homophobia, all veiled as rational

---

* In her book *The War on Cops*, Mac Donald argues against the widespread narrative that racist cops pose the greatest threat to young Black men and maintains that the prevalence of that narrative has had negative effects for Black people.

and fact, and supported by the government and state. In this world today, there is little that is true 'fact.'" The students then chanted, "Shut it down! Shut it down!" until the event was indeed shut down. Then, as the professor hosting the event tried to safely escort Murray to his car, things turned physical. The professor tells the story:

> Most of the hatred was focused on Dr. Murray, but when I took his right arm to shield him and to make sure we stayed together, the crowd turned on me. Someone pulled my hair, while others were shoving me. I feared for my life. Once we got into the car, protesters climbed on it, hitting the windows and rocking the vehicle whenever we stopped to avoid harming them. I am still wearing a neck brace, and spent a week in a dark room to recover from a concussion caused by the whiplash.

Frederick Douglass once said, "To suppress free speech is a double wrong. It violates the rights of the hearer as well as those of the speaker." That's why "censorship" isn't really the right word for what's happening here. People aren't banning speakers from speaking; they can go speak elsewhere. They're preventing their fellow students from *hearing* the ideas. Students pay a lot of money for the privilege of being in a place that expands their intellectual horizons, and SJF idea supremacy robs students of a critical element of their college experience.

Idea supremacy is not unique to Social Justice Fundamentalism or to the Left—there are also stories about campus events being squashed by right-wing activists—but most recent incidents have been the work of the Left. FIRE's disinvitations database shows that the Left has forced twice as many disinvitations and ten times as many event disruptions as the Right.* And in a 2020 survey of over twenty thousand students at fifty-five top US colleges, FIRE found that 60 percent of self-identified "extreme liberals" believe it is acceptable to shout down a controversial speaker on campus, compared with 15 percent of "extreme conservative" students.

---

* FIRE's official metric is not whether protests were "by the Left" or "by the Right" but rather by people "to the left" or "to the right" of the speaker. FIRE notes that many of the blocked speakers would consider themselves progressive.

Idea Supremacy over Other Forms of Expression

When idea supremacy takes hold of a system, it clamps down on all forms of expression.

Protests over campus newspaper op-eds that conflict with SJF thinking have many times led to writers being fired and newspaper budgets being cut. But some papers received backlash for even less. The *Harvard Crimson* was lambasted in 2019 for publishing an article about the controversial border-enforcement government agency ICE. Did the Crimson write positively about ICE? No. They supportively covered campus protests against ICE. The problem was that the article included this sentence:

> ICE did not immediately respond to a request for comment Thursday night.

In a petition signed by over one thousand people, Harvard students demanded that the paper "apologize for the harm they inflicted on the undocumented community" and vow to never contact ICE for comment again. Commenting on the incident, the vice president of the Harvard College Democrats, Isabel Giovannetti, explained: "It's very much in line with our values. It lines up with our commitment to protecting these movements, making sure people's voices can be heard, that intimidation from ICE doesn't prevent these students from exercising their right to mobilize and organize."*

Idea supremacy has come down on campus art scenes. At Mount Holyoke, the annual production of the famous feminist play *The Vagina Monologues* was canceled in 2015, on the grounds that "the show offers an extremely narrow perspective on what it means to be a woman." At Brandeis, playwright Michael Weller was wrong when he thought he'd be able to debut a play that explored the complexities of campus censorship—it was canceled after protests. Accusations of cultural appropriation have

---

* This is a classic example of the motte-and-bailey fallacy we talked about in Chapter 2 (in which someone who makes a hard-to-defend "bailey" argument, when attacked, retreats up to the "motte" castle, swapping out their weak argument for a stronger one). In this case, Giovannetti reframes the bailey position "voices we don't like should never be quoted in the campus newspaper" as the much more defensible motte position "we just want to protect these movements and make sure people's voices can be heard."

attempted to restrict everything from "culinary bigotry" in Oberlin's dining hall to white bands playing afrobeat music at Hampshire College to white girls wearing hoop earrings at Pitzer College.

In 2021, in a large survey conducted by the nonprofit advocacy group Heterodox Academy, 64 percent of students "agreed the climate on their campus prevents students from saying things they believe" (up from 55 percent in 2020). Here's how a Smith College student described things:

> Within a few short weeks, members of my freshman class had quickly assimilated to this new way of non-thinking. They could soon detect a politically incorrect view and call the person out on their "mistake." I began to voice my opinion less often to avoid being berated and judged by a community that claims to represent the free expression of ideas. I learned, along with every other student, to walk on eggshells for fear that I may say something "offensive." That is the social norm here.

Top-Down Idea Supremacy

Since 1990, the number of administrative (nonacademic) staff at US colleges and universities has risen dramatically, alongside the vast increase in student tuition[*] (and student debt) and the replacement of full-time faculty members with part-time faculty and teaching assistants. The largest growth in college staff has been in Diversity, Equity & Inclusion (DEI) departments, which in many top schools have more than one hundred bureaucrats.

The idea of having lots of staff members working to improve the school's "diversity, equity, and inclusion" sounds nice enough on its face. But with powers to enforce vague rules, these departments may be contributing to the rise of idea supremacy on campuses.

Hundreds of US colleges have bias response teams, which monitor and investigate student and faculty speech. Jeffrey Aaron Snyder and Amna Khalid, writing in the *New Republic*, say bias response teams are "committees with unelected members that meet behind closed doors"

---

[*] According to the US Bureau of Labor Statistics, while the overall consumer price index rose 214 percent between 1990 and 2020, college tuition rose 1,184 percent during that stretch.

that "lack both transparency and accountability" and "are rapidly becoming part of the institutional machinery of higher education, but have yet to face any real scrutiny." Some schools have even begun to hire students to report fellow students they see exhibiting some form of bias.

Up-close investigations into how these work in practice have repeatedly produced troubling findings. In 2018, the nonprofit organization Speech First studied how bias response teams work at the University of Michigan. They found:

> More than 150 reports of alleged "expressions of bias"—through posters, fliers, social media, whiteboards, verbal comments, classroom behavior, etc.—have been investigated by the university's bias response team since April 2017. According to Michigan, "bias comes in many forms," can be intentional or unintentional, and "can be a hurtful action based on who someone is as a person." In the school's words, "the most important indication of bias is your own feelings." As a result, a student whose speech is seen by another student as hurtful to his or her feelings may receive a knock on the door from a team of school officials threatening to refer the student for discipline unless he or she submits to "restorative justice," "individualized education," or "unconscious bias training."

When Speech First brought a lawsuit against Michigan, alleging that their bias response teams were unconstitutional and "flagrantly violate the First Amendment," the court agreed, ruling against the school. As of 2022, 456 US colleges have bias response teams (almost double the 2017 total of 232), and very few have been subject to investigations like the one at Michigan.

Providing ammunition for bias response teams are university speech codes, which FIRE defines as a "university regulation or policy that prohibits expression that would be protected by the First Amendment in society at large." Speech codes, enforced by bias response teams, tend to be vaguely worded, granting administrators leeway to suspend or

---

* According to Speech First, which examined 821 US colleges, 66 percent of the public four-year colleges (250) and 46 percent of the private four-year colleges (204) they examined had bias-response teams. Both of these numbers are around double what FIRE had identified in 2017.

expel students who commit microaggressions and anything else staff deem to be offensive. A glance at nearly any university website makes it clear that the "offensive speech" is being defined the SJF way. Miami University, for example, urges students to "speak out when jokes or comments are made that are hateful or demean others because of race, religion, disability, ethnic/national origin, gender, or sexual orientation." This list is repeated nearly verbatim across many college websites, while politics-related hate or discrimination, which has run rampant in recent years, was mentioned all of zero times on the dozens of websites I visited.

After a deep investigation into speech codes at Tufts, FIRE reported that "students have been systematically investigated, interrogated by police, and punished by Tufts for speech the university claims, generally, to permit….Open disagreement isn't just 'social suicide'—it can get you in serious trouble." In response to this climate, a group of Tufts students submitted a proposal to the school government asking that the college's administration "clarify its ambiguous speech-related policies." On the grounds that the *proposal itself* made some students "feel unsafe on campus," it was rejected in a 26–0 vote.

Speech First writes that "the lack of clear and meaningful standards in both the school's speech code and bias response system present a serious risk that it will be enforced in an arbitrary or discriminatory manner and may be used to target speech based on a speaker's viewpoint." We saw this play out, for example, at Emory when a student wrote "Trump 2016" on the ground in chalk during the 2016 election. Responding to student complaints that the "hate speech" made them feel unsafe, administrators took action, offering emergency counseling to the students while launching a manhunt using security camera footage to find out who had written the pro-Trump message.

A sixth of America's four hundred top colleges have implemented "free speech zones" on campus—implying that speech is *not* free elsewhere on campus. But even in these zones, speech that conflicts with campus orthodoxy has been banned. Sam Houston State, for example, sent the campus police to a university-approved "free speech wall," where they told the organizers to take down a message that said "fuck Obama" or face criminal charges.

Free speech, remember, requires a two-piece puzzle: free speech laws and free speech culture. These stories, from the disinvitations and shutdowns to the bias response teams and speech codes, aren't about free speech laws, as very few of them violate the First Amendment. They're stories about an ideology that has crippled free speech *culture* on campuses. Without the critical second puzzle piece, most vocal skeptics become silent skeptics, and campuses transform from Idea Labs to SJF Echo Chambers.

The real power of idea supremacy is that you only have to achieve a little of it through punishments and public shamings. In an environment soon infused with fear, self-censorship does most of the heavy lifting. The stories that make the headlines give just a hint of the problem, because there will never be any headlines about the speakers not invited, the conversations not started, the hands not raised in the first place.

A few years ago, I interviewed a conservative student at Dartmouth College about his experience there. He told me that fellow conservatives he knew were shocked to see stats showing that almost a fifth of graduating students were conservative. "We all keep our views to ourselves," he said, "so in every class, it always feels like we're the only one."

IDEA SUPREMACY ON CAMPUS: RESEARCH

In 2014, a Harvard student wrote an article in the school newspaper called "The Doctrine of Academic Freedom." In it, she wrote:

> The liberal obsession with "academic freedom" seems a bit misplaced to me....If our university community opposes racism, sexism, and heterosexism, why should we put up with research that counters our goals simply in the name of "academic freedom"? Instead, I would like to propose a more rigorous standard: one of "academic justice." When an academic community observes research promoting or justifying oppression, it should ensure that this research does not continue.

This is a standard argument for a religious institution, where the goal is not the search for truth but adherence to a sacred philosophy or scripture. But at a university like Harvard, whose motto means "truth," academic freedom is supposed to be a sacred tenet.

The article went viral, mostly to scathing criticism, on and off the Harvard campus. I remember reading the article and feeling heartened by the negative reaction to it. What I didn't realize at the time was that across much of academia, the writer's wish had already come true.

THE LARRY SUMMERS STORY

In 2005, the National Bureau of Economic Research held a "Conference on Diversifying the Science & Engineering Workforce." They invited then–Harvard president Larry Summers to give a lunchtime talk, not as Harvard president, but as a top economist, to share some of his thoughts on why there weren't more women in STEM professions (Science, Tech, Engineering, Math).

He prefaced his remarks by saying he would take "an entirely positive, rather than normative approach, and just try to think about and offer some hypotheses as to why we observe what we observe." In other words, he'd focus the talk on What Is, not What Should Be.

He then laid out the "three broad hypotheses about the sources of the very substantial disparities…with respect to the presence of women in high-end scientific professions."

The first is the "high-powered job hypothesis," which highlights the fact that "the most prestigious activities in our society expect of people who are going to rise to leadership positions in their forties near total commitments to their work." Summers suggests this could be examined by asking: "What fraction of young women in their mid-twenties make a decision that they don't want to have a job that they think about eighty hours a week? What fraction of young men make a decision that they're unwilling to have a job that they think about eighty hours a week?" and observing the difference between the two figures.[*]

The second hypothesis is about potential differences in ability and interests:

---

[*] Summers acknowledges the obvious normative question that would pop up here—"Is our society right to have familial arrangements in which women are asked to make that choice and asked more to make that choice than men?"—and says that's a question he wants to come back to.

It does appear that on many, many different human attributes—height, weight, propensity for criminality, overall IQ, mathematical ability, scientific ability—there is relatively clear evidence that whatever the difference in means—which can be debated—there is a difference in the standard deviation and variability of a male and a female population. And that is true with respect to attributes that are and are not plausibly, culturally determined....There may also be elements...of taste differences between little girls and little boys that are not easy to attribute to socialization.

The third hypothesis is about discrimination:

To what extent is there overt discrimination? Surely there is some. Much more tellingly, to what extent are there pervasive patterns of passive discrimination and stereotyping in which people like to choose people like themselves, and the people in the previous group are disproportionately white male, and so they choose people who are like themselves, who are disproportionately white male. No one who's been in a university department or who has been involved in personnel processes can deny that this kind of taste does go on, and it is something that happens, and it is something that absolutely, vigorously needs to be combated.

After presenting the three hypotheses, Summers offers suggestions for the kinds of further research that should be done in order to figure out what about the three hypotheses is and isn't true. He finishes his talk with this:

Let me just conclude by saying that I've given you my best guesses after a fair amount of reading the literature and a lot of talking to people. They may be all wrong. I will have served my purpose if I have provoked thought on this question and provoked the marshalling of evidence to contradict what I have said. But I think we all need to be thinking very hard about how to do better on these issues and that they are too important to sentimentalize rather than to think about in as rigorous and careful ways as we can.

This was a controversial talk that could understandably ruffle feathers—especially because Summers believed discrimination was the smallest contributor of the three.* It's also a standard academic analysis. An economist laid out what he believes are the three most prevalent hypotheses in the existing research on a topic, offered some suggestions for further exploration, and in a Q&A after the talk, members of the audience offered their views on those points.

But in the audience was an MIT biology professor named Nancy Hopkins. Hopkins was a long-time advocate for the view that gender disparities in STEM were caused primarily by discrimination, and Summers' points—which contradicted Hopkins' long-held beliefs—did not sit well.

Midway through Summers' remarks, while he explained the second hypothesis (the one about biological differences between the sexes), Hopkins packed up her things and walked out of the talk. Then she started calling reporters.

"I felt I was going to be sick," she told the *Washington Post*. "My heart was pounding and my breath was shallow. I was extremely upset."

She told the *New York Times*: "When he started talking about innate differences in aptitude between men and women, I just couldn't breathe because this kind of bias makes me physically ill."

She told the *Harvard Crimson* that Summers "shouldn't admit women to Harvard if he's going to announce when they come that, hey, we don't feel that you can make it to the top."

The story exploded. A writer for the *Boston Globe* summed up Summers' points as debating whether women were "natively inferior." The *Guardian* headline read "Why women are poor at science, by Harvard president," while others argued that Summers was a sexist and a misogynist.

Plenty of people defended Summers. When author and cognitive psychologist Steven Pinker was asked by the *Crimson* whether he was offended by Summers' remarks, he replied: "The truth cannot be offensive. Perhaps the hypothesis is wrong, but how would we ever find out whether it is wrong if it is 'offensive' even to consider it?" Paula E. Stephan, a professor of economics who was at the talk, scoffed at the

---

* He notes: "I would like nothing better than to be proved wrong, because I would like nothing better than for these problems to be addressable simply by everybody understanding what they are, and working very hard to address them."

notion that she might be offended by the comments: "I think if you come to participate in a research conference, you should expect speakers to present hypotheses that you may not agree with and then discuss them on the basis of research findings." Three others at the conference told the *Globe* that Summers' remarks "reflected mainstream economic theories."

But the defenses had little effect on the backlash Summers received at Harvard. A Harvard board member resigned his post, writing that Summers' remarks were "an insult heard worldwide." The Harvard Faculty passed a vote of "lack of confidence" in Summers. A letter signed by more than one hundred Harvard faculty members lambasted Summers for "reinforc[ing] an institutional culture at Harvard that erects numerous barriers to improving the representation of women on the faculty, and to impede our efforts to recruit top women scholars." It was the straw that broke the back of a tumultuous stint as Harvard president, and Summers resigned the next year.

・・・

A Liberal Social Justice activist might disagree vehemently with the hypotheses Summers highlighted—and in the Q&A, some people did so—but they probably would not object to him expressing them. Liberal science is *fueled* by disagreement.

Social Justice Fundamentalism has a different take on this. First, the SJF narrative already explains exactly What Is and What Should Be. One sacred tenet holds there are no differences of ability or interest between demographic groups. This tenet, combined with SJF's notion of the all-encompassing Force, generates the SJF axiom we discussed last chapter: any disparity of outcome between groups *must by definition* be the result of injustice.*

Second, SJF doesn't just hold these viewpoints—it holds them as *sacred*, believing that someone who challenges these ideas shouldn't be refuted but punished. To Nancy Hopkins and many others, Summers' points weren't merely wrong, they were *blasphemy*. The Summers

---

* As we noted, the axiom only applies when the disparity fits the SJF worldview—i.e., when it negatively affects groups downward on the Intersectional Stack, in the direction of the Force. When a disparity goes in the other direction—like the fact that women make up about 60 percent of today's American college students—the axiom goes away.

story is about more than differing ideas. It's about a struggle between two opposite methods of dealing with ideas: open inquiry and idea supremacy.

Quick tangent because I think it illuminates an important point:

But What About Those Things Summers Said?

After reading more about this story, I dug in a bit to the research myself. Today, the subject remains a work in progress full of fierce debate. Some of the interesting data I came across:

Women and men are, across broad averages, slightly stronger at different things

PISA is a well-known test taken by fifteen-year-olds across over seventy countries and economies. The data from a recent year reveals the following:

	NUMBER OF COUNTRIES WHERE WOMEN OUTPERFORMED MEN	NUMBER OF COUNTRIES WHERE MEN OUTPERFORMED WOMEN
READING	67	0
MATH	24	43
SCIENCE	29	38

So women sometimes scored higher than men at math and science, but they *always* scored better at reading. The reading numbers are so skewed that even in the countries where women outperformed men in math or science, they outperformed men in reading by even *higher* margins.

Data from a thirty-year examination of SAT/ACT scores reveals the same pattern. On average, men do a little better on the math/science sections of the test, women do a little better on the verbal/writing sections.

This is just one of many areas where male and female strengths differ. In an article about the Summers controversy, Steven Pinker lists some more: "Men are, on average, better at mental rotation and mathematical word problems; women are better at remembering locations and at mathematical calculation. Women match shapes more quickly, are better at reading faces, are better spellers, retrieve words more fluently, and have a better memory for verbal material. Men take greater risks and place a higher premium on status; women are more solicitous to their children."

While these discrepancies may partially account for the gender ratio disparity in STEM professions, social psychologist Sean Stevens notes an additional possibility: Of all people qualified to work in STEM fields, "the women in this elite group generally have much better verbal skills than the men in that elite group. This means that these women may be better employees than men who match them on quantitative skills, but because they have such superior verbal skills they have more choices available to them when selecting a profession." Qualified women, perhaps with a more diverse set of cognitive talents, may distribute themselves among fields more widely than their male STEM equivalents.

There's far more variation within the two groups than between them

The way the data is often presented makes the differences seem bigger than they are. For example, in his book *Factfulness*, Hans Rosling shows how SAT math scores are often presented:

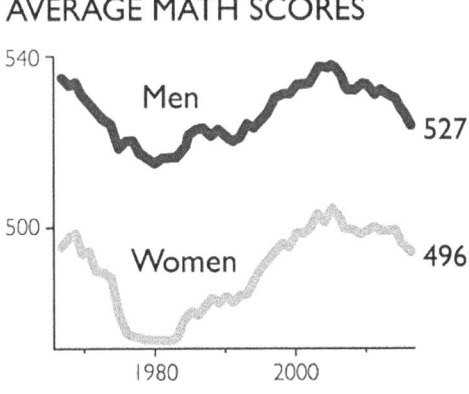

Source: Rosling, Factfulness

Then, using the data from the 2016 SAT, Rosling presents the same data a different way, using overlapping bell curves. He notes: "There is an almost complete overlap between men and women's math scores. The majority of women have a male math twin: a man with the same math score as they do."

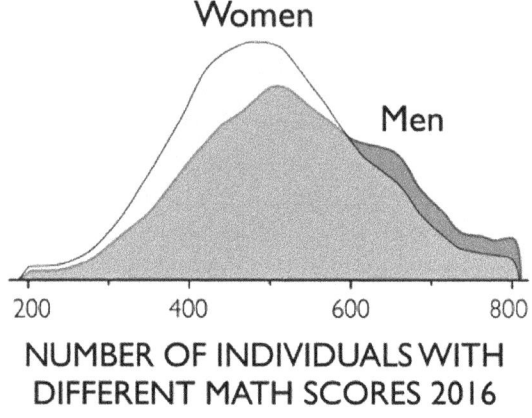

NUMBER OF INDIVIDUALS WITH DIFFERENT MATH SCORES 2016

Source: Rosling, Factfulness

This emphasizes a big point: broad group averages tell you nothing about any individual.

Women and men, across broad averages, display different interests

There are lots of studies that suggest women are, on average, more interested in "people," while men are, on average, more interested in "things," and this likely contributes to differences in career choices. According to a large 2022 study by the Institute for Family Studies, "In every country (without exception), more girls than boys aspired to a people-oriented occupation, and more boys than girls aspired to a things-oriented or STEM occupation."

Considering both the differences in cognition and personality, graphs like this one of US PhD students in 2015, from the Council of Graduate Schools, seem unsurprising:*

---

* It's worth noting that Summers' talk was about sciences like math and engineering. When health and medical sciences are included in the definition of STEM, there are *more* women than men enrolled in STEM grad programs.

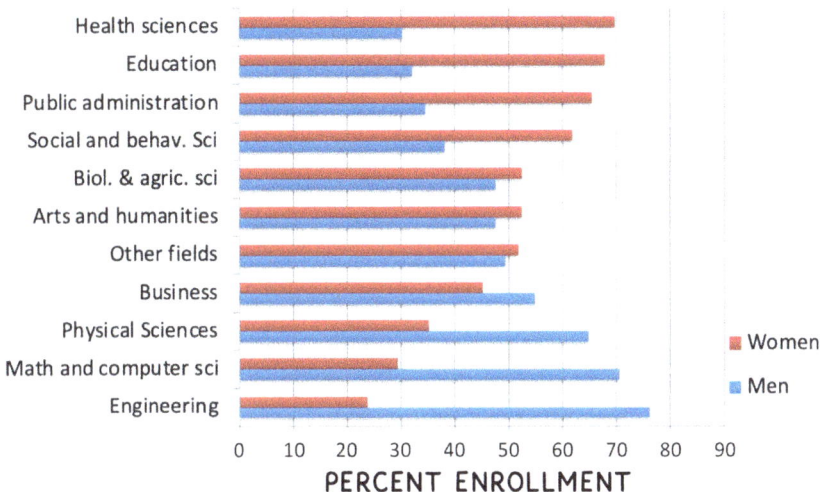

Source: Jonathan Haidt

None of this means other factors like socialization, cultural norms, and discrimination don't play a role in the disparity between men and women in STEM professions (or a role in these differences we just outlined). It just suggests, as Summers said, that the disparity may not *only* be due to socialization, cultural norms, and discrimination.

Let's call this the Nuanced Story, one that is unafraid to consider every factor and takes into account the full array of inputs that may contribute to an output like the gender disparity in STEM. Learning about the Nuanced Story didn't turn me into a misogynist—quite the opposite. It made me feel humble in the face of what is obviously a very complex story. It made me better appreciate the value of gender diversity in any industry. And it made me better prepared to refute inaccurate, harmful gender prejudices and teach misguided people why they're wrong.

But reading article after article about this story back in 2005, I didn't learn anything about the Nuanced Story. Instead, I heard two other stories, repeated ad nauseam.

The first was the straw man version of Summers' talk. The talk itself was never quoted in the articles—just that Summers had said women are, as the *Guardian* had put it, "poor at science," that he doesn't believe, as Nancy Hopkins had put it, that women "can make it to the top," and many more versions of both of these points. The Nuanced Story, which is what Summers actually talked about, says nothing like this.

The second was the SJF alternative to the Summers straw man: that there are no differences between women and men across broad averages and that therefore the STEM disparity must 100 percent be due to discrimination and patriarchal norms.

In suppressing the Nuanced Story, SJF idea supremacy hindered the path toward knowledge and, if anything, *slowed* progress in the arena of women and STEM. But it also did further harm, causing these other two stories to spread: one that feeds misogyny; another that fuels anger and hopelessness.

Since 2005, this double-wrong—the suppression of science and the spread of anti-science—has only become more prevalent.

FORBIDDEN RESEARCH

Social psychologist Jonathan Haidt talks about chairing a bipartisan group of top poverty scholars that worked together to create what he believes is "the best analysis of American poverty in the last thirty years." Haidt explains that, in performing the analysis, scholars on the political left focused on economic changes, systemic racism, and what they saw as a rigged political system. The scholars on the political right focused on the decline of marriage, the rise of dependency and the loss of agency, and irresponsible personal choices. It was specifically the bipartisan nature of the effort that Haidt believes ultimately made it so effective, and by working together, scholars on the left became convinced about typically conservative emphases like the importance of marriage, while those on the right came out in uncharacteristic support of birth control. Sounds great, right?

The thing is, this analysis was done at the AEI-Brookings Working Group (a think tank collaboration), not at a university. Haidt says that it had to be this way, because A) the conservatives on the project were, like most conservative intellectuals today, at think tanks, not at universities, and B) given that people of color are overrepresented among victims of poverty, the conservative scholars' focuses—marriage/dependency/personal choices—would have never been permitted as considerations. In Haidt's words, "Those are blasphemy. You can't blame the victim." He compares partisan lenses to tools in a shed, saying the university's stance is: "One third of the tools, you cannot use them. If you touch it, we shoot you."

Haidt isn't being paranoid. Over the past few years, dozens of scholars from around the US have had their careers tarred or totally derailed for making the mistake of doing research whose results conflict with the SJF narrative.

In 2017, two researchers wrote a mathematics paper that involved the greater male variability hypothesis, the same hypothesis Summers had mentioned in his speech. It was accepted to the academic journal *Mathematical Intelligencer*, but when one of the papers' authors posted a preprint on his website, a protest erupted, leading the journal to cancel the planned publication. One of the authors notes that "in my 40 years of publishing research papers I had never heard of the rejection of an already-accepted paper." The two authors submitted the paper to another journal, where it was again accepted, and eventually published. Three days of backlash later, the journal retracted the paper.

In 2018, physician-scientist Lisa Littman published a paper on the phenomenon of "rapid onset gender dysphoria," which explores the roles of social contagion and social media in the development of gender dysphoria. After intense protests, including a warning that "the conclusions of the study could be used to discredit efforts to support transgender youth and invalidate the perspectives of members of the transgender community," the journal "corrected" and republished the paper.

Incidents like these—and so many others—are stories of moments of truth gone wrong. In each case, a research institution is forced to choose between standing up for their publication criteria (which each paper had already successfully passed through) or ceding those criteria to protesters. And in each case, the protesters won.

In some situations, entire fields are being stalled in their progress by SJF activism. In 2017, science writer Ann Gibbons wrote an article called "There's no such thing as a 'pure' European—or anyone else," about "revolutionary new methods to analyze DNA and the isotopes found in bones and teeth" that are "exposing the tangled roots of peoples around the world." She explains:

> Almost all indigenous Europeans descend from at least three major migrations in the past 15,000 years, including two from the Middle East....Few of us are actually the direct descendants of the ancient skeletons found in our backyards or historic homelands.

Paleogenetic research like this isn't just fascinating, it's important for human health. A 2020 paper, for example, used recent paleogenetic findings to identify populations likely to carry a particular gene cluster that would put them at high risk of severe symptoms from Covid-19.

But over the past few years, paleogenetic research across North America has stalled. Anthropologist Bruce Bourque writes about a 2019 conference at Brown University, where speakers talked about an update to ethical standards in the field:

> They advised audience members to pursue a "commonly agreed set of best practices" with "descendant communities"—especially when paleogenomic conclusions challenge, or conflict with, community knowledge about the past. Folklore and myths must be taken into account, and we must discourage the idea of science "controlling the narrative."...It is preferable, we are told, to put away our scientific instruments, and instead consider the oral histories of local community members. As a result, established academics in this field are not only backing away from future projects, but even apologizing for their invaluable discoveries of the past.

Bourque refers to these new ethical standards as an "insistence that traditional folklore and origin stories be protected from scientific scrutiny." He goes on:

> It is now seen as insulting to bring up the fact that humans arrived in the Americas from Asia via Beringia during the Last Glacial Maximum about 16,000 years ago, as this fact conflicts with spiritual notions that, in many cases, roughly correspond to Christian creationist myths. By demonstrating the degree to which today's Indigenous communities may themselves be entirely separate from ancient precursors, paleogenetics can be seen as a further threat to the ideal of Indigenous communities as homogenous, genetically distinct populations rooted timelessly in specific geographic areas.

When Gibbons wrote about new studies showing "that there is no such thing as a 'pure' European," it almost certainly upset some people who believe they are of pure European ancestry. When she wrote about migrations that happened fifteen thousand years ago, it probably didn't go over well with fundamentalist Christians who believe the Earth was created six thousand years ago. But science isn't concerned with feelings, it's concerned with truth. The history of science is a history of upsetting people by overturning their existing beliefs. A scientific community not willing to do that would not have come very far. Now though, research that might similarly upset indigenous groups—groups low down on SJF's Intersectional Stack—is being halted.

Beyond the many stories like these, we'll never learn about all the would-be research that was never attempted in the first place because of fear of SJF retribution.

The clampdown on academic freedom is only half the effect of idea supremacy in research. There's also the dissent-free path it paves for research that *confirms* the sacred narrative. Trying to expose this, three academics, Peter Boghossian, Helen Pluckrose, and James Lindsay, created an experiment. They wrote a handful of bogus academic papers—papers that intentionally used shoddy methodology, cited ridiculous evidence, and drew inane conclusions (but conclusions that aligned perfectly with SJF)—and they submitted them (using pseudonyms) to prominent social-justice-focused journals. Seven were accepted for publication.

Academic papers are supposed to be judged on rigor and accuracy. That's what keeps research institutions pointed toward truth. When papers are instead filtered based on how well their conclusions align with a particular ideology, journals turn from truth-finding organs into political instruments.

IDEA SUPREMACY ON CAMPUS: EDUCATION

Students interested in learning about social justice will typically be directed to "interdisciplinary departments" like gender studies, whiteness studies, queer theory, or postcolonial theory. These classes will often be taught using the methods of "critical pedagogy," a teaching philosophy whose main tenets mirror the principles of Social Justice Fundamentalism. One of these tenets is that disagreement with SJF isn't really cool.

SJF scholars talk about the problem of "resistance" in the classroom. In a 2007 paper, Syracuse professor Barbara Applebaum argues that "systemically privileged students' resistance to learning and knowing*... reproduces systems of oppression and privilege in the classroom." To Applebaum, "The mere fact that they can question the existence of systemic oppression is a function of their privilege." So disagreement from a privileged person is, in critical pedagogy, itself an act of oppression. But disagreement from non-privileged students is a no-go as well. As we touched on in Chapter 5, DiAngelo and Sensoy say that "when a student of Color claims that racism doesn't affect him," that viewpoint should not be affirmed in a social justice classroom.

Critical pedagogy lies in stark opposition to liberal teaching methods. A liberal education tries to teach students *how* to think and arms them with many different philosophies. University of Pennsylvania history professor Alan Charles Kors describes his time as a student at Princeton in the early 1960s:

> The people who taught me at Princeton...were probably disproportionately individuals of the Left, but none of that was obvious from their curriculum, from their syllabi, or from their teaching. They did not see their task as producing disciples and clones in a classroom.

He recounts one class where the Marxist professor reprimanded the students for answering exam questions "with what you thought I wanted to hear." On the next exam, he insisted students argue from the exact opposite perspective.

But many of today's social justice classes, practicing critical pedagogy, do things the opposite way. They teach students *what* to think and offer only one lens: SJF. Instead of reprimanding students who try to mirror the professor's politics, professors penalize students who don't.

Here's how the dictionary defines "indoctrination": *the process of teaching a person or group to accept a set of beliefs uncritically.*

---

* Applebaum quotes some examples of resistance: "remaining silent, evading questions, resorting to the rhetoric of ignoring color, focusing on progress, victim blaming, and focusing on culture rather than race."

Indoctrination is what idea supremacy looks like in a classroom. And it's an apt description of what happens in many of today's social justice classes.

It would be one thing if this kind of classroom experience were limited to students who choose to take classes in interdisciplinary departments. But that's increasingly not the case.

SJF as a Graduation Requirement

In a 2020 memo, a dean at the University of North Carolina wrote that "it is possible for a…student to graduate without taking a course focused on the question of diversity. Faculty believe that is a problem." She wrote about "the need to accent racism, social justice, and cultural competency throughout the curriculum." This sentiment has swept through college administrations over the past few years, and hundreds of schools have acted, making major changes to graduation requirements.

Many schools have made diversity and inclusion training a mandatory part of freshman orientation—training that teaches students about SJF tenets like power and privilege, microaggressions, and systemic oppression. Students in these orientations are trained to see the campus through SJF's identity-focused lens. A student named Carrie Pritt wrote in *Quillette* about her experience in Princeton's freshman orientation, recalling a session in which the leader told students to "stand up if you identify as Caucasian" and then told the standing students to "look at your community." The leader, wrote Pritt, "went on to repeat the exercise for over an hour with different adjectives in place of 'Caucasian': black, wealthy, first-generation, socially conservative. Each time he introduced a new label, he paused so that a new group of students could stand and take note of one another. By the time he was finished, every member of Princeton University's freshman class had been branded with a demographic."

Hundreds of schools have also begun requiring students to take at least one class in SJF in order to graduate. California State University students are, as of 2020, required by law to take an "ethnic studies" course that guidelines say must "critique dominant narratives of power and their claims to neutrality, objectivity, color-blindness, freedom from bias, and meritocracy in order to examine their harm to Indigenous and other communities of color." Since 2017, Hamilton College has required new students in every department to take a class that analyzes "structural and institutional hierarchies based on one or more of the social categories of race, class, gender, ethnicity, nationality, religion, sexuality, age, and abilities/disabilities." In 2021, Emory began requiring a "race and ethnicity course" in which students would "develop a critical[*] awareness of how racial and ethnic antagonisms and inequality develop historically through individual, institutional, and cultural forces." In every case I examined, it was clear from the course description that what's being taught in these required classes is Social Justice Fundamentalism.

These examples are the norm, not the exception. An analysis of sixty representative US colleges and universities found that fifty-one of them require students to take one or more social-justice-related classes.[†] There's nothing wrong with schools requiring students to take classes in certain core academic areas—but SJF is a specific political ideology, not a core academic area.

Students may also find themselves inadvertently studying social justice in seemingly unrelated departments. Pomona, for example, recently amended its Introduction to Statistics course. The new syllabus reads: "The main goal of this course is to enhance your analytical and statistical skills while exploring topics in social justice." Students taking the course are required to submit mandatory weekly journals that "should contain reflections on both the statistical and social justice topics covered."

Both the mandated SJF learning for all students and the way those courses are taught involve an element of coercion. Students *must* be trained in SJF, and disagreement during those trainings will *not* be permitted. But SJF idea supremacy goes much further than those specific instances—it hangs over *all* classes.

---

[*] When "critical" is used in this kind of way, it almost always refers to the SJF meaning (e.g., as it's used in "critical race theory"), not to the more common usage, as in "critical thinking." In this description, a "critical awareness" essentially translates to "a mindset that sees things through the SJF worldview."

[†] A professor I spoke to believes many of these requirements were created in order to "guarantee tenured employment for social justice professors." She explained it like this: "Social justice classes have a really hard time filling their classes and their majors, but they continue to get new tenure lines and funding. So you have five gender studies professors, with expensive pension and benefits packages, all teaching classes with seven students in them, when those same thirty-five kids could be taught by one political science or history professor."

Forbidden Teaching

William Deresiewicz, a former English professor at Yale, explains how the increase in college administrators, at the expense of full-time faculty positions, has led to a major power shift on campuses:

> Where once administrations worked in alliance with the faculty, were indeed largely composed of faculty, now they work against the faculty in alliance with students, a separate managerial stratum more interested in the satisfaction of its customers than the well-being of its employees. In the inevitable power struggle between students and teachers, the former have gained the whip hand....With the expansion of Title IX in 2011—the law is now being used, among other things, to police classroom content—even tenured faculty are sitting with a sword above their heads....In a conflict between a student and a faculty member, almost nothing is at stake for the student beyond the possibility of receiving a low grade...But the teacher could be fired.

This has led to story after story of professors being held at the whim of students who take offense to their teaching.

Lindsay Shepherd, a teaching assistant at Wilfrid Laurier University, ended up in hot water after she played, for her class, five minutes of a TV debate with clinical psychologist Jordan Peterson about legal issues around gender pronouns and free speech. A student complaint landed Shepherd in a meeting with school diversity officials (which she recorded), where she was reprimanded for creating "an unsafe learning environment for students." When Shepherd said that she had "remained very neutral" in class, she was told, "That's kind of the problem."

Shepherd's experience is not uncommon. A Brandeis professor was the subject of a long investigation for saying the racial slur "wetback" while explaining its use as a pejorative. Duquesne University went a step further and actually fired a professor for saying a racial slur in a pedagogical context (he was talking about how the word has become more taboo over time). A USC professor was removed from his position after saying a Chinese filler word that *sounds* like an English slur during a lesson about filler words in different languages. A University of Illinois Chicago law professor was placed on leave for including *censored* references to two slurs (literally, "N___" and "B___") in an exam hypothetical about workplace discrimination.* The month after George Floyd's death, a white UCLA student emailed their professor recommending that, due to the tragedy, students of color receive extended deadlines and a shortened final exam. The professor sent a response explaining why he saw such a policy as impractical, and the student posted the email online. Twenty thousand petition signatures later, UCLA suspended the professor.†

The nonprofit FIRE documented 471 such attempts to get professors fired or punished between 2015 and 2021, with almost three-quarters of them resulting in some type of sanction (172 of the punished professors were tenured—27 of those were fired).‡ The frequency of these incidents quadrupled during that span (from 30 in 2015 to 122 in 2021).§

The policing of professors by students is encouraged by administrators by instructive signs all around campus and in official surveys. Two professors at Villanova explain how this works:

> Last fall we were notified by the Villanova administration that new "diversity and inclusion" questions would be added to the course and teaching evaluations that students fill out each semester. In addition to the standard questions about the intellectual worth of the course and the quality of instruction, students are now being asked heavily politicized questions such as whether the instructor has demonstrated "cultural awareness" or created an "environment free of bias based on individual differences or social identities." In short, students are being asked to rate professors according to their perceived agreement with progressive political opinion on

---

* Extra note of absurdity: The school then required this professor to participate in months-long "training on classroom conversations that address racism"—and the training materials used *the same redacted slur* the professor was placed on leave for.

† One more because I just have to tell you: A Fordham University professor was fired after he accidentally confused the names of two Black students in class.

‡ By the way, the *primary purpose* of tenure is to protect professors from pressure to conform to whatever ideological fads would inevitably come, so they could remain independent. Firing tenured professors for offending the sensibilities of a particular political ideology directly contradicts that purpose.

§ FIRE's director Greg Lukianoff notes in *Reason* that this trend is especially pronounced in the top-ranked schools. The top ten ranked schools alone account for 15 percent of the total incidents.

bias and identity....All charges of insensitivity, injustice and bigotry will become part of the faculty's permanent record. How long will it be before professors cease to challenge their students for fear of losing their careers and livelihoods?

Of course, this affects how and what professors teach. For example, Harvard law professor Jeannie Suk Gersen says that law professors are increasingly dropping rape law from their curriculums:

> About a dozen new teachers of criminal law at multiple institutions have told me that they are not including rape law in their courses, arguing that it's not worth the risk of complaints of discomfort by students. Even seasoned teachers of criminal law, at law schools across the country, have confided that they are seriously considering dropping rape law and other topics related to sex and gender violence.

Gersen likens the students whose sensitivities forbid the teaching of rape law to medical students who insist on being shielded from the sight of blood. She points out that the victims of these curriculum changes aren't just the majority of students who expect to learn about rape law in law school: "If the topic of sexual assault were to leave the law-school classroom, it would be a tremendous loss—above all to victims of sexual assault."

In some cases, administrators, hearing student protests, have gone so far as to make curriculum changes official. A group of student activists at Reed College caused a stir in 2017 when they interrupted a large humanities class with protests that the syllabus—which covered the philosophy of ancient Rome, Greece, and Egypt—was too white, male, and Eurocentric. Though most of the students in the class were annoyed about the protests, saying it was hurting their opportunity to learn, in a moment of truth at Reed, administrators sided with the protesters and made sweeping changes to the curriculum. In the revised syllabus, half of the material was replaced with books that explored social justice issues.

Introductory courses that focus on Western art, literature, and philosophy have become targets of SJF in schools across the US and UK, and in many cases, the courses have been revised like Reed's, or canceled altogether. When Howard University announced that it would be dissolving its Classics department, renowned professor Cornel West co-wrote an article in the *Washington Post*, lamenting: "Today, one of America's greatest Black institutions, Howard University, is diminishing the light of wisdom and truth that inspired Douglass, King and countless other freedom fighters....Academia's continual campaign to disregard or neglect the classics is a sign of spiritual decay, moral decline and a deep intellectual narrowness running amok in American culture."

Perhaps the most egregious instance of idea supremacy over education happens in the hiring department.

Recruiting

Bret Weinstein's wife and fellow Evergreen professor Heather Heying talks about the sweeping changes enacted by the school in the months leading up to all the "Day of Absence" drama:

> Some of the things from this plan, that no one has seen, are things like: "From now on, not just individuals hired to positions need to have an equity justification, but every single position itself needs to have an equity justification." Which means, how do you hire a chemist? Does chemistry have an equity justification? How do you hire an artist who doesn't happen to be engaged in social justice issues? That is the end of a liberal arts college right there.

It turns out that across the US, this has become a common policy. Here's a sampling* of excerpts from recent faculty job postings:

> **Purdue—Military History/American Civil War Era**, Assistant Professor: *Candidates should address...their past experiences, current interests or activities and/or future goals to promote a climate that values diversity and inclusion.*

> **Lafayette—Electrical and Computer Engineering**, Assistant Professor: *In your cover letter, please address how your scholarship, teaching, mentoring, and/or community service might support Lafayette College's commitment to diversity and inclusion.*

---

* See David Randall's *Social Justice Education in America* report for a long list of similar job postings.

San Francisco State—Ancient Greek/Roman Philosophy, Assistant Professor:...*providing curricula that reflect all dimensions of human diversity, and that encourage critical thinking and a commitment to social justice.*

UMass Amherst—Science Education, Professor: *The person hired will...have a philosophy of teaching and advising that reflects a commitment to social justice, improving learning and instruction, and challenging inequities in science education.*

Michigan—Physics Department, Student Administration Manager: *The selected candidate should have...general knowledge of issues and concepts related to diversity, inclusion, equity, and social justice.*

Military history, computer engineering, ancient philosophy, science education, and physics. These ads are not for social justice classes. And yet, all of these job postings say they are looking for applicants with a commitment to social justice. At first glance, the postings simply seem to aim to hire professors who care about diversity and inclusion. But the specific wording reveals the trademark language of SJF—something that will become clear in a minute.

Ads like these likely go a long way toward dissuading conservatives, non-SJF progressives, and nonpolitical academics from applying. For those who apply anyway, there's another gatekeeper waiting for them at the beginning of the application process.

Diversity Statements

In 1950, the University of California system began requiring its faculty to sign oaths pledging their loyalty to the United States and affirming that they were in no way Communists. Those who didn't were fired or rejected as applicants. This was common for a brief period until 1952, when California's Supreme Court ruled that the loyalty oath was unconstitutional and ordered the UC system to reinstate all employees that had been fired for refusing to sign.

It seems like an absurd moment in ancient history. But in the last few years, hundreds of American colleges have recently added a "diversity statement" to their application process for faculty and administrators, in which applicants must explain how they've contributed to equity, diversity, and inclusion in their previous work and how they plan to continue that work on campus.

UC Berkeley describes its new hiring process in a 2018–2019 report. In the hiring of five life science professors, the first filter was the job ad, which mirrors those listed above: they're looking for "applications from outstanding early career research scientists who also demonstrated strong potential to enhance equity, inclusion and diversity." They received 893 applicants who met basic qualifications.

They then "conducted a first review and evaluated candidates based solely on contributions to diversity, equity and inclusion." For the assessment, they evaluated applicants on three criteria—knowledge about diversity, equity, and inclusion (DEI), track record in advancing DEI, and plans for advancing DEI. Only applicants who received high scores across the board were considered for the next round. This eliminated over 75 percent of the candidates, leaving 214 on the "long list." Finalists were then "asked to describe their efforts to promote equity and inclusion, as well as ideas for advancing equity and inclusion at Berkeley."

The report states that "emphasizing diversity, equity and inclusion in the first review is now an agreed practice" and that "limiting the first review to contributions in DE&I is itself a dramatic change of emphasis in the typical evaluation process which generally focuses primarily on research accomplishments."

So applicants must first score high marks on their diversity statements and then describe, in person, their history as a social justice activist and their plans for future activism. This is the process to hire *science professors*. And Berkeley has made it clear that this isn't just part of the application process but the *very first filter*, meaning candidates who aren't active social justice activists *won't even make it to the stage* where they're reviewed by people who are actually assessing their scholarship.

Let's take a closer look at the specific criteria Berkeley used to make that first major cut from the initial 893 applicants down to 214. For each of the three areas (DEI knowledge, track record, and future plans), Berkeley's rubric describes what entails a score of 1–2, 3, and 4–5. Berkeley states that only applicants who received a combined score of 11 out of 15 or higher made it through to the next round, which means an applicant with one "2" would need to totally crush the other two areas. Let's look at some of the descriptions of what will land someone with a

1–2 and essentially disqualify them from becoming a life science professor at Berkeley:

> Explicitly states the intention to ignore the varying backgrounds of their students and "treat everyone the same."
>
> Defines diversity only in terms of different areas of study or different nationalities, but doesn't discuss gender or ethnicity/race.
>
> May state having had little experience with these issues because of lack of exposure.
>
> Participated in no specific activities, or only one or two limited activities [related to advancing diversity, equity, inclusion, and belonging.]

So you may be a brilliant, accomplished scholar in the life sciences, but if you've spent too much time studying biology and not enough on progressive political activism, you're out. Even if you are a progressive activist, but instead of working on social justice activism, you spend your time on local politics, climate change activism, and gun control activism—you're out. If you're a social justice activist but subscribe to Liberal Social Justice, not SJF, you're out.

The 214 candidates that made Berkeley's "longlist" likely received 4–5s in most areas. Let's look at what a 4–5 means:

> Clear knowledge of, experience with, and interest in dimensions of diversity that result from different identities, such as ethnic, socioeconomic, racial, gender, sexual orientation, disability, and cultural differences.
>
> Consistent track record that spans multiple years.
>
> Organized or spoken at workshops or other events...aimed at increasing others' understanding of diversity, equity, and inclusion.
>
> Clearly formulates new ideas for advancing equity and inclusion at Berkeley and within their field, through their research, teaching, and/or service.

In other words: to teach science at Berkeley, *you must be an experienced progressive activist specifically of the SJF variety, with plans to continue that activism at Berkeley.*

Writing about a similar hiring process at UCLA, Heather Mac Donald points out that if Albert Einstein applied for a faculty job at UCLA today, he almost certainly would be ruled out before anyone had a chance to take a look at his research.

Item 40.3 of the UC Regents Bylaws reads as follows: *No political test shall ever be considered in the appointment and promotion of any faculty member or employee.* These schools are doing something they're not supposed to be doing. But they're doing it anyway. As is Cornell. And Emory. And Denison. And Pomona. And UT Austin. And Washington. And Hartford.*

Beyond using diversity statements as a hiring filter, many schools now require *existing* faculty and administrators to submit a diversity statement in order to achieve tenure and the extra earnings that come along with it.

Outside of academia, the required diversity statement has been referred to as "a political test with teeth," "a public confession of faith," "a new kind of religious creed," and "blatant viewpoint discrimination."

But people *inside* of academia are mostly keeping their thoughts to themselves. And for good reason: those who have attempted to criticize the practice within academia have become targets of ensuing uproars. One vocal critic—the former dean of Harvard Medical School, Jeffrey Flier, only revealed his feelings on diversity statements after he stepped down as dean. He tweeted:

> As a dean of a major academic institution, I could not have said this. But I will now. Requiring such statements in applications for appointments and promotions is an affront to academic freedom, and diminishes the true value of diversity, equity [and] inclusion by trivializing it. Of course, I *could* have said it, but by doing so I

---

* Relevant other thing that happened: In 2017, Republican Iowa senator Mark Chelgren proposed a law that would mandate that Iowa's state universities hire Republicans and Democrats in roughly equal numbers. This law (which didn't advance beyond its introduction) would also require an ideological litmus test—an attempt to remedy one wrong with another wrong.

would have become a target for focused and dedicated opposition, which would have diminished or even ended my ability to serve the functions I was hired to pursue.

Once again, there's an uncanny link between these policies and the writings of Robin DiAngelo and Özlem Sensoy, who wrote a 2017 paper recommending that universities "incorporate language into every job description that signals a critical paradigm to traditional canons" and "operationalize diversity" by requiring "explicit evidence...that the candidate has promoted (rather than simply values) diversity." This is why I keep referencing SJF activists like DiAngelo. Their work may seem obscure to most Americans, but anyone planning to attend or work at an American university is now being deeply affected by what these scholars and activists believe, and by the radical philosophies that underlie those beliefs.

Let's take a step back and look at the big picture.

IDEA SUPREMACY AND THE SOCIAL JUSTICE HORSE

SJF idea supremacy has permeated American college campuses,* rewriting the rules for what's okay to say, research, and teach. We've seen those rules enforced by students, professors, and administrators, *on* students, professors, and administrators.

Like most instances of authoritarianism, all of this bullying is framed as righteousness. Reflecting on the Evergreen fiasco that left her and her husband estranged from a college where they had built their careers, Heather Heying shares her view of the people that took over the school:

> They've wrapped up something that is quite ugly in a very pretty box and put a name on it that sounds beautiful. And it's the wrong name, and it's the wrong wrapping, and it's ugly inside.

It's the classic Trojan horse situation. Or in this case, a Social Justice Horse that SJF rides around in, talking about noble-sounding things like diversity, inclusion, justice, and safety. But inside the Social

---

* Just the small sampling we've covered here has included stories at sixty different colleges.

Justice Horse are all kinds of low-rung, illiberal things like tribalism, bullying, bigotry, censorship, witch-hunting, anti-intellectualism, indoctrination, discrimination, and hypocrisy. All the signs of a big, lumbering golem.

The Social Justice Horse is the common feature in all of the stories we've gone through. In each case, what's being framed as social justice is something very different.

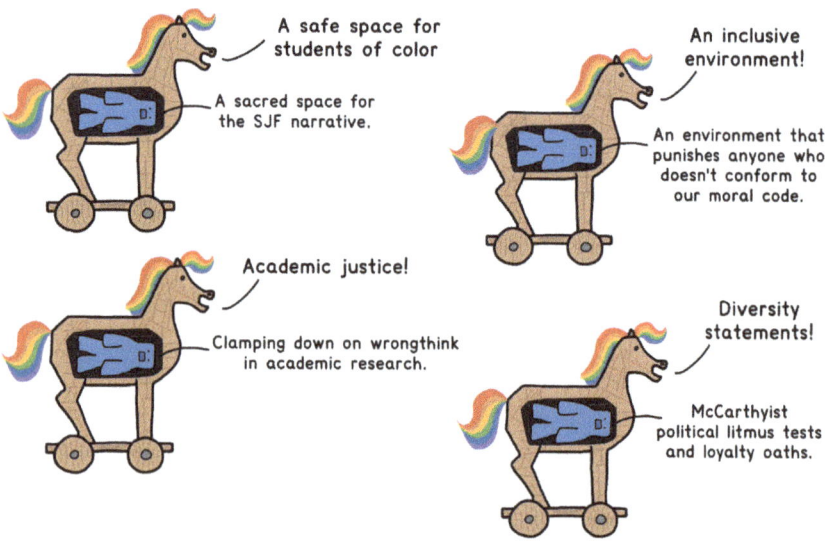

The story of colleges and SJF is a story about how liberal institutions can go wrong. A liberal institution is only liberal when it stands up for liberal values. When a golem figures out how to breach those defenses and break out of its cage, it wreaks havoc on the surrounding environment.

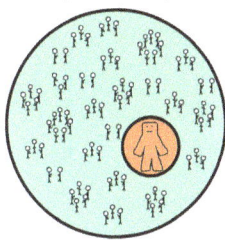  

An Echo Chamber inside a college campus, contained by the high-rung immune system

The high-rung immune system fails to contain the golem, allowing it to tramp through the campus punishing people who defy it

The campus becomes one big Echo Chamber

The victims in this story go well beyond those who have been punished directly.

THE CONSEQUENCES OF CAMPUS IDEA SUPREMACY, FOR STUDENTS

Veteran Penn professor Alan Charles Kors describes the house where he lived as a resident professor at Penn in the 1970s:

> At a time when Penn was probably 3% black, Van Pelt College House…was never less than 20% black because it had a reputation as a place where you could just be an individual and not be a representative of a group. We had the first wave of the gay liberation movement living with Campus Crusade for Christ. We had Maoist revolutionaries. We had New Age Leftists. We had campus Republicans and we had socialist would-be revolutionaries living together. They argued with and offended each other all the time. But freedom is an extraordinary medium, and over time they learned to talk with each other, to understand each other, to humanize their relationships with each other, and even occasionally to change each other's minds. What a terrible price students are paying now for the idea of comfort.

Kors is describing the quintessential Idea Lab—the intellectual habitat of the Higher Mind, full of boxing rings where ideas go at it.

Compare that description from Kors to this one from Concordia student Terry Newman:

Instead of a widening of horizons at university, I experienced there a strange sort of thinning, a constriction of the known world and all of reality into a single, narrow, idiosyncratic and firmly imposed set of perceptions and thoughts, an orthodoxy, a faith.

Newman's testimonial, and so many others like it, describe a classic Echo Chamber.

But colleges still write about their intellectual rigor on website homepages and keep stone *veritas* plaques up on campus gates. Then students arrive to find themselves somewhere very different than advertised. It amounts to a bait and switch, with terrible consequences.

I imagine the path of a maturing thinker looking something like this:*

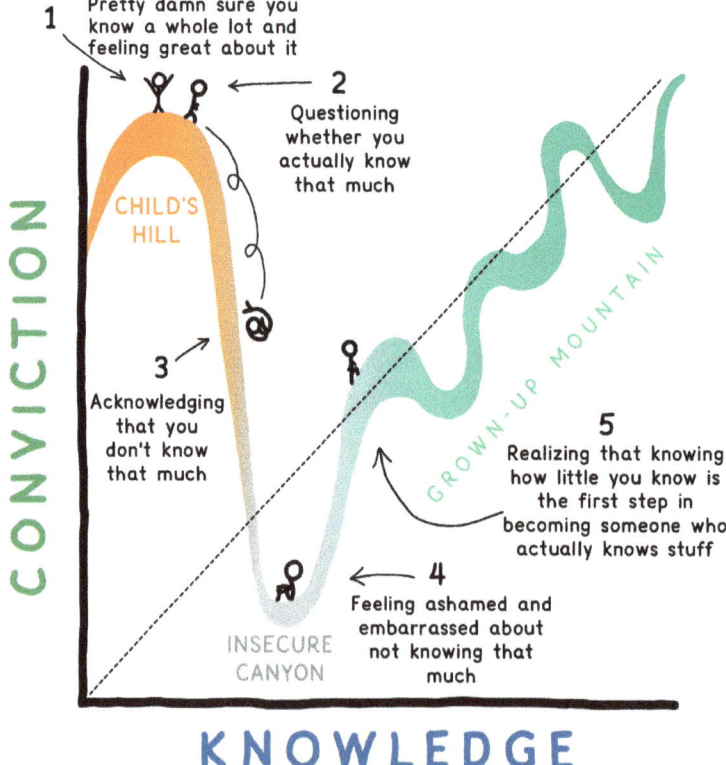

---

* People often refer to the "Dunning-Kruger" phenomenon when describing this kind of path. In fact, Dunning-Kruger refers to something a bit different.

When I headed off to college as an eighteen-year-old, I was pretty close to that proud Position 1 guy up on Child's Hill.

But college changed me. I took classes with professors who held a wide range of worldviews, which offered me a variety of intellectual lenses to keep and use in the future. I made friends with people who loved to disagree, explore the edges of topics, and call each other out on confirmation bias or falling for groupthink. I attended lectures by speakers across the political spectrum and came to realize I was most fascinated hearing from those whose views I disagreed with. It was the ideal safe-but-uncomfortable place for a maturing thinker. Looking back, I see that college provided me with an invaluable service. It shoved me off Child's Hill and sent me tumbling down the cliff.

Albert Einstein once said, "The value of an education in a liberal arts college is not the learning of many facts, but the training of the mind to think something that cannot be learned from textbooks." This was certainly true for me. College taught me how to think, and how to learn, and I came out of college with a foothold on Grown-Up Mountain, ready for a lifetime of climbing.

I graduated in 2004, but my college experience wasn't too far from the way Kors described college in the 1970s. The dramatic shift from Idea Lab campuses to Echo Chamber campuses has mostly happened over the past decade (people who have seen it happen firsthand point to late 2013 as the moment when the shift began to accelerate).

Instead of pushing students off Child's Hill toward more mature thinking, today's colleges are *nailing their feet* to the top of it.

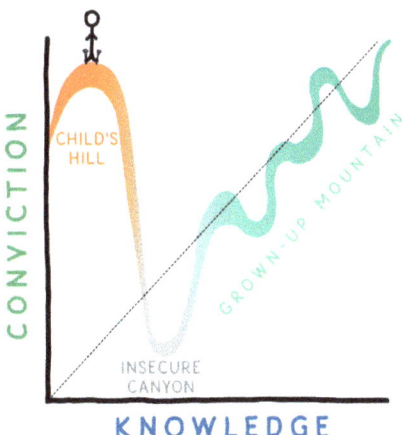

Instead of immersing students in a high-rung intellectual environment and teaching them how to be high-rung thinkers, colleges are immersing them in a low-rung environment and teaching them how to stay there.

Students pay colleges enormous sums of money because they want to grow into better and more knowledgeable thinkers—because they want to, before entering the workforce and adult life, spend four critical years sharpening their most important tool: their brain. And they're not getting what they were promised.

Normally, when brands in an industry stop staying true to their promises, the market catches on and demand heads elsewhere. But at the moment, colleges have a monopoly on a bunch of irreplaceable services for young people: higher education, job application credentialing, the stamp of belonging to the elite class, and for many students, the last great chance to make lifelong friends. So the demand stays level even as the quality of the product deteriorates—which is part of why colleges have been allowed to slip this far without much consequence.

I dedicated this whole chapter to colleges because if we want to understand how a golem can conquer a liberal institution, it's useful to look closely at a specific instance of it. But there's another reason too: what happens on campuses has major implications for the rest of the country.

THE CONSEQUENCES OF CAMPUS IDEA SUPREMACY, FOR SOCIETY

Today's College Students Are Tomorrow's Leaders

Depriving students of a rigorous intellectual boot camp doesn't hurt only them, it makes tomorrow's society a less informed, less intelligent place for everyone. According to a comprehensive study, people are at their most politically and ideologically impressionable between their mid-teens and mid-twenties—so what they're taught in college can stick with them forever. When, during those years, students are encouraged to think like political Zealots, it makes tomorrow's society more politically polarized. And when millions of young people are encouraged to act like idea supremacists, idea supremacy quickly spreads into other parts of society.

Universities Are Society's Primary Mechanism of Knowledge Discovery

Academic research is supposed to be the ultimate genie—a marketplace of ideas unlike any other, with rigorous rules and standards, and processes like peer review that institutionalize collaborative thinking to create a hyperefficient truth-finding machine. But when a research institution is hijacked by a golem within its midst, all of those rules change. Peer review stops filtering out falsehoods and starts filtering out ideas that threaten the golem. The research institution becomes an instrument of the golem, serving not the *veritas* plaque above its gates but the needs of its new golem boss: feeding it with confirmation and protecting it from doubt. This cripples our society's ability to learn new things.

Perhaps even worse, it cripples our society's ability to trust in the new things we *do* learn. Trust is the lifeblood of a healthy society. But while it takes decades to build the public's trust, it doesn't take long to shatter it. Most of today's published research papers are still the product of a high-integrity peer-review process, but they may have a harder time changing minds because of well-publicized corruption in other academic arenas. When the mantra "trust the science" is shown in some cases to mean "trust our ideology," it makes fewer people trust the science.

And finally—

This Story Did Not Happen in Isolation

The Liberal Games is an artificial construct built to protect us from the Power Games. When a major part of a liberal society falls off the wagon and gets swallowed up by the Power Games, it is an ominous sign.

Social Justice Fundamentalism evolved inside of a progressive space and continually mutated until it had developed a resistance to academia's high-rung immune system. It's not a coincidence that the first schools it conquered were the softest targets—those farthest left,

---

* Jonathan Rauch argues that institutions like universities are society's *only* effective truth-discovery mechanisms: "Without the places where professionals like experts and editors and peer reviewers organize conversations and compare propositions and assess competence and provide accountability...there is no marketplace of ideas; there are only cults warring and splintering and individuals running around making noise. This is why the corruption of reality-based institutions is so dangerous."

like Oberlin and Evergreen. As the golem continued to mutate, developing sneakier ways to become more impervious to attack and more lethal to challengers, it began to conquer the next softest targets, and then the next after that. Each time, it learned to more finely tune its takeover abilities.

If you zoom out on all of society, academia is among the farthest-left sectors—the Oberlin of liberal institutions. The decades of evolution in the college incubator did more than optimize the SJF golem to resist the immune systems of progressive universities. It optimized it to conquer *all* progressive institutions.

Golems are endlessly greedy. Until they're stopped by some more powerful force, they'll continue to expand outward. And over the past few years, the SJF golem has come charging out of the campus gates.

INTERLUDE

THE DIGITAL CUDGEL

There was a time, long, long ago, when social media was a nice place. Nice people on Facebook shared stories about their days and photos of their vacations, and nice people wrote nice comments underneath. Other nice people would post tweets about how much they liked coffee or how silly their dog was, while others would post perfectly square, exquisitely filtered photos of mountains on Instagram.

In his TED Talk, journalist and author Jon Ronson talks about the niceness of Twitter back then:

> In the early days of Twitter, it was like a place of radical de-shaming. People would admit shameful secrets about themselves, and other people would say, "Oh my God, I'm exactly the same."

People living in social media's Nice Age would probably be shocked to know only a decade later, social media would be like this:

How, in just a few short years, did a place for nice people to be nice to each other become a place for mean people to scream at each other?

The thing is, social media wasn't just a fun place to hang out, it was a wildly profitable new business model. Social media platforms had struck the internet's version of oil—attention—and the platforms' early versions had only scratched the surface of what was possible. While we were busy sharing our thoughts and being silly with each other, the leaders of the platforms were busy innovating.

In 2009 and 2010, new buttons appeared on social media platforms, allowing people to "like" and "share" and "retweet" each other's posts. Simple chronological social media feeds became algorithmically manipulated feeds, geared toward maximum engagement. The more likes and retweets a post got, the more the algorithms smiled upon them. And guess who suddenly got *real* interested in all this?

Our Primitive Minds crave attention and status, and the new, evolved social media platforms now offered both of these in the form of a quantifiable gamified system. Post the right post and you'll get lots of likes and shares. Do that enough times and you'll get lots of followers, maybe even enough to get *verified*. All of this taps deeply into our primitive psychology, and Primitive Minds across the world became addicted to the game, optimizing their behavior for maximum algorithmic rewards.

Unfortunately, a sizable body of research suggests that the best way to win the social media game is to post things that trigger people's emotions, especially strong emotions like anger, and *especially* tribal anger at the out-group. These incentives have come to flood social media feeds with anger, political tribalism, and general negativity.* Suddenly, we were all exposed to the inner thoughts of way more *strangers* than ever before, and lots of people who choose not to spend time with politically hostile people in real life were getting a large dose of them online.

All of this made social media a less nice place to be, which has made a lot of nice people more timid about posting their thoughts. Some have logged off altogether. Over the years, social media has increasingly become a Primitive Mind playground.

Meanwhile, another story was in progress. At some point in the early 2010s, people discovered that they could use social media to do something incredible: speak truth to power. Here's Ronson again:

---

* There is an ongoing debate among social scientists about the cause of these changes. Some scholars suggest that the social media environment has reshaped the behavior of users, making them more aggressive and hostile in online interactions than they are in offline interactions. Others have found that rather than change people's behavior, online environments allow those who *were already* aggressive and hostile—both online and offline—to dominate online discussions and reach way more people than they ever could before.

Voiceless people realized that they had a voice, and it was powerful and eloquent. If a newspaper ran some racist or homophobic column, we realized we could do something about it. We could get them. We could hit them with a weapon that we understood but they didn't—a social media shaming. Advertisers would withdraw their advertising. When powerful people misused their privilege, we were going to get them. This was like the democratization of justice. Hierarchies were being leveled out. We were going to do things better.

Like, take this boss:

For a long time, bosses like him could sexually abuse their employees, often without consequences. Speaking out about the abuse could leave the employee ostracized at the company or maybe even out of a job. Others might be hesitant to publicly support her out of fear for their own careers. A situation like this is like a glitch in the Liberal Games.

But social media changed the equation. The employee now had a way to tell her story to lots of strangers and rally a swell of public support that could pressure the company to fire the abusive boss. This new source of power—the digital megaphone—helped provide the equation's missing element, and in some cases, repair the glitch.

Each correction like this makes a liberal society truer to its promises, like taking steps up a hill toward justice.

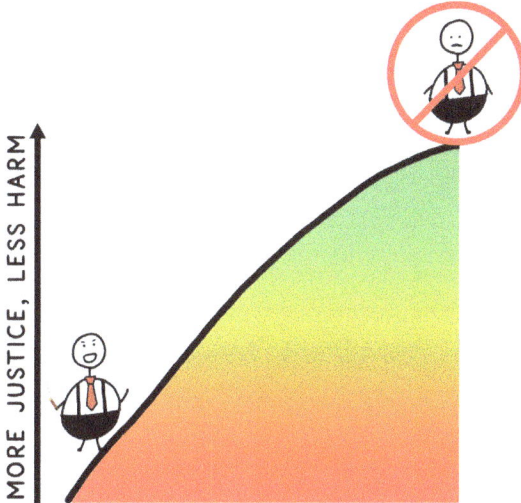

The problem is that it wasn't just the high-minded activists who were exhilarated by this amazing new way to take down bad guys. Millions of social-media-addicted Primitive Minds had just found their new favorite activity. Frothing at the mouth after the latest kill, they asked: *Who's next?*

Intoxicated with the power to be righteous crusaders on a mass scale, Primitive Minds searched for new villains to slay. When there weren't any obvious villains, they'd manufacture them. It works something like this:

Step 1: Find a Villain

What's the difference between a fair accusation and a smear?

A fair accusation plays by liberal rules. It's done in good faith and based on commonly held definitions.

A smear is an accusation not beholden to liberal rules, playing instead by Power Games rules: *everyone can do whatever they want, if they have the power to pull it off.*

The smear is an age-old weapon of the low-rung movement. In 1953, former Communist Bella Dodd explained in a public hearing how Communists use "methods of fear" to fight their enemies:

> Anyone who opposes the Communist line, anyone who is going to hurt them in any way, is bound to get the full impact of the attacks of the Communists plus all of their friends. The attack is always in high-sounding words. The congressional committees of the United States Government become the agents of Fascists, and therefore, everyone is asked to organize against the "agents of fascism"...Or it becomes a McCarranite, or a McCarthyite. Let me assure you that these are just general smear words. They are emotional words. They are words which have no definition, and first you create a sense of fear and hatred and then you apply this word to everyone against you.

Meanwhile, the actual McCarthyites were doing the same exact thing, only swapping out "Fascist" for "Communist" as their Disney movie villain.

A modern social media smear campaign does this too, using similar tactics. Concept creep can make someone into a villain by expanding the definition of damning labels—racist, misogynist, white supremacist, groomer, etc.—to include lesser offenses and a broader range of behavior. Other campaigns will create villains using misrepresentation: out-of-context quotes, willful misinterpretation, or straight-up fabrication.

And then there's a trademark rule of any smear campaign: *guilty because accused*. As tenuous as an accusation may be, once someone is deemed a villain by people in a low-rung movement, there's no need to dig deeper or clarify anything with them or let them defend themselves. *The Handmaid's Tale* author Margaret Atwood writes about this:

> Guilty because accused...tends to kick in during the "Terror and Virtue" phase of revolutions—something has gone wrong, and there must be a purge, as in the French Revolution, Stalin's purges in the USSR, the Red Guard period in China, the reign of the Generals in Argentina and the early days of the Iranian Revolution. The list is long and Left and Right have both indulged.

So an identified target is, with or without evidence, a guilty villain—which also means a villain necessitating severe punishment.

Step 2: Destroy the Villain

During the first decade of the internet, low-rung political groups *wanted* to ruin their enemies' lives—but they had no effective way to do it. If you listened closely, you could faintly hear them screaming in the comment sections of articles or YouTube videos, but they had little power in these pockets of oblivion.

But on social media, the same outrage could be shared and retweeted by others who felt the same way—and faint screams became a lot louder.

For every journalist with a traditional megaphone, there are one hundred random people with large social media followings. Used in a certain way, these followings are like paintball guns loaded with "smear bullets." When a movement has a target in their sights, they can instantly fire a smear at them.

If the smear gets noticed by someone who has a large following, they can retweet to blast out the same smear from a much larger gun. Influential activists follow other influential activists, and quickly, the smear is being simultaneously fired at the target from thousands of accounts. What it amounts to is one giant cannonball launcher, firing an industrial-sized smear at the target.

Social media algorithms pick up on activity, with no regard for the *kind* of activity it is. So quickly, the algorithms crank up the volume on the smear. Shame pours down on the target from a million mouths all at once. Reflecting on his own past as a social media shamer, writer Barrett Wilson says:

> How did I become that person? It happened because it was exhilarating. Every time I would call someone racist or sexist, I would get a rush. That rush would then be reaffirmed and sustained by the stars, hearts, and thumbs-up that constitute the nickels and dimes of social media validation. The people giving me these stars, hearts, and thumbs-up were engaging in their own cynical game: A fear of being targeted by the mob induces us to signal publicly that we are part of it.

When our psyches are down on the low rungs, consumed with this mix of exhilaration and fear, it's easy to forget that something cruel is happening to a real human. The Primitive Mind specializes in dehumanizing members of its out-group, a delusion easier to sustain when the person is just an online avatar. This delusion is responsible for what Ronson calls "a disconnect between the severity of the crime and the gleeful savagery of the punishment."

Then come the news websites. When something goes viral enough on social media, it ignites the media engine, becoming the subject of a slew of articles, appearing on everything from random blogs to sites like Jezebel and HuffPost and Breitbart to national media brands like CNN and Fox News.* The target is quickly being shamed by some of the largest megaphones on the internet. Those articles are then further amplified when *they* go viral on social media.

The target is left with a smear plastered on their forehead.

It doesn't stop there. The Google search algorithm optimizes for relevance and view count, regardless of the whether its front-page results are true or false. The shame storm eventually subsides as the Primitive Minds on social media move on to the next target—but Google search results are forever. One big shame storm is usually all it takes for the smear to be stitched irreparably onto the target's online presence. Forever forward, googling their name will bring the smear front and center along with anything else about them. Google takes the smear and *permanently* brands it onto the target's forehead.

---

* In a 2022 Pew survey of almost twelve thousand journalists, 75 percent of those who use social media cite "identifying stories to cover" as one of the ways it impacts their work. In another question, 67 percent of journalists say social media has a very or somewhat negative impact on the state of journalism as a whole.

Even if the smear itself is overexaggerated or totally fabricated, the damage to the target's reputation is extremely real. Author Chimamanda Ngozi Adichie writes:

> When you are a public figure, people will write and say false things about you. It comes with the territory. Many of those things you brush aside. Many you ignore. The people close to you advise you that silence is best. And it often is. Sometimes, though, silence makes a lie begin to take on the shimmer of truth. In this age of social media, where a story travels the world in minutes, silence sometimes means that other people can hijack your story and soon, their false version becomes the defining story about you.

But speaking out doesn't really work either, even when the target can provide demonstrative proof they're being misrepresented. Author and podcaster Sam Harris, an experienced smear campaign target, explains why:

> It is impossible to effectively defend oneself against unethical critics. If nothing else, the law of entropy is on their side, because it will always be easier to make a mess than to clean it up. It is, for instance, easier to call a person a "racist," a "bigot," a "misogynist," etc. than it is for one's target to prove that he isn't any of these things. In fact, the very act of defending himself against such accusations quickly becomes debasing. Whether or not the original charges can be made to stick, the victim immediately seems thin-skinned and overly concerned about his reputation. And, rebutted or not, the original charges will be repeated in blogs and comment threads, and many readers will assume that where there's smoke, there must be fire.

And for the finishing touch:

Step 3: Make the Villain Radioactive

In a liberal democracy, the hard cudgel of physical violence isn't allowed. You can't burn villains at the stake. But you *can* burn their reputation and livelihood at the stake. This is the soft cudgel of social consequences.

In a human society, the soft cudgel carries nearly as much power as the hard cudgel, but unlike the hard cudgel it comes along with a big asterisk: it only works if everyone decides to let it work. If enough people stand up for the target and push back against the smear campaign, the soft cudgel loses its impact. The pushback is also a soft cudgel of its own—one that can land the smearers with tarnished reputations as cruel bullies.

This is part of the reason those who do business by way of the soft cudgel are always so big on *guilt by association*.

We talked about the important difference between refusing to go see a campus speaker and actually shutting down the event itself, which prohibits *all* students from hearing the speaker. One is a person making individual choices; the other is idea supremacy.

A similar distinction can be drawn with boycotting. A group of people boycotting a business they disapprove of is totally fair game in a country like the US. Boycotts have been a powerful tool of peaceful activism many times in the past. What's less fair game is *pressuring others* to boycott the businesses you disapprove of by promoting the notion that "anyone who doesn't boycott this business is one of the bad guys." Individual boycotting is what high-rung activists do. Coercive boycotting is what low-rung mobs do.

Guilt by association is the coercive boycott of a *person*. Individually boycotting a person means you refuse to work for them, work with them, or employ them. It means you refuse to defend them or listen to them defend themselves. It means you cut off contact with them and cease to be associated with them in any way. Again, all fair game.

But guilt by association—which attacks anyone who *doesn't* boycott the target—takes this to the next level. To the *supremacy* level.

Guilt by association makes a blacklisted target *radioactive*. Those who praise, defend, or attempt to humanize the target, those who work with or employ the target, those who share the target's work or offer them a platform, or even those who suggest that a smear campaign has gone too far, will end up on the blacklist alongside the target. So even people who believe the target to be unfairly maligned will usually keep their distance from the target publicly. The target becomes someone with whom it's "just not worth it" to be involved. This leaves them isolated from society, which can be catastrophic for their career, social life, and mental health.

On the hottest-button topics, during the hottest moments, guilt by association can go further, extending multiple degrees away from the original target, forming a kind of "smear web."

Let's say Bob is a provocative podcaster who likes to criticize a certain low-rung movement and point out ways they're wrong and awful. Now Bob might be an asshole—a tribal low-runger himself who unfairly maligns and misrepresents his enemy movement. Or Bob might be a high-runger whose criticisms of the low-rung movement are cogent, accurate, and consistent with the principles he claims to have. To the low-rung movement, it doesn't matter which of these Bob is. They may not even be able to tell the difference. Bob holds Viewpoints A, B, and C, which makes him a disgusting member of the out-group. A villain. So the movement smears him, and his name becomes radioactive within the movement's sphere of influence.

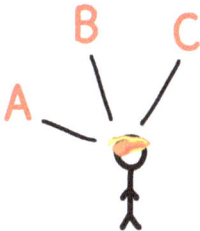

Guilt by association doesn't just travel from person to person—it also travels from people to *ideas*. For our purposes, let's imagine Bob *is* a low-rung asshole, who makes a lot of low-rung asshole points. But Bob makes a *lot* of points and let's say one of those points is something most high-rungers would agree with. We'll call it Viewpoint D. Bob's enemies will apply Bob's smear to *all* viewpoints that he uses to criticize them, not distinguishing between which viewpoints are asshole-y and which aren't. Viewpoint D is plastered with the smear along with his other points.

Now say Angela is a reasonably high-rung journalist who doesn't even know who Bob is—but she also holds Viewpoint D. And one day, she writes an article expressing Viewpoint D. Without realizing it, Angela just touched a radioactive object. The low-rung movement comes across the article and uses it as proof that Angela is a villain with villainous ideas and villainous motives. Soon, the mob is scouring through Angela's other articles, her past tweets, and old photos of her on Google Images. Through a bunch of misrepresentation, Angela is now thoroughly discredited in the mob's sphere of influence. The smear has traveled from Bob, to Viewpoint D, to Angela.

In the midst of all of this, Angela has a guest named Jason on her podcast. When the episode is released, Jason receives a slew of shame on social media for going on a villain's podcast, and fans of Jason, fearful of the mob, become hesitant to share his work or retweet his tweets. The smear manages to make its way all the way to Jason.

Angela's next scheduled podcast guest, not wanting to deal with what Jason had to go through, cancels the interview, saying she's "super swamped with work right now." Other journalists, not wanting to be the next Angela, think twice about publicly expressing Viewpoint D.

This is how a smear, even when applied to a genuine asshole, can spider out into a web that ends up punishing non-assholes and hindering productive discussion.

All of those ecosystem changes we explored in Chapter 3—changes in the media landscape and shifting incentives, the advent of social media and Google search, and a whole lot of algorithms trying to maximize traffic and clicks—inadvertently brought a new weapon into the world: the digital cudgel. No one intended to create a new weapon, but once it came into existence, it was only a matter of time before people picked it up and started using it.

Over time, society develops laws and social etiquette that govern how we behave and keep things contained within the Liberal Games structure. But the digital cudgel dropped into our ecosystem suddenly, catching us off guard, and we've been living for the past decade in the social equivalent of the Wild West. The same new weapon that gave high-rung activists new ways to attack injustice also gave Primitive Minds a new way to play the Power Games. In their hands, the digital cudgel created new harms and new injustices.

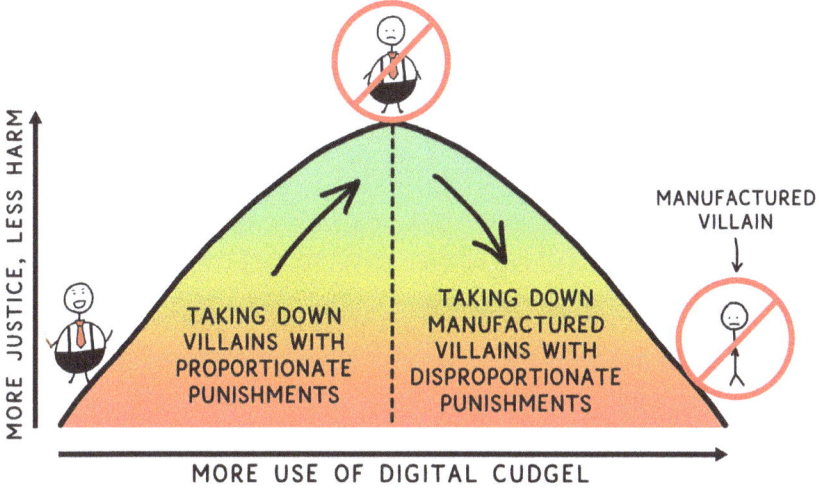

The early social media culture of "radical de-shaming" was a place where it was safe to admit your shameful secrets with laughter. It was a culture that understood that to be human is to be flawed. The kind of culture that happens when Higher Minds are leading the way. As social media fell more and more into the hands of Primitive Minds, the culture of radical de-shaming gave way to its opposite: the Political Disney World culture of righteous heroes and evil villains, of binary 1s and 0s. The culture where a person's shameful secret is proof of their true villainous nature and cause for a permanent smear to their reputation. If likes and retweets made social media unpleasant, the digital cudgel went further and made it *scary*.

As Ronson puts it: "The great thing about social media was how it gave a voice to voiceless people, but we're now creating a surveillance society, where the smartest way to survive is to go back to being voiceless."

When I've talked to people about this, one of the most common retorts is, "This all seems like a big deal on social media, but it's not actually that big a deal in the real world."

It's definitely true that social media is not representative of the real world. According to Pew research, for example, only 23 percent of American adults use Twitter, and this group is disproportionately young, wealthy, and college educated. Social media users also tend to be more politically engaged. Further, 92 percent of all tweets from US accounts come from just 10 percent of users (less than 3 percent of the total population). This tiny group, doing almost all of the tweeting, retweeting, commenting, and liking, is also overwhelmingly politically progressive.* Most of the smearing and the mobbing and the guilt by association on Twitter is the work of a tiny slice of the population.

But history has shown us again and again that a small portion of the population, with a sufficiently large cudgel, can hijack a society.

In the story of colleges, we saw how a small and nonrepresentative group found a way to conquer campuses. And they did so with great assistance from the digital cudgel of social media, as we saw in the many stories that were driven by social media backlash.

What happened in academia provided SJF idea supremacists in greater society with a blueprint for how a small Echo Chamber can take over a much larger entity. With this blueprint in one hand and a digital cudgel in the other, the SJF golem has shown the world just how vulnerable a liberal society really is.

---

* Sixty-nine percent of this group identify as "Democrat" or "lean Democrat," while 26 percent are "Republican" or "lean Republican."

CHAPTER 7

HOW TO CONQUER A SOCIETY

But that was then, and this is, to put it mildly, now.
—LOUIS MENAND

Between when I began writing this book in 2016 and when I finished it, a new term exploded into the public consciousness.

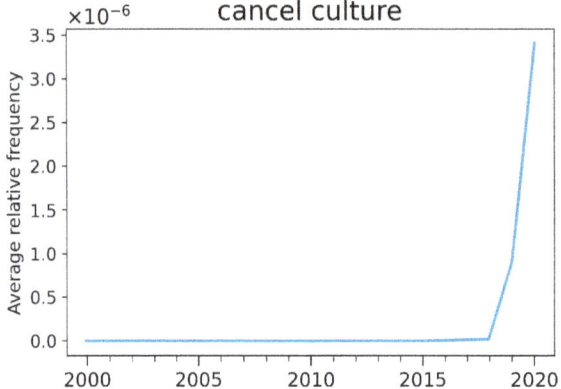

—Average frequency in: *New York Times, Washington Post, Guardian, Los Angeles Times*

Source: David Rozado, "Charts Compiled for Tim Urban"

As Social Justice Fundamentalism spread through US society, Americans were trying to process what was happening. "Cancel culture" was a useful term that gave a concrete label to an abstract phenomenon.

But there are downsides to using a single label to describe a broad array of complex incidents. The term becomes overused and loaded with baggage. And it can box in our conversations. Throughout this book, we've been building a richer language to talk about what's going on in our societies, parsing the terms so we could make single-axis discussions multidimensional.

Just as we added another dimension to the political spectrum with the Ladder and split the concept of "social justice" into "Liberal Social Justice" and "Social Justice Fundamentalism," we need to go beyond the term "cancel culture" in order to capture the larger story.

So I'd like to welcome you to the **illiberal staircase**.

Not all illiberalism is equally illiberal. The staircase allows us to take all the SJF-related incidents that have created buzz in the news or on social media and organize them by degree of illiberalism. A healthy liberal society sits atop the staircase, on the liberal line. When things happen on the steps below, it is a sign that the liberal rules have begun to break down. The staircase is like a ruler that measures how far we've fallen.

HOW TO CONQUER A SOCIETY • 349

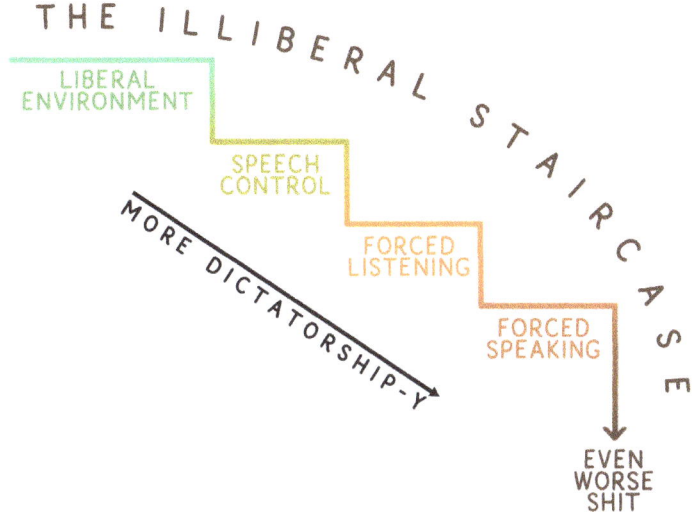

If we want to help repair our societies and restore their defenses, we have to fully understand the problem. So in our final deep dive, let's grab our magnifying glass and our flashlight and head down the stairs to see what's really going on.

ILLIBERAL STAIRCASE, STEP 1: SPEECH CONTROL

The SJF idea supremacy we saw on college campuses has spread to many other pockets of society. We're about to take a tour through some of the hundreds of stories that have emerged over the past few years, across many industries. I tried to include enough stories to show the breadth of the situation, but not so many that you'd want to throw me and this book out the window. Many of these stories are maddening and will probably put you in a bad mood.* But I still feel hopeful about the big picture, and I'll explain why in the book's conclusion, so bear with me.

Okay, let's start with some good old-fashioned cancel culture stories.

---

* I'm in a bad mood too, if it makes you feel better.

McNeil

I remember reading about Donald McNeil back in early 2021. Between 2012 and 2021, the *New York Times* organized educational travel programs that took groups of high school students to other countries during the summer, accompanied by a *New York Times* expert they could talk to and learn from during the experience. After a 2019 program in Peru, some of the students had complaints about one of the experts on their trip: veteran *NYT* writer Donald McNeil.

McNeil, who had worked at the Times since 1976, specialized in plagues and pestilences and had become the paper's lead reporter on Covid-19. According to a 2021 article in the Daily Beast, students said that McNeil "made wildly offensive and racist comments while leading a *Times* student trip." McNeil had, among other "racist and sexist remarks," "used the 'n-word' and suggested he did not believe in the concept of white privilege." One participant made their feelings clear: "I expect immediate action…I think firing him would even be appropriate."

At the time, in 2019, the Times handled the incident internally, reprimanding McNeil and apologizing to the students. The Daily Beast article, published two years later, made the story public. The story exploded on social media and subsequent articles soon appeared in the *Washington Post*, *Vanity Fair*, CNN, Slate, and the *New York Post*. One *NYT* reporter called it "the most explosive scandal I've seen at the paper. It's chaos." Top managers at the Times held meetings with each department at the paper and one with the paper's Black reporters.

As the scandal erupted, the paper's executive editor called McNeil and told him,[*] "You've lost the newsroom. A lot of your colleagues are hurt. A lot of them won't work with you. Thank you for writing the apology. But we'd like you to consider adding to it that you're leaving." Soon, McNeil's editor called to tell him: "If you refused to leave voluntarily, you wouldn't be the lead pandemic reporter anymore…No more big front-page stories."

McNeil resigned. The executive editor sent a memo to the staff informing them about McNeil's departure. He explained: "We do not

---

[*] The following quotes are from McNeil's notes and may not be exact. He explains: "My notes of the conversation are sparser than I normally take, but I also recounted it right afterward to a friend, so I think this is accurate."

tolerate racist language regardless of intent."

I remember thinking that forcing their lead Covid reporter out during the heat of the pandemic for something that happened two years earlier seemed harsh. But it also seemed reasonable. He had gone on racist tirades in front of high school students, even using the n-word. Probably someone who should not be working at a major newspaper in 2021.

Then I dug deeper.

A couple of weeks after resigning, McNeil told his side of the story in detail in a four-part post on Medium.

He explained that, as the "expert" on the trip, his contract obligated him to "be available to talk to the students, including during meals." It was his second time as a trip expert.

> In 2018, some students and I spent hours trying to top each other's bad puns. On the 2019 trip, talk at the table constantly turned to politics.

McNeil engaged the students on their political questions.

> I saw it as answering everyone's questions as frankly as I could. I felt I was trying to show them that the world is a more nuanced place than they assumed.

He told the n-word story.

> A student asked me if I thought her high school's administration was right to suspend a classmate of hers for using the word in a video she'd made in eighth grade. I said "Did she actually call someone a 'offending word'?* Or was she singing a rap song or quoting a book title or something?" When the student explained that it was the student, who was white and Jewish, sitting with a black friend and the two were jokingly insulting each other by calling each other offensive names for a black person and a Jew, I said "She was suspended for that? Two years later? No, I don't

---

* Clarification: In McNeil's post, he wrote "offending word," referring to him saying the actual word at the time.

think suspension was warranted. Somebody should have talked to her, but any school administrator should know that twelve-year-olds say dumb things. It's part of growing up."

McNeil's post addresses a number of other student allegations about offensive things he had said. For each, he gives a fuller story, and in each case, his recounting is far more nuanced than what ended up in the story told by the media.

At the end of his post, McNeil sums up his larger point:

> The portrait the Daily Beast paints of a dyspeptic old man abusing students by spouting "wildly racist and offensive comments" is inaccurate. I was trying to engage them in a serious conversation that opened their eyes….I thought I was generally arguing in favor of open-mindedness and tolerance—but it clearly didn't come across that way….I do not see why their complaints should have ended my career at the Times two years later. But they did.

Throughout the whole ordeal, it was McNeil's utterance of the n-word that was cited most by those calling for his firing. But the critics seemed to be forgetting the difference between *using* and *mentioning* a word—what's known as the "use-mention distinction."

Using a word means saying that word to refer to something the word is supposed to signify—e.g., "Sprite is my favorite kind of **pop**."

Mentioning a word is talking about the word itself, not its meaning—e.g., "People in the Midwest commonly refer to soda as '**pop**.'"

McNeil had *mentioned* the word, not used it. While I assume the n-word has not been *used* in modern American journalism in many decades, it is *mentioned* all the time. Journalist Katie Herzog talked about this after McNeil's firing:

> *Slate* has 700 instances of the word as recently as last year. The *New York Times*, the place where Donald McNeil was fired for saying the word, had printed it the week before. The week before.

In 2019, when this happened, the *New York Times* seemed to agree that mentioning a racial slur in a discussion about whether someone should have been punished for using it was not a fireable offense. Back then, the executive editor had said this about McNeil's case: "He showed extremely poor judgment, but it did not appear to me that his intentions were hateful or malicious."

But two years later, in the face of an explosion of social media outrage and a letter from staff demanding further action, Times management suddenly had a different position on the use-mention distinction: "We do not tolerate racist language regardless of intent." Mentioning the word, regardless of context or intent, was now a fireable offense—*retroactively*.

In the world of Social Justice Fundamentalism, there's no use-mention distinction, and no forgiveness for well-intentioned mistakes.

McCammond

The month after McNeil left the *New York Times*, Alexi McCammond left *Teen Vogue*.

The twenty-seven-year-old McCammond, who in 2019 had been named Emerging Journalist of the Year by the National Association of Black Journalists, had just been hired as *Teen Vogue*'s new editor-in-chief. Then someone found McCammond's old tweets.

Back in 2011, when McCammond was seventeen, she wrote a few racist and homophobic tweets like "thanks a lot stupid asian TA," "now googling how to not wake up with swollen, asian eyes...," and "hahahahah you're so gay lmao." After an uproar on social media, Condé Nast emailed staff letting them know that they and McCammond "agreed that it was best to part ways," and McCammond left the company.

In the Liberal Games, adults are typically forgiven for stupid things they said as a teenager—something many of us are guilty of. Assuming the adult expresses remorse (which McCammond did), a liberal society would treat an incident like that as a teaching moment and move on. But in SJF, bad behavior in the past renders someone a villain today, deserving of severe punishment.

Like the Times in the McNeil incident, Condé Nast executives at first stood by McCammond, writing: "Given her previous acknowledgment of these posts and her sincere apologies, in addition to her remarkable work in journalism elevating the voices of marginalized communities, we were looking forward to welcoming her into our community." But when faced with public outrage, they backed down.

Bennet

In the weeks following George Floyd's murder at the hands of a white cop, a well-publicized scandal erupted at the *New York Times*. The paper had published an article by Arkansas senator Tom Cotton in the opinion section about riots that had sprung up in multiple cities. In the article, titled "Tom Cotton: Send in the Troops," Cotton wrote:

> A majority who seek to protest peacefully shouldn't be confused with bands of miscreants....These rioters, if not subdued, not only will destroy the livelihoods of law-abiding citizens but will also take more innocent lives. Many poor communities that still bear scars from past upheavals will be set back still further.
>
> One thing above all else will restore order to our streets: an overwhelming show of force to disperse, detain and ultimately deter lawbreakers.

Cotton then argued that the situation warranted military involvement, authorized by the Insurrection Act, recalling previous instances when presidents had sent the military to quell unrest, like the LA riots of 1992. Though this was a hugely controversial stance, Cotton pointed out that much of the public supported these measures:

> According to a recent poll, 58 percent of registered voters, including nearly half of Democrats and 37 percent of African-Americans, would support cities' calling in the military to "address protests and demonstrations" that are in "response to the death of George Floyd."

The op-ed was met with furious backlash. The NewsGuild of New York, the union that represents many Times journalists, issued a statement on Twitter arguing that the op-ed "undermines the journalistic work of our members, puts our Black staff members in danger, promotes hate, and is likely to encourage further violence." Dozens of Times staff members tweeted: "Running this puts Black @NYTimes staff in danger."

In response, *Times* Opinion editor James Bennet defended the decision to publish Cotton's op-ed, arguing that it was the job of the op-ed page "to provide a debate on important questions like this" and that "it would undermine the integrity and independence of the *New York Times* if we only published views that editors like me agreed with." He also pointed out that Cotton was an influential senator with real power, and that "the public would be better equipped to push back if it heard the argument and had the chance to respond to the reasoning." The paper's publisher and executive editor both echoed these sentiments.

But when the backlash reached a fever pitch, the Times began to change its tune. One day after Bennet defended the article, he apologized in an all-staff meeting and said the op-ed should not have been published. The same day, the Times added an editors' note to the top of Cotton's op-ed saying that "the essay fell short of our standards and should not have been published." The paper assured staff they would take "steps to reduce the likelihood of something like this happening again."

The first of those "steps" happened two days later, when Bennet resigned from his position as head of *Times* Opinion. That night, Bennet's replacement, Kathleen Kingsbury, wrote a note to Times staff, telling them that anyone who comes across "any piece of Opinion journalism—including headlines or social posts or photos or you name it—that gives you the slightest pause, please call or text me immediately."

Damore

Google was built to be an Idea Lab company. Tech journalist Nitasha Tiku explains:

> Larry Page and Sergey Brin...had designed their company's famously open culture to facilitate free thinking. Employees were "obligated to dissent" if they saw something they disagreed with, and they were encouraged to "bring their whole selves" to work rather than check their politics and personal lives at the door. And the wild thing about Google was that so many employees complied. They weighed in on thousands of online mailing lists, including IndustryInfo, a mega forum with more than 30,000 members...On Thursdays, Google would host a company-wide meeting called TGIF, known for its no-holds-barred Q&As where employees could, and did, aggressively challenge executives.

This was a common culture at a Silicon Valley company in the early 2000s. But as the US spun down the tribal vortex, the same trend we saw within political parties and universities happened in Silicon Valley.

Political donation data in the heat of the 2018 midterms found tech companies looking a lot like universities. At Netflix, 99.6 percent of donation dollars made by employees went to Democratic candidates. For Twitter, the number was 98.7 percent. Apple, 97.5 percent. Google employees donated the most of all—$3.7 million combined—96 percent of which went to the Democrats.*

As tech companies moved toward political purity, hostility toward political difference grew. A 2018 class-action lawsuit against Google included dozens of examples of postings to company-wide message boards that expressed mockery and disgust for political conservatives. One showed a picture of a Republican rally along with George Carlin's line, "Never underestimate the power of stupid people in large groups." Another read, "'America First' is a slogan for American Nazis." One Googler posted this suggestion: "I think only women and poc should be allowed to make hiring decisions at google for a year…look at the resulting hiring data. Google likes experiments? Do an experiment." Another proposed a "moratorium on hiring white cis heterosexual abled men who aren't abuse survivors."

This is the backdrop for the infamous "Google memo" shitshow of 2017. More than the actual memo, the blowup itself is worth looking back on.

James Damore, a fourth-year engineer at Google at the time, had attended a "Diversity and Inclusion" conference at Google. Talking about the conference, Damore later summed up one of the main messages as: "The population has 50 percent women. Google has 20 percent women. Therefore, sexism." He disagreed with this and wrote a memo explaining why. The memo is online in its entirety, but here's the summary he includes at the beginning:

- Google's political bias has equated the freedom from offense with psychological safety, but shaming into silence is the antithesis of psychological safety.
- This silencing has created an ideological echo chamber where some ideas are too sacred to be honestly discussed.
- The lack of discussion fosters the most extreme and authoritarian elements of this ideology.
- Extreme: all disparities in representation are due to oppression

---

* This doesn't tell us the total number of employees who donated, only that those who did were almost all Democrats.

- Authoritarian: we should discriminate to correct for this oppression
- Differences in distributions of traits between men and women may in part explain why we don't have 50% representation of women in tech and leadership.
- Discrimination to reach equal representation is unfair, divisive, and bad for business.

While making some of the same points Larry Summers made at that talk in 2005, Damore was also complaining about the worldview and the coercive tendencies of Social Justice Fundamentalism at Google. In particular, he was addressing the notion that the gender imbalance at Google must entirely be due to discrimination against women at the company—and that, therefore, the hiring process needed to be adjusted until there were equal numbers of men and women at the company.*

The document first went viral on Google message boards. As I dug into the responses, it was like there were two alternative universes.

The first universe showed up in anonymous surveys, like one that asked Google employees what they thought about the content of the memo: 36 percent agreed with it, 48 percent disagreed. Employees shared a wide variety of nuanced views on Google's internal anonymous forum "Blind," ranging from full-throated agreement to passionate disagreement. In standard Idea Lab fashion, people descended upon Damore's hypothesis, examining it, kicking it, defending it, ridiculing it. Universe 1 was deeply divided on the ideas in Damore's memo, with one common thread: no one claimed that publishing the memo was harmful or suggested that Damore should be punished for it.

In the second universe, the memo was seen as an unforgivable act of harm. One ex-Google employee reprimanded Damore, saying: "Not only was nearly everything you said in that document wrong, the fact that you did that has caused significant harm to people across this company, and to the company's entire ability to function." A current employee

---

* In Chapter 5, we talked about SJF's two primary tenets when it comes to racial disparities: *Racial discrimination is the* sole *cause of racial disparities in this country and the* only *remedy to racist discrimination is anti-racist discrimination*. These are those same two SJF tenets, being applied in this case to gender disparities.

wrote: "I'm happy that Googlers have reacted like a body to an infection, surrounding and isolating, trying to contain the damage...Because this is an infection, and this is actively hurting people."

It was clear in Universe 2 that Damore needed to be not refuted but fired. One employee wrote that Damore "should find another place to work." Another asked management: "*What happens* when someone pushes a horrible, bigoted essay that causes widespread hurt? Any consequences?...What will you do about it? What values does the company hold *and is willing to uphold*?" Another suggested that beyond firing Damore, the company should "change our interview processes to notice toxic opinions like that" and "[update] our code of conduct to say not to do anything that looks even a bit like that, ever." If Google didn't fire Damore, those in Universe 2 would force the issue by refusing to work with him. One wrote, "Even in the event that we would hesitate to dismiss a person for espousing repugnant opinions, if nobody is willing to work with them then they cannot be a part of a team and cannot be retained."

Then there was the guilt by association. An employee urged Google management "to send a clear message by not only terminating Mr. Damore, but also severely disciplining or terminating those who have expressed support." Another simply said, "fuck those opinions, and fuck people who think it's okay to have them."

In a healthy high-rung environment, people in Universe 1 (whether they agreed or disagreed with the memo) would stand up for a culture of open discourse, backed by the company's leadership, and those in Universe 2 would be forced to coexist with a variety of viewpoints on a topic they hold sacred. Especially since Universe 1 represented the majority (an anonymous survey asked employees whether they thought the memo "is harmful and shouldn't have been shared": 30 percent agreed that it was, 57 percent disagreed). But this wasn't a healthy high-rung environment, as evidenced by the fact that Universe 1 was only apparent through *anonymous* surveys and on anonymous forums.

The reaction at Google was a microcosm of what would play out days later when the memo was leaked to the wider world. Wandering through Universe 1 online, I read papers discussing the scientific literature on average differences between men and women.* I read papers

---

* Heterodox Academy performed a meta-analysis of twenty-four papers on the topic, highlighting passages that supported and opposed Damore's claims in...

about men being more interested in things and women more interested in people, on average. I read about how talented female engineers were likely to be more versatile than talented male engineers and thus have more options in other fields. Many of these voices argued that the body of data would predictably yield the gender imbalance at Google, as well as the gender disparity in other high-paying fields that are dominated by women, like psychology, pediatrics, veterinary medicine, and physical therapy.

I also encountered people who thought Damore was attributing too much of Google's gender imbalance to innate factors. Some scientists argued that biological sex differences were not that relevant to the kinds of work people do at Google. They pointed to other possible causes, like the masculine culture tech companies have a reputation for—and the ways that it can lead to subconscious discrimination in recruiting and hiring, create a hostile environment for women, and ultimately, create a feedback loop whereby women self-select out of the industry.

There were people who zoomed out and looked at the pipeline, pointing out that the percentage of women at Google was nearly identical to the percentage of women who receive bachelor's degrees in computer science, which suggests that Google's gender disparity was a representative reflection of the applicant pool. Some argued that the disparity in computer science graduates could be caused by embedded cultural stereotypes and early childhood socialization rather than biological differences. Other people rebutted this argument, saying that even if it were true, it wouldn't be Google's responsibility to address broader cultural phenomena. Still others retorted that Google is a cultural leader with a responsibility to help dismantle outdated stereotypes.

Again, Universe 1 was divided on Damore's ideas and no one was calling for Damore's head.*

Universe 2, on the other hand, shared a single united take, expressed by nearly every major media outlet. Headlines in ABC News, *Reuters*,

---

...green and red, respectively. Green and red passages appeared in roughly equal number.

* And again, this seems to have been the majority view. In a survey that asked whether expressing the viewpoint that "psychological differences help explain why there are more male than female engineers" should be a fireable offense, only 34 percent of Democrats and 14 percent of Republicans agreed.

Slate, The Huffington Post, and PBS News all referred to the memo as the "anti-diversity memo." NBC News and *Vice* called it the "anti-diversity manifesto." Engadget and Gizmodo used "anti-diversity screed." Mashable went with "screed against diversity." *Time* magazine called it the "anti-diversity tirade." The *Guardian* called it a "diatribe against women in tech." The *Washington Post* headline read: "A Google engineer said women may be genetically unsuited for tech jobs."

Of the tens of thousands of words I read about the memo in Universe 1, I never heard anyone say it was "anti-diversity." Which makes sense, because the memo isn't anti-diversity.

One line in Damore's memo reads: "I strongly believe in gender and racial diversity, and I think we should strive for more." He later reiterates the point: "I hope it's clear that I'm not saying that diversity is bad, that Google or society is 100 percent fair, that we shouldn't try to correct for existing biases, or that minorities have the same experience of those in the majority." What Damore objected to wasn't diversity itself but 1) the means Google uses to achieve diversity and 2) the notion that Google's gender disparity could only be caused by discriminatory practices and sexist culture.

But Universe 2 didn't deal with the memo's specifics. It constructed a straw-man memo, written by a straw-man villain, and wrote about *them* instead. While the actual memo circulated quietly around academic papers and blogs in Universe 1, the straw-man memo of Universe 2 was going mega-viral on the largest platforms.

Google leadership faced a moment of truth. Which universe would it stand behind? In Universe 1, firing Damore for criticizing company policy in an internal memo was unthinkable—the kind of authoritarianism Google had historically disdained. In Universe 2, firing Damore, the misogynist author of the anti-diversity tirade that made Google an unsafe place for women, was the only reasonable option.

Google fired Damore.

In a letter to staff following Damore's firing, Google's CEO, Sundar Pichai, said parts of the memo "cross the line by advancing harmful gender stereotypes in our workplace" and said he was determined to "create a more inclusive environment for all."

The message was clear: Google may be an Idea Lab in some areas, but in others, everyone at the company now worked within the SJF Echo Chamber.

Of the seemingly endless such stories that have emerged from the world of tech, I told this one because, like the *New York Times*, Google was founded *specifically* as an Idea Lab company. These companies have, under SJF pressure, become the polar opposite of what they used to be.

Shrier

In July 2021, the American Booksellers Association (ABA), a trade organization that supports independent booksellers, sent out its monthly box of books to 750 member bookstores. Included in the boxes was Abigail Shrier's book *Irreversible Damage: The Transgender Craze Seducing Our Daughters*.

Shrier sums up the book's main message like this:

> *Irreversible Damage* argues that transgender identification among teen girls has become a social contagion. Girls who might have encouraged each other in bulimia, anorexia or cutting are today deciding they have "gender dysphoria," pushing for hormones and surgeries—and easily obtaining them.
>
> The numbers are startling: In the nearly 100-year diagnostic history of "gender dysphoria"—severe discomfort in one's biological sex—the disorder first appeared in early childhood (ages 2 to 4) and overwhelmingly afflicted boys. Today, teen girls with no history of childhood dysphoria are suddenly the leading demographic. From 2016–17, the number of gender surgeries on girls and women in the U.S. quadrupled, with biological females accounting for 70% of all gender surgeries.
>
> Part of the reason this has become an epidemic among teen girls is that, unlike bulimia or anorexia, our culture celebrates girls who medically "transition"—and denigrates or cancels all who point out that this can be a mode of self-harm.

The controversial book struck a chord, selling well with high ratings on Amazon and being named one of *The Economist*'s Books of the Year and one of *The Times*' Best Books of 2021.

But when the book was met with outrage from activists on Twitter, Target announced that it would stop selling the book. Writing in the *Wall Street Journal*, Shrier expressed her frustration: "Amid a sea of material unskeptically promoting medical transition for teenage girls, there's one book that investigates this phenomenon and urges caution. That is the book the activists seek to suppress."

A few months later, Amazon stopped allowing the publisher to advertise Shrier's book on the site, on the grounds that it "may not be appropriate for all audiences." But Amazon made no such restrictions when it came to other viewpoints on the same topic—in fact, even a direct search for Shrier's book title turned up results celebrating gender transition, with Shrier's book listed below them. She again expressed her frustration, this time on Twitter: "Celebrate medical transition for teenagers, and Amazon amplifies you. Point out the risks? And they'll mute you."

The American Booksellers Association hates this kind of thing. It has a foundation called American Booksellers for Free Expression, which calls itself "the bookseller's voice in the fight against censorship," with a mission "to promote and protect the free exchange of ideas, particularly those contained in books, by opposing restrictions on the freedom of speech." The association is also a sponsor of "Banned Books Week," a movement that "brings together the entire book community—librarians, booksellers, publishers, journalists, teachers, and readers of all types—in shared support of the freedom to seek and to express ideas, even those some consider unorthodox or unpopular."

So it makes sense that ABA would be willing to include Shrier's unorthodox book in its mailing.

But when the box arrived at bookstores, some of the members were offended by the inclusion of *Irreversible Damage*, and a slew of angry tweets followed. Later that day, ABA tweeted a profuse apology that began: "An anti-trans book was included in our July mailing to members. This is a serious, violent incident that goes against ABA's ends policies, values, and everything we believe and support. It is inexcusable." The organization's CEO, Allison Hill, also sent a letter to members calling the inclusion of the book "horrific harm...that caused violence and pain." She writes: "We traumatized and endangered members of the trans community...and put the authors in danger through a forced association...There is nothing that I can say that will make this right."*

Social media backlash forced ABA into a moment of truth—a test of their long-standing commitment to "the freedom to seek and to express

---

* A whole lot of concept creep in this paragraph.

ideas, even those some consider unorthodox or unpopular." In the face of pressure, ABA sided with the fundamentalists.

Livingston

Journalist Katie Herzog talked to a group of a dozen doctors—a group "so worried about the dangers of speaking out about their concerns" that, like many whistleblowers in these stories, they insisted on anonymity. Herzog wrote:

> Some of these doctors say that there is a "purge" underway in the world of American medicine: question the current orthodoxy and you will be pushed out...."People are afraid to speak honestly," said a doctor who immigrated to the U.S. from the Soviet Union. "It's like back to the USSR, where you could only speak to the ones you trust." If the authorities found out, you could lose your job, your status, you could go to jail or worse. The fear here is not dissimilar.

This stifling of free speech was recently demonstrated by the *Journal of the American Medical Association* (*JAMA*), one of the world's leading medical journals. On a 2021 episode of the journal's podcast, deputy editor Ed Livingston had the nerve to question whether the use of the term "structural racism" in medicine may have adverse effects:

> I think using the term racism invokes feelings amongst people—as I just said, my own feelings earlier on, that make it—that are negative, and that people do have this response that we've said repeatedly, "I'm not a racist. So why are you calling me a racist?" And because they respond that way, they're turned off by the whole structural racism phenomenon. Are there better terms we can use? Is there a better word than racism?

The uproar was scalding. Physician Uché Blackstock, MD, said, "The fact that podcast was conceived of, recorded and posted was unconscionable...I think it caused an incalculable amount of pain and trauma to Black physicians and patients." Brittani James, the co-founder of the Institute for Antiracism in Medicine, said, "They are doing immense harm with their racism and misogyny and ignorance, and I'm not just going to sit here while they are killing folks." A Change.org petition by

James' institute that called for *JAMA* "to rectify this harmful incident and examine the infrastructural makeup that allowed this podcast to pass many stages of evaluation before release" has received more than ten thousand signatures.

The American Medical Association (AMA), the journal's parent company, reacted to the uproar the same way the *Times*, Google, and the American Bookseller's Association did: they tweeted that the podcast was "wrong, false and harmful" and "in no way reflective of the AMA as an independent organization." *JAMA*'s chief editor, Howard Bauchner, issued a statement calling Livingston's comments "inaccurate, offensive, hurtful, and inconsistent with the standards of *JAMA*," and promised that "We are instituting changes that will address and prevent such failures from happening again." Those changes turned out to be asking Livingston to resign from his position as *JAMA*'s deputy editor, which he did, and, after the uproar persisted, Bauchner resigning from his position as *JAMA*'s chief editor.

In a statement following the resignations, *JAMA* made it clear that the SJF narrative would never be questioned or debated again under its name:

> The intersection between society, health, and equity is clear and addressing structural racism, including in medical journalism, is essential to improving health....Today, and for the future, these goals will be accomplished by championing diversity, equity, and inclusion in all aspects of clinical care, biomedical research, health policy, and society.

This is the kind of story those doctors were talking about when they expressed their concerns. Herzog's article continues:

> "We're afraid of what's happening to other people happening to us," a doctor on the West Coast told me. "We are seeing people being fired. We are seeing people's reputations being sullied. There are members of our group who say, 'I will be asked to leave a board. I will endanger the work of the nonprofit that I lead if this comes out.' People are at risk of being totally marginalized and having to leave their institutions."

Wang

It turns out that a political movement that can police what's allowed on a medical podcast can also dictate what is published in medical journals.

In 2020, cardiologist Norman Wang, MD, published a paper in the *Journal of the American Heart Association* (*JAHA*) analyzing diversity policies in cardiology. The paper argued that the industry's affirmative action policies weren't effective at increasing diversity within the field and didn't improve patient outcomes. Wang concluded, "Ultimately, all who aspire to a profession in medicine and cardiology must be assessed as individuals on the basis of their personal merits, not their racial and ethnic identities."

The view that race or ethnicity should not be considered in academic admissions is a mainstream position—one shared by, according to a 2019 Pew poll, 73 percent of Americans, including 63 percent of Democrats, 62 percent of Black Americans, and 65 percent of Hispanic Americans. But the backlash on Twitter was fierce, often coming along with the hashtag #RetractRacists. One cardiologist wrote: "How a paper that is so incompatible with our core values came to be published will be reviewed." One tweet described Wang's paper similarly to how the media described Damore's Google memo: "a 'Minorities are not qualified to be in medicine' diatribe."

A research paper (not an opinion) about policy effectiveness that successfully passed through peer review was met with a swing of the digital cudgel. It was a moment of truth for the University of Pittsburgh, where Wang worked; for *JAHA*, the journal that published the paper; and for the American Heart Association, the journal's parent company.

You can guess how it played out. The dean of the school sent a mass email denouncing the paper as "against equity and inclusivity." The department chair called the article "antithetical to [the school's] values." The journal's editor-in-chief issued a statement that the paper doesn't "reflect in any way my views, the views of the *JAHA* Editorial Board, or the views of the American Heart Association," that "we condemn discrimination and racism in all forms," and reaffirming its commitment "to increase diversity, equity and inclusiveness in medicine and cardiology," and vowing to "prevent future missteps of this type." The American Heart Association tweeted: "[The article] does *not* represent AHA values. *JAHA* is editorially independent but that's no excuse. We'll investigate. We'll do better."

The journal retracted Wang's paper—only the second retraction in the journal's history. And the university removed Wang from his position as Program Director of the Clinical Cardiac Electrophysiology Fellowship and prohibited him from making contact with any students, telling him that any classroom he participated in was "inherently unsafe."

• • •

These stories, and hundreds of others like them, come from many different industries—academia, media, tech, publishing, medicine, the arts, foundations, NGOs, advocacy groups—but they tend to follow a common pattern:

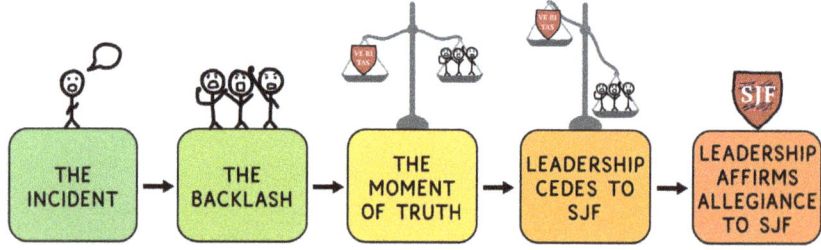

- **The incident**: Someone writes or says something that's acceptable to most of society but blasphemy within SJF.
- **The backlash**: A major protest occurs both within the institution and on social media, often equating the offender's words with harm and demanding punishment in the name of safety.
- **The moment of truth**: Leadership within the institution—in each case, an institution specifically built to play by liberal rules—is forced to either stand up for its liberal ideals or cede to mob demands.
- **Leadership cedes to SJF**: In many cases, leadership initially stands up for liberal values. But when the backlash persists, to avoid being guilty by association, leadership fires the target or retracts their words.
- **Leadership affirms allegiance to SJF**: Public statements say something like, "The incident is antithetical to our values. We vow that it will not happen again. We reaffirm our commitment to diversity, equity, and inclusion."

Across our wider society, SJF is being allowed to play King Mustache. Like in Hypothetica, protesters and social media mobs clamored for punishment—but it was leadership at the New York Times, Google, Amazon, the American Heart Association, and others, by actually *carrying out* the punishments, that turned the clamors into a very real cudgel.

The stories that make the news are, as in academia, only the tip of the iceberg. Most cancellations have happened more quietly, to lower-profile people. You hear them from your friends, your friends' friends, and in tweets that never go viral. And then there are the many thousands of such incidents prevented by fear from ever happening in the first place. Each punishment is a warning to everyone else in the institution: "You are no longer in the safety of an Idea Lab. You are now in an ideological Echo Chamber whose rules will be heavily enforced." In that kind of environment, most people simply go silent.

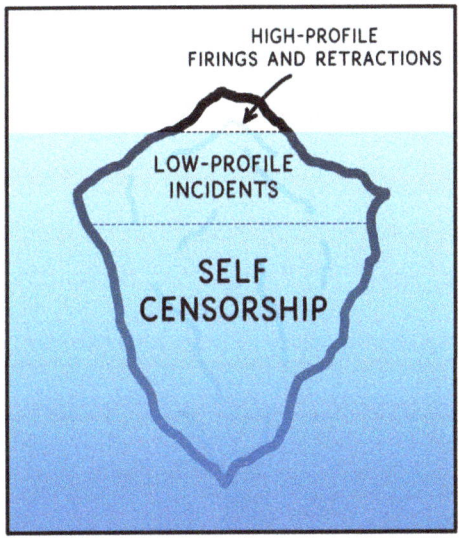

We'll never hear about the article that sits on the editor's desk and never gets published, or the movie that never gets bought. The science too risky to research. The book too risky to write. The memo too risky to send. The op-ed too risky to pen. The opinion too risky to voice. George Orwell called this "the sinister fact" about censorship: "Unpopular ideas can be silenced, and inconvenient facts kept dark, without the need for any official ban."

Surveys consistently show that this fear has become widespread. In a 2020 survey by the Cato Institute, majorities of every political group except the far left ("strong liberals") agreed with the statement "The political climate these days prevents me from saying things I believe because others might find them offensive." In a 2022 survey commissioned by *Times* Opinion and Siena College, 84 percent of Americans said it is a "very serious" or "somewhat serious" problem that some Americans do not speak freely due to fear of retaliation or harsh criticism.

Which brings us to a famous concept:

POPPER'S PARADOX

In his 1945 book *The Open Society and Its Enemies*, philosopher Karl Popper describes a "Paradox of Tolerance" like this:

> If we extend unlimited tolerance even to those who are intolerant, if we are not prepared to defend a tolerant society against the onslaught of the intolerant, then the tolerant will be destroyed, and tolerance with them.

This is only part of Popper's Paradox, but it's the part that's most widely referenced—often quoted more colloquially as, "In order to maintain a tolerant society, the society must be intolerant of intolerance."

The problem here is that tolerance, in itself, is not a principle. "Tolerance" and "intolerance" only take on moral meaning when you add on the "of ___." If the blank is, say, "people who look different than you," then tolerance sounds great. If instead the blank is, "a religious practice that involves sacrificing children," then *intolerance* suddenly sounds a lot better.

When you leave the "of ___" unspecified, Popper's Paradox is inevitably twisted by political or religious groups into some version of: *In order to maintain a tolerant society, the society must be intolerant of [people, ideas, and practices that we don't like].* By labeling their ideological opponents as "intolerant," whoever has the most cultural power in any environment can use Popper's reasoning to justify authoritarianism.

The Economist points out that every authoritarian who suppresses free speech justifies it as a means of protecting people:

Nearly all countries have laws that protect freedom of speech. So authoritarians are always looking out for respectable-sounding excuses to trample on it. National security is one. Russia recently sentenced Vadim Tyumentsev, a blogger, to five years in prison for promoting "extremism", after he criticised Russian policy in Ukraine. "Hate speech" is another. China locks up campaigners for Tibetan independence for "inciting ethnic hatred"; Saudi Arabia flogs blasphemers; Indians can be jailed for up to three years for promoting disharmony "on grounds of religion, race…caste…or any other ground whatsoever."

Each of these cases are essentially framed as "being intolerant of intolerance."

But if we read Popper's Paradox in its fuller context, we see that he's talking about something very specific:

> I do not imply, for instance, that we should always suppress the utterance of intolerant philosophies; as long as we can counter them by rational argument and keep them in check by public opinion, suppression would certainly be most unwise. But we should claim the right to suppress them if necessary even by force; **for it may easily turn out that they are not prepared to meet us on the level of rational argument, but begin by denouncing all argument**; they may forbid their followers to listen to rational argument, because it is deceptive, and teach them to answer arguments by the use of their fists or pistols. We should therefore claim, in the name of tolerance, the right not to tolerate the intolerant.

Popper was specifically concerned by those who refuse to engage in rational argument, instead using intimidation to respond to criticism of their ideas. When he talked about intolerance, he was referring to one kind in particular: *idea supremacy*. Popper believed that liberal societies have to be intolerant when people impede the workings of the marketplace of ideas. Not only is SJF idea supremacy not justified by Popper's Paradox, it is *exactly what Popper was warning about*.

This highlights the massive difference between criticism and cancel culture. Criticism attacks ideas, cancel culture punishes people. Criticism enriches discussion, cancel culture shuts down discussion.

Criticism helps lift up the best ideas, cancel culture protects the ideas of the culturally powerful. Criticism is a staple of liberalism, cancel culture is the epitome of illiberalism.

To be a good liberal means to criticize, not cancel. But it *also* means that you stand up for liberalism—when you see cancel culture happening, you try to *stop* it. This is what Popper's Paradox calls for.

This is all pretty obvious when a society's "big brain" is thinking clearly—but in today's political chaos and confusion, the distinction between attacking ideas and attacking people has blurred. When people have spoken up against idea supremacy—i.e., the good liberal calling out illiberal behavior, as per Popper's Paradox—cancelers have regularly retorted:

If the distinction between criticism and canceling isn't clear, this seems valid. The person trying to stop the canceling seems hypocritical. It seems like an instance of standard political squabbling. Soon, no one can agree on the definition of tolerance or intolerance or criticism or canceling. Confusion enables illiberalism, which enhances confusion, which leaves us in the exact kind of environment where golems thrive.

• • •

Step 1 of the illiberal staircase is about speech control, and cancellations are only half the story here. Remember, King Mustache's cudgel created not one but *two* artificial gaps in Hypothetica's marketplace of ideas.

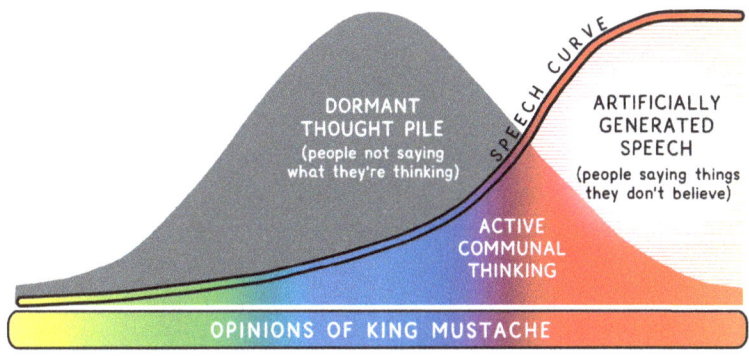

A group with the power to stop people from saying things they don't like also has the power to bellow ideas they *do* like through the country's largest megaphones, unimpeded by the usual market forces.

THE AMPLIFICATION OF SJF IN THE MARKETPLACE OF IDEAS

The American Psychological Association, the organization that controls the education and licensing of most clinical psychologists in the US, wrote on its website in 2020 that "we are living in a racism pandemic." Its language mirrors the way SJF activists in academia talk about the Force: "Every institution in America is born from the blood of white supremacist ideology and capitalism—and that's the disease."

In 2020, the editor of *Science* published a letter arguing that "systemic racism in science permeates this nation" and that "people of color learn better with more inclusive methods"—mirroring the tendency in SJF to talk about people as if they are part of monolithic groups instead of unique individuals. A first step toward addressing these problems, he said, was for "science and scientists to say out loud that they have benefited from, and failed to acknowledge, white supremacy."

In 2020, the Smithsonian National Museum of African American History and Culture published a set of guidelines for talking about race. It included a since-removed graphic called "Aspects and Assumptions of Whiteness & White Culture in the United States." The list of concepts the guidelines attributed to "whiteness" and "white culture" include "self-reliance," "the nuclear family," "objective, rational linear thinking," "hard work is the key to success," "respect authority," "plan for future," "delayed gratification," "follow rigid time schedules," "intent counts," "action orientation," "decision-making," and "be polite." This is straight out of the SJF idea that nearly all elements of a modern liberal society are actually oppression in disguise.*

In October 2021, the American Medical Association (which, remember, said it was "wrong, false and harmful" for Ed Livingston to question the term "structural racism") published a paper titled "Advancing Health Equity: Guide to Language, Narrative and Concepts." The guide asks doctors to replace common terms or phrases with new ones that emphasize the SJF worldview. For example, instead of using the term "vulnerable" for groups, the AMA tells doctors to say "oppressed" or "groups that have been economically/socially marginalized." While "vulnerable groups" just states what the groups are, the new terms also include *how* and *why*, according to the SJF, things got that way.†

This fundamentalist language made its way onto these megaphones not gradually but suddenly, in just the past few years. As philosopher Peter Boghossian tweeted, "A few years ago almost no one had even heard the

---

* I imagine that non-white cultures and countries around the world also might have a quibble with the notion that "white culture" should get credit for all of these basic concepts.

† My personal favorite part of the document: the AMA says that "Low-income people have the highest level of coronary artery disease in the United States" should be swapped out for "People underpaid and forced into poverty as a result of banking policies, real estate developers gentrifying neighborhoods, and corporations weakening the power of labor movements, among others, have the highest level of coronary artery disease in the United States."

word 'equity' outside of a financial context. Now it's ubiquitous—infused in every institution. The lack of suspicion about this now dominant value is striking. It's been accepted wholesale as a universal moral truth."

This terminology has suddenly become common on the largest media platforms. For example, "whiteness," according to Robin DiAngelo and Özlem Sensoy, "refers to the specific dimensions of racism that elevate White people over people of Color." This is a core concept within SJF ideology that hasn't been commonly used or discussed elsewhere until very recently. But recent years saw lots of headlines like "To Understand Trump's Support, We Must Think in Terms of Multiracial Whiteness" (*Washington Post*), "How the Mainstream Media's Whiteness Enabled Trump" (Slate), "Whiteness Is a Pandemic" (The Root), "Understanding Multiracial Whiteness and Trump Supporters" (NPR), and "He Wants to Save Classics From Whiteness. Can the Field Survive?" (*New York Times Magazine*).

To illustrate just how stark these trends are, I asked Associate Professor David Rozado, who has been studying these trends in his own research, to compile data showing how common SJF terms have blown up on major media platforms:

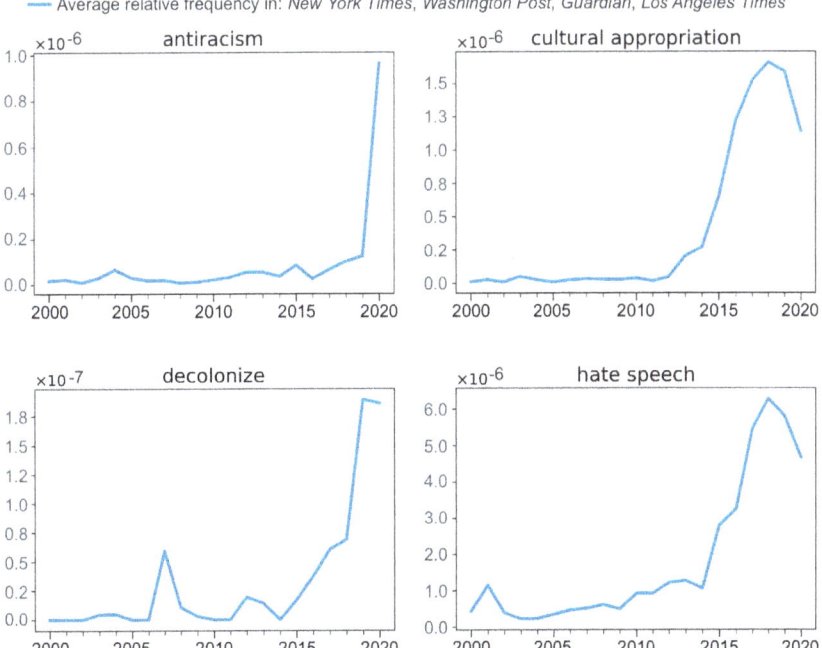

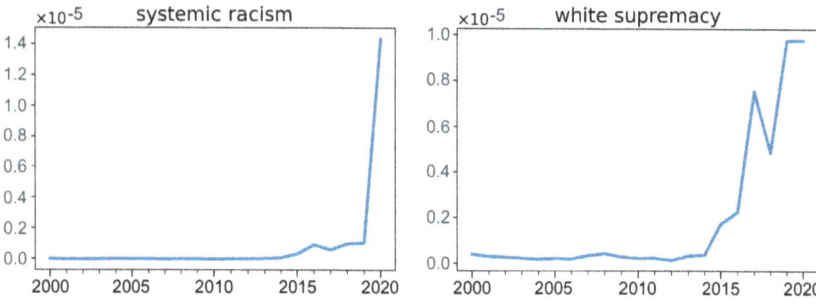

Source: David Rozado, "Charts Compiled for Tim Urban"

This also applies to more general SJF concepts. "A racist policy," writes Ibram X. Kendi, "is any measure that produces or sustains racial inequity between racial groups." Most Americans still use the individual definition of "racist," but SJF's usage has exploded into headlines in the past few years. For example:

> ***Scientific American***: The **Racist** Roots of Fighting Obesity (2020)
> ***Nature***: Computer Science Has a **Racism** Problem: These Researchers Want to Fix It (2022)
> ***Food & Wine***: The Difference between Yams and Sweet Potatoes Is Structural **Racism** (2022)
> **Classic FM**: Is Classical Music **Racist**? (2020)
> **Aeon**: Western Philosophy is **Racist** (2017)
> ***Psychology Today***: Can Dogs Be **Racist**? (2019)
> **Level**: The Unintentional **Racism** Found in Traffic Signals (2020)
> ***The Guardian***: Is Jingle Bells **Racist**? Despite Backlash from the Right, It's Not Black and White (2017)
> ***The Times***: Students Who Look Away Could Be **Racist**, Oxford Says (2017)
> ***The Allegheny Front***: Reckoning with the **Racist** Past of Bird Names (2020)
> ***The Blaze***: Clemson University: Expecting People to Show Up on Time is **Racist** (2017)
> **Book and Film Globe**: Is 'The Muppet Show' **Racist**? (2021)
> ***The Independent***: Your 'Strange' Crush on Rishi Sunak Could Actually Be a **Racist** Fetish (2020)
> ***Washington Examiner***: Student Shares Campus Tale That Soap Dispensers Are **Racist** (2021)

The Sunday Times: Orcs in the Lord of the Rings 'Show Tolkien Was **Racist**' (2018)

Literary Hub: The **Racist** History of Celebrating the American Tomboy (2020)

Global News: Dr. Seuss Books Are '**Racist**,' New Study Says. Should Kids Still Read Them? (2019)

The Independent: M&S Apologises for '**Racist**' Bra Names and Says 'We Have More to Learn' (2020)

Hot Air: San Francisco Board of Education VP: Meritocracy Is a Racist System (2021)

Chicago Tribune: Is Math **Racist**? New Course Outlines Prompt Conversations about Identity, Race in Seattle Classrooms (2019)

The Conversation: How Hollywood's 'Alien' and 'Predator' Movies Reinforce Anti-Black **Racism** (2020)

Today's Parent: Why the Way We Teach Kids Table Manners Is Actually Kind of **Racist** (2019)

BBC: Ex-MP Fiona Onasanya Attacks Kellogg's Cereal Box '**racism**' (2020)

The Guardian: Twitter Apologises for '**Racist**' Image-Cropping Algorithm (2020)

Politico: The **Racist** History of Tipping (2019)

Vox: The Knitting Community Is Reckoning with **Racism** (2019)

Daily Star: Avatar 2 Branded 'Horrible and **Racist**' as Viewers Call for Boycott over 'Tone-Deaf' Plot (2022)

The Telegraph: From Elvis Presley to Patti Smith and The Stones, Rock Music Is Built on **Racism** (2020)

CNN: A Rock That Students Call a Symbol of **Racism** Has Been Removed from University of Wisconsin (2021)

The Spinoff: The Many Problems with Auckland University's **Racist** Coffee (2020)

The New York Post: Why Your Swipes on Hinge and OKCupid Might Be **Racist** (2021)

BBC: Is Italian Fashion **Racist**? (2020)

As we've seen in other places, what happens in the marketplace of ideas is often mirrored in the world of academic research. We looked at the usage of those same SJF terms in scholarly abstracts:

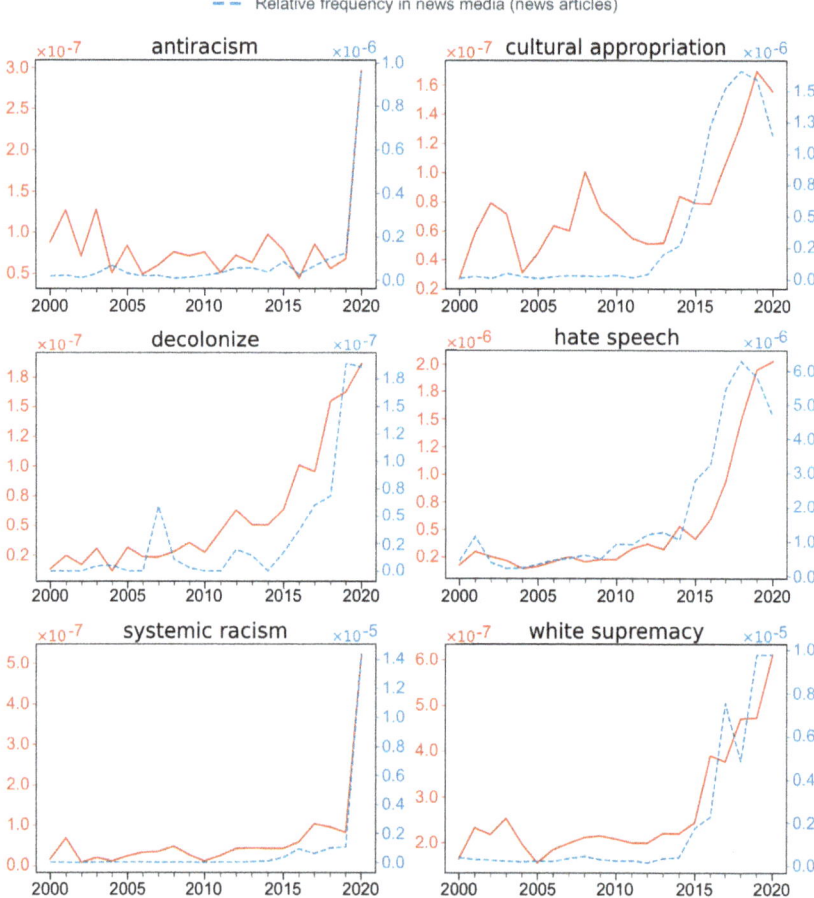

Source: David Rozado, "Charts Compiled for Tim Urban"

For example, a paper published in 2020 in the reputable journal *Proceedings of the National Academies of Sciences* (*PNAS*) analyzed 1.8 million hospital births and came to an eye-opening conclusion: the Black–white newborn mortality gap (the difference in mortality rate between Black and white newborns) is smaller when Black newborns are under the care of Black physicians than when they are under the care of white physicians. The authors called this "a robust racial concordance benefit for Black newborns" (racial concordance meaning the doctor and the patient are the same race) and finished their paper with this recommendation:

Taken with this work, it gives warrant for hospitals and other care organizations to invest in efforts to reduce such biases and explore their connection to institutional racism. Reducing racial disparities in newborn mortality will also require raising awareness among physicians, nurses, and hospital administrators about the prevalence of racial and ethnic disparities, their effects, furthering diversity initiatives, and revisiting organizational routines in low-performing hospitals.

The findings went viral online. CNN wrote that the findings "laid bare how shocking racial disparities in human health can affect even the first hours of a person's life." *Science News* wrote that "for these babies, care from a Black physician does indeed matter." One doctor wrote on Medium: "New evidence reinforces the case that a largely white medical establishment is failing children of color," which may suggest that "recruiting, training, and retaining pediatricians of color is much more than a corrective to centuries of racial inequity; it is literally a lifesaving intervention for our patients."

Much less viral were the people pointing out that these headlines were grossly misleading.

A single study should always be taken with a grain of salt, and this one in particular had some serious limitations. First, the researchers assumed babies were paired with doctors quasi-randomly, but it could be that wealthier Black families are more likely to have the option to choose to work with a Black doctor. A phenomenon like this, not controlled for in the study, could corrupt the results.

Second, there was what one doctor described as the challenge of "ascribing the outcome of the child to one of many doctors who plays a role in the care of that child. Health care is a team sport." In other words, it's not clear in many cases whether the official "physician of record" was even present for the birth. Each hospital also has their own way of organizing personnel—something the study did not take into account.

Finally, there was the inherent difficulty in any attempt to determine the race of doctors in a large study like this. Here, the authors' dataset provided information only about the babies—the race of the doctors was determined by looking at their online photos.

Those who criticized the study didn't mince their words. One doctor told Katie Herzog, anonymously:

It's some of the most shoddy, methodologically flawed research we've ever seen published in these journals, with sensational conclusions that seem totally unjustified from the results of the study. It's frustrating because we all know how hard it is to get good, sound research published. So do those rules and quality standards no longer apply to this topic, or to these authors, or for a certain time period?

To be fair, the study's authors acknowledged many of these shortcomings, underscoring the need for further research. But none of these qualifiers made the headlines, which presented the story as a set of groundbreaking findings and amplified the paper's call for changes in educational and hiring policies at hospitals.

Another anonymous doctor made a comment that perfectly sums up the two connected phenomena we've been talking about:

"Whole research areas are off-limits," he said, adding that some of what is being published in the nation's top journals is "shoddy as hell."

A healthy marketplace of ideas (or research institution) has two basic rules: 1) all ideas are free to be expressed, and 2) all ideas may be criticized. To make it to the biggest stages, ideas have to be persuasive enough to win people over and sound enough to survive a gauntlet of criticism.

"Whole research areas are off-limits" is a violation of Rule 1. Instead of subjecting SJF-unfriendly papers to criticism, SJF activists have subjected their *authors* to punishment, using fear to prevent such research from happening in the first place.

When research is published that is "shoddy as hell," it means something is off with Rule 2. It means SJF-friendly research that would fail to make it through the normal gauntlet is getting a free pass. In the case of the paper we just looked at, on race and infant mortality, one doctor believes that most of the standard criticism was left unsaid: "I am aware of dozens of people who agree with my assessment of this paper and are scared to comment." This is how shoddy research ends up with a gauntlet-free path to publication (and media amplification).[*]

---

[*] While we're here: In October of 2022, the Foundation for Individual Rights...

And it's happening across industries. Whether we look at the world of newspaper op-eds, internal company memos, published books, or medical articles, we've seen "whole areas off limits"—areas that conflict with the SJF narrative or sensibilities. Meanwhile, the radical ideas of SJF are suddenly being amplified across society, often in ways that lack rigorous standards—even though only a small portion of people subscribe to them.

Using low-rung, coercive tactics, SJF has manipulated American society's Speech Curve, creating two sizable gaps between what people are thinking and what they're saying about social justice topics.

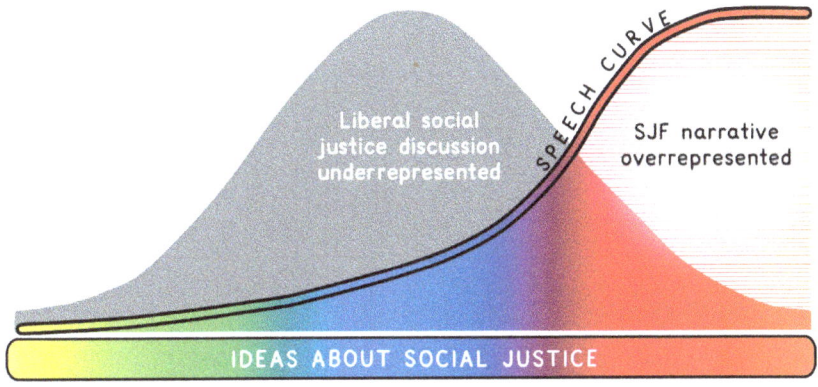

Social Justice Fundamentalism isn't unusual as a movement that wishes to strong-arm society's Speech Curve to match its own Echo Chamber. What's unusual is that it currently has the power to do so.

Movements with a Power Games mindset, like animal species in an ecosystem, don't have an "okay we've gone far enough" setting. If the high-rung immune system isn't working the way it's supposed to, they will push the envelope further and further until something stops them.

...and Expression surfaced a video showing an auditorium of medical students at the University of Minnesota reciting not the Hippocratic Oath but an SJF Oath. In unison, they vowed: "We commit to uprooting the legacy and perpetuation of structural violence deeply embedded within the healthcare system. We recognize inequities built by past and present traumas rooted in white supremacy, colonialism, the gender binary, ableism, and all forms of oppression....We pledge to honor all indigenous ways of healing that have been historically marginalized by Western medicine."

ILLIBERAL STAIRCASE, STEP 2: FORCED LISTENING

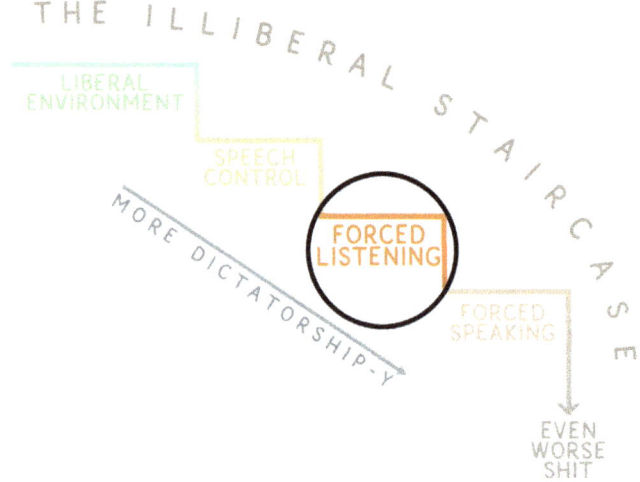

With Step 1's Speech Curve manipulation, at least any citizen is welcome to check out. Maybe people are scared to speak their minds, and maybe they're seeing a lot of SJF in news headlines, on social media, and elsewhere, but they can ignore it if they so choose.

Down on Step 2, checking out is not an option.

FORCED LISTENING FOR GROWN-UPS: SJF PROFESSIONAL TRAININGS

In March of 2022, conservative staff members at the Walt Disney Company issued an open letter about the rapidly changing political atmosphere at the company. Disney, they argued, should remain apolitical, as it is "uniquely situated to provide experiences and entertainment that can bridge our national divide and bring us all together." But they said the company had become "an increasingly uncomfortable place to work for those of us whose political and religious views are not explicitly progressive. We watch quietly as our beliefs come under attack from our own employer, and we frequently see those who share our opinions condemned as villains by our own leadership."

It's in this kind of environment, increasingly common at large companies across the US, that a new kind of (usually mandatory) training has emerged.

Since 2020, according to internal company materials, Disney employees from departments across the company have participated in anti-racism trainings, where they're instructed to "take ownership of educating yourself about structural anti-Black racism." They're told to "challenge colorblind ideologies and rhetoric" and "work through feelings of guilt, shame and defensiveness to understand what is beneath them and what needs to be healed." They're taught about America's "racist infrastructure" and the importance of going beyond equal treatment to strive for "equity" and "equality of the outcome." Employees are told that it's not okay to say "politics don't belong at work" and instructed to "be a change agent by calling out microaggressions and other racist behavior when you witness them."

American Express employees were told in mandatory trainings to create an "identity map" by writing their "race, sexual orientation, body type, religion, disability status, age, gender identity, citizenship" in circles surrounding the words "Who am I?" Verizon employees were taught about intersectionality, microaggressions, and institutional racism, and asked to write a reflection on questions like "What is my cultural identity?" with "race/ethnicity, gender/gender identity, religion, education, profession, sexual orientation" beneath. CVS Health hourly employees were sent to a mandatory training where keynote speaker Ibram X. Kendi explained that "to be born in [The United States] is to literally have racist ideas rain on our head consistently and constantly…We're just walking through society completely soaked in racist ideas believing we're dry." Employees were asked to fill out a "Reflect on Privilege" checklist and told they should "commit to holding yourself and colleagues accountable to consistently celebrate diversity and take swift action against non-inclusive behaviors."

You can read dozens of eerily similar stories about trainings in corporate America—an estimated 80 percent of which are mandatory.

These kinds of trainings have also swept through the public sector, from the Department of Homeland Security, where employees were warned about "color blindness" and the "myth of meritocracy," to the federal financial agencies like the Treasury and the Federal Reserve, where white employees were advised not to "perpetuate white silence" or "shy away from using language like 'whiteness,' 'racism,' 'white supremacy,' and 'allyship,'" to the City of Seattle, where employees were taught about "internalized racial superiority" and "internalized racial inferiority" and told that white people's "anger, self-righteousness and defensiveness mask fear, shame and guilt for the harm of [their] actions."

Less publicized are the many similar stories at smaller companies. One former employee of an arts nonprofit talked on a podcast about a year-long series of DEI trainings at her company—which she said were "very, very mandatory." No one dissented during the trainings, she said, because doing so would put their jobs in danger. As she put it: "We're being told that there's only one very specific way to have that conversation, and if you don't happen to agree with it, then it feels like you can't have the conversation, you're not included. There's no room for dissent." This included employees of color, one of whom was immediately "shut down" by the instructor when she said she had not experienced racism.

The same trainings are happening at hospitals across the country. One doctor at a New England hospital sent me a portion of a mandatory training he was attending that included a very specific definition of racism:

> Racism is a system of structuring opportunity and assigning value based on the social interpretation of how one looks (which is what we call "race") that unfairly disadvantages some individuals and communities, unfairly advantages other individuals and communities, and saps the strength of the whole society through the waste of human resources.

After the training—which, by the way, he said took the place of "our most useful teaching conference"—he and his colleagues had to answer a multiple-choice quiz about the presentation. One question, for example, stated, "Focusing on race and racism just makes the problem worse" and offered two options: "true" and "false." What would happen, I asked him, if you believed the answer was "true" and clicked that option? He replied, "I don't know but I definitely don't want to find out."

Over in the United Kingdom, mental health nurse Amy Gallagher found out. She tells the story of training to be a psychotherapist at the Tavistock and Portman NHS Trust (the NHS is England's publicly funded healthcare system). The training included lessons based on

Robin DiAngelo's work, on concepts like "white ignorance" and "white fragility." In one of the lectures, the trainer told students "to let go of the myth of our white innocence and purity and acknowledge the darkness at its heart."

At the time of this writing, all we have is Gallagher's story. She says she expressed her discomfort with the trainings to the program leaders, telling them: "I personally don't agree with these views, and we need to be aware that patients might not agree with these either."

After speaking out, she says, "the Tavistock staff threatened, suspended, harassed, bullied, victimised me and tried to destroy my career over a two-year campaign of abuse which is ongoing." She was told she was "not fit to become a therapist" and that "if I continued to speak inappropriately about race, I would be suspended, I would be barred from entering the profession of psychotherapy."

When I've discussed these stories with people, a common response is: "What's the big problem with this? Is it so bad for white people to be made more aware of the subtler aspects of racism?"

There are two problems:

1. Diversity trainings are usually ineffective and often backfire

Diversity trainings have been around since the 1960s, with noble goals like, according to sociologist Musa al-Gharbi, "rectifying inequalities, improving the organizational climate and employee morale, increasing collaboration across lines of difference, fostering free exchange of ideas and information, enhancing the hiring, retention, and promotion of diverse candidates, and more."

The problem is that diversity trainings aren't very effective. Al-Gharbi writes:

> Unfortunately, a robust and ever-growing body of empirical literature suggests that diversity-related training typically fails at its stated objectives. It does not seem to meaningfully or durably improve organizational climate or workplace morale; it does not increase collaboration or exchange across lines of difference; it does not improve hiring, retention or promotion of diverse candidates. In fact, the training is often counterproductive with respect to these explicit goals.

Study after study after study has come to the same conclusion: there is little evidence that diversity trainings work.*

On the other hand, there is significant evidence that the trainings can be counterproductive. Diversity trainings can reduce sympathy, reinforce bias and stereotypes, cause claims of discrimination to be taken less seriously, drive a wedge between demographic groups,† and decrease morale.

Al-Gharbi points to mountains of research that suggest ways to make diversity trainings more effective and less damaging. Rather than focus trainings on the broader problems in American society and American history, or on often controversial progressive stances like equality of outcome or the myth of meritocracy, "training should instead be tightly connected to specific organizational objectives and the specific tasks different team members are responsible for." Rather than discuss bias and prejudice exclusively in the context of how privileged groups perceive oppressed groups, he says, discuss these phenomena as what they really are: general cognitive tendencies that all people are susceptible to. Rather than training people to avoid conflict—by teaching members of minority groups to be extra sensitive to perceived slights and leaving members of privileged groups walking on eggshells—trainings should teach people how to *manage* conflict. While conflict can bring people together and drive innovation when

---

* One of the most common elements of today's diversity trainings, the "implicit association test," has repeatedly been shown to lack both reliability and validity. The test's popularity is based on the premise that implicit biases revealed by the test translate to unconscious discriminatory behavior in practice. But, as Jesse Singal observed in a 2017 article for *New York Magazine*, a number of meta-analyses suggest the opposite.

† Remember the former nonprofit employee from a few pages back? In her conversation on the podcast *Blocked and Reported*, she explains how she experienced this firsthand. She was initially on board with the DEI trainings, some of which (including the discussions of race) were led by Robin DiAngelo. But in retrospect, she says, they caused her to disengage from her coworkers of color: "I believed that there was sort of an intrinsic racism to me in my interactions and I was worried as I interacted with my POC coworkers—I was worried, am I gonna say something wrong or can I compliment my coworker's hair?...And faced with the choice of, do I stick my neck out and go for this interaction and then potentially have to pull like a Robin DiAngelo apology with a script she gave us, or do I just put my head back down and sit back down at my computer? It was often easier to do the latter."

managed constructively, trying to rid the workplace of conflict is not only futile, it stifles creativity.

If diversity trainings are not effective and are often counterproductive, and if we know what would make them more effective—why are they proliferating?

This is a question that has exasperated many researchers. Writing about implicit bias testing, professors Gregory Mitchell and Philip Tetlock emphasize that it is "difficult to find a psychological construct that is so popular yet so misunderstood and lacking in theoretical and practical payoff." Harvard social scientist Frank Dobbin, who has spent decades studying diversity trainings, laments, "We're doing a lot of things that are pretty well known not to work....If we know that the existing modules we have aren't really doing anything, I'm just perplexed as to why we keep doing them."

The most charitable explanation for why the bad programs persist is some combination of inertia and ignorance about their ineffectiveness. But there are other explanations as well. Having diversity training in place provides companies with critical legal protection against discrimination lawsuits. It provides the company with positive PR, suggesting to the world and to their staff that they care about diversity and are doing something about it. The diversity industry is now also worth billions of dollars, with popular trainers making millions per year. If the companies and the trainers are both getting what they need from maintaining the status quo, why would they do anything to change it?

2. Modern diversity trainings are mostly SJF trainings and violate the principle of secularism

Reading through documents from recent diversity trainings across society, I was struck by how they use the same wording, the same materials, and the same exercises. Some common themes:

- Racial oppression is encoded in America's DNA and permeates every aspect of American life
- Efforts should focus on achieving not merely equality of opportunity but equality of outcome
- All white people contribute to racism, no matter how they act or what they believe about themselves

- Phenomena like timeliness, individualism, perfectionism, and hard work are elements of white supremacy culture and tools of oppression
- White people who feel uncomfortable or defensive during trainings are simply exhibiting white fragility; marginalized people who disagree are exhibiting internalized oppression

These are not broadly accepted ideas, or even typical progressive ideas. This is Social Justice Fundamentalism. As SJF has pushed its way through colleges and out into the larger world, it has also become the ubiquitous ethos in diversity trainings. Employees are being trained on ideas that are, at best, unproven and massively controversial, as if they were well-established truths—often in mandatory sessions, with no dissent allowed.

I doubt many Americans have any problem with company trainings on why racism and harassment are unacceptable in the workplace. But few Americans would be okay with companies training employees on why they must be devout Christians or zealous Marxists or staunch libertarians.

This is because most Americans share a belief in *secularism*. British author Helen Pluckrose describes the essence of secularism like this:

> I don't believe what you believe, and I don't have to. I defend your right to hold, express and live by your own belief system, but you have no right to impose any of it on me.

It's not a violation of secularism for governments or companies to train employees not to racially discriminate because this maps onto the widely shared American ideal of equal opportunity. But training on why it's wrong to vote Democrat or wrong not to worship Jesus *would* violate secularism, because these are specific, controversial belief systems. Unless a company is explicitly centered around politics or religion, imposing these kinds of worldviews on employees is entirely inappropriate.

The trainings we've looked at fall squarely in the inappropriate category, violating the principle of secularism. A company can and should demand that employees are not racist at work. But whether employees reject racism for SJF reasons, for liberal reasons, or for any other reasons is not a company matter.

When engineers, accountants, nurses, intelligence officers, and graphic designers are being put through mandatory trainings on a single political lens, asked to uncritically accept the worldview of a single ideology, our secularism alarm bells should be blaring—even if it's all being framed as something much nicer-sounding.

At least employees of companies are grown-ups. What happens when similar trainings are forced upon far more impressionable children?

FORCED LISTENING FOR KIDS: SJF IN SCHOOLS

In 2021, the topic of politics in K–12 education burst onto the main stage of American political squabbling. As with most hot political topics, the discussion has become oversimplified, weaponized, and full of confusion. Let's take a look at the story behind the headlines.

To start, let's revisit the concept of critical pedagogy. Alison Bailey is a professor at Illinois State University whose scholarship "engages issues at the intersections of feminist theories, philosophy of race, critical whiteness studies, and social epistemology." In a 2017 paper titled "Tracking Privilege-Preserving Epistemic Pushback in Feminist and Critical Race Philosophy Classes," Bailey talks about "the distinction between critical thinking and critical pedagogy." She writes:

> The critical-thinking tradition is concerned primarily with epistemic adequacy. To be critical is to show good judgment in recognizing when arguments are faulty, assertions lack evidence, truth claims appeal to unreliable sources, or concepts are sloppily crafted

and applied. For critical thinkers, the problem is that people fail to "examine the assumptions, commitments, and logic of daily life... the basic problem is irrational, illogical, and unexamined living."...

Critical pedagogy begins from a different set of assumptions rooted in the neo-Marxian literature on critical theory commonly associated with the Frankfurt School. Here, the critical learner is someone who is empowered and motivated to seek justice and emancipation. Critical pedagogy regards the claims that students make in response to social-justice issues not as propositions to be assessed for their truth value, but as expressions of power that function to re-inscribe and perpetuate social inequalities. Its mission is to teach students ways of identifying and mapping how power shapes our understandings of the world. This is the first step toward resisting and transforming social injustices. By interrogating the politics of knowledge-production, this tradition also calls into question the uses of the accepted critical-thinking toolkit to determine epistemic adequacy.

Critical pedagogy is fundamentally different from critical thinking. While critical thinking teaches students general thinking skills, critical pedagogy teaches students to analyze the world through the SJF lens, in the service of "resisting and transforming social injustices." In critical pedagogy, the tool kit of critical thinking may itself be problematic. Bailey continues:

> To extend Audre Lorde's classic metaphor, the tools of the critical-thinking tradition (for example, validity, soundness, conceptual clarity) cannot dismantle the master's house: they can temporarily beat the master at his own game, but they can never bring about any enduring structural change.

Most American parents who assume their kids are learning critical thinking in schools would be surprised to learn about the increasing prevalence of critical pedagogy in K–12 education.

The Roots: How Teachers Are Trained

In a 2020 issue of the popular publication *Education Week,* English and social studies teacher Larry Ferlazzo had a stern message for teachers:

> If you as a teacher have not committed to doing the work of understanding your internal racism, implicit bias and prejudice, you are complicit in the deaths of Black people, and people of color broadly, across the nation. If you are not committed to the work of being actively anti-racist, you are complicit in validating the physical and spiritual murders of Black men, women and children daily. If you espouse the ideology of colorblindness and champion the myth of meritocracy, you are complicit in the vilification and denigration of Black people in this country.

This is representative of a message that teachers across the US are hearing from the moment they embark down a career path in education.

It starts with the education schools—schools that teach teachers how to teach. Here's what a graduate of the University of Washington's Secondary Teacher Education Program (STEP), writing in 2019 under a pseudonym, has to say about his experience in the program—a program that he says "demands total intellectual acquiescence":

> The first three of STEP's four quarters address social constructivism, postmodernism, and identity politics through flimsy and subjective content…imploring students to interpret every organization and social structure through the paradigms of power and oppression via gender, race, and sexuality….Students are segregated by race to discuss their place in the intersectional hierarchy of oppression….
>
> Above all, the program emphasizes that diversity and inclusion are the most important considerations in education, and that equity—equality of outcome rather than equality of opportunity—ought to be the primary goal of public policy.

We've talked about *White Fragility* author Robin DiAngelo and how she says a lot of stuff like "over-smiling allows white people to mask an anti-Blackness that is foundational to our very existence as white." DiAngelo's day job? She trains aspiring teachers.

We talked about Derald Wing Sue and his landmark paper on microaggressions that frames ideas like "America is the land of opportunity" and "I believe the most qualified person should get the job" as a form of bigotry. Sue trains teachers for a living.

In fact, many of SJF's leading scholars aren't undergrad professors but professors at education schools—which has made the above description of STEP common at education schools around the country.

Stanford's Teacher Education Program "aims to cultivate teacher leaders who share a set of core values that includes a commitment to social justice." The University of Pennsylvania's Graduate School of Education is committed to "preparing anti-racist educators and researchers." Students at Harvard's Graduate School of Education "will engage deeply with key concepts around equity, systems of power and oppression, cycles of socialization, identity, and transformation within the context of education writ large." By the time an aspiring teacher receives their master's degree, many have already been thoroughly trained in Social Justice Fundamentalism.

SJF training comes at the expense of time that might have been spent learning about other things. One teacher in Canada said there had been "blatant efforts to indoctrinate" prospective teachers, adding: "Meanwhile, what's being sacrificed is a real understanding of the pedagogical processes...Every single lecture within is focused on systems of oppression, intersectional identities, and critical ___ theories."

After getting their degrees, many teachers will be tested on their SJF knowledge right out of the gate, when they apply for a job. We looked at the way many university departments have begun using "diversity statements" as a euphemism for politically discriminatory hiring, as a way to ensure that only proven SJF believers and activists make it onto their payroll. In the past few years, we've begun seeing this in K–12 schools too. In Newton, Massachusetts, where I grew up, one of the application questions for prospective teachers reads, "What values and experiences would you bring to support the Newton Public Schools in becoming an active anti-racist school system?" According to a teacher I spoke to who works at one of Newton's schools, questions like these are ideological litmus tests. She says: "In the ten years since I've been at the school, the hiring process has transformed to one that hires based on ideology first, teaching second. Applicants are required to write about their plans for integrating anti-racism into their teaching. And having conservative views and espousing them would destroy you socially at the school with the faculty."*

---

* Her response when I asked whether this affects her on a day-to-day basis: "I'm afraid to speak openly and truthfully at meetings, full faculty or small groups,...

For teachers that are hired, the trainings continue once they enter the classroom.

I recently spoke to a teacher on the East Coast who had just been sent to his second annual "Workshop for Antiracist Culturally Responsive Teaching," where he and his colleagues were instructed to "normalize talking about racial identity in their classrooms." On the West Coast, the California Teachers Association published advice on its website "to look at everything they do and teach through a racial and social justice lens," offering workshops on how to introduce social justice activism to preschoolers.

Similar to the corporate trainings we looked at, teacher trainings often center specifically around SJF. Springfield, Missouri's public school district asked teachers to locate themselves on an "Oppression Matrix" that mirrored SJF's Intersectional Stack and told them that progress comes in the form of student "empowerment," which the district defines as teaching students to "refuse to accept the dominant ideology and their subordinate status and take actions to redistribute social power more equitably." A teacher training in Santa Clara County explained the "foundational concept" of "critical pedagogy," in which "the kids become a subject and you are intending to awaken them to the oppression that they aren't aware of but that they are actively participating in....Then, how do we 'destroy, dismantle' and change those systems?" Notes from the training's Q&A include an explanation that this awakening of students can start "as early as 1st grade," as a way of "cashing in on kids' inherent empathy."

Naturally, training teachers and administrators in SJF leads to schools training *students* on SJF. And as with colleges, the stories from K–12 classrooms number in the hundreds, spanning the country, from public schools in low-income districts to the most elite private schools in New York City and Los Angeles. These are recent developments—nearly all of the below anecdotes are from 2020 or later.

...due to job fears and the social stigma of being labeled to the right. I'm not even conservative, but the centrist/left-of-center doesn't fit the mold here. There are a few of us like me, but when political issues come up, we speak almost in hushed tones behind closed doors so as not to be overheard."

Curriculum Changes

In a 1998 paper, cited more than one thousand times, prominent critical race theorist Gloria Ladson-Billings explained that "critical race theory sees the official school curriculum as a culturally specific artifact designed to maintain a White supremacist master script." A quarter century later, many schools are taking action to alter their curricula.

Harvard-Westlake, one of the top private schools in Los Angeles, recently announced plans for "redesigning the 11th grade US History course from a critical race theory perspective." A top New York City school, Fieldston, teaches a class called "historicizing whiteness," and according to journalist Bari Weiss, the school's physics classes no longer use the term "Newton's laws," opting instead for "the three fundamental laws of physics" in order to "decenter whiteness." At a 2021 conference held by the National Association of Independent Schools, which sets standards for more than 1,600 independent schools in the US, participants were told that "failing to explore the intersection of STEM and social justice" constitutes an act of "curriculum violence."

Unlike the wealthy parents of private school students, public school parents rarely have another option. They have to trust their district. And the list of public school districts that have instituted new programs and new curricula—all using nearly identical SJF language—is long.

California public school districts have implemented a required ethnic studies course. Like the ethnic studies courses being required for California's state college students, the curriculum is filled with SJF.

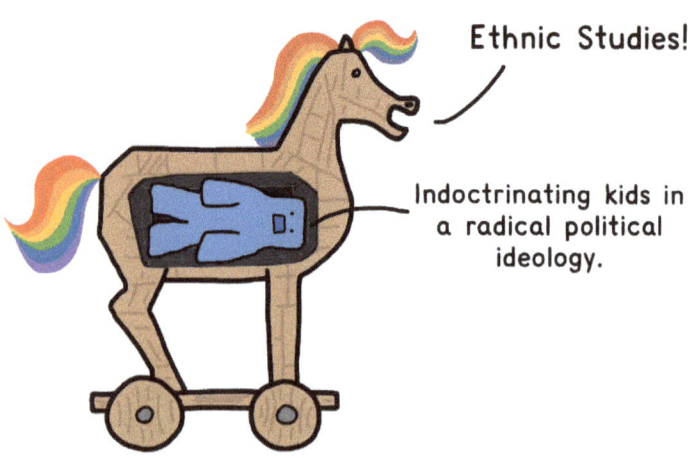

Teachers are instructed to "challenge racist, bigoted, discriminatory, imperialist/colonial beliefs and practices" on "ideological, institutional, interpersonal, and internalized" levels, to teach and "critique empire-building in history and its relationship to white supremacy, racism and other forms of power and oppression." A specific and radical political worldview being taught as a required course to California public school students.

The same thing is happening in Oregon and Washington. In North Carolina and Virginia. All over New York and California.

Seattle public schools now teach a "Math Ethnic Studies" course whose description is also straight from the SJF narrative:

> Power and oppression, as defined by ethnic studies, are the ways in which individuals and groups define mathematical knowledge so as to see "Western" mathematics as the only legitimate expression of mathematical identity and intelligence. This definition of legitimacy is then used to disenfranchise people and communities of color. This erases the historical contributions of people and communities of color.

The curriculum instructs teachers to explore the following questions:

> How can we use data to resist and liberate people and communities of color from oppression?
> How can we change mathematics from individualistic to collectivist thinking?
> Where does Power and Oppression show up in our math experiences?
> Who holds power in a mathematical classroom?
> Who gets to say if an answer is right?
> How important is it to be Right? What is Right? Says Who?
> Why/how does data-driven processes prevent liberation?

Some curriculum changes are less obvious at first glance. Many schools incorporate "Social-Emotional Learning" (SEL) into their curricula—a teaching method "by which children and adults acquire and effectively apply the knowledge, attitudes, and skills necessary to understand and manage emotions, set and achieve positive goals, feel and show empathy for others, establish and maintain positive relationships, and make responsible decisions." SEL, which has been around since the 1960s, is controversial because its efficacy is questionable and it comes at the expense of other learning. But it is widespread and had, until recently, enjoyed bipartisan support.

But around 2019, a new term began to make waves: *Transformative SEL*—"a specific form of SEL implementation," according to the American Federation of Teachers,* "that concentrates SEL practice on transforming inequitable settings and systems, and promoting justice-oriented civic engagement…This form of SEL is aimed at redistributing power to promote social justice through increased engagement in school and civic life."

In June of 2020, the same month so many companies were making eerily uniform statements about their commitment to antiracism, Karen Niemi, president and CEO of the leading SEL organization CASEL, explained that "we see SEL as a tool for antiracism." SEL has the potential, she said, "to help people move from anger, to agency, and then to action." The older definition of SEL (the one I quoted above) has been removed from CASEL's website, while materials have been added to the site describing the way transformative SEL can help students construct an "ethnic/racial identity," which "should be understood to be multidimensional, multifaceted, and intersectional." CASEL sees "untapped opportunity for SEL to serve as a lever for equity, addressing issues such as power, privilege, prejudice, discrimination, social justice, empowerment, and self-determination…elevating student assets and agency to resist oppressive forces and circumstances and advocate for and co-create equitable solutions."

To an untrained eye, these changes may sound great. But when you're familiar with this terminology, what you see is a decades-old teaching method (SEL) now being used as a tool to train and even recruit students into a very specific political ideological movement: SJF.†

---

* Side note: In 2022, 99.99 percent of political donations from the American Federation of Teachers went to Democrats.
† According to a report by educational consulting and investment firm Tyton Partners, between November 2019 and April 2021, SEL school and district spend grew about 45 percent, from $530 million to $765 million. Much of this increase was paid for by federal stimulus dollars.

For every official change, there are dozens of reports from whistleblower parents about what they've discovered unofficially happening in their child's classroom.

During "privilege walks," K–12 students stand in a line and the teacher reads out statements like, "If you have ever been the only person of your race/ethnicity in a classroom or place of work, take one step back," or "If you grew up with people of color or working class people who were servants, maids, gardeners, or babysitters in your home, take one step forward."

There are even white privilege lessons for elementary school children. In 2020, for example, third graders in Cupertino, California, were instructed to assign themselves a power and privilege score, based on characteristics like their race and gender identity. Schools in Evanston, Illinois, integrated an illustrated children's book called *Not My Idea*. The book features the devil offering a white child a "contract binding you to whiteness," which promises the child "stolen land," "stolen riches," and "special favors." In return, whiteness gets "to mess endlessly with the lives of your friends, neighbors, loved ones, and all fellow humans of *color*," along with the white child's "soul."

One grandfather tweeted a picture of a chart in his three-year-old grandson's preschool classroom, which displayed eight skin pigments, drawn in crayon, and pictures of every child lined up below their skin tone. Bari Weiss shares the story of the mother of a four-year-old in New York: "One day at home, in the midst of the application process, she was drawing with her daughter, who said offhandedly: 'I need to draw in my own skin color.' Skin color, she told her mother, is 'really important.' She said that's what she learned in school."

Teaching a Single Lens

In 2021, a public school district in Evanston, Illinois, held its third annual "Black Lives Matter at School Week of Action," during which students learned about the movement using curriculum created by Black Lives Matter activists and the local teachers' union. The program is a nationwide effort, having been rolled out in over twenty school districts across the country as of the 2017–2018 school year.

Teaching students about a major movement of their era makes sense. But especially when the movement is based on a radical ideology that only a small portion of Americans subscribe to, it should be taught alongside the larger context. In an article for *The Atlantic*, journalist Conor Friedersdorf argues that students receiving a proper education on the movement would be able to "accurately explain not only the values and beliefs of Black Lives Matter but also the strongest criticisms of the movement's approach. Can children describe how it compares with other forms of civil-rights activism, why many anti-racists embrace it, and why other anti-racists partly or wholly reject it?"

This program, though, teaches children that Black Lives Matter is the one and only correct approach to social justice. As one lesson's slide deck puts it in the first slide, "Today I'm going to teach you about what the Black Lives Matter movement is and why it's necessary." The part of the curriculum designed for preschoolers and kindergarteners states its goal as "students will understand that our country has a racist history that is grounded in white privilege."*

Most Americans would have no problem with their children being taught, unequivocally, that Black lives matter, that racism is an enduring problem, and that racial equality is a goal we should all be striving for—because these reflect broad liberal values. But it's something very different when students are taught that the particular neo-Marxist, postmodern political lens of the Black Lives Matter movement is the *only* acceptable worldview, as opposed to one of many competing ideologies.

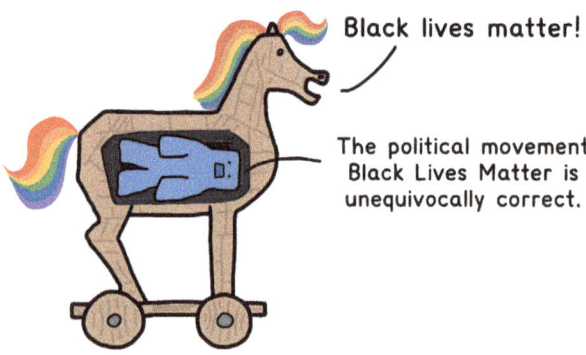

---

* A look at the curriculum makes it clear that while it's named after Black Lives Matter, a more appropriate name would be "SJF week" because the curriculum includes many aspects of SJF. The preschoolers and kindergarteners in the program, for example, have a day dedicated to "Queer, Trans-Affirming, & Collective Value," during which they are taught about gender expression, gender identity, LGBTQ+, and non-binary.

This isn't teaching—it's indoctrination.

When students are taught, their minds expand and open. When students are indoctrinated, their minds narrow and close. Friedersdorf quotes a parent of a child in the program—a parent who was generally supportive of the school's "BLM week":

> They present every issue with such moral certainty—like there is no other viewpoint. And we're definitely seeing this in my daughter. She can make the case for defunding the police, but when I tried to explain to her why someone might have a Blue Lives Matter sign, why some families support the police, she wasn't open to considering that view. She had a blinding certainty that troubled me. She thinks that even raising the question is racist. If she even hears a squeak of criticism of BLM, or of an idea that's presented as supporting equity, she's quick to call out racism.

The problem in all these cases is not the inclusion of SJF ideas in a student's education—it's the teaching of those ideas as if they're Bible verses in a religious school, not to be challenged or questioned.

Recent data suggests that this may be more the rule than the exception. In 2022, Manhattan Institute analysts Zach Goldberg and Eric Kaufmann commissioned a study on a nationally representative sample of 1,505 eighteen- to twenty-year-old Americans (82.4 percent of whom had attended public schools). They presented participants with eight SJF-y concepts (e.g., "America is a systematically racist country"; "Gender is an identity choice, regardless of the biological sex you were born into") and asked whether they had learned about them in school. Eighty-five percent of respondents reported that they had been taught about at least one of the eight concepts in class, and the average respondent had learned about half of the eight concepts.

Then the survey asked students whether they were taught these ideas alongside opposing arguments. Of those who had been taught at least one of the concepts, 68 percent reported that they were either not taught about opposing arguments (27 percent) or that they were taught that any opposing arguments were "not respectable" (41 percent). So—according to this survey at least—*most* students are learning about SJF in school, and well over half of students are learning about it in a single-lens, indoctrinate-y way.

When a political lens is taught this way, in state-run public schools, it violates the principle of secularism.

Punishing Pushback

As you might expect, many teachers have furious objections to this rapid onslaught of changes to how children are taught. But like the once-vocal dissenters in academia, media, and tech, most teachers have learned to shut their mouths—and for good reason. In April of 2021, Paul Rossi, a teacher at New York City's Grace Church School, published an article on Bari Weiss' Substack protesting the changes happening in his school. He wrote:

> My school, like so many others, induces students via shame and sophistry to identify primarily with their race before their individual identities are fully formed. Students are pressured to conform their opinions to those broadly associated with their race and gender and to minimize or dismiss individual experiences that don't match those assumptions. The morally compromised status of "oppressor" is assigned to one group of students based on their immutable characteristics. In the meantime, dependency, resentment and moral superiority are cultivated in students considered "oppressed."

According to Rossi, he was reprimanded by a school official a few days later, and the head of the school "ordered all high school advisors to read a public reprimand of my conduct out loud to every student in the school." Then he was relieved of his teaching duties and eventually left the school.

In this kind of environment, most teachers simply cannot afford to protest. A teacher I spoke to felt passionately that his school was doing bad things to students in the name of social justice, but speaking up? "It would be career suicide, and with two children I cannot afford to lose health insurance." Instead, he said, "I just keep my head down. Too much to lose." When vocal dissenters like Rossi are punished, it scares others into silence.

Concerned parents face the same quandary. An anonymous mother of a Brentwood student lamented to Bari Weiss, "The school can ask you to leave for any reason. Then you'll be blacklisted from all the private schools and you'll be known as a racist, which is worse than being called a murderer." An anonymous student from a top NYC private school sang the same tune: "If you publish my name, it would ruin my life. People would attack me for even questioning this ideology."

Twisting Words

Perhaps even more effective than punishing pushback is twisting the words of critics and creating straw men who are then easily demolished.

When I hear the quotes of these teachers, parents, and students, I see people who most likely fully support Liberal Social Justice but object to something very specific: Social Justice Fundamentalism—its ideas, its worldview, its teaching methods, and its coercive tactics.

But the Social Justice Horse can be used as a weapon, not just a shield. The Social Justice Horse says that what's being taught is "ethnic studies" or "the history of racism" or the notion that "Black lives matter"—so, therefore, the protesters must be trying to eradicate *those* ideas from schools.

This was especially on display in 2021, when these issues bubbled up into mainstream consciousness in what became known as the battle over "critical race theory in K–12 schools." Conservative activist Christopher Rufo catalyzed the discussion by publishing a series of whistleblower documents from teacher trainings and class handouts. Rufo framed the issue as critical race theory (CRT), and the term quickly went from relative obscurity to a mainstay on conservative programming (according to archive.org, the term was mentioned all of four times on Fox News in 2019, followed by 77 times in 2020 and a whopping 1,821 times in 2021).

In June of 2021, Kimberlé Crenshaw, who coined the term "critical race theory" and originated the concept of intersectionality, appeared on MSNBC as a guest of host Joy Reid. Here's what she said:

---

* Parents who can't talk the SJF talk may have trouble getting their kids into certain schools in the first place. A friend of mine shared this story: "Just caught up with a friend of mine from college who has been interviewing at top schools in NY for his four-year-old son, and he said the head of one of the most prestigious schools told him, 'If you aren't thinking about gender identity 24/7 then this is not the place for you.' Another asked him, 'When was the last time you discussed gender identity with your son?'"

I'm one of the co-authors on one of the few books on critical race theory—I think I would know if we were being taught in K–12.... This is not about whether anything called critical race theory is being taught in K–12.

On one hand, there seems to be evidence contradicting this. In 2021, Crenshaw's own organization, African American Policy Forum, put out a pamphlet that said: "Critical race theory originated in law schools, but over time, professional educators and activists in a host of settings—K–12 teachers, DEI advocates, racial justice and democracy activists, among others—applied CRT to help recognize and eliminate systemic racism." Likewise, in 2021 the National Education Association (NEA) approved a plan, which would roll out to its fourteen thousand local communities in all fifty states, with goals like "increasing the implication of culturally responsive education, critical race theory, and ethnic studies curriculum in pre-K–12."

On the other hand, Crenshaw's point is probably technically correct. CRT originated in law schools and explores how America's history of slavery, segregation, and discrimination may be embedded in the nation's laws in ways that continue to marginalize and oppress people of color. Whatever might be taught in K–12 classrooms wouldn't be a perfect representation of CRT, but a simplified version of it or something that shares its principles—what John McWhorter has termed "C.R.T.-lite." These organizations also typically talk about "applying" CRT's lens to education, which isn't necessarily the same as actually teaching CRT to students.

Either way, what certainly *has* entered hundreds of schools is Social Justice Fundamentalism, and everything that comes along with it: the idea that disparities always imply injustice and equality of opportunity must lead to equality of outcome; the view that identity characteristics like race, gender, and sexual orientation are the primary axes of advantage and disadvantage, and identity diversity is the only meaningful form of diversity; the equating of basic liberal values and institutions like free speech, science, and meritocracy with "whiteness"; the belief that oppression pervades every institution, every interaction, and every norm; the notion that disagreeing with SJF is violence and punishing such behavior is nothing more than self-defense; the gloomy outlook that sees a world where racism, sexism, homophobia, and transphobia are forever present and barely improving.

So the "Is CRT in schools?" debate is mostly a squabble over semantics. CRT is not synonymous with Social Justice Fundamentalism, but they share a common ancestor, and many of the principles of SJF are derived from the principles of CRT. While activists like Rufo incorrectly use CRT to refer to what we've been calling SJF, their argument that CRT has entered schools is only a semantic distinction away from the truth.

But in her MSNBC appearance, Crenshaw went beyond issuing a technical rebuff to the arguments about CRT in schools. She went on to say:

> What they're calling critical race theory doesn't exist anyway. It is a backlash effort to reverse the racial reckoning unlike anything we've seen in our lifetime….They can't say: "We're for racism."… So they looked around and found a strange-sounding theory that they could put all of the grievances and resentments in and mobilize people around this bogeyman.

Later in the conversation, Crenshaw explains how she sees the larger stakes in play:

> The biggest risk is that this tried-and-true framing of antiracism as racist against white people is going to win again. It won at the end of the Civil War when civil rights were framed as reverse discrimination against white people. It won after *Brown vs. Board of Education* when integration was framed as damaging white children. And it could win now if people don't wake up and have a sense of what's at stake.

Crenshaw frames what's being taught in schools as the latest in a long line of Liberal Social Justice movements—a category that includes the abolition of slavery and the outlawing of racial segregation in public schools. The implication: If schools are merely teaching basic ideas about race and racism in America, then that's what these CRT critics *really* want to eradicate. Using CRT as a front for their real intentions, the reasoning goes, these are today's version of the historical racists who used similar tricks to fight against Reconstruction and the Civil Rights Movement. This is captured in a popular meme:

> So, the folks who tried to prevent a black girl from going to school in 1957 are opposed to their grandchildren learning about how they tried to prevent a black girl from going to school in 1957.

This framing of the conflict has been repeated ad nauseum on Twitter:

This is pretty consistent with the Republican base. Whether it is trying to fight teaching basic history around racism, the role of racism in U.S. history—you know there is a direct through line from that to denying Juneteenth.
—Alexandria Ocasio-Cortez, US representative

The new Republican position seems to be that in America absolutely no one should ever be censored unless they are talking about race and in that case they should [be] like super duper censored.
—Chris Murphy, US senator

Opposition to critical race theory is obviously rooted in racism and has just become the newest dog whistle for racists.
—Rashida Tlaib, US representative

Open question to those who are afraid of "critical race theory" (which isn't being taught in K-12 schools…) What do you WANT taught about U.S. slavery and racism? Nothing?
—MSNBC host Joy Reid

US conservatives 2021: "It is illegal to teach about the history of racism."
—Jacob T. Levy, McGill political science professor

The message in each case is the same: wanting to fight against "critical race theory in schools" is actually code for wanting to forbid *any* discussion of racism or racial injustice in the classroom. It's the same Social Justice Horse trick: depicting SJF as basic social progress, and therefore also depicting critics of SJF as the kind of people that would fight against basic social progress: in our language, the Lower Right.*

But swapping out teacher training with ideological training is not basic social progress. Infusing schooling for children as young as four with politics, using one and only one political lens, is not basic social progress. Indoctrinating students, instead of teaching them critical thinking skills, is not basic social progress. Imposing severe penalties on teachers, parents, and students who stray from the orthodoxy is not basic social progress.

On Step 2 of the illiberal staircase, we've seen examples of something worse than the punishments for dissent on Step 1: people being *forced* to sit and listen to SJF ideas, whether they like it or not. Americans of all ages—from public elementary schools to private high schools to colleges to adults in public- and private-sector jobs—are currently having SJF forced upon them in a way that would have been unthinkable just a decade ago.

On Step 3 of the staircase, things get even worse.

ILLIBERAL STAIRCASE, STEP 3: FORCED SPEAKING

Even the most stable societies are jolted from time to time into moments of chaos when emotions are heightened and political tensions are through the roof. These moments, often filled with excitement, fear, confusion, and hope, are like social earthquakes—tectonic plates that have been jammed together in a stubborn status quo are suddenly on the move.

---

* To complicate things further, the Lower Right is *also* involved in all of this. Alongside the protests I'm referring to here are certain right-wing efforts that *are* overly restrictive. We'll come back to this later in the chapter.

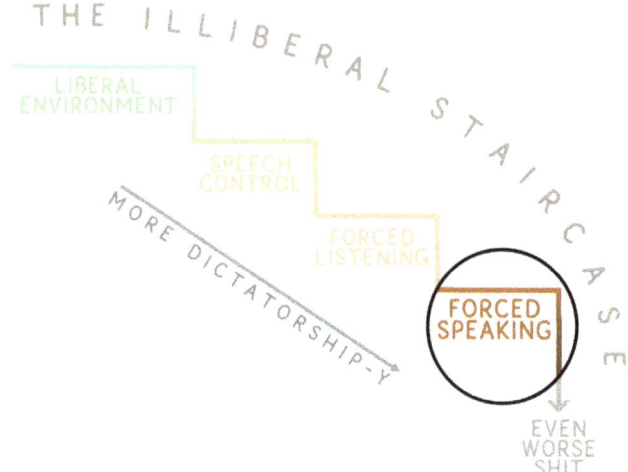

Social earthquakes provide a rare opportunity for social movements—whose goals, by definition, are to enact change. It's often a race, in these moments, to push long-wished changes forward before the plates slow back down and settle into a new status quo. Depending on which movements win the race, social earthquakes can be giant leaps forward for a society, or big steps backward.

The social earthquake caused by the Great Depression opened up a rare opportunity for the sweeping changes of the New Deal. The social earthquake of 1960s America yielded the Civil Rights and Voting Rights Acts. One of the enduring criticisms of the Bush administration is that it used the seismic social earthquake caused by 9/11 to launch an opportunistic war and enact surveillance policies that in normal times would have seemed unjustifiable.

The second half of 2020, following the murder of George Floyd and subsequent nationwide protests, at the height of a pandemic, was a social earthquake, and a whole lot of change happened very quickly, undoubtedly some positive and some negative. But one movement—Social Justice Fundamentalism—seized the opportunity better than any other. Proponents of SJF would call these particular changes a leap forward—the 2020s version of the Civil Rights Movement. But I see those changes more like Bush after 9/11—forcing through *negative* change that would not be possible during normal times.

Idea supremacy ramped way up, and SJF tenets suddenly blared from the largest platforms, presented as unqualified truth, while the voicing of any conflicting ideas was more severely punished than it had been before. Companies and schools across the country preached SJF ideas, in unison, to captive audiences.

During this period, an even more extreme concept began to gain traction.

Silence is violence.

By now, we're familiar with "dissent is violence"—the highly illiberal SJF tenet that justifies the censorship of ideological opponents, pressures vocal dissenters into silence, and chills discourse.

"Silence is violence" is next-level coercion, taking aim at everyone who's not a *vocal SJF activist*.

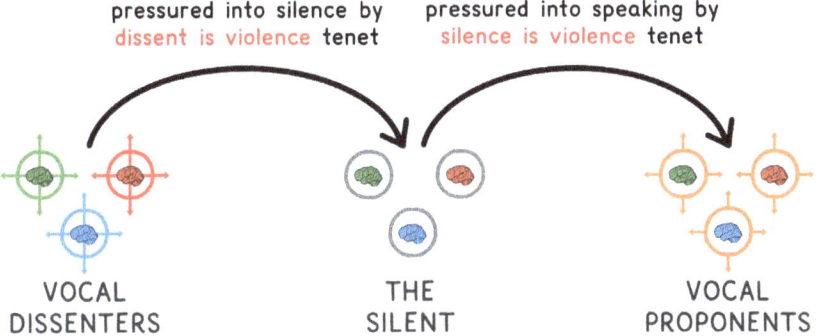

There are plenty of reasons people might stay silent about a given political topic. Maybe they're afraid to voice an unpopular opinion. Maybe they hold popular opinions but they're not the vocal type. Maybe they don't feel they know enough about the topic to have a strong opinion, or the political tribalism surrounding the topic has made them want to check out. Maybe they're just not that interested in politics. In a liberal society, it's totally okay to be silent on any topic, for any reason at all.

But by 2020, silence on sacred SJF topics was no longer permissible in many arenas. To be considered a nonviolent, non-reprehensible person, at least within progressive circles, you had to outwardly preach the SJF gospel.

The business world is full of stories of employees being pressured by their bosses to publicly express allegiance to the SJF worldview. One tweet in June 2020 read:

> My friend is being told by higher ups at her work that silence on her personal social media accounts is her being complicit in perpetuating injustice...how is this not harassment?

In an article in *Areo Magazine*, Helen Pluckrose published some of the emails she had received, like:

> I work for a tech company. My boss just announced that he is white, male & privileged and that we all need to do more to show we are addressing this kind of privilege. I don't understand what I'm supposed to do, but I really want to keep my job.

And

> I am a marketing executive & we have all been required to join a Slack channel to talk about racism and any white person not contributing to say they are racist and trying to do better is called out for their white silence.

In June of 2020, while protests were happening in the street, most tech companies put out statements using eerily similar wording—something along the lines of Amazon's "we stand in solidarity with the Black community—our employees, customers, and partners—in the fight against systemic racism and injustice." These typically came along with a pledge of millions of dollars to fight racial injustice and a commitment to establish or expand the company's office of Diversity, Equity, and Inclusion. There's nothing wrong with a company doing this. But when nearly *every* tech company does it, in the same month, using the same language, I can't help but think that companies know *not* doing it would land them in hot water with their staff and the media.

Sometimes, even repeating the uniform statement didn't suffice. In June 2020, both the president and the chairman of the Poetry Foundation resigned after a letter signed by hundreds of poets expressed outrage that the foundation's statement—which said it "stands in solidarity with the Black community, and denounces injustice and systemic racism"—wasn't strong *enough*.

In the world of sports, 2020 saw every NBA team playing a video before early-season games in support of Black Lives Matter. The BLM logo appeared on every NBA court, teams kneeled in unison during the singing of the national anthem, and nearly all players elected to put a social justice slogan ("Black Lives Matter," "Equality," "Say Their Names") on the back of their jersey. Again, nothing wrong with this, but the coercive pressure of "silence is violence" was hovering above it all. When one NBA player, Jonathan Isaac, elected to wear his normal jersey and stand for the anthem while the rest of his team kneeled, he was subject to a media inquisition following the game. One reporter asked, "You didn't kneel during the anthem but you also didn't wear a Black Lives Matter shirt. Do you believe Black lives matter?" On Twitter, he was called a "coon" and a subject of "white brainwashing."

As we discussed on Step 2, being pressured to publicly support the organization Black Lives Matter is not the same as being pressured to support the idea that Black lives matter. The BLM website makes it clear that BLM is a political organization, founded by self-proclaimed "trained Marxists," that pushes for radical reforms, like defunding the police and disrupting the nuclear family structure, that are unpopular with majorities of Americans of all races. If NBA teams want to support a radical political organization, that's their right. When one player chooses not to, either because he doesn't agree with the movement or simply because he chooses to practice activism in a different setting, and is all but accused by the media of not believing that Black lives matter, that is a problem. That's "silence is violence" in action.

It has also become common for students and faculty to be pressured to publicly affirm SJF ideas.

A Las Vegas parent filed a lawsuit in 2020 alleging that the school had been "repeatedly compelling" her son to speak and write about "intimate matters of race, gender, sexuality and religion," "to reveal his identities in a controlled, yet non-private setting, to scrutiny and official labeling," and "to accept and affirm politicized and discriminatory principles and statements that he cannot in conscience affirm." The lawsuit includes a host of class slides displaying all the usual SJF tenets and alleges that the school "repeatedly threatened the student with material harm including a failing grade and non-graduation if he failed to comply with their requirements."

When Paul Rossi published his article about what was going on at NYC's Grace Church School, he described a number of similar scenes:

> These concerns are confirmed for me when I attend grade-level and all-school meetings about race or gender issues. There, I witness student after student sticking to a narrow script of acceptable responses….It is common for teachers to exhort students who remain silent that "we really need to hear from you."…A recent faculty email chain received enthusiastic support for recommending that we "'officially' flag students" who appear "resistant" to the "culture we are trying to establish."

A list of demands at NYC's Dalton School—signed by 120 teachers and staff—included a similar item, this one directed at staff: "Administrators, faculty, and staff should produce individual public anti-racism statements."

Teachers have reported being required to add to their curricula a "Pyramid of Racism" graphic that includes "remaining apolitical" and "avoiding confrontation," while other classes have taught students that "white silence" is among the descriptions of "covert white supremacy."

These examples all go further than the forced listening on Step 2—they're stories of people being forced to express outward allegiance to a single ideology.

"Silence is violence" did not come out of nowhere. It is a core principle of SJF.

In Robin DiAngelo and Özlem Sensoy's 2012 book, *Is Everyone Really Equal?*, their definition of "passive racism" includes "silence," "lack of interest in learning about racism," and "not getting involved in any antiracist efforts or in continuing education." In a 2012 paper about "white silence in racial discussions," DiAngelo writes that "regardless of the rationale for white silence in discussions of race, if it is not strategically enacted from an antiracist framework, it functions to maintain white power and privilege and must be challenged."

This is the fancy theoretical underpinning of "silence is violence."

Then there's Ibram X. Kendi, whose name was everywhere in the months following George Floyd's death.

In *How to Be an Antiracist*, Kendi writes: "There is no in-between safe space of 'not racist.' The claim of 'not racist' neutrality is a mask for racism."

In his 2020 TED Talk, Kendi talks again about this idea:

> What I'm trying to do with my work is to really get Americans to eliminate the concept of "not racist" from their vocabulary and realize we're either being racist or antiracist....The heartbeat of racism itself has always been denial, and the sound of that heartbeat has always been, "I'm not racist."

Silence is violence. "Not racist" is racist. Different wording—same idea. Both reduce the world to good vs. bad and eliminate the possibility of neutrality, equating the neutral position with the "bad" position.

When most people hear "anti-racist," they think of being "against racism," which of course sounds great. But when we listen to more of what Kendi has to say, we see that "anti-racist" means much more than that.

Kendi defines a "racist individual" as "someone who is expressing a racist idea or supporting a racist policy with their actions or even inaction." Contrast that with Kendi's definition of anti-racist: to "spend your time transforming and challenging power and policy is to spend your time being antiracist."

So "inaction" (like silence) lands someone in the "racist" pile, while to be an anti-racist requires "spending your time" as an activist.

Kendi calls racism and capitalism "conjoined twins," arguing that "the life of racism cannot be separated from the life of capitalism...In order to truly be antiracist, you also have to truly be anti-capitalist."

So "you're either anti-racist or racist" also means "you're either anti-capitalist or racist."

Kendi has also said, "I can't imagine a pathway to being antiracist that does not engage critical race theory."

So "you're either anti-racist or racist" also means "you either engage critical race theory or you're racist."

You either engage in activism using Ibram X. Kendi's precise worldview, precise politics, and precise way of diagnosing and solving problems—or you're racist.

You're either a vocal, active member of the SJF army—or you're a harmful person.

---

* DiAngelo and Sensoy echo this point in *Is Everyone Really Equal?*, noting that there's no such thing as "passive antiracism"—that "antiracism requires action—by definition it cannot be passive."

"Silence is violence"—in all its forms—is textbook coercion. The same exact "you're with us or you're against us" mentality Grover Norquist used to coerce 1990s Republicans into signing his pledge. The same "struggle session" technique 1960s Maoists used to force their opponents to declare their allegiance to the movement, or else. *No neutrality allowed* is a trademark of every low-rung movement with way too much power.

• • •

Having descended down this staircase, let's recall that a society's "big brain" is made up of the brains of its individuals—those are its "neurons." It's why free discourse is so important: the big brain can only think when people are free to *speak* their minds. So beyond violating the basic spirit of a liberal society, slipping down this staircase comes along with a major consequence.

IDEA SUPREMACY MAKES SOCIETY'S BIG BRAIN DUMB

The stories from Steps 1, 2, and 3—policing the marketplace of ideas, instituting mandatory political indoctrinations in workplaces and schools, pressuring people into vocal political support—are all examples of idea supremacy in action. In a liberal society, most effective movements succeed by stoking a mind-changing movement that moves the Thought Pile, not by using bullying tactics to muscle the Speech Curve to their desired shape. When a movement like SJF is allowed to do things the Power Games way, it cripples the society's ability to make knowledge. In his book *The Constitution of Knowledge*, Jonathan Rauch writes:

> Ideas in the marketplace do not talk directly to each other, and for the most part neither do individuals. Rather, our conversations are mediated through institutions like journals and newspapers and social-media platforms; and they rely on a dense network of norms and rules, like truthfulness and fact-checking; and they depend on the expertise of professionals, like peer reviewers and editors—and the entire system rests on a foundation of values: a shared understanding that there are right and wrong ways to make

knowledge. Those values and rules and institutions do for knowledge what the U.S. Constitution does for politics: they create a governing structure, forcing social contestation onto peaceful and productive pathways.

We've seen how SJF has been able to hijack the "governing structure" of America's knowledge-making mechanisms. The society's big brain—the national genie—relies on these mechanisms, and when they're disabled, the genie is disabled too. The country's big brain becomes fractured, spreading confusion and delusion.

In his book *Inside the Third Reich*, Adolf Hitler's architect and Minister of Armaments Albert Speer wrote about how he and so many others descended into the alternative reality of the Nazis:

> In normal circumstances people who turn their backs on reality are soon set straight by the mockery and criticism of those around them, which makes them aware they have lost credibility. In the Third Reich, there were no such correctives, especially for those who belonged to the upper stratum. On the contrary, every self-deception was multiplied in a hall of distorting mirrors, becoming a repeatedly confirmed picture of a fantastical dream world, which no longer bore any relationship to the grim outside world.

I bring this up not to compare Nazi ideology to Social Justice Fundamentalism but to point out that the ideas themselves barely matter. If flat-earthers gained enough power to punish those who argued against the flat-earth worldview and intimidate most round-earthers into silence, continually amplify the flat-earth worldview from the most prominent and reputable platforms, teach people that the earth is flat in companies and schools, and pressure people to outwardly proclaim their belief in flat-earthism, the number of people who believed the earth was flat would rise dramatically. When people lose the ability to speak openly or to criticize falsehoods, it becomes difficult to separate truth from fiction.

In real life, we can't see the Thought Pile, so when a small group has the ability to bend the Speech Curve to their will and control what's being said, people tend to assume that the viewpoints they're hearing again and again must be "what everybody thinks." As more and more people come to believe the viewpoints, the social cost of being a vocal dissenter to that view rises. Delusion begets silence and silence begets more delusion.

This kind of vicious cycle will naturally be most pronounced when it comes to the most sensitive, controversial topics, riddled with the most taboo land mines.

Take police killings. Between 2016 and 2022, 326 unarmed white men and 232 unarmed Black men were killed (by any means) by police in the US. Media coverage of these incidents has been highly skewed, with the median story about a Black victim receiving nine times the coverage as the median story about a white victim. When we look at the ten most written-about cases for each category (between January 2013 and November 2021), the numbers are even starker:

COPS KILLING UNARMED PEOPLE
THE 10 MOST COVERED WHITE AND BLACK VICTIMS BY NUMBER OF ARTICLES WRITTEN

Victim	Articles
David Kassick	148
Autumn Steele	165
Deven Guilford	172
Dillon Taylor	187
Daniel Shaver	197
Andrew Finch	299
Jeremy Mardis	404
Bijan Ghaisar	504
John Geer	667
Tony Robinson	1,622
Eric Harris	1,773
Akai Gurley	1,816
Botham Jean	2,118
Stephon Clark	2,184
Justine Diamond	3,590
Walter Scott	7,390
Tamir Rice	12,241
Breonna Taylor	26,812
Eric Garner	30,426
George Floyd	178,465

Source: Data from mappingpoliceviolence.org, compiled by Zach Goldberg

This kind of vast distortion in coverage leaves people with a vastly distorted picture of reality—one that is then broadcast from society's largest megaphones.

> egins with the former vice president raising a question: "Why do Black Americans wake up knowing they could lose their life if just living their life?"
> — KAMALA HARRIS

> We're literally hunted EVERYDAY/EVERYTIME we step foot outside the comfort of our homes!
> — LEBRON JAMES

> Black people are being slaughtered in the streets.
> — JULIANNE MOORE

> Why would any person of color ever comply with a police officer when there is a 50/50 shot of getting "accidentally" shot?
> — CHELSEA HANDLER

> less to police, and that the next victim of a police shooting could be just about any black American.
> — VOX

A 2019 survey asked 980 people from across the political spectrum how many unarmed Black men they believed were killed by police (by shooting or any other means) in 2019. That year, thirty-one unarmed Black men were killed by police. All groups overestimated the number, with those on the political left being the farthest off. Fifty-four percent of the "very liberal" group were off by a factor of over 30X, including 22 percent of the "very liberal" group who were off by a factor of over 300X.

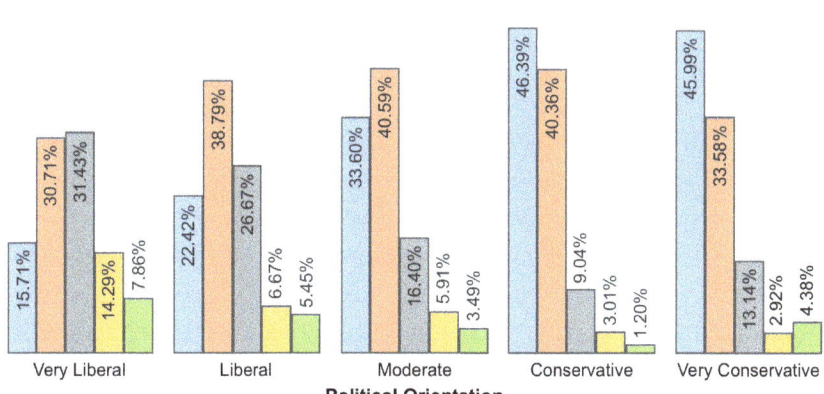

How many unarmed Black men were killed by police in 2019?

Source: Skeptic Research Center

The survey also asked participants what percentage of total people killed by police in 2019 they believed were Black. The actual number, according to the Mapping Police Violence database, was 25.9 percent (285 out of 1,099). Again, all groups overestimated the percentage, with those on the left being the farthest off (the "liberal" and "very liberal" groups answered 56 percent and 60 percent, respectively).

Anonymous surveys like these are graphical depictions of a Thought Pile driven toward delusion by a distorted Speech Curve.

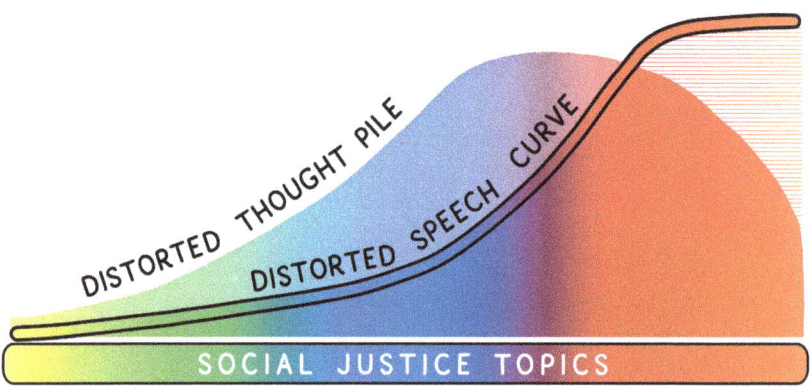

This particular distortion can be especially harmful by feeding into a self-fulfilling prophecy, as people who believe cops are more dangerous than they are become less trusting of police, which may make them more likely to resist arrest. And more generally, people who feel that the state is out to get them are more likely to feel separate and rejected and fall into an antisocial culture.

There are all kinds of statistics that suggest that racism in America, while still very present, is moving in the right direction overall. The percentage of non-Black Americans who stand in opposition to a close relative marrying a Black person has dropped from 65 percent to 14 percent since 1990. The percentage of white Americans who agreed with the statement that Black Americans shouldn't "push themselves where they're not wanted" has also dropped precipitously, as has the percentage who agree that it is permissible to racially discriminate when selling a home. During the same decades, the percentage of Americans who support racial equality in jobs, schools, and public accommodations has risen dramatically.

But the Thought Pile is bending toward a very different viewpoint. Over the past decade, the percentage of white liberals who believe racism is a big problem has doubled:

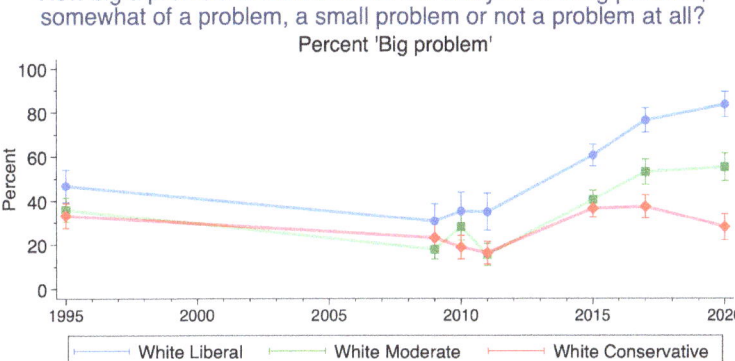

Source: Tablet

Over the same stretch, the percentage of Black Americans who believe Black–white relations are good or somewhat good has been slashed almost in half:

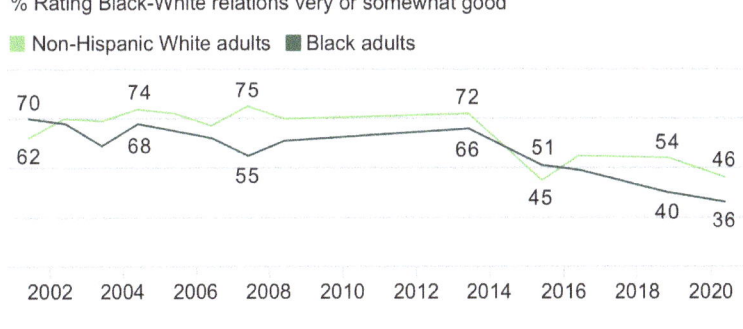

Source: Gallup

A Pew question asks Americans whether they believe "racial discrimination is the main reason why many Blacks can't get ahead." The percentage of Black respondents answering "yes" steadily decreased starting in the mid-1990s, suggesting that Black Americans' feeling of agency was on the rise. This makes sense, given the amount of promising data pointing to improving conditions for Black Americans—both the Black poverty rate and the Black unemployment rate have dropped to all-time lows, while both the Black incarceration rate and the disparity between the Black and white incarceration rate have been steadily declining over the past twenty years. But the SJF narrative tells the opposite kind of story, and this could be contributing to a sharp reversal in Black Americans' sense of empowerment in recent years.*

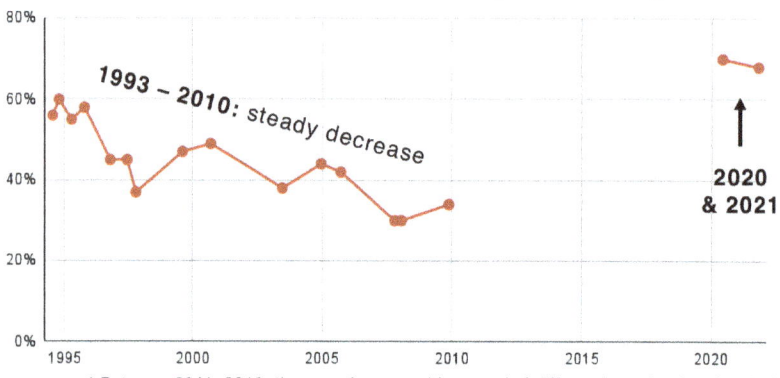

Percentage of Black Americans who believe "racial discrimination is the main reason many blacks can't get ahead"

*Between 2011–2019, the question was either worded differently or the data is missing.

In another realm, the SJF narrative says that women are routinely paid significantly less than men for doing the same work. But the statistics this claim is based on—often cited as "77" or "80" or "83 cents on the dollar for the same work"—are highly misleading. Namely, the figure compares the median wages earned by all American women who worked full-time year-round to the median for all American men who worked full-time year-round. Under that crude calculation, the average

---

* While I believe that these trends are caused, at least in part, by the SJF narrative making people think things are worse than they are, the SJF activist would likely argue that they're caused by people becoming more aware of racism that was always there. Whatever the case, people feeling worse about their society and their prospects has many negative effects, so it's especially important that if a narrative is making people feel that way, it is solidly based in reality. I don't think SJF passes that bar.

working woman earns 82 percent of what the average working man earns. This number doesn't account for specific occupations, positions, education, or a number of other relevant variables.

According to the website Payscale, when controlling for "all compensable variables"—i.e., when comparing apples to apples—the gender wage gap drops dramatically, from 18 percent to 1 percent. Women earn 99 cents—not 77 or 80 or 83 cents—for every dollar a man makes, for the same work.

But in a society with a distorted Speech Curve, the 1 percent statistic is spoken at a whisper while the larger misleading statistics ring from the largest platforms, including the largest megaphone of all. In his 2014 State of the Union address, Barack Obama said, "Today, women make up about half our workforce. But they still make 77 cents for every dollar a man earns. That is wrong, and in 2014, it's an embarrassment. A woman deserves equal pay for equal work."[*] Implying an apples-to-apples comparison, he overstated the gap by more than 7x. In 2019, on CBS's *Late Show with Stephen Colbert*, Kamala Harris said that "in America today, women on average are paid 80 cents on the dollar for what men are paid for the same work"—a 10x overstatement of the gap (the actual figure at the time was 98 cents).

The figure that doesn't account for differences in occupation still matters. It's important to look into the reasons men and women end up on differing career paths that leave the average working woman making 18 percent less money than the average working man. But what is accomplished by repeatedly conflating it with the variable-controlled "equal work" gap, effectively overstating that measure by seven- or tenfold? The same thing accomplished by overstating the number of Black men killed by cops—it distorts the Thought Pile. It makes Americans believe their country suffers from significantly more gender inequality than it does. It makes women feel angrier and more discouraged than they otherwise would.

---

[*] After Obama's 2014 address, McClatchy reported that using the same methodology, the White House's female employees made ninety-one cents for every dollar made by its male employees. White House spokesman Jay Carney responded by explaining that McClatchy's calculation didn't control for variables—that it just "looked at the aggregate of everyone on staff, and that includes from the most junior levels to the most senior." But that's also the case for Obama's seventy-seven cents figure, which he called "an embarrassment."

This is a theme throughout the world of SJF. In 2018, the LGBTQ advocacy group GLAAD wrote on its blog: "In America, trans women of color have a life expectancy of 35 years of age while that of their cisgender counterparts is around 78. This horrifying statistic is just one example of why standing with all those in our trans community is essential to our survival." This statistic has been thrown around dozens of times—by *USA Today*, *The Guardian*, the Huffington Post, *Fast Company*, the *Los Angeles Review of Books*, and many others. The thing is, most of these articles don't report a source, and a quick investigation reveals that in fact there is no source. Of the articles that did include a citation, many linked to a report that had nothing to do with the US and doesn't provide any support for the claim. Violence against trans women of color is a very real problem, but again, what is accomplished by repeating a fake statistic?

We can simplify people's first instincts on these kinds of issues—police shootings, the gender wage gap, violence against trans women of color, and so many others—to three categories:

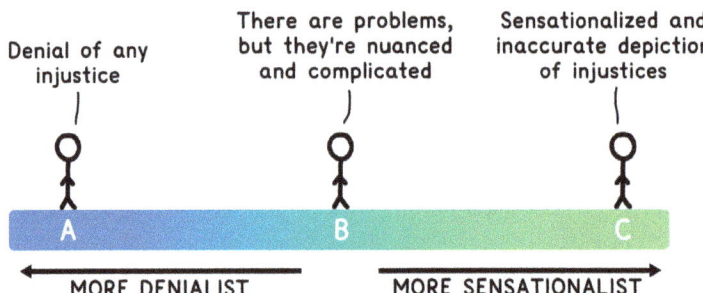

SJF hinders productive discussions on complex social topics in two ways: it spreads Position C far and wide, and it makes it taboo to take Position B. It is a Political Disney World narrative with no room for gray area—you're either part of the in-group and fully aligned with SJF, or you're Person A—an out-grouped right-winger and an enemy of social justice. By conflating Person B with Person A, SJF puts a target on the back of anyone who pushes back against its gospel.

If you happen to point out that there's not an epidemic of unarmed Black men being killed by cops, you will gain an instant reputation as a racist who believes racial injustice is a thing of the past. Talk about issues with the 18 percent wage gap figure, be branded a misogynist who believes women belong in the kitchen.

In normal conditions, cheap straw-man tricks like these don't work. But when the Speech Curve is distorted, we have a hard time getting on the same page about basic notions of what's true or false or right or wrong.

When the big brain isn't working correctly, zealotry can look like righteousness. Nuance can look like bigotry. Free speech can look like violence, and violence can look like free speech. Fairness can look like discrimination, and discrimination can look like fairness. Anecdotes look like trends and trends look like anecdotes. Bullying can look like self-defense. And censorship can look like civility.

Paralyzed by the past few years of cultural chaos and confusion, America has allowed a political group to hijack the discussion on so many important issues—to spread falsehoods that foster fear, gloom, hopelessness, and anger, and shut down the nuanced, evidence-based discussions that are so critical to problem-solving. All in the service of promoting and protecting their narrative.

There's another consequence to the descent down the stairs: the illiberal staircase doesn't stop at Step 3. When a movement is able to impose idea supremacy all across a liberal society, it's a sign that the normal defenses are out of order. Soon, more liberal structures begin to crumble.

IDEA SUPREMACY IS THE GATEWAY TO EVEN WORSE SHIT

In a 2019 piece in *Politico*, Ibram X. Kendi proposed a constitutional amendment that would outlaw racism as it's defined by Social Justice Fundamentalism. Here's what he said:

> To fix the original sin of racism, Americans should pass an antiracist amendment to the U.S. Constitution that enshrines two guiding anti-racist principals: Racial inequity is evidence of racist policy and the different racial groups are equals. The amendment would make unconstitutional racial inequity over a certain threshold, as well as racist ideas by public officials (with "racist ideas" and "public official" clearly defined). It would establish and permanently fund the Department of Anti-racism (DOA) comprised of formally trained experts on racism and no political appointees. The DOA would be responsible for preclearing all local, state and federal public policies to ensure they won't yield racial inequity, monitor those policies, investigate private racist policies when racial inequity surfaces, and monitor public officials for expressions of racist ideas. The DOA would be empowered with disciplinary tools to wield over and against policymakers and public officials who do not voluntarily change their racist policy and ideas.

If enacted, Kendi's proposal would be undemocratic, authoritarian, and in blatant violation of the First Amendment. The proposal is an affront to liberal values, but that's the whole point: SJF is an ideology that thinks liberalism is inherently bad and should be replaced with a new system that limits freedom of speech and uses the law to ensure not equality of opportunity but equality of outcome.

Nothing happening in 2022 America is quite as illiberal as Kendi's Department of Antiracism—but we're moving in a bad direction. Little stories keep popping up that should sound any liberal-minded person's alarm bells.

Recall these two quotes from Kendi's book *How to Be an Antiracist*:

> A racist policy is any measure that produces or sustains inequity between racial groups. An antiracist policy is any measure that produces or sustains racial equity between racial groups.

> The only remedy to racist discrimination is antiracist discrimination.

In 2020, the *New York Times* published an article arguing that orchestras should end blind auditions, because they produced orchestras that were not diverse enough, with too many Asian and white musicians. The writer was adhering to Kendi's definition of an anti-racist. The policy of auditioning musicians without seeing who they were was producing an outcome with a racial disparity—and was therefore a racist policy.

The proposed solution—to get rid of blind auditions to ensure proportional racial representation among orchestra musicians—would inherently discriminate against some Asian and white musicians who would have made the cut under blind auditions. This is, according to SJF, the anti-racist way.

This was just an op-ed, and it was just about orchestras. But the same logic has in recent years informed actual government policy.

Covid Vaccination Protocols

In a 2021 article on the Substack newsletter *Common Sense*, journalist Katie Herzog writes about a major disparity:

> [Covid-19] has killed black, Hispanic, and Native American people at three times the rate as whites. These discrepancies are likely due to an array of factors, including income, housing, work, language, pre-existing conditions, access to health care, and, yes, possibly some degree of racism.

While Herzog listed a whole host of potential causes of the group disparity around Covid deaths, in SJF, correlation implies causation: discrepancies in Covid deaths must be due solely to systemic racism. And there's only one remedy: anti-racist discrimination. A counterforce to balance out the Force, in the name of equity.

After the Covid vaccine became available, many policies came to reflect the SJF logic.

In 2021, the State of Vermont made Covid booster shots available to "BIPOC Vermonters" who were eighteen or older, while restricting the booster for white people to those sixty-five and older (unless they met another eligibility condition). Hamilton, a city in Canada, did something similar, tweeting in April 2021 that vaccine appointments were "now available for Black and other racialized populations/people of colour ages 18+." When New York State authorized oral antivirals in

December 2021, it did so for all people of color but only white people with risk factors, under the premise that being non-white "should be considered a risk factor."

Many of these follow the lead of FDA documentation, which labels "race or ethnicity" as factors that "place individual patients at high risk for progression to severe COVID-19." This reasoning—that membership in a demographic group that's disproportionately affected by Covid should itself be considered a risk factor that warrants preferential access to treatment—is the basis of the above policies. Minnesota, for example, whose scoring system gives "BIPOC status" the same weight as "age sixty-five and older" and double the weight of "hypertension in a patient fifty-five years and older," cites the FDA when justifying the policy: "FDA's acknowledgment means that race and ethnicity alone, apart from other underlying health conditions, may be considered in determining eligibility for [monoclonal antibodies]." The same logic would seem to warrant preferential treatment for men over women, given that American men have been shown to be about 60 percent more likely than American women to die of Covid. Likewise for factors like socioeconomic status. But neither the FDA nor any of the above states applied the reasoning consistently—only when it came to "race and ethnicity." In most cases, the preference applied to all non-white races, which includes ethnicities like East Asian that have *not* been disproportionately affected. It all reeks of SJF inconsistency and disregard for basic liberal rules.

We see the same thinking over at the CDC, which in late 2020 proposed vaccinating essential workers as the very first group instead of the elderly, even though the elderly were by far the most at-risk population. Among the reasons for this included in their official report: "promote justice" and "mitigate health inequities." Talking to the *New York Times*, University of Pennsylvania ethics and medical policy scholar Harald Schmidt explained what this meant: "Older populations are whiter. Society is structured in a way that enables them to live longer. Instead of giving additional health benefits to those who already had more of them, we can start to level the playing field a bit."

Some legal scholars have argued that the policies themselves violate the Fourteenth Amendment, which forbids states from treating individuals differently based on race. The government—the FDA, the CDC, the White House—is also a driver and participant in these trends.

Protests During Covid

Another Covid-related controversy surfaced around the topic of public protests. Up until June 2020, the medical industry had been promoting a singular message regarding protests. This message was captured by Dr. Tom Frieden, the former director of the CDC, in a March 2020 *Washington Post* article:

> People need to shelter in place. Otherwise, there will be explosive spread as occurred in Wuhan, China, and in Italy, and as is occurring in New York. Sheltering in place has two benefits. The first is to reduce transmission....The other crucial and under-recognized value of sheltering is to buy time to strengthen healthcare and public health systems....More than the economy will be hurt if we get this wrong. Reopening the floodgates could overwhelm healthcare facilities, killing doctors, nurses, patients and others.

Medical professionals were resolute about the rules: There should be no large public gatherings or in-person religious services or students in classrooms or nonessential travel. For the sake of the greater good, people would need to cope with loneliness, with economic hardship, even with mourning a lost loved one away from the rest of their family. When large public protests against these rules began in some conservative states, the experts rebuked them as ignorant, selfish, and dangerous (when Georgia's governor loosened restrictions in his state, it was dubbed "Georgia's Experiment in Human Sacrifice" in a viral *Atlantic* article).

Then came the George Floyd incident. As the streets filled with a new kind of protest, the medical world faced a moment of truth.

One position was articulated in an open letter, signed by 1,288 "public health professionals, infectious diseases professionals, and community stakeholders" that called for a unified "anti-racist public health response to demonstrations against systemic injustice occurring during the COVID-19 pandemic." According to the letter, this messaging "must be wholly different from the response to white protesters resisting stay-home orders....Protests against systemic racism, which fosters the disproportionate burden of COVID-19 on Black communities and also perpetuates police violence, must be supported." This full reversal on protest policy during lockdown received widespread support from the media.

It also received support from many medical experts. "People can protest peacefully AND work together to stop Covid. Violence harms public health," tweeted Dr. Frieden—the same person I just quoted above saying the opposite.

Stanford infectious disease doctor Abraar Karan, MD, had a stern message about anti-lockdown protests on May 12, tweeting:

> We are having people scream and protest in large crowds with no masks on all around the country—these are literally all possible set-ups for super-spreading events…The great irony of protesting during an epidemic, only to create more epidemics.

Nineteen days later, he performed the same about-face as Dr. Frieden, tweeting (sorry in advance about all his annoying hashtags):

> For those who see #covid19 & the #protests2020 as separate—they are not. They are deeply interlinked[.] Until the deepest inequities are addressed—#racism being at the center of those #covid19 will not go away. Failing to treat every person w/ justice, respect, fairness, & humanity is a part of a *failed* epidemic response. Epidemics like #covid19 are not solved in vacuums.

Johns Hopkins epidemiologist Jennifer Nuzzo tweeted a similar stance: "We should always evaluate the risks and benefits of efforts to control the virus. In this moment the public health risks of not protesting to demand an end to systemic racism greatly exceed the harms of the virus."

In many parts of the country, new policies were enacted that fell in line with the new messaging. Hillsborough County, Florida, passed a resolution "declaring racism a public health crisis." In Contra Costa County, California, updated guidelines read: "social outdoor gatherings of up to 12 people" but "protests of up to 100 people." An Oregon county made a new rule exempting "people of color who have heightened concerns about racial profiling" from their existing mask order. New York City Mayor Bill de Blasio, who one month earlier had instructed the NYPD to arrest Hasidic Jews who were continuing to gather in large numbers for funerals, now instructed the city's contact tracers not to ask Covid patients if they had attended a BLM protest.*

To many people watching, it looked like this:†

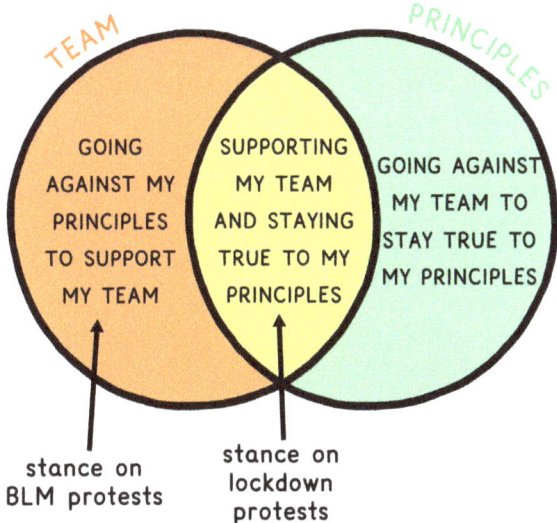

Condemning protests when it's politically popular to do so and then pulling a 180 on that position when the political winds are blowing in the opposite direction makes both positions look like bullshit to the public. When this comes from the media, it makes people lose trust in the media. When it comes from the medical community, it makes people lose trust in the medical community. When it comes from the government, it makes people lose trust in the government. All in the midst of a pandemic when public trust was a critical resource.

With both vaccination protocol and the rules around protests, SJF reasoning rose to become both expert advice and official policy.

---

* In 2021, five US senators, led by Elizabeth Warren, aimed to take this to the federal level, introducing a bill that would establish a "National Center on Antiracism and Health" within the CDC. A stipulation of the bill: "the new center must declare racism a public health crisis."
† Or, perhaps, they always believed outdoor protests did limited harm, in which case the stance on BLM protests was in the yellow zone and the stance on lockdown protests was in the orange zone. Either way, it's hypocritical.

The SJF Social Credit Score

In a late 2020 blog post, Yelp—the restaurant reviews site critical to any modern restaurant's business—announced that it flagged hundreds of restaurants for "racist behavior." In future cases, a large "Business Accused of Racist Behavior" warning would appear front and center on the restaurant's Yelp page. In a statement to the site Eater, a Yelp spokesperson clarified their criteria: "We're taking a firmer stance against racism with the Business Accused of Racist Behavior Alert that will be placed when we learn of reports of egregious, racially-charged actions such as the use of racist language, symbols or sentiment that clearly discredits the Black Lives Matter movement." A business owner who read this would come away with a clear warning: *Don't say or do anything that discredits Black Lives Matter.*

In 2021, PayPal partnered with the Anti-Defamation League's Center on Extremism on a new initiative "to fight extremism and hate through the financial industry and across at-risk communities." Specifically, the initiative would target "racism, hate and extremism across its platforms and the industry." That sounds reasonable, but consider the fact that a year earlier, in 2020, the Anti-Defamation League deleted from their website the widely held definition of racism—

> Racism is the belief that a particular race is superior or inferior to another, that a person's social and moral traits are predetermined by his or her inborn biological characteristics.

—and replaced it with the SJF definition of racism:

> Racism: the marginalization and/or oppression of people of color based on a socially constructed racial hierarchy that privileges white people.

PayPal, an indispensable utility to so many businesses, would now be potentially targeting people and businesses who are racist not in the traditional sense, but in the eyes of SJF.

Having read about this, I wasn't surprised by a June 2022 article in *Quillette*, when evolutionary biologist Colin Wright explained that PayPal, out of the blue, blocked him from his account and restricted his ability to access the funds in it for 180 days. PayPal's reasoning was vague ("after a review, we decided to permanently limit your account, as there was a change in your business model or your business was considered risky"), but Wright just happens to write articles about biological sex that conflict with the SJF narrative on transgenderism. For example, in 2020 he criticized the rising concept that sex is "assigned," rather than observed, at birth (check out the endnotes for more about this). I encourage you to read Wright's articles and tweets. Only through an SJF lens would anything he says constitute "extremism" or "hate."

In October of 2022, PayPal announced an impending policy change that would deduct $2,500 from the accounts of users who sent, posted, or published materials that "depict, promote, or incite hatred or discrimination of protected groups or of individuals or groups based on protected characteristics (e.g., race, religion, gender or gender identity, sexual orientation, etc.)" or those who "promote misinformation." David Marcus, former PayPal president, criticized the policy, tweeting: "A private company now gets to decide to take your money if you say something they disagree with. Insanity."

Liberals around the world recoil when they hear stories about China's "social credit score," which is said to blacklist people who aren't deemed to be "trustworthy citizens." Blacklisted people, unable to buy train tickets, buy a house, or do a large number of other basic things, are essentially banned from society.

Tech companies, with the ability to block people from reaching their followers, selling their books, marketing their restaurants, or accepting payments for their business, have the same kind of blacklist power. America doesn't have a social credit score—but these are stories of people *effectively* being blacklisted.

The Shadow of Jim Crow

In the US, we're not living in the era of racial apartheid—but under SJF guidance, *apartheid-like* policies are becoming more common.

When Kila Posey, a mother in Atlanta, called her daughter's elementary school to request that her daughter be placed in the class of a specific

---

* In November of 2022, the Chinese government released a draft law that offered more information on the Social Credit System, which suggested that perhaps the system would not be as *Black Mirror*-y as many Westerners previously thought.

teacher for the upcoming school year, she got a surprising response: the school told her it wouldn't work, because her daughter was Black and that classroom wasn't "one of the Black classes." When Posey asked for clarification, she was told that the school had begun grouping all of the Black students together in certain classes to help them build a community. Posey, in disbelief, explained the obvious: "It's segregating classrooms. You cannot segregate classrooms. You can't do it."

This policy, which would have seemed unfathomable in America as recently as ten years ago, is akin to the SJF concept of "affinity groups"—a practice that has spread across the country, from elite private schools in New York to public schools in California and Massachusetts. The City of Sacramento, which promotes affinity groups in their schools, explains it as a way for white people to "discover together their group identity"—a place where "they can cultivate racial solidarity and compassion and support each other in sitting with the discomfort, confusion, and numbness that often accompany white racial awakening." This concept has carried over to other settings, like a "Students of Color Field Trip" at a public high school outside Chicago or a "Families of Color Playground Night" at an elementary school in Denver.

Discriminatory policies, reminiscent of those we associate with the deep past, have also been popping up over recent months. In May of 2022, Dropbox's Senior Director of Product Design Jasmine Friedl tweeted about her intention to apply racial discrimination in her hiring: "[I] deeply care about equity in hiring. Therefore, I choose to prioritize folks in our BIPOC and [Underrepresented Minority] communities."

In July of 2022, a job posting for a physics position at Canada's University of Guelph made it clear that white men need not apply: "Candidates *must* be from one or more of the following equity-seeking groups to apply: women, persons with disabilities, Indigenous peoples, and racialized groups."

In August of 2022, an agreement between the Minneapolis Federation of Teachers union and the city's school district stated that should teacher layoffs happen, those first on the chopping block should not be the least senior, as is typical, but those who are "not a member of an underrepresented population" among licensed teachers—a policy that likely translates to "lay white teachers off first." As part of the reasoning behind this policy, the agreement includes that same SJF corollary: "to remedy the continuing effects of past discrimination."

Some of these policies are likely in place to satisfy dictates from above. In 2021, for example, Nasdaq began requiring companies, in order to be listed by the exchange, "to have at least one woman director, as well as a director who self-identifies as a racial minority or as lesbian, gay, bisexual, transgender or queer." Beyond the SJF-ness of these requirements—focusing the new requirements entirely around race, gender, and sexual orientation, and not the hundred other ways a company board can be diverse—it's a bit weird, when you take a step back, that board members would have to disclose information like their sexual orientation to Nasdaq. In 2020, the investment bank Goldman Sachs similarly announced that it would refuse to facilitate the IPOs of companies whose board of directors were all straight, white men (at the time, 499 of the five hundred Fortune 500 companies had at least one woman on the board, which makes the announcement seem more performative than meaningful). In early 2021, *Forbes* Chief Content Officer Randall Lane went so far as to threaten any company that hired a former member of the Trump administration, writing: "Hire any of Trump's fellow fabulists above, and *Forbes* will assume that everything your company or firm talks about is a lie. We're going to scrutinize, double-check, investigate with the same skepticism we'd approach a Trump tweet. Want to ensure the world's biggest business media brand approaches you as a potential funnel of disinformation? Then hire away."

In Washington, DC, a 2021 proposal from House Democrats aimed to make banks subject to an independent "racial equity audit" once every two years or they'd face a $20,000 daily fine. A 2021 letter from Senate Democrats urged Alphabet Inc., Google's parent company, to do the same. In its announcement about the letter, New Jersey senator Cory Booker's website quotes the president of advocacy group Color of Change: "It is past due that Google makes the structural changes necessary to eradicate the racism ingrained in their business practices and on their platform." Color of Change, the force behind racial equity audits at companies like Airbnb and Facebook, is a political group whose philosophy aligns with SJF principles.

The government has implemented discriminatory policies of its own. In 2019, New York State granted a tax credit to the salaries of writers and directors—but only for women or members of minority groups. San Francisco has initiated a number of publicly funded programs resembling a universal basic income that are available only to non-white residents.

In January 2021, President Joe Biden announced that his administration would take the unusual approach of constructing economic policy around not individual need but group categories like race and sex: "Our priority will be Black, Latino, Asian, and Native American owned small businesses, women-owned businesses." In June of 2021, his administration created a program that would forgive the debt of farmers who are "Black, American Indian/Alaskan Native, Hispanic, Asian and Pacific Islander," but not the debt of white farmers. (The program was later blocked by a judge, who could not confirm that it was constitutional.)*

In October of 2022, America's largest research funder in physical sciences, the Energy Department's Office of Science, began mirroring the new hiring practices at universities. In order to be considered for funding, all applicants now must "describe the activities and strategies of the applicant to promote equity and inclusion as an intrinsic element to advancing scientific excellence." Writing about this new policy in the *Wall Street Journal*, physicist Lawrence Krauss asks, "Are we at a point where the heart of the nation's scientific research enterprise is to be held hostage to ideology? Will the U.S. government refuse to fund major national-laboratory initiatives to explore forefront fundamental and applied science because scientists show insufficient zeal for fashionable causes?"

We're not living in the Jim Crow era. We don't have a social credit score or a Department of Antiracism. We're not in the surveillance state of North Korea or the dystopian world of George Orwell's *1984*.

But we're closer to all these worlds than we should be.

In some cases, cultural pushback—or court rulings—have fended off dystopian policies or proposals. In other cases, the policies are currently in effect. But all of these stories are signs of a society in a dire struggle to maintain the Liberal Games.

Which brings me to one last institution.

---

* On Black Lives Matter's website, a 2022 article talked about BLM's involvement in the creation of many of these policies: "Biden's action plan is a major win for the organizations like [Black Lives Matter Global Network Foundation (BLMGNF)] who have been working with the White House to help develop it since the end of 2020. The solutions in the plan are the result of tireless advocacy and organizing from the grassroots level and beyond, and we are heartened to see the result of so many racial justice advocates' hard work be written into federal policy today."

What About the ACLU?

What *about* the ACLU? With all of this illiberalism going on, where is the organization that was famously built to protect society from slipping down the illiberal staircase?

Since it was founded in 1920, the American Civil Liberties Union has staunchly defended Americans' constitutional rights. The ACLU has stood up for everyone from Communists to the civil rights activists to the Nation of Islam. The ACLU even famously fought in 1977 for the rights of neo-Nazis to march in Skokie, Illinois (a town with lots of Holocaust survivors). For David Goldberger, the ACLU lawyer who led the case at the time, doing so was a no-brainer. He wrote, "Though I detested their beliefs, I went into court to defend the First Amendment." Ira Glasser, who led the ACLU from 1978 to 2001, hammers the point home another way: "What happened in Germany didn't happen because there was a good First Amendment there. It happened because there wasn't."

In other words, the ACLU doesn't care about the "horizontal" dimension in politics—only their founding mission to defend the Constitution.

But times have changed. For most of its existence, free speech was the ACLU's most sacred cause. Today, their focus has shifted. Journalist Michael Powell writes in the *New York Times*:

> One hears markedly less from the ACLU about free speech nowadays. Its annual reports from 2017 to 2019 highlight its role as a leader in the resistance against President Donald J. Trump. But the words "First Amendment" or "free speech" cannot be found. Nor do those reports mention colleges and universities, where the most volatile speech battles often play out.

The organization's long-time stance regarding staying *politically impartial* has also completely changed. The ACLU has recently taken on a handful of causes, like coming out in support of canceling student debt, that aren't related to protecting civil liberties. And most of the organization's stances now align with the stances of SJF activists. The ACLU opposed a motion that would reinstate due process for those accused of sexual harassment and assault on college campuses*—the opposite

---

* As SJF has taken over campus justice systems it has become disturbingly common for students accused of sexual assault to be found guilty without a...

of the stance the previous ACLU would take. In another instance, when a woman filed a request with the Washington State Department of Corrections for data on the number of transgender inmates who had been granted transfer from men's to women's prison, the ACLU filed a lawsuit to block the data from being released. In other cases, the ACLU has aligned with SJF activists to take a public stance that presumed the guilt of people accused of sexual assault, racism, or murder—even though they hadn't been found guilty. And on social media, it's becoming difficult to see the difference between ACLU's Twitter page and the Twitter page of an organization distinctly devoted to progressive activism.*

Reflecting on these two changes—the focus away from free speech and toward partisan politics—the former director Glasser lamented: "There are a lot of organizations fighting eloquently for racial justice and immigrant rights. But there's only one ACLU that is a content-neutral defender of free speech. I fear we're in danger of losing that."

Glasser's fears were further validated when a confidential internal document was leaked to the press in 2018. In the document, senior ACLU staff wrote about the tension between defending free speech and the political activism they had committed themselves to: "Our defense of speech may have a greater or lesser harmful impact on the equality and justice work to which we are also committed." Before deciding whether to take on a free speech case, the ACLU would now consider "factors such as the (present and historical) context of the proposed speech; the potential effect on marginalized communities; the extent to which the speech may assist in advancing the goals of white supremacists or others whose views are contrary to our values; and the structural and power inequalities in the community in which the speech will occur."

Former ACLU board member Wendy Kaminer wrote in the *Wall Street Journal* that these new guidelines "reflect a demotion of free speech in the ACLU's hierarchy of values." To prominent First Amendment lawyer

---

...chance to defend themselves. Writer Judith Shulevitz believes that in these cases, the university acts as "cop, prosecutor, judge, and jury—and also hears the appeals"—a conflation of roles Harvard Law School professor Janet Halley says is "fundamentally not due process."

* In March 2021, journalist Michael Tracey compiled the topics covered in the ACLU's recent tweets, finding that only 1 percent were on the topic of free speech, compared with 63 percent about transgender rights and 9 percent about police reform/racial justice.

Floyd Abrams, it reflected a full reversal: "The last thing they should be thinking about in a case is which ideological side profits. The ACLU that used to exist would have said exactly the opposite."

Author James Kirchick sums it up like this: "Like so many other institutions whose worthy missions we naively assumed to be inviolable—the ACLU is no longer itself."

Like so many other institutions, the ACLU is no longer itself.

This is the distinct feeling I've had reading about what's happening at companies and institutions across society—from Harvard to the *New York Times*, Disney to Google, the American Medical Association to the American Booksellers Association. So many institutions are suddenly behaving nothing like themselves—and often in direct contradiction to their stated values. The reason, in each case, seems to me to be the same: the entity's telos—its core founding purpose—has been superseded by Social Justice Fundamentalism.

Remember the 1960s Republican Fundamentalists in

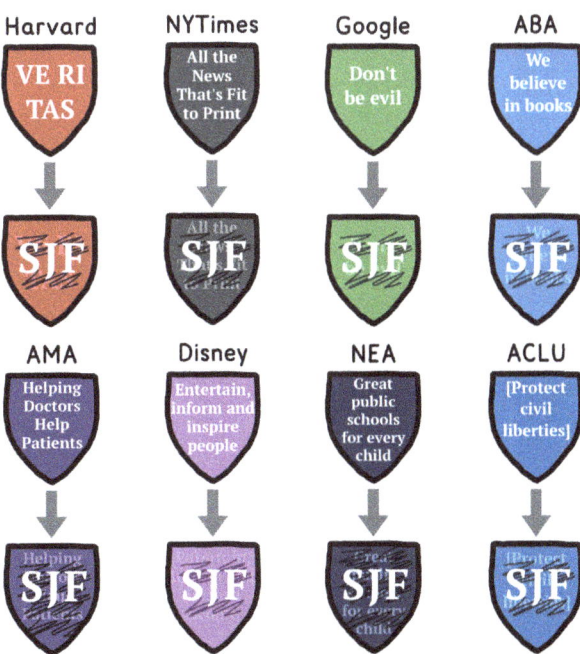

Chapter 4? They were an example of how, as historian Geoffrey Kabaservice describes it, "a small, disciplined minority, uninhibited by bourgeois scruples over fair play or tradition or truth, could defeat a majority and bend an organization to its will." This is also a good description of what we've seen SJF do, again and again, over the past few years.

Through a combination of Social-Justice-Horse trickery and mafia-like coercion, the SJF golem has managed to hijack institutions from within and transform them into instruments of SJF activism. The hijackings don't happen all at once but gradually, in a series of "moments of truth," when SJF issues a challenge to an entity's culture and core values *and* the entity fails to stand up for itself. An institution is only what it is willing to stand up for. If it lets an unscientific, anti-free-speech, morally inconsistent, illiberal ideology take over, the institution itself becomes unscientific, anti-free-speech, morally inconsistent, and illiberal.

Many of these companies have spent decades building up hard-earned trust with the public, trust that SJF leverages to bring power and legitimacy to itself, its worldview, and its ethical framework. In the lag time between when a brand is co-opted by an ideology and when the public's trust in the brand has been eroded, the ideology spends that trust like currency and can do a lot of damage.

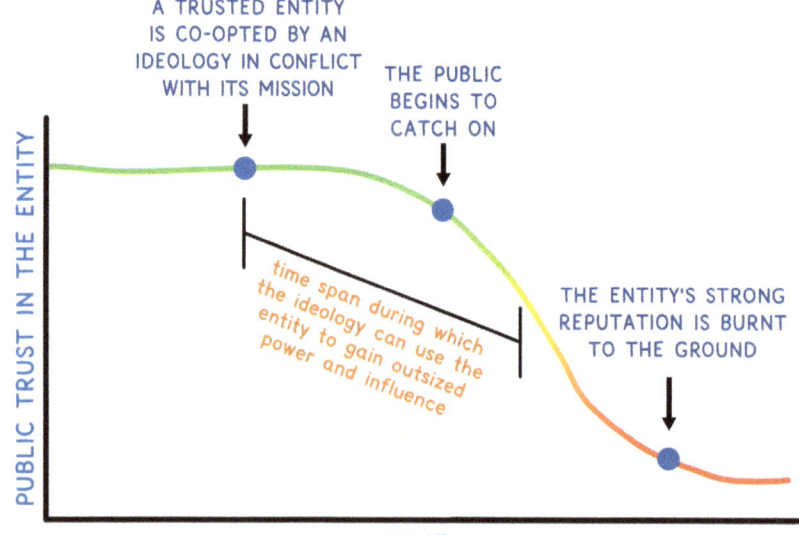

I said earlier that my problem with Social Justice Fundamentalism isn't the ideology itself. I strongly disagree with most aspects of SJF, but there are hundreds of ideologies floating around today's world that I don't like. My problem is with SJF's tactics—the fact that it's an *expansionist golem* that attempts to spread itself not through persuasion but through bullying, smear campaigns, loyalty oaths, guilt by association, and other coercive measures.

Liberal societies are built to constrain this kind of threat, and they're usually great at it, which is why so few expansionist golems succeed. The fact that SJF is succeeding, to the amazing extent that it is, is evidence that something is very wrong. The high-rung immune system that normally keeps movements like SJF in check has gone MIA. With that counterforce missing, SJF has pushed the envelope farther and farther down the illiberal staircase.

This is what we have to remember when we read about some high-profile person getting canceled for defying SJF. No political group in a liberal society should have the power to destroy a person's livelihood or reputation at will. When a group does have that power, it reveals a big crack in the society's liberal armor. Once that crack becomes apparent, it will be exploited again and again, to increasing degrees, like a spear pushing deeper and deeper into the society's vital organs.

. . .

Let's revisit those three former Obama voters from the beginning of Chapter 5.

2022

| Wokeness is a huge problem, causing a lot of damage. | What you're calling "wokeness" is today's version of the 1960s Civil Rights Movement, and you're on the wrong side of history. | I agree that wokeness is over the top, but I disagree that it's this HUGE problem. Also you're both kind of stressing me out. |

I spent Chapters 5, 6, and 7 explaining why I'm the person on the left. I hope to reach both the middle and right person with this book. But as I wrote this, I especially had the person on the right in mind—the person who's not especially woke themselves, but they don't think wokeness is a huge deal and tend to think people like me are way too worked up about it.

Over the six years I worked on this book, I've had what feels like eighty thousand discussions with this person on the right. I've heard their arguments many times.

You're cherry-picking the worst anecdotes. Every movement has its share of awful stories.*

What people call "cancel culture" is just the marketplace of ideas doing its thing.†

If free speech were really in peril, people like Joe Rogan, Jordan Peterson, and Bill Maher wouldn't be able to regularly criticize wokeness on their huge platforms.‡

Progressive movements are always intense and often radical, but that's how change happens—you're making the "old man on the wrong side of history" mistake.§

You've been spending too much time on Twitter. Out in the real world, this stuff just isn't that big of a deal.¶

---

* I'm sure I didn't do a perfect job, but I worked very hard not to cherry-pick stories. I intentionally left out dozens of extreme examples because they seemed to be outliers. Instead, I only included examples I believed were representative of a broad trend in order to present an accurate, not-sensationalized depiction of what's really happening.

† As we talked about in this chapter, there is a difference between a culture of criticism (which enriches discussion) and cancel culture (which shuts down discussion).

‡ The fact that famous people on independent platforms can freely speak certain ideas does not mean those ideas can be freely spoken by millions of students, employees, and others without the same privilege. The "Joe Rogan" argument, to me, is akin to seeing Caitlyn Jenner appearing on the cover of *Vanity Fair* as evidence that transgender people no longer face difficulties, or seeing Obama winning the presidency as evidence that Black Americans no longer face injustice.

§ Radical progressivism can be good and effective, when it's the high-rung type—evidence based, experimental, and open to being wrong. But low-rung golems (like, I argue, SJF) are rarely productive, and their extremeness isn't simply a good thing gone a little too far: it's regression in the opposite direction of progress.

¶ Spending time on Twitter does have a tendency to make you think the world...

I understand the thinking behind all of these arguments, and part of why I wrote this book is that it's not easy in a discussion to fully explain why I believe those arguments are so badly misguided. I hope I've been able to do so here.

I don't know everything there is to know about this topic, and I undoubtedly have blind spots—but after spending a whole lot of time grappling with this story and studying it from every angle I could, I feel pretty confident in a basic overarching point:

SJF IS BAD FOR ALMOST EVERYONE

We've seen a lot of people hurt by SJF in these stories.

There are its direct targets: the people who have been smeared, publicly shamed, and punished.

There are the employees SJF is being forced upon, in mandatory trainings.

There are the millions of kids, from preschool through college, who are being denied important lessons in favor of ideological training—taught, by grown-ups they've been told to trust, how to think like Zealots and bully like idea supremacists.

There are all those industries and institutions whose core functions have been impeded by SJF, like a disease spreading through the organs of a body—something that affects all of us.

But think about where SJF has done the most harm: academia, media, tech, publishing, healthcare, the arts, and left-wing politics. They're all traditionally politically progressive. As I mentioned at the end of last chapter, Social Justice Fundamentalism evolved for decades within academia to become resistant to the particular immune defenses of the progressive environment. SJF's use of straw men and smearing and trojan horses was, with time, precisely tailored to exploit progressive vulnerabilities. By the time the movement exploded out of college

---

...is ending, but I don't think this particular story is an illusion of the Twitter addicts. It has serious breadth, being widespread across industries, and it has serious depth, reaching deep into those industries and altering the telos of so many companies and organizations. We've also seen how what happens on social media directly influences what's amplified by news media and what happens inside companies.

campuses into the world, SJF had perfected the art of taking over a progressive institution.

In a podcast episode about the infamous brutal executions carried out by the Catholic Church in the 1600s, Dan Carlin made a point that stuck with me: "The most horrible procedures were done on devout Christians by even more devout Christians." It seems to be a similar story with SJF. This radical left movement has directed most of its bullying toward the less-radical left. And progressive America has suffered terribly for it. In particular:

SJF IS BAD FOR SOCIAL JUSTICE CAUSES

Productive social justice movements use a big tool kit, and SJF has deprived progressive America of many of its most important tools. Like:

Nuance

Earlier, I compared social movements to earthquakes. A certain cause gathers more and more momentum until eventually, the stubborn status quo gives way and society's tectonic plates shift. A lot of change happens quickly, and chaos ensues. This is the movement's "hammer phase," which smashes old norms, old systems, and old laws. But this is only part of the job.

Imagine you're trying to fill a glass to the very top with water. You can fill the first 80 percent of the glass quickly, but then you have to slow down and get cautious and precise—otherwise you'll overfill the glass and make a mess.

Movements work the same way. The hammer phase is like filling the glass to that first 80 percent. To finish the job, movements need to put down the hammer and pick up the sandpaper. Major progress has been made, but edges still need to be sanded, new policies still need tweaking, and new cultural norms need to be pressure tested.

During the hammer phase of a progressive movement, it can be hard to tell the difference between the Upper Left and the Lower Left, as both are charging ahead fiercely. But when it's time for the subtler "sandpaper phase," the difference becomes crystal clear.

Golems don't use sandpaper. They only know how to hammer. As the Upper Left tries to get nuanced, the Lower Left keeps charging full steam ahead breaking things. For a progressive movement to prevail, it has to succeed on two fronts: its struggle against conservative resistance, and its struggle against Lower Left excess.

And it's here that America's Upper Left has faltered in recent years. Instead of engaging in the full two-front battle, they only engaged with their conservative opponents, losing their nerve when it came to a major threat down on the Lower Left: Social Justice Fundamentalism.

In failing to stand up to SJF, the Upper Left has allowed SJF to take sandpaper out of its tool kit. When the high-rung world has attempted to engage in productive discussions around complicated topics like fairness, accountability, bias, discrimination, diversity, forgiveness, and affirmative action, SJF has smeared every argument other than its own doctrine as a right-wing attempt to uphold the status quo.

Optimism

Successful American movements have been fueled by optimism and hope. But there's no place for positivity in SJF, which is rooted in the idea that liberal societies are hopelessly and irreparably oppressive. When it comes to the state of our politics, negative sentiment like grievance and outrage are shorthand for righteousness in SJF, while positive sentiments like optimism and gratitude are taken as a sign of false consciousness, callous privilege, or both. When positivity is shamed out of the conversation, the air ends up filled with gloom, resentment, and nihilism—not sentiments that energize people to fix problems.

Common-Humanity Rhetoric

Look at a successful progressive movement of the past and you'll hear a lot of "common-humanity" rhetoric—the kind captured by civil rights activist Pauli Murray in her essay "An American Credo":

> I intend to destroy segregation by positive and embracing methods. When my brothers try to draw a circle to exclude me, I shall draw a larger circle to include them. Where they speak out for the privileges of a puny group, I shall shout for the rights of all mankind.

This kind of language, which speaks directly to people's Higher Minds, builds the broad coalitions that can create seismic change.

SJF speaks instead to people's Primitive Minds using the "with us or against us" language of "common-enemy" rhetoric—while stigmatizing common-humanity rhetoric like "there is only one race, the human race" as bigotry. Common-enemy rhetoric creates division and limits the movement's size and ability to make enduring change.

Credibility

To win people over, a movement has to maintain a reputation for integrity. But the unscientific, illiberal, hypocritical nature of SJF has hurt the credibility of today's social justice movements.

When SJF activists argue that trans women swimmers, bikers, and weight lifters have no physical advantage over their cis-women counterparts, in the face of clear scientific evidence about sex differences in things like bone density and muscle mass, it hurts high-rung LGBTQ movements. When Black Lives Matter's stance remains that Jussie Smollett is telling the truth, in the face of overwhelming evidence that he is not, it makes it harder for the high-rung activists calling for police reform to be persuasive. As SJF concept creep has continually expanded the definitions of critically important terms like "racism," "misogyny," and "violence," it has diminished the impact of those words and cheapened their meaning. When a movement continually cries wolf, it weakens our defenses against actual wolves.

Deprived of these critical tools, many social justice efforts have stalled. Worse, many have begun to move backward.

Counterproductive Results

Social justice activism is aimed, above all, at improving the lives of marginalized people. But Social Justice Fundamentalism has been shown time and again to be counterproductive to that cause.

There's research showing that diversity training makes companies less diverse and can reinforce stereotypes.

Creating a distorted perception of how dangerous cops are diminishes trust in law enforcement and makes police encounters potentially *more* dangerous and less effective, and making people feel like the system is hopelessly rigged against them logically makes them more likely to engage in criminal activity and other antisocial behavior.

SJF screams from the hilltops that standardized tests like the SAT are biased against women and people of color. While there's little evidence that this is true, there *is* evidence that when people are led to believe a test is biased against them, it hurts their performance.

Sometimes SJF seems to mimic bigoted traditions that Liberal Social Justice activists have worked so hard to knock down. As we've discussed, SJF insists that virtues like niceness, punctuality, and evidence-based thinking are qualities of "whiteness"—which sounds a lot like the kinds of things white supremacists say.

The SJF narrative also reinforces rigid gender stereotypes. In an article called "As a Gay Child in a Christian Cult, I Was Taught to Hate Myself. Then I Joined the Church of Social Justice—and Nothing Changed," Ben Appel writes:

> Young boys and girls, not to mention impressionable adults, are being led to believe that if, say, a boy likes to wear skirts or put on makeup, he might really be a girl on the inside; or if a girl would rather play football than cheerlead, then perhaps she's not a girl, but really a boy, or nonbinary. By means of this "progressive" ideology, we regress to a time in which the categories of "boy" and "girl" were defined in a narrow and reactionary manner.

This regressive SJF concept is now the messaging of most major medical institutions. The American Psychological Association, for example, defines "transgender" as "an umbrella term for persons whose gender identity, gender expression or behavior does not conform to that typically associated with the sex to which they were assigned at birth." So if you were born a girl but you behave or express yourself in a way typically associated with boys (aka a tomboy), the APA definition seems to imply that this makes you less of a girl. The same messaging rang out in a video on Boston Children's Hospital's YouTube page, in which a doctor talks about signs your child might be transgender, including "playing with the 'opposite gender's' toys."*

When any movement—no matter how noble—falls into the hands of a low-rung tribe, it ends up in a backward place, usually hurting the people the original movement wants to help.

---

* One meme sums up the logic like this:
   Sexism: the woman should do the dishes
   Feminism: men or women can do the dishes
   Gender ideology: whoever is doing the dishes is a woman

SJF IS AN AFFRONT TO THE PROGRESSIVE SPIRIT

Beyond the most basic definition of "pushing for change," when I think of "progressivism," a couple of defining characteristics come to mind:

1. Fighting for the Little Guy

Progressives—from the moderates to the radicals—are supposed to speak truth to power and advocate for the powerless, the downtrodden, the oppressed. Those categories are broad and fluid, so effective progressivism should be as well.

But SJF isn't broad or fluid. Who's the little guy and who's the big guy is determined by one thing: the Intersectional Stack.

The road upward in modern America runs through college campuses, but children of America's large white working class are dramatically underrepresented among college students. For universities so hell-bent on "diversity and inclusion," this underrepresented group is invisible—because on the Intersectional Stack, they show up in the powerful, privileged category.

The same working class voted overwhelmingly for Donald Trump. When it came to white voters, the less educated the neighborhood, the more likely they were to vote for Trump. And the districts where Trump made gains over Romney were in notable economic despair. But SJF, with its single-axis lens, saw only one story: *White people voted for Trump. The privileged part of the country voted for the racist, xenophobic candidate.* Clean and simple. The fact that it was specifically the least privileged whites who voted for Trump didn't register.

A 2019 paper found that "among social liberals, learning about White privilege reduces sympathy, increases blame, and decreases external attributions for White people struggling with poverty." Being white is surely a source of privilege in today's American society but learning about privilege only through the lens of intersectionality leaves would-be progressives with a blind spot toward America's white working class that, on most other metrics, qualifies as one of the country's "little guys."

SJF's one-dimensional lens also ends up neglecting the non-white poor. According to scholar Richard Kahlenberg, 71 percent of the Black and Hispanic students at Harvard come from wealthy backgrounds. It's well-known that colleges privilege applicants whose parents are alumni—an overwhelmingly wealthy, white group—but it seems that the college admissions process favors the wealthy across *all* backgrounds. When "diversity" is only thought about from a one-dimensional perspective, the distinction between the wealthy and poor person of color goes unnoticed.

Homicide is the leading cause of death among young Black men in America, while growing up in a single-parent home is one of the best predictors of poverty. But violence and one-parent homes aren't phenomena easily explained by SJF's notion of the Force, so they are left out of much of today's progressive discussion.*

There's also SJF's attitude toward free speech. As Jonathan Rauch wrote in 2013, "History shows that, over time and probably today more than ever, the more open the intellectual environment, the better minorities will do. It is just about that simple." Free speech is always most important to those not in power. Free speech is the only nonviolent tool for criticizing and challenging the status quo. It is the engine behind every social justice movement in American history, from the abolition of slavery to gay marriage. In any society, it is the little guy who relies most on free speech. But SJF takes the opposite stance, framing free speech as a tool of the powerful and something marginalized groups need protection *from*.

SJF leaves a lot of little guys in the dust. Maybe it comes down to disagreements about what constitutes a little guy or what helps the little guy. Or, less charitably—maybe SJF just isn't really focused on the little guy.

Being part of the elite class does not in itself make one an elit*ist*. Elitism is an attitude: one that looks down upon those who don't have elite wealth or an elite education, who don't have the right table manners or the right hobbies. Or...one that looks down upon those who don't hold the elite's political views or use the proper elite words and terms. Elitism is a social club with very specific codes and rules, and SJF sure seems like the current set of code words and code views to signify membership. Which is, of course, the very opposite of what progressivism is supposed to be about.

---

* In 2022, Pew asked Black Americans what the most important issue was facing their community. "Violence/crime" (17 percent) and "economic issues" (11 percent) were the two most common answers, with only 3 percent answering "Racism/diversity/culture."

2. Open-Minded

When I think of the best kind of progressivism, I think of the ultimate *safe space*. There should be nowhere easier to be yourself, to be weird, or to be different than a progressive environment. Progressivism, at its best, *celebrates* difference. There should be nowhere safer to ask dumb questions or make mistakes—because progressivism is compassionate and forgiving and super-duper humane. This is the kind of hyper-evolved environment young people growing up in a strict home with rigid, close-minded parents can't wait to escape to.

Compare that with this passage from a queer activist named Yarrow Eady as he reflected on his days as an SJF hard-liner:

> Thinking this way quickly divides the world into an ingroup and an outgroup—believers and heathens, the righteous and the wrong-teous....Members of the ingroup are held to the same stringent standards. Every minor heresy inches you further away from the group. People are reluctant to say that anything is too radical for fear of being seen as too un-radical. Conversely, showing your devotion to the cause earns you respect. Groupthink becomes the modus operandi. When I was part of groups like this, everyone was on exactly the same page about a suspiciously large range of issues. Internal disagreement was rare. The insular community served as an incubator of extreme, irrational views.

He's describing the *opposite* of a safe space—the exact kind of space a kid with strict, rigid parents wants to escape *from*.

From every angle, SJF is a complete and utter departure from open-minded progressivism. It is highly authoritarian, laying down rules about how to speak, how to think, how to teach, how to hire. It doles out severe penalties for minor infractions. It's the opposite of diverse and inclusive, enforcing strict conformity. It's vindictive and promotes medieval-style public-shaming campaigns. It assumes the worst about people's intentions.

Like elitism, rigidity is supposed to be what progressives make fun of *conservatives* for.

Most progressive Americans are not SJF adherents. But *many* of them have been scared into silence by SJF. The result is that SJF is writing a lot of the rules about what modern-day progressivism is and isn't.

In allowing SJF to do that, high-rung progressives have betrayed a lot of the people who have always relied on progressives to fight for them.

And finally—

SJF IS BAD FOR SJF BELIEVERS

Over recent decades, Americans began spending less time immersed within communities and more time being isolated and lonely. This broad trend may be especially pronounced in progressive America, which has also seen a sharp decrease in religion. According to Gallup surveys, in 2000, 71 percent of Democrats were church members. By 2020, that had dropped to 48 percent.

For a species that craves meaning, purpose, community, identity, and a sense of belonging, these trends leave a lot of holes.

Meanwhile, hypercharged political tribalism was on the rise, and during the 2000s, religiousness became strongly associated with the religious Christians of conservative America. This ignited a passionate movement called New Atheism. But around 2015, it transformed into something different. Blogger Scott Alexander writes:

> [New Atheism] had been felled by social justice, which was a sort of Liberal Ideology 2.0, filling the same social role [of] New Atheism, only better. Most atheists jumped ship to join the winning team—"this atheism blog is now a feminism blog" was kind of the unofficial slogan of the 2015 blogosphere—and thus was the empire forged.

Just like that, the New Atheists were born-again social justice evangelicals.

Critics of what we've been calling SJF often compare it to religion, and not without reason. SJF talks about "whiteness" as an original sin and emphasizes the need for anti-racist confession. SJF views its narrative like scripture and wrongspeak like blasphemy. The way activists like Robin DiAngelo talk about racism—"24/7 the forces around us push and seduce and compel us to participate and the only way to not collude is to actively, intentionally, and strategically seek to resist those forces, and as soon as we're complacent, we get sucked back in"—sure sounds a lot like the way Christians talk about Satan.

There's nothing necessarily wrong with a political religion. There are religions that improve the lives of their adherents and provide them with a moral structure that makes them better people. But I don't think SJF is one of those religions.

In their book *The Coddling of the American Mind*, Jonathan Haidt and Greg Lukianoff share a list of "common cognitive disorders" that cognitive behavioral therapy practitioners believe cause anxiety and depression, and they note that many of today's young people are actively being trained *into* the precise kinds of thinking CBT aims to eradicate—like overgeneralizing, all-or-nothing thinking, blaming others, and focusing on the negatives.

The world of SJF is also laden with shame. We talked about the way high-rung politics sees people: as a mess of gray complexity, an evolving jumble of virtues and flaws. Through a high-rung lens, all people are worthy of compassion, and no one is above criticism. On the low rungs, people are either perfectly righteous 1s or morally reprehensible 0s. The problem with that is that no one's actually a 1, and most people, deep down, know that about themselves. If a person is taught that there are only 1s and 0s, and they know they're not a 1, then they might start to think of themselves as a secret 0 and feel horribly ashamed of it. The notion that a person would be made to feel shame because they were born gay is reprehensible to progressive sensibilities. But SJF also teaches its adherents to feel shame for things they cannot help: for their privilege, for unconscious bias inherent to every human, for atrocities committed by their ancestors or the ancestors of people who look like them.*

So SJF fosters grievance in those low down on the Intersectional Stack and shame in those higher up—or in the case of, say, a white woman or a gay man, a little of both. Either way, it seems like a recipe for misery.

And then there's the social aspect. There are so many testimonials about the way SJF diminishes a feeling of trust and safety among friends. Here's one from an activist on Twitter:

---

* Shame may translate to firepower for SJF: research suggests that moral outrage is often "a means of reducing guilt over one's own moral failings and restoring a moral identity" and that "personal guilt uniquely predicted moral outrage [at] harm-doing and support for retributive punishment."

> So many of my friends and comrades and I have discussed how we are all virtually afraid of being abandoned by people we care about for saying the "wrong" thing, but if we name this then we are all lumped together with abuse apologists....It doesn't feel good to know that people will no longer talk to people they have conflict with, they will instead convince everyone that you're "bad" and everything you touch is bad....The conflict becomes all-consuming.

The same ideology that encourages adherents to police and punish its enemies also encourages them to do it to their own friends and fellow activists.

Many ideologies prey on people's worst instincts. SJF also preys on people's best—their empathy, their desire to help the marginalized and make the world a better place, their determination to stand up to forces of evil.

And it preys on people's deepest human needs—for meaning, purpose, community, identity, and a sense of belonging. SJF, it tells them, can fill every one of those holes. But the testimonials speak a different story: that SJF is a more like a get-rich-quick scheme that ends up backfiring and making those holes even more gaping, that floods adherents with grievance, shame, and paranoia, squashes their individuality, drives them away from nonbelievers in their lives, and tears the trust out of their friend groups—all while generating a deep dependence that makes SJF very hard to move on from.

To recap: Social Justice Fundamentalism is bad for those who are canceled by it, for those who are silenced by it, for kids and employees indoctrinated by it, for those affected by its illiberal policies, and for everyone relying on the core values of companies and institutions across the country. SJF is *also* bad for social justice itself, for progressivism in general, and even for the people who believe and promote it.

So who is SJF *good* for?

Beyond the tiny group of people profiting handsomely off of SJF, I see only one: the Lower Right.

GOLEMS, INC.

Nothing has been more of a boon to America's big red golem than the rise of Social Justice Fundamentalism.

Just as the rise of Donald Trump was the greatest gift to SJF activists, SJF is continual fuel for right-wing low-rungness, providing endless content for *Fox News* segments, political campaigns, and QAnon forums. A rallying cry of Lower Right politicians is that white Americans are being treated unfairly—a claim often used to inflame racism and xenophobia.* But when states do things like making vaccines available only to people of color, it adds firepower to these fears and boosts those politicians.

The enduring goal of white supremacists is to get as many white people as possible to view themselves as part of a white identity group—a mission hugely aided by SJF forcing concepts like whiteness, white privilege, white complicity, and white silence into the mainstream.

Right-wing provocateur Rush Limbaugh preached in 2013 about "the Four Corners of Deceit in our culture…government, academia, science, and the media." This is an over-the-top conspiracy theory designed to shatter trust in US society's core knowledge-making institutions (with the convenient implication that the only sources that *can* be trusted are people like Limbaugh himself). But when those core institutions actually *do* allow a political group like SJF to corrupt their integrity, it makes conspiracy peddlers like Limbaugh all the more convincing.

According to Pew research, distrust in media was the #1 predictor of voting for Trump. When major media brands increasingly lend their giant megaphones to a radical ideology that only a small portion of Americans subscribe to, it just enhances these feelings and hands votes over to Trump and other politicians like him.

In case after case, SJF has been a great enabler of the Lower Right.

On Step 2 of the illiberal staircase, we saw how SJF had infiltrated hundreds of classrooms around the US and how any pushback against this has been distorted as pushback against *all* discussions of race in the classroom. What we didn't talk about was the response from Republican state legislatures.

---

* Almost two-thirds of the 21 million Americans who believe the 2020 election was stolen from Trump agreed that "African American people or Hispanic people in our country will eventually have more rights than whites."

In early 2021, Republican legislatures across the country started passing bills to ban concepts associated with CRT from being taught in K–12 classrooms. Tennessee has banned lessons that teach students they "should feel discomfort, guilt, anguish or another form of psychological distress solely because of the individual's race or sex"—other states, including Iowa and Oklahoma, have passed bills with nearly identical language. Pennsylvania attempted to ban requiring "a student to read, view or listen to a book, article, video presentation, digital presentation or other learning material that espouses, advocates or promotes a racist or sexist concept." In November of 2021, North Dakota passed a law that banned teaching *about* "the theory that racism is not merely the product of learned individual bias or prejudice, but that racism is systemically embedded in American society and the American legal system to facilitate racial inequality." Similar bills have been passed in Montana, Texas, New Hampshire, and other states.

Proponents of the bills argue that they are simply trying to curb the recent trends we've been discussing, putting an end not to all discussions on these topics but to schools indoctrinating students on what they believe is a radical and divisive ideology. They also point out that such bills do not violate the Constitution when aimed at K–12 schools, as K–12 teachers have limited First Amendment rights inside the classroom, and states and school boards do have a lot of discretion over what can and cannot be taught to K–12 public school students.

But while these points may be technically correct, the language in most of the bills is broad and vague, and critics of the bills have correctly pointed out that they are likely to have a general chilling effect on race discussion in the classroom. If lessons that teach students that they "should feel discomfort, guilt, anguish or another form of psychological distress solely because of the individual's race or sex" are banned, might that lead teachers to avoid a wide range of topics, well beyond those that fall into the SJF bucket? As a white person, I certainly felt discomfort

---

* Higher education is a different story. Republican legislatures have also proposed bills aiming to restrict what can be taught at universities, like Florida's Stop WOKE Act. These are unconstitutional affronts to academic freedom, which is why very few have been able to pass. As FIRE president Greg Lukianoff has put it, "Many of the efforts by conservatives to turn the tide on campus have mutated into approaches that look uncomfortably like the very speech codes they battled for decades."

learning about Jim Crow laws in school. As a Jew, I felt plenty of anguish learning about the Holocaust. If it's no longer allowed to teach about "the theory that racism is systemically embedded in American society and the American legal system," wouldn't that rule out lessons on, say, housing discrimination or criminal justice reform?

Even *if* the wording were somehow specific enough to contain banned lessons to SJF, that's not a good idea either. SJF (or, again, as it is popularly referred to in this discussion, CRT) is a political lens, and a very relevant one in current events, and if a teacher wants to teach students about it, they should be able to. Rather than instituting overly restrictive bans, parents and government officials should insist that any political lenses taught to students are presented as single lenses among many, as part of a well-rounded education. The problem isn't the lens, it's the indoctrination.

These bills are a classic example of fighting illiberalism with more illiberalism, and it adds credibility to the straw-man argument that the whole countermovement to "CRT in schools" is a front for eradicating all discussion of race in K–12 classrooms.

In 2022, this pattern repeated itself around the issue of gender ideology in schools. To sum it up briefly:

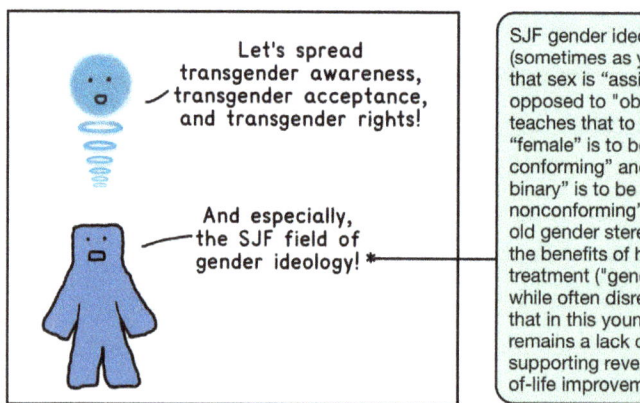

---

* Some of the bills, like North Carolina's House Bill 324, ban highly illiberal practices like "compelled speech." As we've discussed on Step 3, forcing students or teachers to outwardly affirm any particular belief is definitely not okay—but this is already illegal. It can be successfully fought with lawsuits, so banning it with additional bills is redundant.

HOW TO CONQUER A SOCIETY • 451

The Lower Right joins the party, pushing back against gender ideology, especially for young children. But in many cases, this morphs into backlash against broader trends around transgender awareness and even LGBTQ in general. Some activists make an effort to conflate all discussion of gender identity in schools with indoctrination or sexual exploitation. Republican legislatures around the country enact bills banning books from school libraries. While some books have been removed for being highly sexually explicit, others have been targeted simply for exploring LGBTQ topics.

On issue after issue, a similar pattern has emerged: Golem A does something illiberal, which is met by both *liberal* pushback from the high rungs and *illiberal* pushback from the opposing Golem B. Golem A then leverages Golem B's involvement by framing *all* pushback against it as the work of the other golem.

We've seen the same pattern going in the other direction. The Left's information bubble, for all its issues, is informed by a wide variety of sources. Many progressive-leaning media outlets, like the *New York Times*, the *Washington Post*, and the *Atlantic*, publish opinion pieces criticizing popular progressive narratives. America's right-wing information bubble is much more airtight. Someone can go months watching Fox News, reading Breitbart, and listening to conservative talk radio without confronting a compelling challenge to the predominant narratives of the political Right. This makes the right-wing bubble fertile ground for outlandish conspiracy theories.

Most famous is QAnon—the family of wacky conspiracy theories that gained steam throughout the Trump presidency and persists today. In February of 2022, research organization PRRI conducted a large survey asking participants about three core QAnon theories:

> The government, media, and financial sector are controlled by a group of Satan-worshipping pedophiles who run a global child sex-trafficking operation.

> There is a storm coming soon that will sweep away the elites in power and restore the rightful leaders.
>
> Because things have gotten so far off track, true American patriots may have to resort to violence in order to save our country.

Twenty-five percent of Republicans (compared with 9 percent of Democrats) agreed with all three statements.

When Covid rolled around, a new crop of conspiracy theories started circulating around the right-wing bubble. *Fox Business* anchor Trish Regan referred to Covid worries as "yet another attempt to impeach the president." Others began to insist that Covid vaccines were part of a secret government plot to implant 5G microchips in millions of American bodies.

A bubble where these theories can thrive is also a bubble primed to believe Donald Trump when he declares himself the true winner of the 2020 election. According to polling done in mid-2022, only around 25 percent of Republican voters believe that Joe Biden was legitimately elected.

This widespread doubt is at the foundation of a movement that is hijacking the Republican Party. The Republican National Committee has referred to the violent January 6 assault on the Capitol as "legitimate political discourse." Since 2020, dozens of election officials in battleground states have been subject to harassment, even death threats, for their decisions to uphold the 2020 election outcome. The result may be that, come the 2024 election, these offices are staffed by people less likely to defy a candidate like Trump.

Republican politicians are facing similar pressure to support the #StopTheSteal narrative or be branded as a traitor by party machinery—and over half of Republican nominees who campaigned in the 2022 midterms deny or question the 2020 results (and 61 percent of these nominees won their races). In the 1990s, politicians like Newt Gingrich made it taboo for Republican politicians to legitimize the opposition. Today it has become taboo among Republicans to legitimize American democracy itself.

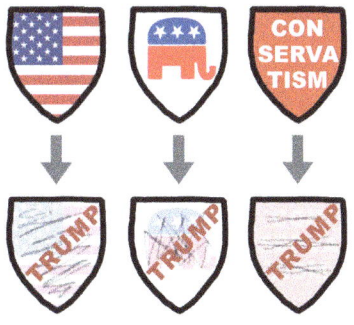

Through it all, Trump has continued sowing doubt in the electoral process. In October of 2022, he told a Michigan crowd, "I don't believe we'll ever have a fair election again."

But the Democratic Party has responded, in part, by engaging in its own Orwellian behavior. In July 2021, the White House announced that the government was "working to combat misinformation that's traveling online." Surgeon General Vivek Murthy explained: "Modern technology companies have enabled misinformation to poison our information environment….We're asking them to monitor misinformation more closely. We're asking them to consistently take action against misinformation super-spreaders on their platforms." Press Secretary Jen Psaki added: "We're flagging problematic posts for Facebook that spread disinformation."

"Our biggest concern here," Psaki explained the next day, "is the number of people dying around the country because they're getting misinformation that is leading them to not take a vaccine."

But one year earlier, while Trump was in office, the most prominent Democrat politicians were saying this:

> **Joe Biden**: "If and when the vaccine comes, it's not likely to go through all the tests and all the trials that are needed to be done."
>
> **Kamala Harris**: "If Donald Trump tells us that we should take it, I'm not taking it."

Andrew Cuomo: "I think it's going to be a very skeptical American public about taking the vaccine, and they should be....You're going to need someone other than this FDA and this CDC saying it's safe."

Their point was more about Trump than the vaccine. They were expressing their skepticism about taking a vaccine that the Trump administration in particular deemed to be safe.

But a sizable portion of Americans feels the same lack of trust in the Biden administration that Democrat leaders felt about the Trump administration. When those Americans express similar sentiments in 2021 with Biden in office, the White House labels it as "misinformation." In an infographic on their website, the US Department of Health and Human Services encourages people to "check with the CDC" to ensure that information they hear about Covid is real and not misinformation—the same CDC Democratic leaders encouraged Americans not to trust during the previous administration.

And if the government can pressure tech companies to censor what they deem to be misinformation, there's no reason to believe that their definition of "misinformation" or "disinformation" would be limited to Covid-related information. The government isn't supposed to be able to police content on private platforms. But as tech entrepreneur Vivek Ramaswamy and Yale Law School's constitutional scholar Jed Rubenfeld wrote in a 2021 *Wall Street Journal* op-ed, "Congress has co-opted Silicon Valley to do through the back door what government cannot directly accomplish under the Constitution."

The spread of baseless conspiracy theories within the Right's bubble is a dangerous trend. An authoritarian response by the Left only makes the problem worse. It makes it much easier to convince Republican voters that Covid is a Democratic plot or that the 2020 election results were manipulated. In the same way authoritarian measures by Republican legislatures undermine the high-rung pushback against SJF in schools, authoritarian behavior by the Democratic Party undermines the high-rung efforts to combat false right-wing narratives.

---

* A draft copy of a Department of Homeland Security report revealed plans for the department to target "inaccurate information" on topics including "the origins of the COVID-19 pandemic and the efficacy of COVID-19 vaccines, racial justice, U.S. withdrawal from Afghanistan, and the nature of U.S. support to Ukraine."

• • •

It's said that desperate times call for desperate measures, but it turns out that "desperate measures" are quite useful in normal times as well. The modern era's political Echo Chambers have a special knack for making all times seem desperate, which makes the breaking of shared rules seem like justified desperate measures.[*]

America's golems have seized the opportunity, increasingly breaking with liberal norms to snag short-term victories. Each step down the illiberal staircase by one golem justifies a similar downward step by the other, as trust breaks down into cynicism, suspicion, and a cycle of revenge. Soon, everyone is playing the Power Games and, like any prisoner's dilemma gone wrong, everyone ends up losing. But the golems themselves only grow more powerful.

Low-rung movements are driven by fear and hatred of a common enemy, and each low-rung narrative centers around its most important character—its Disney villain. The red golem and blue golem, while hating each other, also *need* each other. They are each other's greatest asset.

On the other hand, the *actual* enemy of a political golem is the genie above it. The real threat to SJF comes not from white supremacy or Fox News mockery or Republican bans but from vocal pushback from principled progressives. The real threat to Trump's mission to discredit the electoral process comes from vocal conservatives who value conservative principles over loyalty to Trump.

This is why we see America's political golems patrolling their own political neighborhoods like intellectual warlords, inflicting heavy penalties on anyone who dares step out of line. The blue golem hits blue dissenters where it hurts, smearing them as racists, transphobes, right-wing conspiracy theorists, Uncle Toms. The red golem brands red dissenters with words no conservative wants to be called: groomers, traitors, RINOs ("Republican In Name Only"). The two golems, alternating taking positions A and C, tend to direct their fiercest ire to those taking position B.

---

[*] As we saw in Chapter 4, Goldwater played into the same psychology in his 1964 nomination acceptance speech: "Let me remind you that extremism in the defense of liberty is no vice. And let me also remind you that moderation in the pursuit of justice is no virtue."

Most high-rungers don't have the stomach for this, so they go silent. Those who continue to speak up for position B mostly have their voices drowned out in the chaos. What's left is a battle of good-vs.-evil narratives. Few people have the time to dig deeply into the nuances of the topic, so millions end up adopting these low-rung narratives as their reality by default.

Earlier I compared the US to a giant trudging its way up a mountain toward a more perfect union. At the heart of the US is a macro version of the tug-of-war inside each of us, and right now, the warring golems are functioning as a unit pulling the whole system in the wrong direction.

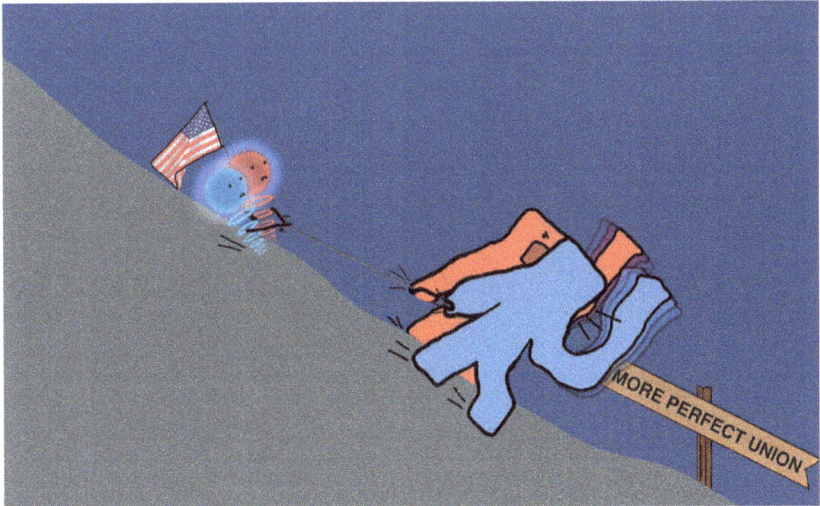

This is how American society is being conquered. Not by a foreign enemy. Not by the Left or by the Right. But by its own worst nature.

Which brings me to one more counterargument I anticipate this book will generate: *bothsidesism*.

In my conversations, in person and on social media, I've been accused by people on both my right and left of framing the problem as "both sides are bad," when in fact, they believe, one side is much worse and more dangerous than the other.

I believe this is misunderstanding my entire point. "Bothsidesism" is a horizontal accusation, but my analysis is *vertical*. This book is about low-rungness, and low-rungness spans the horizontal political spectrum.

The Lower Right and Lower Left both *are* illiberal. They're both anti-science. They're both hypocritical. They're both authoritarian. They're both bigoted. The political uniform that low-rung movements wear is just a façade under which lies a golem with all the trademark low-rung qualities. If one golem is causing more trouble than the other during any given year, it speaks not to that golem being worse but to that golem having more power to do damage at that time. US history is a roller coaster of oscillating power between Left and Right. It would not surprise me if a decade from now, the lion's share of cancel culture stories were the work of the political Right and it was the Left electing the demagogue president.

My problem isn't with progressivism or conservatism but the fact that, at the moment, Americans are being deprived of the high-rung version of *both* by low-rung groups wearing blue and red uniforms. Plenty of people will disagree with my horizontal assessments, which is totally fine, but also beside the point. Whether the Lower Left or Lower Right is doing more damage is dwarfed by the much bigger phenomenon: that across the political spectrum, high-rungness seems to be losing its grip on our society's thinking, its norms, its behavior. Across the whole country—and across many parts of today's world—*low-rungness is on the rise.*

CHANGING COURSE

So what's our problem?

We started this book talking about moths. Moths navigate using moonlight, and in the world they were programmed to live in, that system worked fine. The issue for today's moths is that their environment has changed but their programming has not, so now they spend their nights doing pointless circles around your porch light.

I'm pretty sure this is our situation too. Human nature is a specific software program optimized for a specific purpose: survival in a small tribe, a long time ago. The modern world is nothing like the environment we were made for. This is why we made liberal democracies.

Remember this?

The liberal democracy is an artificial environment, carefully crafted to both contain human nature and convert it into an engine of progress. Like all environments, it's a behavior-shaping mechanism.

It's natural to take our environment for granted—to assume that that's "just the way things work." But a liberal democracy is a human construct, held in place not only by laws but by the "support beam" of the high-rung immune system—by shared notions of what is and isn't tolerable or harmful and by shared determination to uphold those standards. When that support beam weakens, the environment can quickly collapse back to the more natural human habitat of the Power Games.

In our era of exponential progress, rapid changes to our environment have put liberal democracies under great strain. Primitive Minds have instinctually rushed in to fill many of the new power vacuums. New golems have congealed together and have begun stomping through our societies like Godzilla, growing more emboldened with each passing year. These golems have infected the societies' vital organs—their institutions—impeding their ability to function properly and causing a mass crisis of trust.* In the chaos of exponential progress, our societies are beginning to lose their grip.

This is an unfortunately common pattern through history. People who live through bad times, like the world wars, witness the fragility of human civilization firsthand. This harsh dose of reality has them saying, "never again," which gets their priorities in order and leads to wise decisions. These wise decisions protect future society from the kind of bad times they experienced.

But when times are good for long enough, we start to get cocky. We forget that the only reason times are good is because of principles fervently agreed upon by people who had been through hell. When we grow complacent about those principles, the safeguards put in place by older generations deteriorate. And the people of good times never see the rise of new bad times until it's too late to stop them.

It's kind of like a merry-go-round that societies get stuck on:†

---

* Jim Baker, the director of the Office of Net Assessment in the US Department of Defense, told me in a conversation that he believes "the loss of trust in our institutions is the number one threat to our national security."

† Based on the quote from an anonymous meme: "Hard times create strong men, strong men create good times, good times create weak men, and weak men create hard times."

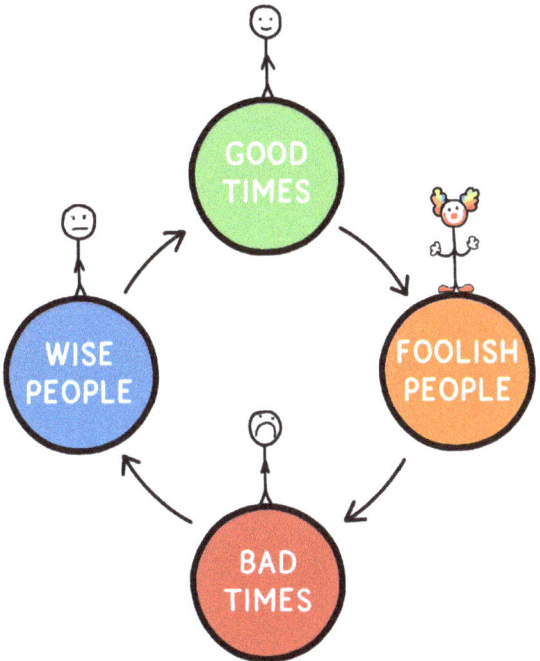

American poet Carl Sandburg once wrote: "When a nation goes down, or a society perishes, one condition may always be found; they forgot where they came from. They lost sight of what had brought them along." This is a pretty good description of the "foolish people" part of the merry-go-round, and also a pretty good description of where I worry we are right now.

The stories we've talked about—of the decline of the Republican Party and the election of a demagogue willing to undermine trust in the electoral process; of Social Justice Fundamentalism hijacking institution after institution and rewriting the way our children are educated—aren't really stories about political parties or political movements. They're stories of millions of people standing on the sideline as people bully their Idea Labs into becoming Echo Chambers, as companies betray their founding missions, as politicians fail their constituents, as mass shaming roars back into fashion; silently thinking, *That's not how we do things here!*

When a person is intimidated into silence, their mind's light disappears from the world and is contained only to their head.

As millions of people have gone dark, the light in the national brain has dimmed.

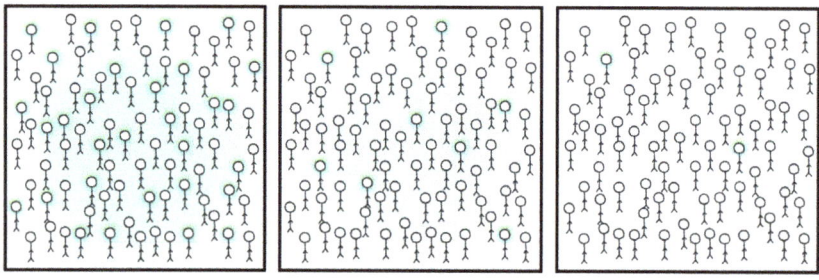

Mass confusion allows divisive ideologies to indoctrinate more people, who join their armies of intimidation, causing more people's lights to go dark as the danger of speaking your mind rises. Silence is contagious, and as it spreads, the big brain loses its ability to think straight and society grows ever more confused. This is the vicious cycle that makes a society forget history. This is how good times can lead to foolish people, who create bad times.

No society wants to enter the "bad times" phase of the merry-go-round. In a super high-tech era like ours, it's an *especially* scary prospect. We live in a time of magical technology, and the power of the human species grows more godlike every year. This power is a double-edged sword, simultaneously paving one road to utopia and another to dystopia. As we move into the deeply uncertain future of page 1,001 of *The Story of Us*, there's never been a *more important time* to have our wits about us.

Which is also why there's never been a *worse time* for us to be spiraling down a vortex of confusion and fear. Exponential technology has given us countless gifts. But in the frenzy, we're forgetting the most important lesson of all: the worst of our nature never lies far beneath the surface.

We really can't afford to get ourselves from foolish to wise the usual way, via bad times. Somehow, we have to figure how to become wise people directly.

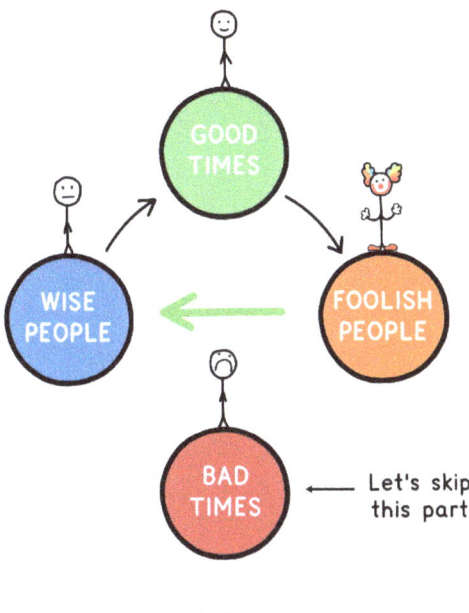

. . .

People have asked me if I'm optimistic or pessimistic about our future. Truthfully, it depends on the day.

While I can't say I'm *confidently* optimistic, I believe there's a strong case for optimism. A few reasons why:

The exhausted majority is sick of this shit. Both my own life experience and a mountain of data point to an enduring truth: Most people—old and young, Black and white, progressive and conservative, American and non-American—are good-hearted, highly reasonable, and yearning for unity much more than division. Most people want free speech, dislike cancel culture, and prefer respectful elected officials. The exhausted majority is a sleeping giant with immense potential energy.

The internet is a double-edged sword. The internet gave birth to a digital cudgel that has given power to mobs, but that same internet also means it's almost impossible to truly silence free speech today. The kinds of tactics that have allowed extreme movements or authoritarian demagogues to conquer nations of the past are up against far greater odds in today's ultra-connected environment.

Most of these bad stories are very recent. The majority of stories in this book happened in 2020 or later. We're in the beginning of the story, not the end. There have been periods of chaos and instability throughout American history, and in each case, the country ultimately prevailed. There's a reason liberal democracies have persisted for centuries: they're remarkably robust and resilient.

The tide seems to be slowly turning. In the time between when I started this book and today, I watched confusion and fear swell up and then more recently, appear to wane a bit. Companies that have held strong in the face of SJF pressure, like tech giant Shopify, have not only survived but thrived. Voices in the media are beginning to show signs of their old integrity, like Erik Wemple's late-2022 *Washington Post* op-ed acknowledging that James Bennet's firing at the New York Times was wrong ("[It's] long past time to ask why more people who claim to uphold journalism and free expression…didn't speak out then in Bennet's defense. It's because we were afraid to."). The exhausted majority spoke with their votes in 2022, when they denied seats to every 2020-election-denying nominee for state offices that hold authority over the voting process. Over at Evergreen, the exhausted majority has spoken as well. Since the 2017 debacle, enrollment has fallen by 50 percent. The ACLU may not be what it used to be, but FIRE has picked up the mantle defending Americans' civil liberties—and they'll soon be expanding their work beyond college campuses. Every year, new organizations are popping up dedicated to civil discourse and bridging political divides—you can find dozens of them on bridgealliance.us.

But for this story to actually have a happy ending, this tide reversal needs much more momentum. And every person reading this can play a part in making it happen.

SO WHAT'S OUR SOLUTION?

How does a society get out of a downward spiral of confusion and fear? With its opposite: an upward spiral of awareness and courage.

Awareness

While writing this book, I found myself in countless discussions about the various topics in it. Some were productive, others weren't. The unproductive discussions always felt the same at the time: *I'm trying to reason with someone, but they're a hopeless low-rung thinker. It's like arguing with a brick wall.*

But this is how unproductive discussions always feel. Even when *you're* the brick wall.

Looking back, I've been writing and talking about the high rungs and low rungs while sometimes battling to stay up on the high rungs myself. There have been moments during research when I've caught myself judging academic papers by whether they confirmed or disconfirmed my hypotheses. There have been times during arguments when I couldn't help but get emotional, when my ego was way too involved, when I was only listening to what the other person was saying in order to come up with my next response.

The first part of our solution is awareness, and the gateway to awareness is humility.

We all spend time in Unconvinceable Land as Attorneys, sometimes even as Zealots. We all identify a little too much with certain ideas. We're all unknowingly standing on Child's Hill with at least a few topics, where our level of conviction far exceeds our level of knowledge. When it comes to the beliefs we hold most sacred, we're all prone to confirmation bias. In one way or another, we're all gullible, all in denial, all delusional Disney protagonists. We all have out-groups and we all dehumanize the people in them. We're all tribal. We're all hypocrites. We're all wrong. Because we're all human.

The most important thing for us to remember is that we do our rational and moral thinking with a not-that-smart tool that was designed to keep an ancient primate alive. Staying aware of this can help us be our wisest selves and reach our potential.

So the first call to action is: *Put your own mask on before helping others.*

Do a self-audit. Where in your internal life is your Primitive Mind holding the reins? What are the triggers that activate your Primitive Mind and leave you buried in fog? Where do you tend to be at your best—consistently high rung, wise, and grown up? What is it about those moments that gives your Higher Mind such a strong advantage? Can you replicate that elsewhere?

Think about your beliefs. Play the "why" game with them, like an annoying four-year-old. Why do you believe what you believe? When did those ideas *become* your beliefs? Were they installed in you by someone else? Are they beholden to some tribe's checklist of approved ideas?

If they are authentically yours, when were they last updated? Your Primitive Mind thinks your beliefs are sacred objects carved in stone, but they're not—they're hypotheses written in pencil, and if you're thinking up on the high rungs, you should probably be pretty active with the eraser.

Think about your values. If you love a political party or a movement because it stands for your values, and that party or movement slides away from those values, are you sticking with it out of tribal loyalty? Or because your values have truly changed alongside it? If the party or movement has departed from your real values, stick with your values. If you do, you'll be accused of having changed—of having "left" the party or movement. But that's not what happened. It left you, and you stayed true to yourself.

Think about the beliefs of those you disagree with. Do they have any merit? Could you state them to your opponent, in all their complexity, in a way that would make your opponent say, "Yup, that's what I believe"? Or would you oversimplify or misrepresent those beliefs? If you can't steel-man your opponent's beliefs, you don't yet *know* whether you disagree with them or not. Everyone believes they are fighting on the side of the good, the right, the vulnerable—even your opponents.

Think about your identity. The truth is, you're not a progressive or a conservative or a moderate or radical or some other political noun. Those are words for ideas, not people. Your mind is way too weird and particular to be locked in a noun or adjective prison. Attaching a political category to your identity is a heavy piece of baggage to carry around, and putting it down makes learning and exploring much easier and less stressful.

Think about people or groups you *hate*. Who are you disgusted by? Remind yourself that this is almost always a delusion of your Primitive Mind. You certainly don't have to like everybody. But when you're *disgusted* by a person or a group of people, you've gotten swallowed up by human craziness. When you find yourself here, try one of these exercises to snap yourself out of it:

Think small. Imagine the little details of the life of the person you're hating: the sticky note they leave in their kid's lunch box, the calendar on their wall with little plans written in the squares, the leftovers in their fridge from last night's home-cooked meal. Like you, everyone else is ultimately just trying to be happy.

Think big. Read about the universe. Nothing makes hatred seem more ridiculous than internalizing how vast time and space are. Doing so makes me want to turn to anyone who will listen and hug them and say, "We both exist! On the same tiny planet at the same exact time! Hi!"

Think outside yourself. Every person has a unique childhood, a unique set of traumas, unique mental health issues. There are many people not lucky enough to be born as intellectually or emotionally intelligent as you were, not lucky enough to have an upbringing like yours. You have no idea what kind of grief, heartbreak, or other misfortune another person may be suffering through. However awful someone is acting, it would probably make a lot more sense if you could spend a few minutes inside their brain.

I've been using a little mantra. When I'm down on the low rungs and I have a moment of self-awareness where I realize I'm on the low rungs, I say in my head: *Climb*.

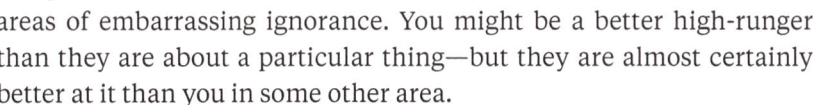

It's not a scolding moment, it's a moment of self-compassion. I'm doing that thing that every human does sometimes. It's okay. I caught myself. Climb.

Once you've begun to address your internal tug-of-war, turn your attention outward. What do your surroundings look like through the Ladder lens?

Think about the people you love. Where are they great at being high-rungers? Where do they struggle down on the low rungs? When someone is acting like a monster, they're not a monster, they're a human mired in an internal tug-of-war and losing. We all have topics that bring out our most biased, irrational selves. We all have areas of embarrassing ignorance. You might be a better high-runger than they are about a particular thing—but they are almost certainly better at it than you in some other area.

Think about your relationships, your friend groups, your work environment. In what ways is each an Idea Lab, and in what ways an Echo Chamber? Where are you being intimidated into silence by a social bully? Where are you the bully?

Think about the media you read or watch. Where does it fall in the Media Matrix?

Rather than search for the perfect media source, right at the intersection of accuracy and neutrality, assume that every company, every journalist, every podcaster, every talking head is flawed—because they are, because they're all human—and diversify your media portfolio. Try to get a sprinkling from across the spectrum. Think of the various voices as the biased lawyers in the courtroom of your mind. Watching their ideas clash will help you, the juror, get closer to the truth.

Practice thinking "vertically" about your society, its industries, its cultures, its politics. Slap the Ladder onto all these things and see what they look like. Where do you see high-rung and low-rung psychology or behavior playing out? Where are people seeking truth vs. seeking confirmation? Where do you see moral consistency and where do you see hypocrisy? Who's using persuasion to get what they want and who's using coercion?

Awareness is an Inner Self project.

But the stories from this book were all made possible by millions of people *not saying* what they were really thinking. Awareness is a necessary but not sufficient condition for us to right the ship. Because awareness + silence changes nothing. This is where the second ingredient comes into play.

Courage

Courage is an Outer Self project.

We looked at story after story of companies and institutions facing what we called "a moment of truth"—situations in which leaders were forced to choose between integrity and popularity. In story after story, these moments went wrong, not because leadership didn't know the right thing to do but because they lacked the courage to lead. My hope is not for the demise of the institutions we talked about in this book but that they'll have the guts to start acting like themselves again.

Each of us faces the same kinds of moments of truth too, in our everyday interactions. These moments are hard because our not-that-smart brains are wired to be afraid of certain things it was good to be afraid of in 50,000 BC—like not pleasing authority, not fitting in, or being socially out-grouped. In many instances, having courage today doesn't require putting yourself in danger—it just requires you overriding your Primitive Mind's incorrect assessment of danger. Because a lot of what the Primitive Mind is terrified of *isn't actually dangerous at all.*

One of the most consistent themes in the stories in this book is that people who have been attacked by a political golem—smeared, shunned, threatened, fired—said they received a lot of private but little public support. The invisible elephant in all of this is the giant mass of silent skeptics. In an environment like that, every time a silent skeptic starts speaking out and becomes a vocal skeptic, it has a *huge* impact.

But you don't need to go that full distance to have an impact. There are different degrees of courage.

Courage level 1: Stop saying stuff you don't believe

Marcus Aurelius once wrote, "If it's not right, don't do it. If it's not true, don't say it." Refraining from participation in something you don't believe in is just a small step in the right direction—but if everyone did it, the world would be a whole lot better.

If everyone is expressing a certain political sentiment you don't agree with or dehumanizing an out-group in a way you find distasteful, try to stay quiet and not participate. This can be easier said than done, because low-rung social environments put a lot of pressure on everyone to pledge outward allegiance to the tribe's sacred beliefs or express hatred of the tribe's enemies. Try it anyway. Think of it like this: saying things you don't believe because others want you to is disrespecting your Inner Self. And your Inner Self deserves better.

If you find yourself being forced to speak up in a training or classroom in a way that will misrepresent yourself, or being pressured to apologize about something you don't think you should have to apologize for, see the situation for what it is: a Maoist-style struggle session. And struggle sessions are fucked up. Unless it'll have truly dire consequences for you, stand your ground.

Courage level 2: Start saying what you really think, in private, with people you know well

This is when you begin letting your Inner Self show itself in public. Start with the people you're closest with. Are there political or social topics you have to be in the closet about with them? If so, consider whether your relationship might become better and more interesting if you stopped self-censoring. Becoming more authentic usually seems scarier than it proves to be. And it might make the relationship closer, more fun, and less stressful.

This can also have another benefit: collaborative growth. Try explaining the Ladder to people and promise that you'll tell each other when the other is being low rung or acknowledge your own low-rungness when you become self-aware of it. You're building a support network, which can be incredibly productive. It's not only great for everyone involved, helping to fast-track personal growth, it can help the group become more of an Idea Lab and less of a boring Echo Chamber.

Of course, sometimes a person or relationship or group just isn't ready for these discussions yet, and that's okay too. Be as high rung as you can around those people, and some of it just might rub off.

Courage level 3: Go public

Class. Work. Church. Book clubs. Dinner parties. This isn't an encouragement to become the insufferable person who always brings up politics. But if you're in a setting where a conversation is happening and your Inner Self is screaming "I disagree!"—start saying, "I disagree." I can almost guarantee that at least some other people in the room will secretly be harboring the same thoughts, and they'll respect the shit out of you for saying it out loud.

You could go even bigger. Start a blog. Start a podcast. Write a book. Tweet a tweet. Spend six years writing a 120,000-word book. If you already have a platform, start laying your Inner Self on it.

This is not for everyone. If you want to be a full hero and throw your career away going down in flames, all power to you (and you'll have a soft landing into a group of awesome new friends), but I'm talking here to everybody else—everyone who can take their ideas public without any major consequences.

For many of us, the fear of putting it all out there is mostly in our own heads. Specifically, in our Primitive Minds.

If that's you, here's a tip for getting your Primitive Mind on board with the plan. Remind yourself that whatever you're putting out there in the world will win you the respect of some people and lose you the respect of some others. And ask yourself: Whose respect do I care about?

For me, that question had an obvious answer. The people whose respect I care about are people who think it's cool to say what you really think, who think it's cool to throw hypotheses out there, the people who like to play around with all kinds of ideas. If I put myself out there, in conversations, in larger settings, and publicly, I'll end up surrounding myself with those kinds of people.

Conversely, if you're hiding your Inner Self out of fear, you're going to end up surrounded by people who like the person you're *pretending* to be. Meanwhile, the people who actually like you don't realize they like you. I can pretty much guarantee that your Inner Self has some major admirers out there. Why not find out who they are?

You don't need to upend your whole life, lose your job, or destroy your friendships to exhibit courage. Taking any of these steps is *way, way* better than taking none of them.

Awareness is about looking out at the world and being able to discern the difference between the low-rung virus and the high-rung immune system. Courage is about becoming *part* of the immune system instead of enabling the virus. As the virus tries to push the national giant off the mountain's steep cliffs, courage keeps your hands at the giant's back, pushing it upward toward a more perfect union.

Just as confusion and fear are contagious, so are awareness and courage. When a person finds the courage to share their real ideas, those ideas spread and build awareness in others. Golems rely on the delusion of pluralistic ignorance (when no one believes but everyone thinks everyone believes). A few brave people speaking out shatters the delusion and makes others realize they're not alone. When more people start saying what they think, it becomes less scary for others to follow in their footsteps. Soon, heads begin to light back up in droves as Inner Selves venture out into the world.

THE BRIGHT SKY IN THE DISTANCE

Earlier, I quoted Josiah Lee Auspitz, writing in 1970 about "the struggle for the soul" of the Republican Party. This is a fitting description of what's going on all around us today: a struggle for the souls of long-trusted companies and institutions, political parties, and in many ways, whole nations themselves.

In the chaos of our modern era, the Primitive Mind raced out of the gates and snagged a cheap victory in Round 1 of many of these struggles. But in the long run, I'd bet on the Higher Mind. The danger we face is not an asteroid racing toward Earth or an impending alien invasion—but only ourselves. We got ourselves into this, and I'm pretty sure we can get ourselves out of it.

There was no shortage of ideas in this book, but I believe one stands out above all: Us vs. Them is always a delusion. *The Story of Us* isn't a story of good guys vs. bad guys but one about the tug-of-war that exists within each human head, each community, each society. In this epic story, heading together toward an uncertain fate, there is no Them. Just one big Us.

CAST OF CHARACTERS • 475

THE UPPER LEFT	THE UPPER RIGHT	THE LOWER LEFT	THE LOWER RIGHT
helpful	helpful	not helpful	not helpful
THE STRONG ARGUMENT	**THE WEAK ARGUMENT**	**BROTHERS, COUSINS, AND STRANGERS**	**THE MOB**
fierce in combat	prefers a peaceful life	worst family ever	please don't tell them about this book
KING MUSTACHE	**THE INNER SELF**	**THE OUTER SELF**	**THE THOUGHT PILE**
a tiny but brutal tyrant	what you think	what you say	what we think
THE SPEECH CURVE	**THE IDEA SUPREMACIST**	**THE TROJAN HORSE**	**THE HARASSY BOSS**
what we say	those who can't persuade, coerce	how the golem gets around	not an important character but such a good drawing
THE SMEARED PERSON	**THE ILLIBERAL STAIRCASE**	**THE MERRY-GO-ROUND**	**THE INSTANT GRATIFICATION MONKEY**
it's not coming off	so slippery	less fun than it looks	my co-author

THE END

ACKNOWLEDGMENTS

There are a lot of people to thank, so settle in.

Wait But Why's Patreon supporters: Your consistent, patient support allowed me to do this book the way I wanted to, with no compromises—something that, with these topics, could have only happened via self-publishing. That kind of creative freedom is a luxury I am continually grateful for.

Wait But Why's readers: You are the reason I can spend all my time thinking and writing in the first place. When I wrote this book, I entirely had you in mind as my audience. Thanks especially to those who read the first iteration of these ideas—the online series *The Story of Us*—and offered piles of feedback through comments and emails. Your negative feedback showed me the weak spots and made me determined to improve them. Your positive feedback drove me to double down on the effort and write this book. Extra thanks to Bakari Kafele, whom I first became aware of when he was writing long, critical comments on the blog series. After begrudgingly accepting that many of his comments were on point, I asked him if he'd read a draft of the book and offer even more feedback, which he generously, thoroughly did.

I'd also like to thank Wait But Why's Twitter followers. A ton of the ideas, terms, and drawings in this book had their first test on Twitter. A writer can't ask for a better gift than to get instant feedback on something they're working on.

I'm in massive debt to dozens of writers whose books and articles informed and influenced this book. Thanks in particular to Jonathan

Haidt and Greg Lukianoff, both for their mountains of inspiring work and for their words of advice along the way.

I got lots of help throughout from professional book people. Thanks to Andy Ward and Drew Cullingham for structural edits, Trish Hall and Sara Lipincott for copyediting, Rubén Rodriguez and several people at Whitefox for ideas and feedback, Andy Young and Joao Fabiano for fact-checking. Joao in particular is an annoyingly hard-ass fact-checker who never missed a chance to tell me I was wrong about something. This book is a lot less wrong because of him. Thanks as well to David Rozado and Zach Goldberg for providing customized data and graphs.

My agent Richard Pine—aka my work dad—is the best mentor I could possibly ask for. That he has played it cool during every one of our "I have a totally new plan (and deadline)" meetings is a luxury no writer (but especially not me) deserves. He has given me grace and sage advice in the most difficult moments of this process. I also want to thank Andy Ward and Larry Finlay for continuing to believe in me when others would have thrown in the towel.

This book probably wouldn't exist without Tobi Lütke, whose enthusiasm for the project is a big reason I turned it from a blog series into a book in the first place. Tobi has also been a shining example of the real-world courage and leadership we so badly need right now, and I hope many others follow in his footsteps.

So many friends have helped in so many ways, and there's no way I'll do them justice here. I am a way better writer and thinker because I am surrounded by thoughtful independent thinkers who love to argue and analyze the world for fun. So many of the ideas I write about were incubated in my friend Idea Labs over the years. Jesse Hartman, Ali Block, Andrew Finn, Hugh Auchincloss, Adam Lunin, Ryan Pakter, Will Levine, Will Bressman, Eliah Seton, Danny Wurwarg, Noah Waxman, Brian Matthay, Eve Marson, Liv Boeree, Igor Kurganov, Isabelle Boemeke, Joe Gebbia, E, C, Philipp Dettmer, Grey, Adam Grant, Risa Needleman, Dave Wallace-Wells, Kate Ballard-Rosa, Chris Anderson, Coleman Hughes, Ezra Klein, Pamela Paresky, and Tony Hsieh have all been a big part of developing the ideas in this book, through thousands of cumulative hours of conversations. Each of these people also loves to disagree with me, which is both infuriating and superbly valuable.

Special thanks to Liv Boeree, Philipp Dettmer, and Grey, who have continually bullied me into moving faster on this project and taken large sums of my money when I fail at a goal after using having to pay them if I fail as motivation.

In addition to conversations, a bunch of people read drafts of this book (some almost twice as long as the finished book) and offered thorough feedback. Philipp Dettmer, Ryan Pakter, Adam Grant, Pamela Paresky, Jesse Hartman, Lizzy Steib, Clemens Strottner, Bailey Edwards, and Andrew Finn put in especially long hours.

Speaking of Andrew Finn—Wait But Why's co-founder and my fifteen-year work husband—he has managed to remain patient and supportive during the eon I took to finish this project. Andrew and I like to refer to our partnership as "two monkeys trying to figure out how to drive a spaceship," and for the past six years (and twenty before that), Andrew has helped me navigate the unpredictable and stay sane in the process. His friendship, and his continued willingness to show up, are an invaluable anchor.

Over the past six years, my parents, sisters, and in-laws proved the "unconditional" part of unconditional love, as I subjected them to a lot more political debate than they ever asked for and spent far too many family vacation hours at my laptop. I pledge to be less shitty on the next long project. Special shoutout to my ninety-seven-year-old nana, who has provided additional motivation by threatening to die before the book comes out every time I see her.

Alicia McElhone has been my right-hand woman at Wait But Why since 2016, and she has been intimately involved in every element of the creation of this book. She's played the role of ideation partner, editor, copyeditor, researcher, fact checker, schedule maker, IT support, and me-starting-writing-at-9:30 a.m. enforcer. She pulled many all-nighters in crunch-time moments, even when I pleaded with her not to, out of sheer dedication to her work and determination to keep Wait But Why at an A+ level. Her fingerprint is on every page of this book.

Finally, there's my wife, Tandice. She's been there for every moment of not just this process but my entire writing career—every high, every moment of doubt and despair, every delusional timeline. Everything I write passes through the Tandice filter before it sees the light of day. She even edited these acknowledgments (though she refused to edit her own acknowledgment [although adding that at the end of her acknowledgment was her idea]).

NOTES

There are over 100 pages of notes for this book, where you'll find all the sources as well as many additional examples and further explanations. Lengthy, full-color books like this are super expensive, so to keep the cost of the book as low as possible, we've put the notes online. You can see them here:

WAITBUTWHY.COM/WOP-NOTES

BIBLIOGRAPHY

WAITBUTWHY.COM/WOP-BIB

ABOUT THE AUTHOR

Tim Urban has been writing stick-figure-illustrated posts on his blog *Wait But Why* since 2013. This is his first book, and he's about to start another book now, but after that one he probably shouldn't write more books, because he's a procrastinator and books are a procrastinator's nightmare. But at least this one is done, thank god. It was extra hard because as he was writing it, the world kept rapidly changing, and then he'd have to incorporate what was happening, which changed the outline, and he'd end up just rewriting big parts of it, and this kept happening, which is why he's pretty sure he'll never write a book about current events again. In Tim's free time, he likes to count how many weeks he has left to live, tell people how many stars there are, and sit at the computer dicking around.

Anyway he wants to thank you for reading this book, especially since if you're reading this right now it means you probably read the whole book (unless you're the kind of person who reads the About the Author page before finishing the book), which is good because people who don't read the whole book really won't get the big point he tried to make in it. He hopes you'll read more of his stuff in the future. K bye.

· · ·

Come say hi:
- **The main place he writes stuff**: waitbutwhy.com
- **Things he thinks of in the shower**: @waitbutwhy (X/Instagram)